GERMANS ON DRUGS

To Mom and Dad,
with love and deep
appreciation. This
project would not have
been completed w. that
your love and support.
I thank you both.

17 September 2007

Recent Titles

For a complete list of titles, please see www.press.umich.edu

GERMANS ON DRUGS

The Complications
of Modernization
in Hamburg

ROBERT P. STEPHENS

THE UNIVERSITY OF MICHIGAN PRESS   *Ann Arbor*

2010   2009   2008   2007   4   3   2   1

A CIP catalog record for this book is available from the British Library.

Library of Congress Cataloging-in-Publication Data

Stephens, Robert P., 1971–
    Germans on drugs : the complications of modernization in Hamburg /
Robert P. Stephens.
        p.   cm. — (Social history, popular culture, and politics
in Germany)
    Includes bibliographical references and index.
    ISBN-13: 978-0-472-09973-3 (cloth : alk. paper)
    ISBN-10: 0-472-09973-6 (cloth : alk. paper)
    ISBN-13: 978-0-472-06973-6 (pbk. : alk. paper)
    ISBN-10: 0-472-06973-x (pbk. : alk. paper)
    1. Drug abuse—Germany—Hamburg.   2. Drug control—Germany—
Hamburg.   3. Drug traffic.   I. Title.
HV5840.G3S73   2007
362.290943'515—dc22   2006028157

Chapter 2 includes material previously published in both "Drug Use and Youth
Consumption in West Germany during the Sixties," *Journal for Cultural Research* 7,
no. 2 (April 2003): 107–24, http://www.tandf.co.uk/journals, and "Drugs, Consumption,
and Internationalization in Hamburg, 1960–1968," in *Consuming Germany in the Cold
War: Consumption and National Identity in East and West Germany, 1949–1989,* edited by
David F. Crew (New York: Berg, 2003): 179–207.

Chapter 9 is adapted from an article in *Selling Modernity: Advertising and Public
Relations in Modern German History,* edited by Pamela Swett, Jonathan Weisen,
and Jonathan Zatlin (Durham: Duke University Press, 2007).

Contents

Acknowledgments

This book would not have been possible without generous financial support from the German government, the University of Texas at Austin, and Virginia Polytechnic Institute and State University. A Deutscher Akademischer Austausch Dienst (DAAD) dissertation fellowship allowed me to undertake a year of research in Hamburg, while an Alice Jane Drysdale Sheffield Fellowship in European History from the University of Texas allowed me to complete the research in a timely manner. At Virginia Tech, I received generous financial support from the Department of History and the Humanities Summer Stipend program; these grants allowed me to undertake further archival research and the time to write.

Writing is always a collaborative project that depends on the kindness of other scholars. While undertaking my research in Hamburg, I received support and encouragement from a number of people. The late Arnold Sywottek, director of the Forschungsstelle für Zeitgeschichte and professor at the Universität Hamburg, acted as my mentor and offered help at key junctures when it seemed the project had hit a dead end; he always managed to find the right answer to my queries. Also at the Forschungsstelle, Uwe Lohalm welcomed me to Hamburg and always pointed me in the right direction, while Axel Schildt offered useful advice as well as personal memories of growing up in the Federal Republic. Alf Lüdtke at the Max Planck Institute in Göttingen provided encouragement and suggested new ways of thinking about my project. More recently, Klaus Weinhauer acted as an intellectual companion in a lonely field.

Many of the documents used in this study were officially sealed. Several of Hamburg's state authorities granted me special permission to see the relevant material. First and foremost, Kurt-Jürgen Lange at the Referat Drogen und Sucht not only helped me navigate the Hamburg bureaucracy but also kindly answered my questions about his experiences working in Hamburg during the seventies and opened up his personal files for my inspection. Without his help, this book could not have been written. I must also thank the Behörde für Arbeit, Gesundheit und Soziales, the Staatsanwaltschaft, the Behörde für Inneres, and the Rauschgiftdezernat of the Hamburg police for permission to see documents that were officially sealed. The Hamburg State Archive, the Berlin State Archive, and the Federal Archive in Koblenz provided assistance and a comfortable place to work.

Beyond the state agencies, the Hamburg Landesstelle gegen die Suchtgefahren allowed me access to its library and press clippings collection. The former director of the Landesstelle, Dieter Maul, answered my vaguely formulated questions at an early point in the research and loaned me his personal collection of press clippings from the early 1970s, which proved to be an invaluable source.

The librarians at Virginia Tech's interlibrary loan department filled numerous, often complicated, requests. Likewise, the librarians at the Stanford University Library Special Collections and University Archives helped me navigate their superb collection of underground newspapers. The librarians at Hamburg's Carl von Ossietzky State and University Library as well as at Berlin's State Library provided helpful assistance.

Many of the images that appear in this book were created in the late 1960s and early 1970s and distributed without attribution through various underground publications that have long since disbanded. Every effort has been made to locate the rights holders for these pieces and to secure permission for their use. Grateful acknowledgment is made to anyone originally involved with this artwork whom I was unable to locate for permissions purposes.

Many people helped me hone my arguments over the last decade. A number of my colleagues at Virginia Tech commented on various portions of the manuscript. In particular, Amy Nelson and Tom Ewing gave encouragement in the right doses at the right time. Many colleagues elsewhere also read substantial parts of the manuscript and offered suggestions and encouragement, including Judy Coffin, Standish Meacham, David Imhoof, Paul Hagenloh, and Clayton Whisnant. David Crew was there when the project began and remained supportive throughout, offering sage advice and mentoring with a sure hand. Their contributions made this a better book. Geoff Eley, series editor of the Social History, Popular Culture, and Politics in Germany series at the University of Michigan Press, took a chance on a young author, inviting me to submit my manuscript and advocating for its publication. At the University of Michigan Press, my editors, Jim Reische and Chris Hebert, showed remarkable enthusiasm for the project and bent over backward to deal with the problems of working on the "underground," while Amy Fuller dealt with my mistakes and omissions kindly and with a generous spirit.

Acknowledging aid in intellectual matters and in the gathering of information is simple; debts are owed and can be repaid. Far more complex is the acknowledgment of the emotional supports that allow the solitary work of the historical monograph to remain rewarding. I owe a debt that cannot be repaid to friends and family who have lived with me through this process. These friends know who they are. Even if they are geographically distant, they sustain me. My parents' support was always unconditional, and, for that, I owe them my gratitude. Finally, Heather Gumbert arrived when this project was in its infancy; she lived with it for too many years; she read and commented and critiqued; and she offered a place of refuge. For this, I am in her debt.

Introduction

On a spring morning in March 1972, Norbert Harmsen from Poppen-büttel and a friend of his who lived in a youth home in Hütten met an older member of the Hamburg drug scene, a certain Claus A., at the Alster shopping center. The three left and proceeded to Claus's apart-ment in Hummelsbüttel. According to the statement Claus later made to the police, he left Norbert sleeping in his apartment. When he returned later that evening, he found Norbert dead. Though he was only eighteen, Norbert had been involved in Hamburg's drug scene for some time. The police knew Norbert as a "fixer," one of approximately a thousand drug addicts listed in the police registers. His parents and members of the Hamburg Youth Authority had tried time and again to rid Norbert of his habit to no avail. Next to the young man's body, police found an empty hypodermic, on his arms fresh tracks. Norbert met his death alone. His parents were understandably distraught at the death of their only son. He was a "good kid," they said.[1]

This is all we know about Norbert. He died almost anonymously, another victim of Hamburg's growing drug scene. His was not the first drug-related death in Hamburg. The authorities claimed he was the twelfth since 1967, though other observers of the scene believed that the number was much higher. Norbert's death was not an isolated inci-dent. In all of Germany's big cities, as well as in cities all over Europe and the United States, drug use had become a part of daily life by the early seventies, a legacy we still live with. How do we make sense of Norbert's death? How does his short life fit into our understanding of

1. Private Press Clipping Collection from Dieter Maul: "Schon wieder starb ein junger Mann an Rauschgift," *Die Welt*, 15 March 1972; "Viele wollen jetzt los von der Droge," *Hamburger Abendblatt*, 15 March 1972; "Wer gab ihm das tödliche Mittel?" *Hamburger Abendblatt*, 15 March 1972.

German history? It would be wrong to dismiss Norbert's death as an aberration—as a footnote in the history of crime, as an unfortunate result of the cultural libertinage that emerged from the turbulent sixties, or as simply an exemplar of the dangers of addiction. Norbert's death was neither abnormal nor exceptional; it was part of a larger set of trends that coalesced throughout the capitalist West over the course of the "long sixties" (ca. 1958–74). Indeed, it is my central contention that the emergence of a new youth drug culture in Hamburg during the long sixties was a product of the inherent complications of global capitalist modernization in the Federal Republic. Norbert's death ought to make us pause and reconsider the interpretation of the Federal Republic as a simple "success story."

The history of the Federal Republic is an ongoing project and one that bears the complications of living in an uneasy relationship with its neighbor to the east.[2] While there is no one hegemonic historical narrative of the Federal Republic, in (West) Germany the theme of modernization has become the dominant historical explanation for the postwar period. Modernization, taken largely from the work of Max Weber, emphasizes corporate capitalist economic growth, the rationalization and bureaucratization of social life, and the development of a liberal political framework.[3] Under this interpretation, the Bonn Republic managed to rebuild from the devastation of the war, to construct a modern consumer economy, and—albeit slowly—to successfully democratize its citizenry,[4] while the German Democratic Repub-

2. On the relationship between the historiographies of the two Germanies, see Christoph Klessmann, *Zwei Staaten, eine Nation: deutsche Geschichte 1955–1970* (Göttingen: Vandenhoeck & Ruprecht, 1988); Christoph Klessmann, *Die doppelte Staatsgründung: deutsche Geschichte 1945–1955* (Göttingen: Vandenhoeck & Ruprecht, 1982); Christoph Klessmann and Georg Wagner, eds., *Das gespaltene Land: Leben in Deutschland 1945–1990: Texte und Dokumente zur Sozialgeschichte* (Munich: Beck, 1993); Christoph Klessmann, ed., *The Divided Past: Rewriting Post-war German History* (New York: Berg, 2001); Mary Fulbrook, *Interpretations of the Two Germanies, 1945–1990* (New York: St. Martin's Press, 2000); A. James McAdams, *Germany Divided: From the Wall to Reunification* (Princeton: Princeton University Press, 1993).

3. On the concept of modernization and Weber's influence, see Detlev Peukert, *Max Webers Diagnose der Moderne* (Göttingen: Vandenhoeck & Ruprecht, 1989); Detlev Peukert, "Die 'Letzten Menschen': Beobachtungen zur Kulturkritik im Geschichtsbild Max Webers," *Geschichte und Gesellschaft* 12 (1986): 425–42.

4. For an overview of this narrative, see Axel Schildt, *Ankunft im Westen: Ein Essay zur Erfolgsgeschichte der Bundesrepublik* (Frankfurt am Main: S. Fischer, 1999). On the modernization paradigm for the history of the Federal Republic, see Axel Schildt and Arnold Sywot-

lic, saddled with an authoritarian police state and a command economy, failed to modernize properly. As Robert Moeller has noted, the historians of West Germany's success story believe that "West German society represented a dramatically new and unprecedented construction in modern German history, a 'normal' nation, comparable to other liberal-democratic regimes."[5]

There are problems with this version of German history. As Michael Geyer and Konrad Jarausch have recently pointed out, "The danger of post–Cold War triumphalism is a myopic self-congratulation that assumes that the victorious Western system is perfect as it presently exists and that it no longer needs serious reform."[6] Indeed, this kind of triumphalist narrative has been challenged from a number of directions. Historians of the Third Reich have questioned the modernization narrative itself, arguing that the National Socialist period, rather than being an anomaly, represented a "pathology of modernity."[7] Rather than Nazi rule being either the culmination of a peculiarly backward German "special path" (*Sonderweg*) or an exceptional variant of antimodernism, it marked one particularly brutal version of modernization, a version that contained many similarities to the modernization of the postwar period (i.e., the rapid economic expansion of the 1930s, the promise of consumer abundance, and the popular desire for political stability). Although "modernization" continues to hold a certain explanatory power as a shorthand for the development of the Federal Republic, many historians note that there is no one developmental model that can serve as the "right" path of modernization.[8]

---

tek, eds., *Modernisierung im Wiederaufbau: Die westdeutsche Gesellschaft der 50er Jahre* (Bonn: J. H. W. Dietz, 1993), and Ulrich Herbert, ed., *Wandlungsprozesse in Westdeutschland: Belastung, Integration, Liberalisierung 1945–1980* (Göttingen: Wallstein, 2002); Bernd Faulenbach, "'Modernisierung' in der Bundesrepublik und in der DDR während der 60er Jahre," *Zeitgeschichte* 25 (1998): 282–94.

5. Robert G. Moeller, "Introduction," in *West Germany under Construction: Politics, Society, and Culture in the Adenauer Era*, ed. Robert G. Moeller (Ann Arbor: University of Michigan Press, 1997), 7.

6. Konrad Jarausch and Michael Geyer, *Shattered Past: Reconstructing German Histories* (Princeton: Princeton University Press, 2003), 84.

7. The most explicit statement of this theme remains Detlev Peukert, *Inside Nazi Germany: Conformity, Opposition, and Racism in Everyday Life* (New Haven: Yale University Press, 1989). On Peukert's thesis, see David Crew, "The Pathologies of Modernity: Detlev Peukert on Germany's Twentieth Century," *Social History* 17 (1992): 319–28.

8. Since the publication of the *Peculiarities of German History* in 1984, there has been a concerted attack on the Sonderweg thesis, but the same kind of problems plague the debates

Indeed, the very success of the creation of a consumer economy and a democratic populace was not inevitable. As a number of historians have noted, the majority of West Germans did not become what we would consider modern consumers until the very end of the 1950s.[9] Likewise, as public opinion polls showed, democracy remained a suspect concept for most West Germans until the early 1960s.[10] That West Germans did create a stable, democratic society out of the ashes of the war was an accomplishment. Yet this very success carried its own contradictions. Capitalist, consumer modernization did not represent a panacea. "The development of consumption and democratization in West Germany after 1945," Michael Wildt points out, "reminds us that modernization is not an irreversible process and that modernity itself may yet have an unsettling, imponderable undercurrent."[11]

The processes that were at work in the construction of a stable, democratic society—economic expansion, the development of new consumer mentalities, and economic globalization—contained a set of contradictions that have tended to be walled off as anomalous. Likewise, resistance to the currents of capitalist economic expansion and partial democratization have been seen as either foolhardy and dangerous, as for instance in the treatment of the Red Army Faction, or important and ultimately incorporated into the fabric of society, such as the Greens and the women's movement.[12] At the end of this narra-

---

over the Federal Republic. Instead of industrial England acting as the foil for the "backward" Kaiserreich, the United States becomes the "proper" model for modernization against which all other industrial countries are measured (David Blackbourn and Geoff Eley, *The Peculiarities of German History* [Oxford: Oxford University Press, 1984]). For a recent critique of the Sonderweg thesis, see Edward Ross Dickinson, "Biopolitics, Fascism, Democracy: Some Reflections on Our Discourse about 'Modernity,'" *Central European History* 37 (2004): 1–48, esp. 34–35.

9. Michael Wildt, *Am Beginn der 'Konsumgesellschaft': Mangelerfahrung, Lebenshaltung, Wohlstandshoffnung in Westdeutschland in den fünfziger Jahren* (Hamburg: Ergebnisse, 1994); Victoria de Grazia, "Changing Consumption Regimes in Europe, 1930–1970," in *Getting and Spending: European and American Consumer Societies in the Twentieth Century,* ed. Susan Strasser, Charles McGovern, and Matthias Judt (New York: Cambridge University Press, 1998).

10. Jarausch and Geyer, *Shattered Past.*

11. Michael Wildt, "Consumption as Social Practice in West Germany," in *Getting and Spending,* ed. Strasser, McGovern, and Judt, 315–16.

12. Sabine von Dirke, *All Power to the Imagination! The West German Counterculture from the Student Movement to the Greens* (Lincoln: University of Nebraska Press, 1997); Andrei Markovits and Philip Gorski, *The German Left: Red, Green and Beyond* (New York: Oxford University Press, 1993).

tive of modernization in Germany, the defeat of Leftist "terrorism," the incorporation of the "new social movements" into the polity, and finally the fall of the "second dictatorship" in the German Democratic Republic mark the triumph of economic modernization and democratization in which Germany "returns" to the correct path and takes its rightful place in the "normal" capitalist democratic community of nations, or as Axel Schildt has put it, Germany finally "arrives in the West."[13]

The story of drugs in Germany, and in much of the industrial West, is a story about the complications of modernization. Rather than being understood merely as a peculiar form of crime, a type of sociological deviance, or a physical or psychological malady, drug consumption ought to be understood as a set of consumer practices deeply embedded in the ongoing process of global capitalist modernization. Though the commodities involved in this complex market were, for the most part, illegal, their legal status did not define wholly the meaning ascribed to drugs. Indeed, drugs, both as a group of commodities and as a set of discourses, offer a particularly clear lens through which we can examine the social and cultural changes of the postwar period.[14] The debates about drugs demonstrate the contentious nature of the principal aspects of modernization: consumer culture, globalization, and democratization.

The development of consumer culture in the postwar period has spawned an enormous amount of research over the last decade.[15] This outpouring of work has not been limited to the postwar period but, as

13. Axel Schildt, *Ankunft im Westen.* The idea of Westernization has been criticized by a number of historians. See, for instance, Hanna Schissler, "Writing about 1950s West Germany," in *The Miracle Years: A Cultural History of West Germany, 1949–1968,* ed. Hanna Schissler (Princeton: Princeton University Press, 2001), 5.

14. This is, of course, true of many commodities. The world of things often serves as an entry point into an investigation of social values. See Victoria de Grazia, "Introduction," in *The Sex of Things: Gender and Consumption in Historical Perspective,* ed. Victoria de Grazia and Ellen Furlough (Berkeley: University of California Press, 1996).

15. See, for example, Michael Wildt, *Am Beginn der "Konsumgesellschaft,"* and *Vom kleinen Wohlstand: eine Konsumgeschichte der fünfziger Jahre* (Frankfurt: Fischer Taschenbücher, 1996); Erica Carter, *How German Is She? Postwar West German Reconstruction and the Consuming Woman* (Ann Arbor: University of Michigan Press, 1997); David F. Crew, ed., *Consuming Germany in the Cold War* (New York: Berg, 2003); Martin Daunton and Matthew Hilton, eds., *The Politics of Consumption: Material Culture and Citizenship in Europe and America* (Oxford: Berg, 2001); Hartmut Berghoff, ed., *Konsumpolitik: die Regulierung des privaten Verbrauchs im 20. Jahrhundert* (Göttingen: Vandenhoeck & Ruprecht, 1999).

Jarausch and Geyer have recently argued, presents a possible new narrative to explain the German twentieth century.[16] Yet the path to a successful consumer culture proved to be a difficult one with its own contradictions. Youth drug consumption, which began in the early 1960s and became defined as a serious threat by the end of the decade, posed a serious dilemma to the notion of consumer society, one that was in fact quite contradictory. For the state, widespread drug consumption exposed a paradox inherent in the modernization project: how could the state promote and control consumption at the same time? For a new postwar generation, drug consumption meant something quite different; young consumers began to see "turning on, tuning in, and dropping out" as a way of opting out of consumer society. Yet the results of this project also proved to be paradoxical because their ethos amounted to a rejection of consumption through consumption, and rather than providing a viable alternative to consumer society their actions constructed a global market in recreational pharmaceuticals.

Although the history of consumption has become a new touchstone in defining the course of modernity, consumption on its own is not enough to explain the broad changes in habits and mentalities over the course of the twentieth century. Since the turn to the "new cultural history," the power of the consumption narrative has eclipsed the study of production, which seems to have been jettisoned along with the Marxist paradigm.[17] Yet commodities are not merely consumed. Instead of examining drugs as merely a new mode of youth consumption, I take seriously the need to explain the circuits of commodities: the complex ways in which commodities are produced, distributed, and consumed. The eruption of demand for drugs in the industrial West in the sixties prompted global shifts in the production and distribution of raw materials that involved peasant production and variegated, hierarchical modes of distribution.[18] And many of these changes worked in con-

16. Jarausch and Geyer, *Shattered Past,* 269–317. See also Alon Confino, "Régimes of Consumer Culture: New Narratives in Twentieth-Century German History," *German History* 19 (2001): 135–61.

17. See "Interview with David Blackbourn and Geoff Eley," *German History* 22 (2004): 229–45; Jarausch and Geyer, *Shattered Past.*

18. The literature on drug distribution has been dominated by lurid accounts of trafficking and by a criminology literature focused on deviance. The commodity value of drugs has been largely ignored, and its relationship to "normal" trade has been largely ignored.

gress with larger shifts in production and distribution that were the result of the long process of postwar globalization. As the world—or at least the world of goods—became smaller due to new technologies and methods of transportation, distributors of illicit drug commodities—from wholesale distributors to street dealers to "mules"—were able to utilize legal means of distribution for their own purposes. Modernization, which allowed an increased international circulation of commodities, proved to be a necessary precondition to the emergence of an international market in drugs.

The emergence of an illicit drug economy also highlights the difficulties of modernization's third and most difficult and contentious hallmark: democratization. Much of the literature on the 1950s in West Germany has portrayed the Federal Republic as an essentially conservative state best characterized as "modernization under a conservative guardianship."[19] The sixties, on the other hand, have been seen as a period of dynamic rejection of the conservatism of the Adenauer era in which generational conflict led to greater democratization, as seen in the increased public acceptance of the essential tenets of democracy, the creation of the Great Coalition, the events of 1968, and, eventually, Brandt's *Ostpolitik*.[20] And while the Federal Republic undoubtedly was more firmly democratic in 1970 than it had been in 1949, this new liberalization during the long sixties held its own contradictions, which the drug problem laid bare. While the populace increasingly embraced democracy, deviations from the norm, which certainly increased across the 1960s, became more problematic, and criminal sanctions for a whole gamut of deviance increased in the late sixties and early seventies.[21] Yet the issue of drug use provoked a wide debate over the limits of state power as politicians and the press argued over the seeming criminalization of a substantial portion of the youth population. At

19. Axel Schildt and Arnold Sywottek, "'Reconstruction' and 'Modernization': West German Social History during the 1950s," in *West Germany under Construction,* ed. Moeller, 415. See also Christoph Klessmann, "Ein stolzes Schiff und krächzende Möwen: Die Geschichte der Bundesrepublik und ihre Kritiker," *Geschichte und Gesellschaft* 11 (1985): 476–94; Axel Schildt, *Moderne Zeiten: Freizeit, Massenmedien und "Zeitgeist" in der Bundesrepublik der 50er Jahre* (Hamburg: Christians, 1995).

20. See Axel Schildt and Detlef Siegfried, eds., *Dynamische Zeiten: die 60er Jahre in den beiden deutschen Gesellschaften* (Hamburg: Christians, 2000).

21. See Klaus Weinhauer, *Schutzpolizei in der Bundesrepublik: zwischen Bürgerkrieg und innerer Sicherheit: die turbulenten sechziger Jahre* (Paderborn: Schöningh, 2003).

the same time, young drug users saw their own conduct as a test case for the German democratic spirit and the criminalization of their consumer choices as evidence of the continuing fascist nature of the German state.

This study focuses largely on the city-state of Hamburg for a number of significant reasons. First, because of the illicit nature of the commodities in question, the markets in drugs proved to be international and intensely local at the same time. Writing of a German national market in illicit drugs makes little sense; each major city had its own drug scene that tapped into a larger international market in goods but also had its own peculiarities, hierarchies, and even drug preferences. Furthermore, because of the profound form of federalism instituted in the *Bundesrepublik,* the decisions about social welfare, treatment, and policing were largely left to the states; the federal government created broad policy guidance, such as the promulgation of the new Narcotics Law (Betäubungsmittelgesetz), and poured a substantial amount of money into the problem, but the vast majority of decisions were made at the state level. Hamburg, being a city-state, allows a close examination of the relationship between the implementation of drug policy and the practices of the local drug scene. Hamburg sat at a crossroads of intellectual currents and distribution networks: young Hamburgers looked outward to Stockholm, Copenhagen, and London, while, because of its free port, Hamburg sat at a strategic node of the international trafficking routes. Moreover, Hamburg, with its generous and comparatively progressive social welfare system, acted as a test case for much of the Federal Republic, instituting innovative projects in social work, outreach, and treatment and founding the first coordinating office for drug issues.

In the Federal Republic, the expansion of a consumer economy and democratization was a process fraught with complications. In the end, instead of seeing the history of the Federal Republic as the natural result of Westernization, I argue that the project of capitalist modernization was fundamentally ambiguous and that there were real costs associated with the "return to the West."[22] Or, more troubling, per-

---

22. On Westernization, see Anselm Doering-Manteuffel, *Wie westlich sind die Deutschen? Amerikanisierung und Westernisierung im 20. Jahrundert* (Göttingen: Vandenhoeck & Ruprecht, 1999).

haps Norbert Harmsen's death in 1972 provides a particularly stark symbol of Germany's arrival in the West.

This book is organized into two parts. The first five chapters set out, roughly chronologically, the development of the Hamburg drug scene and the state's attempt to deal with this new social problem. Chapter 1 briefly outlines the history of drugs in Germany from the Second Empire to the early 1960s, focusing on the long decline in drug consumption after the Second World War. Chapter 2 traces the connection between the transformation of Germany into a consumer culture and the emergence of an organized drug scene during the sixties. Chapter 3 shifts to the global political economy of drug production and distribution, examining Germany's place in the larger shifts in the production and distribution of intoxicants over the course of the twentieth century. The politics and construction of the "drug problem" serves as the central issue of chapter 4, while chapter 5 examines the practice of trying to deal with an entrenched urban drug problem.

The last three chapters approach the question of drugs thematically. Chapter 6 raises the question of the ideology and praxis of the "counterculture" in the early seventies by closely examining Hamburg's radical drug help organization, Release. Gender and the paradoxical role of the drug scene in maintaining a conservative gender ideology is the subject of chapter 7. The last chapter examines the failures of Germany's first antidrug campaign as an example of the limits of control in a consumer economy. Finally, a short epilogue uses two films from the early eighties to examine how drugs became a potent way to critique the "success" of the Federal Republic.

1. Drugs in the Age of Classical Addiction

In January 1964, the world stood at the edge of a profound transformation in popular culture. The Beatles were taking off in America, where "I Want to Hold Your Hand" reached number one on the pop charts on the first day of February. Yet many of the cultural transformations that were taking place were far more profound and far less public than the Beatles. Young people throughout the industrial West were creating new styles, new mannerisms, new fashions, and new and assertive ways of thinking about their place in the world. One of the most significant of these new cultural forms of consumption was taking place quietly on the streets and in the clubs of big cities all over Europe: young Europeans were buying and consuming recreational pharmaceuticals.

In Hamburg on the night of 25 January 1964, patrolmen from the Youth Protection Unit, during a regular inspection of a club called Vera Cruz on Balduinstraße, questioned sixteen-year-old Christiana V. from Braunschweig. Obviously intoxicated, the girl admitted she had purchased several twenty-tablet packages of the controlled stimulant Preludin[1] for fifty deutsche marks apiece from a twenty-three-year-old man named Peter. The officers turned Christiana over to her parents and forwarded her case to the Criminal Police for further investigation.[2] Christiana certainly was not the first case of youth drug consumption in Hamburg; in fact, youth drug consumption of various stimulants had been growing in the clubs of Hamburg's red-light dis-

---

1. Preludin was the German trade name for the drug phenmetrazine.
2. StAH, 354-5 II, Jugendbehörde II, Abl. 11.11.1992, 356-04.04 Band 1, Jugendschutztruppe Report, 26 January 1964.

trict since the late 1950s.[3] Yet Christiana's case marks the first incident of a new type of drug use in Hamburg recorded by the Youth Protection Unit and symbolizes an important turning point in one of the most significant social phenomena of the late twentieth century.

From the end of the Second World War through the Adenauer years, illegal drug use had been confined to an insignificant proportion of the population. Made up of physicians, nurses, and the chronically ill, this group was not viewed by authorities as a threat but as a class of individuals in need of medical treatment whose numbers had shown a slow, constant decline. This two-decade trend ended in 1964, when the police and youth authorities first noticed small groups of young people in Hamburg and in other large cities throughout Europe buying, selling, and using illegal drugs. Criminal statistics illustrate this dramatic change. In 1963, the Hamburg Criminal Police investigated 74 individuals for drug offenses, all of whom were adults. Seven years later, the number of investigations had risen to 1,884, an astonishing increase of 2,546 percent.[4] Perhaps even more striking, more than two-thirds of these cases involved teenagers.

In a broader sense, the transformations in the youth drug markets of the 1960s mark a turning point in a longer and, from today's vantage point, surprising story: the long decline in worldwide drug consumption between the mid-1920s and the 1960s. In order to understand the profound changes that took place in the 1960s, we need to first examine this long denouement and its contradictions. This development was a product of the growth of international cooperation; modernization and professionalization in the medical and pharmaceutical communities; new forms of policing and administrating the trade in pharmaceuticals; and political choices both in the centers of colonial power and on the drug-producing and drug-consuming periphery. These changes took place on a global scale yet proved to be uneven, asynchronous, and fraught with complications, many of which held unforeseen and

3. On Hamburg's rock clubs, see Ralf Busch, ed., *Die Beatles in Harburg* (Hamburg: Christians, 1996); Barry Miles, *Paul McCartney: Many Years from Now* (New York: Henry Holt, 1997), 56–78; and Devin McKinney, *Magic Circles: The Beatles in Dream and History* (Cambridge, MA: Harvard University Press, 2003), 3–51.

4. Gerhard Mäckelburg and Hans-Jürgen Wolter, *Jugendkriminalität in Hamburg: Ein Bericht des Landeskriminalamtes über Umfang, Erscheinungsformen und Ursachen der Jugendkriminalität mit einer Übersicht über die statistische Entwicklung der Jahre 1963 bis 1974* (Hamburg: Landeskriminalamt, 1975), 67–69.

unintended consequences. But significantly, they were primarily experienced on an intensely local scale. While the structures of the production and distribution of illicit drugs underwent profound changes, the experiences of drug users and notions about drug addiction showed a discernable continuity in Germany.

The intent of this chapter is not to provide an exhaustive history of drug use and public policy in Germany before the drug wave of the sixties. Instead, the purpose is to establish a foundation from which to discuss the radical transformations in drug production, distribution, and consumption during the 1960s and to introduce the central questions and assumptions that had to be reexamined and reworked by the authorities and the public during the l960s and 1970s. In a sense, it is impossible to understand the significance of the explosion in drug consumption in the sixties and seventies without understanding the long denouement that preceded it.

From the Kaiserreich to the Third Reich

The substantial increases in drug consumption seen in the sixties and early seventies were not novel. Germany had experienced a substantial rise in drug consumption before. While the decadent tales of hedonistic cocaine consumption in Weimar Berlin are well known, these lurid stories are only a small part of a much larger global rise in drug consumption between the 1880s and the mid-1920s.[5] As the colonial powers, beginning with the Anglo-American antiopium movements in the 1870s, started down the long path toward the elimination of the Asian opium trade that had benefited all of the colonial powers for most of the nineteenth century, global drug consumption paradoxically increased. In the industrial West, the reasons for this development were complicated but include the growth of patent medicine industries, the professionalization of pharmacology and the standardization of new painkillers and anesthetics, the rapid rise of injecting technology, and the growth of a modern pharmaceutical industry.

Germany, and Hamburg specifically, played an important part in

5. See David Courtwright, *Forces of Habit: Drugs and the Making of the Modern World* (Cambridge, MA: Harvard University Press, 2002); Alfred W. McCoy, "Coercion and Its Unintended Consequences: A Study of Heroin Trafficking in Southeast and South West Asia," *Crime, Law & Social Change* 33 (2000): 191–224.

this increase in the production and distribution of intoxicating pharmaceuticals. German pharmaceutical firms—such as C. H. Boehringer Sohn in Nieder-Ingelheim, C. F. Boehringer & Söhne in Mannheim, and E. Merck in Darmstadt—played a central role in the production and distribution of opium alkaloids and especially of cocaine.[6] Though most of these drugs were exported, either legally or illegally, to the large drug-using populations in East and Southeast Asia and Iran, a substantial increase in drug consumption was noted in Germany before the First World War. Between 1910 and 1924, for example, the number of drug addicts in German hospitals and asylums rose by a factor of four to eight.[7]

Although drug addiction was on the increase before the war, the number of wounded soldiers with long-term problems coupled with the chaos of the immediate postwar period and the constant increase in pharmaceutical production certainly did little to deter drug use. This continued rise in drug consumption occurred despite legal attempts to control the trade. As a little-known condition of the Treaty of Versailles, Germany was obligated to pass a drug control law in accordance with the Hague opium convention of 1912. The legislature satisfied this demand on 30 December 1920, passing Germany's first opium law despite the complaints of German pharmaceutical producers. While under the 1920 law certain drugs became controlled substances—opium, morphine, and cocaine but not cannabis—that required a doctor's prescription, this seems only to have promoted illicit distribution, and substantial amounts of morphine and cocaine were constantly diverted from the legal trade into the black market through both thefts at wholesalers and semilegal export and reimportation of pharmaceuticals from countries that had not signed the Hague convention.[8] In 1924, the German legislature, in an attempt to strengthen drug laws, increased the penalties for drug crimes from six months to three years in prison.

During the brief flowering of a demimonde drug culture in the 1920s, writers, artists, and intellectuals experimented with drugs: Ernst Jünger, Walter Benjamin, Hans Fallada, and Klaus Mann, just to

6. See Werner Pieper, ed., *Nazis on Speed—Drogen im 3. Reich,* vol. 1 (Löhrbach: Grüne Kraft, 2002), 27.
7. Pieper, *Nazis on Speed,* 31.
8. See Pieper, *Nazis on Speed,* 28, 30.

name a few.[9] Drug consumption also became a prominent theme for popular culture, providing an exotic subject for German silent filmmakers such as Robert Reinert.[10] Yet the majority of drug consumers came from the working class. And the effects of the illicit trade in morphine and cocaine by the mid-1920s had set off a panic. Reports like Hans Wolfgang Maier's *Kokainismus* in 1926 showed the dramatic and devastating effects cocaine could have on the human body; it was filled with case studies of patients with severe maladies brought on by cocaine use.[11]

Yet cocaine consumption seems to have reached its peak both worldwide and in Germany by the mid-1920s. In a thorough examination of the global cocaine trade, David Musto argues that drug prohibitions do not help explain the decline in cocaine consumption after the midtwenties. Instead, he argues that the effects of cocaine use led to a larger cultural turn away from cocaine before international agreements had any substantial effect.[12] Morphine addiction, on the other hand, proved to be a more intractable problem, and German pharmaceutical companies continued to produce and export large quantities of narcotics, particularly of uncontrolled drugs such as codeine, throughout the twenties.[13] Yet opiate addiction also seems to have begun to decline in Germany by the late 1920s, but whether this was a result of the Depression, better drug control, or changes in medical proscribing practices remains unclear.

Following the Second Geneva Opium Conference, in the summer of 1929 the German government passed a more flexible drug control law

9. See Pieper, "Mann, Benjamin, Benn, Jünger & Co.: Dichter und Denker, Kiffer & Junkies," in *Nazis on Speed,* 55–58; and Scott J. Thompson, "From 'Rausch to Rebellion'— Walter Benjamin on Hashish," in *Nazis on Speed,* ed. Pieper, 59–70. See also Anton Kaes, Martin Jay, and Edward Dimendberg, *The Weimar Sourcebook* (Berkeley: University of California Press, 1995).

10. Jack Stevenson, ed., *Addicted: The Myth and Menace of Drugs in Film* (n.p.: Creation, 1999), 14–15.

11. Hans Wolfgang Maier, *Der Kokainismus: Geschichte, Pathologie, Medizinische und behördliche Bekämpfung* (Leipzig: G. Thieme, 1926). For the English translation, see Hans W. Maier and Oriana Josseau Kalant, *Maier's Cocaine Addiction* (Toronto: Addiction Research Foundation, 1987).

12. David Musto, *The American Disease: Origins of Narcotic Control,* exp. ed. (New York: Oxford University Press, 1987).

13. Hans Cousto, "Verbotene Früchte oder Die Verordnungsflut," in *Nazis on Speed,* ed. Pieper, 204–5.

that consolidated previous drug laws, outlawed cannabis preparations, and allowed the government to add drugs to the controlled substances list without having to pass a new law.[14] Then, the following year it passed the Ordinance for the Prescription of Narcotic Medicines and Their Distribution in Pharmacies, which "set maximum daily doses of controlled substances, required written prescriptions for morphine, forbade the distribution of cocaine, and threatened doctors with up to three years in prison."[15] These control measures came into effect as Germany slumped into political chaos following the onset of the Great Depression. And the pressure on drug users soon increased as the Nazi Party came to power.

Drug addiction did not fit neatly into the Nazi worldview. After the seizure of power in 1933, the Nazis set out to protect and encourage the health of the *Volk*. This included campaigns against smoking, drinking, and drugs.[16] Hitler—an abstinent, vegetarian nonsmoker— believed that these vices were outward signs of cultural decline. And the widespread acceptance of notions of racial hygiene and genetic determination in both medical and policing circles made it easy for the state to increasingly marginalize drug consumers as asocial, psychopathic, or genetically deficient. New measures were taken to strengthen the existing policing and social welfare work against addiction. And new groups, such as the Imperial Committee for the Struggle against Drugs (Reichsarbeitsgemeinschaft für Rauschgiftbekämpfung), were created to bring the medical, policing, and political experts together in the war against drugs. Starting in 1935, the Nazi government created the Imperial Center for the Struggle against Drug Crimes (Reichszentrale zur Bekämpfung von Rauschgiftvergehen) at the Prussian Criminal Police Office in Berlin, which acted as a central information-collecting office for drug crimes from the various district police offices.[17] Over the course of the thirties and during the war, the German government created a substantial welfare and policing bureaucracy to deal with issues of addiction, though drug addiction always took a backseat

14. Ibid., 205.

15. Pieper, *Nazis on Speed,* 32.

16. On smoking and the health campaigns, see Robert Proctor, *The Nazi War on Cancer* (Princeton: Princeton University Press, 1999).

17. StAH, Gesundheitsbehörde, 696 Band 3, "Schärferer Kampf gegen Rauschgiftvergehen," *Hamburger Nachrichten,* 3 December 1935.

to the much more pervasive problems of alcohol and tobacco consumption. Like alcoholics, drug users faced a number of possible sanctions, from conviction under the Opium Law to findings of mental and
legal incompetence resulting in forced internment in a treatment or
withdrawal center or, in the worst-case scenario, in a concentration
camp.[18] In the end, the Nazi war on drugs developed out of a larger
worldview. If Nazi Germany can best be understood as a "racial state,"
then drug addiction acted as a powerful metaphor of disease and
degeneration within the body politic, and drug addicts, like so many
other groups deemed "asocial," paid a steep price for a set of morally
bankrupt principles.

While National Socialist drug policy seems to have maintained and
even promoted a long-term decrease in the incidence of drug consumption, in other ways the state promoted drug use. Paradoxically, at the
height of the Nazi struggle against narcotic addiction, German pharmacology and the pharmaceutical industry were busy creating new
generations of abusable drugs. In the 1930s, pharmacologists throughout the industrial West were investigating the properties of stimulants,
the most successful of which was amphetamine, marketed in the
United States by the Lilly drug company under the name Benzedrine.
In 1934, a group of German pharmacologists synthesized methamphetamine, an analog of amphetamine that proved to be twice as effective.
In 1938, the Temmler pharmaceutical company in Berlin began mass
production of methamphetamine under the trade name Pervitin. Marketed as a balm for a number of physical and psychological symptoms,
Pervitin remained an over-the-counter drug until 1941, when studies
indicated that users developed a tolerance to the drug.[19] Yet even after
Pervitin became a prescription-only drug, much of the population
received the stimulant directly from the government. Starting with the
invasion of Poland in 1939, troops were regularly provided with the
drug to keep them alert and awake, and military medical personnel

18. Holger Mach, "Ausschluß and Ausmerzung: Rauschgiftbekämpfung im Dritten
Reich," in *Nazis on Speed,* ed. Pieper, 212. For Hamburg, see StAH, 351-10 II, Sozialbehörde
II, Abl. 3, 135.20-0 Band 1, Memo from Sieveking, 23 August 1941.
19. See E. Speer, "Das Pervitinproblem," *Deutsches Ärzteblatt* 71 (1941): 4–6, 15–19; F.
Dittmar, "Pervitinsucht und akute Pervitinintoxikation," *Deutsche Medizinische Wochenschrift* 68, no. 11 (1942): 266–68; F. Kalus, I. Kucher, and J. Zutt, "Über Psychosen bei chro-
nischem Pervitinmissbrauch," *Nervenarzt* 15 (1942): 313–24.

widely prescribed the drug to soldiers. Between April and Decemeber 1941 alone, the Temmler factory delivered twenty-nine million doses of Pervitin to the military. Then after the defeat at Stalingrad, more and more Germans were provided with Pervitin, not only soldiers but also those on the home front in antiaircraft crews, blackout patrols, and other civil defense squads.[20]

Drug consumption patterns changed significantly between the time of German unification and the fall of the Third Reich. In the waning years of the nineteenth century, drug consumption increased, led by significant changes in production, technology, and marketing. This rise in the availability of narcotics and cocaine continued through the first quarter of the twentieth century, boosted by the cataclysm of the First World War. Yet even as production and consumption rose, forces were at work that led to a gradual decrease in consumption after the mid-1920s. A new international control regime haltingly began before the war, while wartime concerns spread control measures to most European countries. After the war, consumption of narcotics and cocaine rose, but the effects of drug addiction became more apparent, particularly in the large cities. For this reason, drug consumption appears to have begun decreasing even before substantial legal controls were in place. After the Nazi seizure of power, a racial hygiene campaign to rid the country of all forms of addiction led to a continued decrease in consumption of "intoxicating poisons." Yet at the same time, continued pharmacological research created new classes of abusable drugs, which with their simulative effects proved helpful in the service of the Nazi war machine.

The Reimposition of Control after the Second World War

The Second World War marked a turning point in drug addiction. With the outbreak of global war, what little was left of the drug underground of the twenties and thirties disappeared. Cut off from supplies, the illegal trafficking of the interwar period did not outlast the war.[21]

20. Wolf-R. Kemper, "Pervitin—Die Einsteig Droge?" in *Nazis on Speed,* ed. Pieper, 122–29.

21. See Alan Block, "European Drug Traffic and Traffickers between the Wars: The Policy of Suppression and Its Consequences," *Journal of Social History* 23 (1989): 315–38, reprinted in Alan Block, *Space, Time and Organized Crime,* 2d ed. (London: Transaction, 1994), 93–128.

Yet as drug trafficking reached a thirty-year low, there was reason for concern. Years of fighting had left an enormous number of soldiers injured, many of whom were dependent on one form of painkiller or another. As early as 1941, fearing a repeat of the widespread addiction at the end of the First World War, the German Department of the Interior required troop doctors to report any soldier addicted to drugs or considered at risk for addiction to the soldier's home district.[22] At the same time, however, the Wehrmacht was creating its own addicts. Though many soldiers came home from the war addicted to narcotics, what little evidence exists suggests that most did not stay addicted for long.[23] The monumental levels of addiction that authorities feared during the war never surfaced. In fact, after the initial rise in drug consumption, the postwar period saw an unprecedented period of decline in drug use. Yet in the difficult years of rebuilding following the war, drugs became an integral part of a society and economy in ruins.

On 3 May 1945, the British army occupied the Free and Hanseatic City of Hamburg. After three years of Allied bombing, the city lay in ruins. The British Military Government faced the immediate problem of feeding and housing a population of 1.6 million.[24] With a city in ruins and an urban population facing a subsistence crisis, there is little reason to think that controlling drugs would have been a priority. Yet during the first month of the occupation the British Military Government in Hamburg sought to bring German narcotics control into alignment with the prewar international agreements, announcing that since the Opium Office in the National Health Department in Berlin had been disbanded, the Pharmacists' Board in Hamburg would take immediate control of the narcotics import and export certificate system mandated by international convention. At the same time, the president of the German Civil Government of Schleswig-Holstein placed the pharmacies of his district under the direction of the Hamburg board.[25]

---

22. "Bekämpfung des Mißbrauchs von Betäubungsmittel," *Ministerialblatt des Reichs- und Preußischen Ministeriums des Innern*, 12 November 1941.

23. By the early 1950s, ex-soldiers still made up a sizable percentage of the addict population, but their numbers seem small given the numbers of those injured during the war. See StAH, 352-6, Gesundheitsbehörde, 696 Band 3, "Meldungen an das Bundesgesundheitsamt auf Grund internationaler Betäubungsabkommen," 7 March 1953.

24. See Michael Wildt, *Der Traum vom Sattwerden: Hunger und Protest, Schwarzmarkt und Selbsthilfe* (Hamburg: VSA-Verlag, 1986), esp. 25–35.

25. StAH, 352–6, Gesundheitsbehörde, 696 Band 1, memo from von Fisenne, Apothekerkammer Nordmark, 25 August 1945.

During 1945, the crisis in procurement of goods proved particularly acute in the case of narcotics. Want was widespread in Hamburg; even the most common necessities were in desperately short supply. Hospitals and pharmacies were hard-pressed to supply their patients with even the most commonplace drugs such as antibiotics and analgesics. By early September, officials at the Nordmark Pharmacists' Board warned that they were rapidly running through their stores of both processed and unprocessed narcotics. They urged all doctors to prescribe narcotics only in "especially urgent cases." With the return of large numbers of injured soldiers to Hamburg, they warned, large amounts of narcotics would be required and physicians should modify their prescribing habits accordingly.[26] Despite the warnings, by the end of 1946 the shortages of narcotics were still desperate, so much so that the police asked the district attorney's office to send narcotics seized as evidence in criminal cases to the Health Department.[27]

A year into the occupation, the British Military Government established the basis for a postwar drug policy in Hamburg with Military Order Number 95 on 24 June 1946. The order sought to impose a rational drug policy, focusing on two main goals. First, it sought to reinstitute an institutional structure that could fulfill the requirements of the various international narcotics conventions of the 1920s and 1930s and comply with the League of Nations—and the subsequent United Nations—certificate system, an arrangement for the international control of the import and export of narcotics and other dangerous drugs.[28] Second, it placed local control of both the narcotics traffic and addicts in the hands of the Criminal Police and, to a lesser extent, the Health Department. In effect, the British Military Government merely rubber-stamped the continuation of the prewar German organization.

26. StAH, 352-6, Gesundheitsbehörde, 696 Band I, memo from von Fisenne, Apothekerkammer Nordmark, 7 September 1945; StAH, 352-6, Gesundheitsbehörde, 696 Band I, memo from von Fisenne, Apothekerkammer Nordmark, 25 August 1945, and memo from Stadtoberinspektor Worthmann, 14 December 1946.

27. StAH, 352-6, Gesundheitsbehörde, 696 Band I, letter from Breuer, Polizei Hamburg, Kriminalamt to Gesundheitsverwaltung, 31 December 1946.

28. This story has been exhaustively explored elsewhere and need not detain us here. The standard book on the international movement and the influential role of the United States is Musto's *The American Disease*. See also Kettil Bruun et al., *The Gentlemen's Club: International Control of Drugs and Alcohol* (Chicago: University of Chicago Press, 1975), and Arnold Taylor, *American Diplomacy and the Narcotics Traffic, 1900–1939* (Durham, NC: Duke University Press, 1969).

Though the reimposition of the League of Nations certificate system brought Germany back into compliance with its international obligations, in retrospect it showed a certain lack of foresight. The certificate system had been set up to deal with the specific problems of international drug trafficking during the first quarter of the century: the gradual cessation of legal, nonmedical drug consumption and the reduction of the diversion of legal pharmaceuticals into the international black market.[29] By requiring countries to issue import and export certificates for every transaction, the League of Nations system improved both of these dilemmas. On the other hand, the certificate system by its very nature could do little to stem the subterranean trade in illicitly produced drugs. While it is certainly true that the organizations charged with carrying out the certificate system had a substantial impact, not only on the import and export of narcotics but also on the control of the distribution of medically necessary narcotics through the regulation of doctors and pharmacists, the very success in solving the problem of drug diversion—*the* problem of the first half of the twentieth century—led creative entrepreneurs to develop new sources of production and new patterns of distribution over the course of the postwar period.

In order to set up a system of zonal control, the British Military Government resurrected the Opium Law of 10 December 1929. This Weimar-era law and its amendments under the Nazi regime placed raw opium, processed opium, various pharmaceutical derivatives and synthetics of opium, cocaine leaves and their processed derivatives, and *cannabis indica*—in its many forms—under strict control. Military Order Number 95 created a system of control that focused on crime control. It required that all controlled substances be kept in locked cabinets and that exact records be kept, threatened that infractions would be severely punished, and placed responsibility for the oversight of these regulations with the Criminal Police in four major cities: Hamburg, Hannover, Münster, and Düsseldorf. The order also created a zonal system of police drug intelligence. Local police were required to report all real or suspected infringements of the law by either firms or individuals to the British Zone's Central Criminal Police in Hamburg. This central office regularly distributed lists of suspected narcotics

29. See Block, "European Drug Traffic."

addicts and dealers to police throughout the British Occupation Zone. Doctors, public health officers, and the local medical boards were obligated to report any narcotics addicts or any persons suspected of being an addict to the police. Furthermore, producers and distributors were likewise obligated to report any infraction or suspicion of an infraction against the Narcotics Law to the police. The inspection of pharmacies was placed under the control of the Criminal Police rather than the Health Department; at least once every three months, each pharmacy's books were to be examined. Any suspicion that a pharmacy was aiding or abetting either addicts or dealers was to be reported immediately to the central office.[30]

The zonal system set up by Military Order Number 95 stayed in effect throughout the official occupation period only to be replaced in 1952, three years after the founding of the Federal Republic, by the newly formed Federal Opium Office in Koblenz. Placed under the aegis of the Federal Health Office, the new control body's responsibilities remained much the same as the earlier zonal Opium Offices: the implementation of the United Nations certificates system, the observation of the national and international trade in legal narcotics, the supervision of producers and wholesalers as well as pharmacies and hospitals, the creation of the reports required by international conventions, and the support of local and state offices.[31]

The attempt to bring order and control to the legal production and distribution of illicit substances through the Opium Office in Kiel and its successor in Koblenz proved a limited success. It was successful insofar as it managed to do what it set out to do: control the legal trade in narcotics. By the late 1950s, the amount of narcotics entering the illicit economy through diversions from the licit economy had mostly dried up. Physicians were less likely to prescribe maintenance doses of narcotics for patients, and both hospitals and pharmacies were more secure. Yet it remained a flawed system. While drug consumption and addiction declined under the control system, by focusing on halting

30. StAH, 352-6, Gesundheitsbehörde, 696 Band 1, regulation from CCG, 24 June 1946.

31. StAH, Gesundheitsbehörde, 696 Band 3, memo from Redeker, Bundesministerium des Innern, 15 November 1952. Gewehr, "Die gesetzlichen Grundlagen der Bundesopiumstelle und ihr Aufgabenbereich," in *Rauschgift: Arbeitstagung im Bundeskriminalamt Wiesbaden Vom 21. November bis 26. November 1955 über Bekämpfung von Rauschgiftdelikten,* ed. Bundeskriminalamt Wiesbaden (Wiesbaden: Bundesdruckerei, 1956), 55–58.

diversions from the licit trade, the system proved to be unable to detect or deal with new challenges when sources of supply and patterns of distribution changed.

The Black Market

Although the establishment of the central Opium Offices went far in coordinating and rationalizing the legal trade in narcotics, the extensive black market proved to be a major force in the years immediately following the war. From the end of the war until the currency reform in 1948, the economy of Germany was an unmitigated disaster. Rationing was a way of life, and in the hard winters of 1946 and 1947, even with ration cards, goods were scarce. Hunger became a daily reality for many. To survive this crisis, Germans developed a number of strategies, both legal and illegal. One of the most important was the black market. With almost all conceivable consumer goods under rationing, the black market became an extensive alternative economy. Hamburg and other *Großstädte* such as Berlin, Hannover, Düsseldorf, Munich, and Frankfurt developed as important centers of the underground economy. In April 1946, the police chief in Bremen wrote: "The black market in the streets, which is practically dead in Bremen, is a normal, obvious, and more or less accepted phenomenon in Hamburg. Everyone you ask in the street can tell you when the best trading time is in the different squares."[32] In St. Georg, the district around the main train station, and St. Pauli, the port area on the north bank of the Elbe, almost anything could be had for the right price. In addition to daily necessities, consumers particularly desired luxury consumables such as coffee, alcohol, and tobacco. Cigarettes were in such demand and so easily traded that they became in many ways "the measure of all things."[33] Police seizures give only a hint of how enormous and varied this illegal economy was. In 1946 alone, police in Hamburg confiscated over 1 million kilograms of various foodstuffs, 172 kilograms of sweets, 28 cows, 25 horses, nearly 200,000 cigarettes and ration coupons good for another 1 million, and cigars by the tens of thousands; they also

32. Quoted in Willi A. Boelcke, *Der Schwarzmarkt 1945–1948: Vom Überleben nach dem Kriege* (Braunschweig: Westermann, 1986), 85–86.
33. Ibid., 114.

recovered more than 3,000 liters of spirits, over 30,000 liters of wine, over 5,000 meters of fabric, nearly 2,000 pieces of clothing, and 26 cars, among countless other items. Drugs were also widely traded; police seized nearly 5,000 ampoules of narcotics and an incredible 40 million doses of penicillin; the black market value of all of these confiscated wares was estimated at 16.5 million reichsmarks.

In this atmosphere of constant want and insecurity, the black market in narcotics flourished. There were reports in Hamburg that it was less expensive to buy morphine than schnapps.[34] Almost any drug could be had on the black market: raw opium, medicinal opium, morphine, heroin, and cocaine; other opiate derivatives and synthetic painkillers, such as hydrocodone, hydromorphone, oxycodone, pethidine, codeine, and ethylmorphine; as well as stimulants such as amphetamine and methamphetamine. It seemed to authorities as if there was an almost endless supply of these drugs in circulation.

For the authorities, the reason for the widespread availability of drugs was clear. At the end of the war, as the Allied armies closed in, workers in hospitals and in pharmaceutical companies as well as members of the German armed forces had simply walked away from their jobs with anything and everything they could lay their hands on. Similarly, workers stole the stocks of drug factories that had been dispersed to avoid the bombing attacks. The single most important source of narcotics was the many abandoned *Sanitätsparks,* the temporary medical depots of the German army. Narcotics were stored in bulk at these facilities, and in the chaos of early 1945, employees and looters pilfered most of these stores as the army pulled back. Though it is impossible to estimate the amount of narcotics stolen from these facilities, the quantities were significant. In one of the few army medical depots that was not looted, for example, authorities found over three million tablets, ampoules, and suppositories of the powerful synthetic painkiller pethidine.[35] The drugs from these army depots supplied the illicit narcotics market for five years and continued to have a measurable effect on the market a decade after the war.

34. Wildt, *Traum,* 106–13, and StAH, 352-6, Gesundheitsbehörde, 696 Band 1, "Tätigkeitsbericht der Beratungsstelle für Nerven-, Gemüts- und Rauschgiftkranke des Gesundheitsamtes Hamburg für 1947/1948."

35. United Nations, *Summary of Annual Reports of Governments Relating to Narcotic Drugs and Psychotropic Substances,* E/NR/1948/Summary, 45.

The motivation of these opportunistic thieves was equally clear. It was obvious to many in the last months of the war that the currency would not hold its value. People feared a recurrence of the hyperinflation of the 1920s. In anticipation of a devalued currency, goods seemed stable. Even if the currency lost all its value, goods remained tangible and could be bartered. Hoarded narcotics were often not consumed by their owners but instead treated like a speculative investment. Individuals bought drugs hoping either to sell them in a different area or to hold on to them until their value increased. The reason for this type of speculation was the enormous profit to be made. In 1947, dealers were asking as much as one thousand reichsmarks (US$100) for a single gram of morphine and up to two hundred reichsmarks (US$20) for one ampoule.[36] The British government went so far as to claim in 1948 that stolen narcotics "for the past three years formed the high-denomination currency of the black market."[37]

Evidence suggests that there was a significant intranational trade in drugs in Germany from the end of the war until the early years of the Federal Republic. But drug trafficking in the late 1940s and early 1950s little resembled the type of organized hierarchical trade that developed in the 1970s. Drug trafficking consisted mostly of individuals trying to dispose of various pharmaceuticals at a profit, with little intention of making a business of it. In 1949, for instance, police in the British Zone investigated 423 persons for illicit trafficking. The next year the number fell to 337, of whom only 5 were previously known as traders in narcotics.

The case of Adolf S. offers an example of this type of semicriminal intranational trafficking of the late 1940s and early 1950s. Adolf and a friend, Clemens F., worked at a textile factory in Gronau, Westphalia. When the factory stopped paying its employees near the end of the war, Adolf and Clemens hatched a plan with another employee, Willi C. The woman whom Adolf lived with at the time, Margarethe L., had managed to acquire 5 kilograms of opium powder and asked him to find a buyer for 2 kilograms of the drug. The three coconspirators, Adolf S., Clemens F., and Willi C., wanted to sell the opium and use

36. United Nations, *Summary of Annual Reports of Governments Relating to Narcotic Drugs and Psychotropic Substances,* E/NR/1947/Summary, 37–39.
37. United Nations, *Summary of Annual Reports,* E/NR/1948/Summary, 44.

the money to reopen the textile factory. Clemens and Willi visited Hamburg in May 1949, where they met a man named Wilhelm H. in a bar. They offered him the opium for nine thousand deutsche marks per kilogram. Unable to meet the price for the 2 kilograms, Wilhelm bought 200 grams for two thousand deutsche marks. Early the next year, Adolf took the remaining opium to Kiel to look for a buyer. A farmer in Kiel told Adolf that he knew someone in Hamburg who would want the opium. The trip to Hamburg came to nothing, however, as they failed to find the customer. After returning to Kiel, they met an Italian named Bernard B. who knew someone in Frankfurt who might be interested in the contraband. The two made the trip to Frankfurt, but the buyer was not interested. Adolf then returned to Kiel to look for another buyer. This time he was not so lucky. He offered the opium to an undercover police officer and was arrested at Eckernförde with 1,180 grams of the opium.

Adolf S.'s story is indicative of the opportunistic type of drug dealing that went on in the 1940s and early 1950s. He certainly was not a hardened criminal. Difficult times and seemingly fortuitous circumstances coupled with naiveté led Adolf, Clemens, and Willi to try their luck, do something illegal, and hope that they could reopen the textile factory in which they had previously worked. They saw the opium as a means to begin earning an honest living once again. They were in no sense part of "organized crime"; they were merely individuals trying to make do in bleak times.

International smuggling in the late 1940s and early 1950s had little in common with that of the prewar period. The Second World War destroyed the relatively sophisticated international drug-smuggling networks of the interwar period.[38] It was not until the early 1950s, when the legendary French Connection began trafficking drugs through Marseilles to New York, that French, Corsican, Italian, and Turkish traffickers reestablished a substantial international traffic. But even though this organized illicit traffic was absent during the "rubble years," there was a limited European market for stolen pharmaceuticals. Not surprisingly, the primary source of these narcotics was the looted German army stores, from which the drugs were either stolen during occupation or smuggled out of Germany. The centers of this

38. See Block, "European Drug Traffic."

trade, outside Germany, were Paris, Amsterdam, Rotterdam, and Antwerp. In January 1947, for example, a worker at a Parisian bakery and two accomplices were arrested while trying to sell a large amount of morphine, 85.6 kilograms, for 1,290,000 francs (US$10,848.90). The baker had stolen the drugs from a German army rail car while he was employed as a porter for the French National Railway. After liberation, he brought the vials to Paris, hoping to sell them on the black market.[39]

The largest international trade by far was between the British Zone and the Netherlands. By 1947, Dutch authorities were complaining about the large amounts of narcotics being smuggled into their territory from the British Zone, primarily through Aachen and Maastricht.[40] In February, a Dutch citizen was arrested at Losser with seventeen ampoules of morphine. He claimed to have purchased the drugs from an acquaintance in Germany and attempted to smuggle them across the border in his belt. A month later, a Rhine river tug fireman was arrested in Rotterdam with a substantial stash: ten grams of morphine, ten grams of codeine, and assorted other painkillers. The fireman admitted that he had traded foodstuffs for the drugs in the Ruhr region. At the beginning of May, 247 ampoules of morphine and synthetic painkillers from German army stores were confiscated in Amsterdam.[41] As the plundered stocks became scarce in the early 1950s, the international trade dwindled.

The local drug trade in Hamburg was similar to both the domestic and international trade but much smaller in scale. Most dealing took place in the bars and hotels of the area around the main train station, St. Georg, and the red-light district around the port, St. Pauli. A few dealers were professional black marketeers; others were waiters, bartenders, and toilet or coat check attendants. Most, however, were simply people who had come into the possession of a certain amount of narcotics and wanted to dispose of them or exchange them for other commodities. In December 1948, for example, a sixteen-year-old car-

39. United Nations, *Summary of Illicit Transactions and Seizures,* E/NS/1948/Summary, 1 April–30 June 1947, 37–38, and 1 July–31 August 1948, 3.

40. Ironically, the exact opposite was true in the 1960s and 1970s, as Germans lamented loudly the role of Amsterdam in the corruption of Germany's youth.

41. United Nations, *Summary of Illicit Transactions and Seizures,* E/NS/1948/Summary, July–August 1948, 3, 17, 30.

penter's apprentice was apprehended on the Reeperbahn—the main street of Hamburg's red-light district—trying to sell nine ampoules of morphine he had found by the train tracks near Eidelsted. Fifteen days later, police arrested a Greek newspaperman in the main train station with fifty grams of cocaine. He had acquired the drug in Augsburg and planned to sell it on the black market in Hamburg. Two months later, in March, police arrested a thirty-four-year-old businessman in the Hamburg subway. During the war, he had headed an army section that supplied troops in Schleswig-Holstein and appropriated a substantial supply of narcotics. In November, a forty-four-year-old gardener and a fifty-year-old laborer tried to sell two hundred ampoules of morphine at the main train station for six deutsche marks (US$1.80) apiece.[42]

As stolen supplies began to dry up at the end of the forties, some dealers began to cheat their customers, offering various ersatz substances as narcotics. In 1949, eighty-five people in the British Zone were arrested for dealing in false wares. The next year this number had fallen to thirty-eight. Dealers sold novocaine, caffeine, quinine, or insulin in cocaine ampoules; homeostatic drugs were passed off as ampoules of morphine. Some dealers filled original drug packaging with potato meal or other benign substances, and in one case poppy cake was offered to one unsuspecting consumer as opium.[43]

While the black market in the red-light district remained the focus of policing activities, rampant drug trafficking in the displaced persons camps in the half decade after the war particularly troubled authorities. Though most of the drugs came from stolen Wehrmacht stocks, there were reports of thefts from the clinics at the camps. The British Occupation Government reported in 1948 that

A number of the cases led one to suppose that in certain camps there was an organized business in the bartering of narcotics for coffee and cigarettes supplied to the camps for welfare purposes through IRO [international relief organizations].[44]

42. United Nations, *Summary of Illicit Transactions and Seizures,* E/NS/1948/Summary, May–June 1949, 14, 33, 34, 53.

43. StAH, 352-6, Gesundheitsbehörde, 696 Band 2, Government of the United Kingdom, Zonal Narcotics Office, "Report by the Office of the U.K. High Commissioner for the Calendar Year 1950."

44. United Nations, *Summary of Annual Reports,* E/NR/1948/Summary, 44.

Hamburg police occasionally arrested residents of the camps on drug charges. In March 1949, for example, a twenty-three-year-old Ukrainian truck driver was arrested in Hamburg after a woman claiming to be his fiancée reported him to the police. When police searched his belongings at the displaced persons camp, they found thirteen tablets of morphine in his locker. The truck driver claimed that the camp quartermaster had ordered him to store the effects of an ethnic Polish, Ukrainian national and that the drugs must have belonged to him.[45]

Drugs were also being smuggled into the camps from Hamburg. In the spring of 1949, a former employee named Emil T. approached Werner K., the owner of a chemical and wholesale drug company in Hamburg. Emil claimed that he could obtain 1,440 ampoules of the painkiller hydromorphone for around DM 3 apiece. Werner agreed to fund the adventure, and the deal finally went through in July, when Emil purchased the hydromorphone from a druggist named Hans W. for DM 4,320 (US$991). Werner, seeing an opportunity to unload the drugs at a profit, then sent Emil to attempt to sell the hydromorphone to pharmaceutical firms in the Russian Zone. Emil failed to find a buyer and returned the ampoules to Werner in Hamburg in March 1950. Desperate to recoup his investment, Werner tried to sell the ampoules to one of his Latvian employees, named Jaseps K., who thought he could sell the narcotics at one of the displaced persons camps. Werner left him with eight ampoules as samples, which Jaseps then attempted to sell for DM 3.80 apiece to buyers at the displaced persons camp at Bergen-Belsen, a former concentration camp. Before he could conclude the transaction, the police captured him. On evidence from Jaseps, Hamburg police had Emil arrested. He had twenty ampoules of painkillers on his person at the time. Emil claimed that they were a gift from the druggist Hans and "that they were to be used by his family and himself as a last resort if the Russians should overrun the British Zone." Police then arrested Hans in Hannover at the request of the Hamburg police and searched his residence, where they found small quantities of various narcotics. According to his confession, Hans had worked as a pharmacist in the Wehrmacht during the

45. United Nations, *Summary of Illicit Transactions and Seizures,* E/NS/1949/Summary, November–December 1949, 50.

war and had absconded with the drugs. Drug trafficking in the displaced persons camps was, in any case, fairly short lived.[46] In the early
1950s, the camps began to be dismantled and reports of their role in the
drug trade began to disappear.

Another source of drug trafficking was the port. As in most port
cities around the world, Hamburg had a small number of transient and
semitransient Chinese sailors, many of whom were frequent opium
smokers, even in the postwar period. In April 1949, police in Hamburg
arrested a sixty-year-old man named Chung Chong for attempting to
sell a kilogram of opium. Upon further investigation, the police determined that Chung had established an opium-smoking den in his cellar
room on Schmuckstraße. He admitted that he was addicted to opium
and had bought the kilogram on the black market. He was eventually
sentenced to one year in prison. Three years later, in August 1952,
Chung sold 100 grams of raw opium to an undercover U.S. agent. The
next month he sold him another 380 grams. Unable to supply any
more, Chung gave the agents the address of one Chong Kok Low in
Rotterdam, claiming they could find more opium there. After the lead
failed to produce results, the agents returned to Chung. He promised
them another kilogram of raw opium. After the first 880 grams were
delivered, the agents arrested Chung. He claimed to have purchased
the opium from a sailor from the steamer *Indian Trader*. The Chinese,
as Chung's story shows, played a role in the drug trade in Hamburg.
Yet unlike other ports with larger Chinese populations, such as London or Amsterdam, the fears of "yellow contagion" or the effeminacy
brought on through the "oriental" vice never really seized the public
imagination.[47]

The 1948 currency reform represented a watershed, both in real
terms and in people's imaginations.[48] With the currency reform and the
gradual removal of rationing through 1949 and 1950, the black market

46. United Nations, *Summary of Illicit Transactions and Seizures,* E/NS/1950/Summary,
May–June 1950, 87–88.

47. See Marek Kohn, *Dope Girls: The Birth of the British Drug Underground* (London:
Lawrence & Wishart, 1992); Virginia Berridge, "East End Opium Dens and Narcotic Use in
Britain," *London Journal* 4 (1978): 4–28.

48. See Michael Wildt, "Plurality of Taste: Food and Consumption in West Germany
during the 1950s," *History Workshop Journal* 39 (1995): 22–41.

withered away. When goods became available in stores and people had money with which to buy them, there remained little need for the type of extensive underground economy that existed in the first few years after the war. This general expansion of legal and practical access to commodities had little direct effect on the illegal drug trade, but it did have indirect effects. Whereas during the years of want narcotics had been just another illegal commodity in a sea of illegal commodities, the return of free availability for most goods highlighted the illegal nature of the drug trade. By the middle of the 1950s, drugs had taken on a new meaning. During rationing they were one illicitly traded good in a gigantic illicit economy; by the mid-1950s they were *the* illicit commodity.

Not surprisingly, the world of drug addicts changed as well during the course of the 1950s. As the flood of drugs available in the late 1940s slowly bled itself dry, many addicts turned to the traditional means of procuring their drugs; they went from doctor to doctor feigning pain or sent friends and family to do the same, and they stole and forged prescriptions. Officials claimed that by the end of the 1940s, 95 percent of all addicts were using narcotics diverted from the legal supply, either through drugs stolen from wholesalers or through prescription theft and falsification. This number probably increased throughout the course of the decade.[49] The number of addicts under the care of the public health service in Hamburg reached a high point of 375 in 1958 and then slowly declined to a low of 241 in 1968.[50]

As the number of addicts stabilized over the course of the 1950s and then began to decline, new choices became available as pharmacologists continued to churn out new forms of psychoactive drugs and pharmaceutical companies produced and marketed these new drugs. Particularly troublesome to the authorities in the early 1950s was an increase in the consumption of synthetic drugs not yet included under the Opium Law. Whereas in the 1920s and 1930s, most illicit drug consumption had been limited to opium alkaloids, cocaine, and amphetamines, by the middle of the 1950s, addicts who could not find a stable

49. StAH, 352-6, Gesundheitsbehörde, 696 Band 2, Bericht des Ausschußes für Rauschgiftbekämpfung, 25 March 1950.
50. Hamburg Bürgerschaft Drucksache, VI, Nr. 2474, 4 November 1969, "Suchtkrankenheit," 2.

source for opiates often used various new synthetic opiates, stimulants, barbiturates, and tranquilizers.[51] The increase in the number of addictive drugs freely available outstripped the ability of authorities to control them. There was a knowledge lag. Drugs came into general circulation and use before experts or authorities knew their addictive properties. Consequently, addicts, always quick to find new ways of getting high, shared information freely with other addicts so that, by the time authorities became aware of new drugs being abused, addicts were either on to the next drug or had discovered ways to get around regulations.

The case of a thirty-five-year-old war victim shows the process of addiction to these new, over-the-counter drugs. In 1944, Michael received a head wound in battle and became addicted to morphine. His condition took a turn for the worse in 1959, at which time he began using at least ten ampoules of morphine a day. Because of his increasing drug use, the Health Department in Hamburg interned Michael at the General Hospital at Ochsenzoll for detoxification. Believing that the new drug dextromoramide was nonaddictive, doctors tried to treat Michael's morphine addiction by switching him to the new drug. The doctors were wrong. Dextromoramide was available without a prescription, and soon after his release, Michael was injecting 150 ampoules of the drug a day, spending two to three thousand marks a month. As Michael's story illustrates, addicts' strategies changed rapidly, while officials and doctors fumbled to keep up. An explosion in the number of drugs available coupled with an ignorance of their effects hampered the authorities and sometimes, as in Michael's case, hurt addicts.

A few addicts turned to what remained of the underground black market, which was becoming more and more a part of the criminal underground. In the autumn of 1953, for example, two convicts, Kurt K. and Siegfried M., were arrested for a number of pharmacy break-ins in Hamburg and the area around Lichtenfeld. Two years later, Hamburg police arrested a supervisor and three workers at a pharma-

51. StAH, 352-6, Gesundheitsbehörde, 696 Band 3, "Report by the Office of the U.K. High Commissioner," and [Bundeskriminalamt], "Bericht über den illegalen Handel mit Rauschgiften und über den illegalen Erwerb von Rauschgiften durch Süchtige im Jahre 1952 in der Bundesrepublik." United Nations, *Summary of Annual Reports,* E/NR/1956/Summary, 51; E/NR/1959/Summary, 32; E/NR/1960/Summary, 36.

ceutical factory. The four had stolen a precursor chemical necessary to produce the stimulant methamphetamine. Between 1953 and 1955, their average monthly production was sixteen thousand tablets; occasionally they reached thirty thousand. They sold these to four middlemen for sixteen to eighteen pfennigs apiece, who sold them on the street in St. Pauli, mostly to the prostitutes, for fifty pfennigs.[52]

For those who had to resort to the streets, drug addiction was expensive. If one could not find a sympathetic doctor or manage to steal a prescription book, the financial cost of drug addiction could be devastating. In 1950, an ampoule of morphine on the black market cost between ten and twenty deutsche marks and one gram of powder cost around forty. A gram of cocaine usually brought fifteen to twenty deutsche marks. For those who could not afford such expensive drugs, an ampoule of the synthetic narcotic hydromorphone could be purchased for around three deutsche marks. Tablets of the stimulant methamphetamine were comparatively inexpensive, usually less than one mark each. On the wholesale level, an entire kilogram of morphine would go for fifteen thousand deutsche marks, while a kilogram of codeine was worth eleven thousand deutsche marks.[53] At a minimum, morphine addicts would use three or four shots a day. Even at only five deutsche marks a dose, an addict could expect to spend at least fifty-five hundred deutsche marks per year.

After the supply of stolen army narcotics disappeared in the first years of the Federal Republic, the illegal trade in drugs dwindled.[54] By the end of the 1950s, drug abuse and drug trafficking had, for the most part, disappeared as an issue. There were still a number of registered addicts, but most of these continued to be individuals who had become addicted through medical treatment. A drug market probably also survived among certain groups, such as the sailors living around the port

52. Eschenbach, "Erscheinungsformen der Rauschgiftdelikte," in Bundeskriminalamt, *Rauschgift,* 83–84.

53. StAH, 352-6, Gesundheitsbehörde, 696 Band 2, Government of the United Kingdom, Zonal Narcotics Office, "Report by the Office of the U.K. High Commissioner for the Calendar Year 1950."

54. See StAH, 331-1 II, Polizeibehörde II, Abl. 2, 40.75, "Rauschgiftdelikte in der BRD und in West-Berlin," 1957 and 1960. United Nations, E/CN.7/254, "Memorandum by the International Criminal Police Commission on Illicit Traffic in Narcotic Drugs in 1952." United Nations, E/CN.7/310, "Illicit Traffic: Memorandum by the International Criminal Police Commission for 1955," 12.

and members of the sex trade. But for the most part, addicts, if they could not convince a physician to prescribe for them, lied about illnesses, stole and falsified prescriptions, and took uncontrolled drugs as substitutes. As a public issue, drugs faded into the background. In 1960, no one would have predicted that merely a decade later drug abuse would be a problem of enormous proportions. To many, illegal drug abuse seemed to be a problem of the past.

The Addicts

Although it would stand to reason that addicts and the market were intrinsically linked, during the 1950s most drug addiction, as the authorities defined it, was largely removed from the illicit trade. For the most part, the addicts who came to the attention of the authorities were not the denizens of Hamburg's slums and waterfront, prowling the streets searching for that next fix. Quite the contrary, they represented a broad cross-section of society. Many of the higher echelons of society were, if anything, overrepresented. Since these addicts were not seen as a threat to public order and normally procured their drugs through licit channels, though not necessarily licit means, police were fairly uninterested in imposing a punitive solution to drug addiction. Instead, police charged health authorities with dealing with addicts who came to the attention of the police.[55] Health officials in turn followed a strategy that emphasized treatment and registration. The first strategy was viewed as an attempt to cure the addicts. The second was more pragmatic; the authorities despaired at the incredibly high relapse rate after treatment and kept track of addicts in order to prevent the acquisition of narcotics and, when prevention failed, to track usage patterns. Addicts undoubtedly tried to keep their name off the register, if only to avoid legal penalties or the social stigma attached to

55. The identity of drug consumers is very difficult to pin down, not just because of the relative paucity of sources from this period but also because of the type of sources. The only significant source of information on these individuals consists of the statistical reports to the United Nations from the British Zone and, subsequently, the Federal Republic. Information about addicts included in these reports came from the register of addicts kept by the various Health Authorities and forwarded to the Bundesopiumstelle (Federal Opium Office). The statistical reports are all that is available. Access to the actual rolls of addicts is prohibited under the various information protection laws (*Datenschutz*). According to the State Archive, the Hamburg rolls were destroyed after passage of the Datenschutzgesetz in 1984.

drug abuse. Yet even though addicts utilized a number of strategies to avoid being detected—such as forging and stealing prescriptions, using more than one doctor, having friends or family members feign injury—the regular audit of pharmacy books by the police and the centralization of record keeping often foiled even the best-laid plans.

Efforts to keep accurate national records of addicts acted not only as a matter of surveillance; they were also a specific form of policing. The central card catalog of addicts was an attempt to deal with the problem of addicts visiting multiple doctors. Many addicts maintained their habits by traveling from doctor to doctor, receiving prescriptions from each one, and therefore prolonging their high or at least fighting off withdrawal. Some of these trips required remarkable stamina. Dramaturge Sepp K., for example, became addicted to oxycodone after being wounded in the war and losing his right leg. In 1947, he traveled around Stuttgart, Tübingen, and Munich. Then he hitchhiked north, around Braunschweig, through Hamburg and Schleswig-Holstein. Turning south again, he traveled around Münster, through the cities in the Ruhr area, down to Frankfurt and back toward Munich. In all, he visited 116 doctors. By keeping a national roll, authorities tried to curtail this type of strategy. He was finally caught in late 1949 and was interned in a sanitarium in southwest Germany. Two years later he committed suicide.

Those who did end up on the register of addicts were usually reported by a physician, fell afoul of the law, or were discovered during the periodic inspections of prescriptions filled at pharmacies. The first case usually entailed a physician maintaining a patient with a chronic disease on pain medication. Although the various health authorities and the Physicians' and Pharmacists' Boards discouraged long-term maintenance of patients on narcotics, it did occur and was regulated only in that addicts were limited to one prescribing physician and one pharmacist.[56] Until 1952, doctors were required to report anyone they suspected of being an addict to the Criminal Police. But after the founding of the Federal Health Department, Military Order Number 95 was rescinded and doctors were merely asked to report any patient receiving a controlled substance for more than six weeks to the appro-

56. See United Nations, *Federal Republic of Germany Annual Report for 1952*, E/NR/1952/97, 3–4.

priate state Health Authority.[57] Despite these requirements, doctors often refused to follow the directives for the registration of addicts or simply ignored the mandates.[58] The second group of addicts consisted of those reported by the police either for stealing and falsifying prescriptions or for being suspected of another infraction against the Opium Law.

Probably the largest group, however, included those discovered during the audits of pharmacists' books. In addition to discovering the identity of patients who were being maintained on narcotics by physicians, these inspections allowed authorities to monitor physicians' prescribing practices. Overprescribing often led to an investigation. Indeed, throughout the 1950s this was one of the largest categories of drug investigation. In 1949, 150 cases against the Prescription Ordinance were investigated in the British Zone; in 1950, this number rose to 234. By the late 1950s this number had dropped, in all likelihood due to long-term changes in the prescribing culture among physicians. By 1960, there were only 144 investigations under the Prescription Ordinance in the entire Federal Republic.[59]

The only extant source as to the social makeup of addicts in Hamburg is a 1953 report from the senior medical officer (*Obermedizinalrat*) to the Federal Health Department. At the end of 1952, there were 230 registered addicts in Hamburg, 137 male and 93 female. Most were middle-aged: 81 percent were between the ages of thirty and sixty; 12 percent were between the ages of twenty and thirty; only 8 percent were over the age of sixty; and none were younger than twenty years old. Women tended to be younger than men. More than half of the female addicts were between the ages of twenty and forty, and most were probably addicted after childbirth, since obstetric complications remained common and morphine was the typical solution. The profes-

57. See United Nations, *Federal Republic of Germany Annual Report for 1953*, E/NR/1953/105, 1–2.

58. See, for example, StAH, 352-6, Gesundheitsbehörde, 696 Band 3, Amtsgericht Hamburg, "Strafsache gegen den Nervenarzt Dr. Buss, Hbg-Harburg wegen Vergehens gegen das Opiumgesetz."

59. StAH, 352-6, Gesundheitsbehörde, 696 Band 2, Government of the United Kingdom, Zonal Narcotics Office, "Report by the Office of the U.K. High Commissioner for the Calendar Year 1950"; Bundeskriminalamt, "Rauschgiftdelikte in der BRD und in West-Berlin im Jahre 1957," and StAH, 331-1 II, Polizeibehörde II, Abl.2, 40.75, "Rauschgiftdelikte in der BRD und in West-Berlin im Jahre 1960."

sions of addicts varied, but particularly high percentages grouped around the medical professions (27 percent), salaried employees (13 percent), housewives (13 percent), and laborers (13 percent). The sources of their drug supply varied: 27 percent received their supply legally, 15 percent received it primarily from the black market, and 26 percent received it from both legal and illegal sources. What we have, then, is a picture of older people iatrogenically addicted to narcotics, who used both legal and illegal means to maintain their habits.[60]

In 1952 the social makeup of addicts in the new Federal Republic mirrored that of Hamburg almost exactly. The breakdown by gender was almost identical. Statistically, both sets of addicts were employed in similar fields, with the exception of a significantly lower percentage of housewives in Hamburg. On the other hand, two significant differences stand out. First, the prevalence of addicts in Hamburg was much higher than the national average. In fact, only West Berlin had more addicts per capita than Hamburg. Second, many more addicts in Hamburg procured their drugs through illicit means. While in the Federal Republic as a whole 64 percent of addicts received their drugs entirely through licit channels, in Hamburg this number was only 12 percent. Taken together, this suggests what one would expect: larger cities were centers of illicit drug use, and addicts lived in large cities because it was easier to find drugs.

Taking the period from 1952 to 1964 as a whole, an image emerges of a dwindling and aging population of drug users who became addicts due to chronic illness. The number of addicts between 1952 and 1955 rose largely as a result of the promulgation of the 16 June 1953 amendment of the Opium Law, which placed a number of synthetic drugs under the law.[61] After 1955, Germany witnessed a slow but constant decline in the total number of registered addicts, and the addict population grew older. While the number of addicts in most employment groups fell, there was a significant rise in addiction within the ranks of the elderly, including pensioners, the war wounded, and the disabled. Registered addicts were increasingly therapeutically addicted and received their drugs legally. Attempting to explain those not therapeu-

60. StAH, 352-6, Gesundheitsbehörde, 696 Band 3, Obermedizinalrat Hamburg, "Meldungen an das Bundesgesundheitsbehörde," 7 March 1953.
61. See United Nations, *Federal Republic of Germany Annual Report for 1953,* E/NR/1953/105, 2.

tically addicted, authorities blamed "factors such as bad influence, love of sensation, curiosity, domestic, professional or financial difficulties, emotional stress, anxiety and, in the cases of doctors, to overwork."[62] At the same time, doctors' traditional reliance on morphine as a general palliative began to diminish as they began shifting toward prescribing synthetic narcotics. Of course, there were probably a number of addicts who managed to stay off the addicts' register, but declining arrest rates suggest either that there was a reduction in underground drug use or that drugs ceased to be a major policing priority. The answer probably lies in a combination of the two. In the final analysis, the evidence points to a simple conclusion: addiction to controlled substances in Germany—what little of it existed—was on the wane.

For the purpose of my larger argument, the point is not so much what drug addicts were as much as what they were not. First, they did not constitute a significant portion of the population. Even in Hamburg, where the concentration was high, registered addicts made up only 0.01 percent of the population. Second, the most significant shared characteristic of almost all addicts in this period was that they were *not* young. The model of the problem drug user seen in the United States during the 1950s—that of the younger, urban male hustler addicted to heroin—did not exist in Germany.[63] Drug addicts simply were not a significant public problem. And despite the theft of prescriptions and a very small number of pharmacy break-ins, they were not criminals. The image of the drug addict breaking into houses and stealing purses to support his or her habit just did not exist in Germany.

Treating Addiction

Even if drug use did not represent a major threat, authorities still had to decide what to do with addicts. Surprisingly, there was little debate about this crucial issue. For experts and policymakers alike the answer seemed clear: the system of (often forcible) rehabilitation set up under

62. United Nations, *Summary of Annual Reports,* E/NR/1959/Summary, 32.
63. David Courtwright et al., *Addicts Who Survived: An Oral History of Narcotic Use in America, 1923–1965* (Knoxville: University of Tennessee Press, 1989), 144–47, and H. Wayne Morgan, *Drugs in America: A Social History, 1800–1980* (Syracuse: Syracuse University Press, 1981), 145–48.

the Weimar Republic and augmented during the National Socialist period should remain in place. For their own good, addicts must be "cured," whether they liked it or not. Forced institutionalization represented, according to one legal commentator, "the most effective method of fighting drug addiction and its criminality."[64] It seemed to many the most legitimate method as well. Medical and legal experts as well as government authorities agreed that addicts were mentally ill. One legal expert put it this way:

> In most all cases, narcotics addiction strikes abnormal personality types, the so-called psychopaths. Physical and mental illness seize these individuals against their will and make them incapable of living an orderly and moral life, even incapable of doing their duty within the human community.[65]

Officials in Hamburg went so far as to accuse addicts not only of depravity and extreme egotism but also of sexual perversity.[66] Yet it was not that drug abuse caused mental illness; quite the contrary, mental illness led to drug addiction. More specifically, the experts believed that the people at risk were those who were somehow already psychologically damaged.[67] And since these people were ill, a public health approach would prove most effective. This was not a new idea. Indeed, the basic attitudes toward drug abuse did not show a substantial change between the Weimar period and the middle to late 1960s. The basic premise—that drug addiction must be treated as a medical problem rather than as a criminal problem—proved to be the most lasting aspect of German drug policy.[68]

Forced institutionalization was a policy well established by the post-

64. Karl Ewald, "Die Rauschgiftsucht im geltenden Strafrecht," *Nervenarzt* 19 (1948): 266.

65. Ewald, "Die Rauschgiftsucht," 266.

66. StAH, 352-6, Gesundheitsbehörde, 696 Band 1, "Tätigkeitsbericht der Beratungsstelle für Nerven-, Gemüts- und Rauschgiftkranke des Gesundheitsamtes Hamburg für 1947/1948."

67. Elke Hauschildt, *Auf den richtigen Weg zwingen—: Trinkerfürsorge 1922 bis 1945* (Freiburg im Breisgau: Lambertus, 1995). Hauschildt argues that, in the case of alcoholics, the trend to see addiction as a result of a psychological defect began in the 1890s and reached its apotheosis under the Nazi's racialist conception of addiction as evidence of genetic inferiority. See esp. 133–34.

68. Hauschildt points out that forced institutionalization also remained the preferred method for treating alcoholics until the early 1970s, ibid., 216.

war period. During the Weimar era, forced institutionalization had been the method of last resort to deal with addicts, most of whom were alcoholics.[69] When the Nazis came to power, they began enforcing their biological view of society and characterized addiction—like so many other social "problems"—as a clear sign of genetic inferiority. Alcoholics and drug addicts suffered the same maltreatment as other groups considered genetically inferior, including sterilization, forced labor, and occasionally euthanasia.[70]

In November 1933, the Nazi government passed the Law against Habitual Criminals and on Measures of Safety and Rehabilitation as an extension of the Code of Criminal Procedure (Reichsstrafgesetzbuch [RStGB] and subsequently the Bundesstrafgesetzbuch [StGB]) in order to facilitate action against certain "asocial" groups. Paragraph 42 of the law circumscribed the scope of "Safety and Rehabilitation." Social welfare authorities used this statute to institutionalize chronic alcoholics or drug addicts for "cure or care." According to the law, anyone committing a punishable act, other than a misdemeanor, in a state of mental incapacity or diminished capacity could be committed to an institution if, according to a judge, such confinement was necessary to protect the public security. Furthermore, addiction could be used as a reason for incarcerating persistent offenders.

> The court shall order, in addition to punishment, the confinement in an institution for chronic alcoholics or drug addicts of anyone habitually and excessively indulging in intoxicating liquors or other stupefying substances, who has been convicted of, and sentenced for, a felony or gross misdemeanor committed while under the influence, causally connected to his addiction, or committed while fully intoxicated . . . if such confinement is necessary to condition him for a lawful and orderly way of life.

The main difference between the two sections of the statute lay in the possible length of commitment. Addicts judged under the latter section, for committing an offense as a result of addiction, were remanded to a detoxification clinic (*Entziehungsanstalt*) for a limited period. If found mentally incapacitated, on the other hand, the law

69. Ibid., 86–90.
70. Ibid., 146–51, 193.

allowed for the internment of the addict in a sanitarium (*Heilanstalt* or *Pflegeanstalt*) for an indeterminate period. Public health officials recommended to doctors a treatment period of six months to two years. Under the statute, chronic alcoholics and drug addicts could also be forced into compulsory labor, and many of the institutions were indeed centers of forced labor.[71]

In the immediate postwar period, the responsibility for drug addicts in Hamburg fell to the Social Authority and its Counseling Center for the Mentally Ill, Emotionally Disturbed, and Drug Addicted.[72] Authorities there developed a number of strategies to deal with the growing number of drug addicts. Options ran the gambit from outpatient counseling to long-term incarceration. Ambulant care was seen as a total failure. In its report for the years 1947 and 1948, the Counseling Center claimed they knew of no case in which ambulant care had been successful. Long-term internment proved enormously expensive and was used only in the worst cases. Brief forced withdrawal treatments became the preferred method.

Though some individuals admitted themselves for voluntary withdrawal treatment in the psychiatric clinic at the University Hospital at Eppendorf, the General Hospital at Rissen, or private sanitariums in Bonn and Cologne, most in-patient treatments were court ordered. The criminal process for drug addicts was complicated because they were normally considered sick rather than criminal. At the arraignment, the accused could either be held over for trial under paragraph 114 of the Criminal Procedure Code (Strafprozessordnung [StPO]) or temporarily interned in a treatment center under paragraph 126 of the StPO, which allowed for immediate institutionalization of addicts in the cases of a compelling suspicion of the commission of a punishable crime, or a legitimate assumption that a court would order forced institutionalization, or as demanded in order to protect the public security. After the war, the official policy of the Hamburg police was to push for this type of temporary restraining order.[73]

---

71. Ibid., 160–64; the use of alcoholics, and probably drug addicts as well, for forced labor was continued in the Federal Republic, 220–21.

72. StAH, 352-6, Gesundheitsbehörde, 696 Band 1, Beratungsstelle für Nerven-, Gemüts- und Rauschgiftkranke, Memo, 1948.

73. StAH, 331-1 II, Polizeibehörde II, Abl.2, 40.75, Report from Kriminalamt-Leitung Hamburg, 30 July 1946.

Gretchen M.'s story illustrates how this process worked in practice. During war service as a nurse, Gretchen became addicted to methamphetamines. In 1940, she was sentenced to six months in a Magdeburg jail. The next year she was arrested in Berlin for forging prescriptions and was sentenced to three and a half months in a sanitarium. She managed to stay out of trouble until 1947, when she was caught in Hamburg forging stolen prescriptions for various opiates. Found incompetent, she was sent to a sanitarium. Soon after her release, she was treated with morphine for gall bladder problems and relapsed. She began to get her supply from the black market and quickly amassed a debt of DM 480. In 1948, she received a job at an English daycare facility. Soon she began stealing phenobarbital tablets and was subsequently fired. The next year, a judge sentenced her to five months and two weeks in jail and one year in an institution for theft and acquisition of narcotics. At the end of 1951, Gretchen relapsed again while working at a hospital, where she stole sixty or seventy ampoules of morphine in ten weeks. After being discovered and fired by the hospital, she found a sympathetic doctor who prescribed six hundred ketobemidone tablets for her in just four months. Later, she found yet another job at a hospital but was fired by the sixth day for stealing morphine. In 1953, a court in Lüneburg again found her legally incompetent but declined to have her institutionalized.[74] Gretchen's story illustrates the cyclical nature of drug abuse and of attempts to deal with problem drug use. Repeatedly, Gretchen went through forced withdrawal treatment, and repeatedly she relapsed. Rather than being a path to an "orderly life," forced institutionalization tended to be merely a revolving door, dealing with the same problem cases again and again.

For those who came into contact with the Counseling Center without committing an offense—usually by being reported by the family or a doctor—other methods had to be used. At first, the center pursued a strategy of temporarily remanding addicts, arguing in front of a judge that it was urgent that the patients be forced to undergo treatment to prevent them from becoming criminals. Soon, though, the center decided that it was more efficient to utilize the strategy that had been used throughout much of Weimar and throughout the Nazi period by pursuing a legal deprivation of the right of decision (*Entmündi-*

74. Eschenbach, "Erscheinungsformen," 77.

gungsverfahren). In effect, the addict was placed under the guardian-ship of the state,[75] which then admitted the addict for "voluntary" treatment. Unlike a temporary order, the patient did not have to be released as soon as he or she no longer posed an immediate danger to himself or herself or others. The social welfare workers also liked the fact that the writ could be obtained relatively easily within a day.[76]

During the forties and fifties, the withdrawal treatment itself was often a terrible experience for addicts in Hamburg. They were incar-cerated in the psychiatric department of a public hospital, often Lan-genhorn Hospital or the University Hospital at Eppendorf, for a period ranging from a few weeks to a few months, depending on the doctors' recommendations. Patients always found the first few days the worst. They suffered through the nausea, shaking, sweating, sleepless-ness, and pain of withdrawal. Many complained of terrible mistreat-ment by the staff. And as if to amplify all of the difficulties, the addicts were often housed indiscriminately among the seriously mentally ill. Many of these addicts had been soldiers in the war and considered themselves victims; the idea that they be imprisoned along with the insane seemed to many an "unbearable load."[77]

On top of the pain and indignity of forced institutionalization, the treatment was a shambles. There were widespread reports that visitors smuggled narcotics into the hospitals and that certain patients showed "unbelievable ingenuity" in developing a thriving narcotics trade within the closed wards. If that was not bad enough, many of the patients were allowed holiday leave. These *Urlaub* passes often turned into drug holidays, with patients returning in worse shape than when they had arrived.[78] The most dire and perhaps most lasting conse-

---

75. This is found under §1631 of the Bundesgesetzbuch. See also Karl Ewald, "Die Rauschgiftsucht im geltenden Strafrecht," *Nervenarzt* 19 (1948): 266. The *Sammelvormünd-schaft* (collective guardianship) fell to the Sozialbehörde.

76. StAH, 352-6, Gesundheitsbehörde, 696 Band 1, "Tätigkeitsbericht der Beratungsstelle für Nerven-, Gemüts- und Rauschgiftkranke des Gesundheitsamtes Ham-burg für 1947/1948"; Untitled Report, and "Ausschuß für Rauschgifte," 29 July 1948. See also StAH, 331-1 II, Polizeibehörde II, Abl. 2, 40.75, Lecture given by Ackermann, 13 August 1946.

77. StAH, 352-6, Gesundheitsbehörde, 696 Band 1, "Tätigkeitsbericht der Beratungsstelle für Nerven-, Gemüts- und Rauschgiftkranke des Gesundheitsamtes Ham-burg für 1947/1948."

78. This last problem was improved in 1948 when the treatment of addicts was shifted to the psychiatric department at Heiligenhafen.

quence rested in the forced treatment of the unwilling: relationships developed during treatment often did not lead to an environment of mutual support of abstinence but rather facilitated a network of drug contacts after release. In short, forced treatment helped expand the web of drug suppliers and consumers.

The worst part of involuntary treatment was not the inefficiency of the program, the ineptitude of providers, or the inadequate planning. The worst part was that it just did not work. Most patients quickly relapsed. Some were deemed "hopeless" and "no longer capable of integration" into society and were committed to the long-term institution (*Versorgungsheim*) at Farmsen.[79] Others cycled in and out of care for any number of years; still others simply disappeared from public oversight.

Forced institutionalization illustrates not only how addicts were treated but also how experts and the authorities understood addiction. Even before the Second World War, the basic framework for the understanding of addiction and the treatment of addicts was in place. Addicts were mentally ill and deserved medical treatment rather than punishment. They should be interned and treated by psychiatrists for their illness or, if all else failed, placed in a long-term medical facility. This remained the basis of treatment until the radical changes in both the quantity and quality of drug use at the end of the 1960s made doctors, academics, the police, the government, and the public question the meaning of addiction and the treatment of addicts.

Conclusion

When police searched sixteen-year-old Christiana from Braunschweig on that night in January 1964, drug addiction, like many social problems at the edge of the *Wirtschaftswunder* (economic miracle) years, seemed on its way to extinction. With better control of physician prescribing practices, a continuation of close surveillance of current and past addicts, a tighter control of emerging drugs, and a strong international commitment to stopping the international traffic in narcotics,

---

79. StAH, 352-6, Gesundheitsbehörde, 696 Band 1, "Tätigkeitsbericht der Beratungsstelle für Nerven-, Gemüts- und Rauschgiftkranke des Gesundheitsamtes Hamburg für 1947/1948."

German authorities believed that they were on the right track. They projected that the number of addicts would continue to decrease, that the average age of addicts would continue to increase, and that drug abuse on a significant scale might remain limited to Asia and North America. The heyday of the classic morphinist that dominated much of the history of drug use in twentieth-century Germany was indeed in the past. There was also a broad consensus about what drug addiction meant and how to deal with it. The therapeutic model based on drug abuse as a symptom of mental illness that deserved psychiatric care had become unquestioned dogma. Yet at the end of the Adenauer era, in the unsupervised spaces where adolescent sociability took place—in homes, parks, and bars—new forms of drug use were beginning to appear. In the decade that followed, officials in Hamburg, and in the rest of Germany, would be forced to rethink radically their response to drug abuse and addiction in general. The therapeutic model of addiction, in place since Weimar, would be fundamentally challenged by rapid shifts in both the rise of youth drug consumption and the globalization of the market to satisfy their demand.

2. Creating a Drug Scene

As is well known, it was the Germans who invented methamphetamine, which of all accessible tools has brought humans beings within the closest twitch of machinehood, and without methamphetamine we would never have had such high plasma marks of the counterculture as Lenny Bruce, Bob Dylan, Lou Reed and the Velvet Underground, Neal Cassady, Jack Kerouac, Allen Ginsberg's "Howl," Blue Cheer, Cream, and *Creem,* as well as all of the fine performances in Andy Warhol movies not inspired by heroin. So it can easily be seen that it was in reality the *Germans* who were responsible for *Blonde on Blonde* and *On the Road;* the Reich never died, it just reincarnated in American archetypes ground out by holloweyed jerkyfingered manikins locked into their typewriters and guitars like rhinoceroses copulating.

—Lester Bangs, 1975

Between 1964 and 1968, Germany experienced a rapid rise in drug consumption among its young citizens. Youth consumption of drugs was largely a product of two closely tied phenomena that emerged at the end of the 1950s and continued unabated throughout the 1960s: the creation of new youth consumer markets and the internationalization of youth culture. Both of these trends arose from the success of economic expansion and globalization after the Second World War, and both had broad implications. If there was, as Arthur Marwick has argued, a "cultural revolution" between 1958 and 1974, then young people were the avant-garde of this revolution, and their attempts to break free from what they saw as the stifling conformity of the fifties and the long shadow of the Third Reich led to broad changes throughout German society. In particular, this early period witnessed the emergence of a new international youth culture based around the consumption of illicit substances. Drug use may have represented only a part of the larger social transformation in Germany and the Western world, but it was a central and quite conspicuous facet of these broad changes.

Western youths' broad rejection of the social values of the immediate postwar period led to the emergence of a new culture of refusal. Young people throughout the industrialized countries adopted drug use because it was pleasurable, because it proved to be a potent symbol of rebellion against their parents' and grandparents' generations, and because they saw drug use as a means of refusing to follow well-worn paths to the adult world. Drug consumption threatened authority; more important, it represented, perhaps more than any other phenomenon, a broad-based rejection of the rule of law. Simply by taking drugs, a substantial minority if not a majority of young people transgressed the legal boundaries of the state. Individuals who would never consider committing property crimes, for example, saw drug consumption as a private issue and therefore proved willing not only to break the law but often to flaunt their lawbreaking openly. Drug consumption and the related social problems that increasingly took center stage as the sixties reached their close illustrate the complications of broad capitalist consumerism. Indeed, drugs represent the dark side of the consumerist ideal. The radical shifts that took place at the intersection of consumption, internationalization, and the culture of refusal lie at the root of the contemporary drug problem.

Shifting Consumer Regimes and Genußmittel

Illegal drug use in Germany in the 1960s grew within the context of rising affluence and changing patterns of consumption. At the end of the 1950s and the outset of the 1960s, West Germany saw a drastic change in what the historian Victoria de Grazia has termed "consumption regimes"—the social process of consumption as well as ideas of what consumption meant. Throughout the decade of the 1950s, the fear of the hunger years haunted the generations that had lived through them. Since the war, this "hunger mentality," with its concomitant frugal consumption of goods, had praised the virtues of savings and economy.[1] Yet within a decade this pattern, which had held sway since at least the First World War, was replaced by a modern "consumer economy" focused on consumption as a social duty and the key to economic prosperity.[2] The shift in basic values of what consumption and

1. See Wildt, "Plurality of Taste," 24–26.
2. See Erica Carter, *How German Is She? Postwar West German Reconstruction and the Consuming Woman* (Ann Arbor: University of Michigan Press, 1997).

goods meant was among the most rapid and most sweeping in history.[3] The generation that had lived through the war and rationing could not have imagined the pleasure of consuming anything as unproductive and ephemeral as drugs. The generation of '68ers, those born during or after the war, grew up with very different ideas about their role as consumers. Their formative years fell well within the scope of Germany's Wirtschaftswunder. Without the basic and drastic changes in fundamental patterns of consumption and in basic social attitudes, the spectacular increase in drug use in the late 1960s simply would not have occurred.

Although the economy of the Federal Republic showed unprecedented improvement in the 1950s, the benefits did not reach consumers until the end of the decade. Rising income was the most immediate effect of the German Wirtschaftswunder. In 1950, the average working-class family of four in Hamburg made only DM 343 a month; by 1963 this had almost tripled to DM 975. Despite the rise in income, consumption patterns did not change rapidly. Through the entire period, the single most important category of expenditure remained food. At the beginning of the 1950s, families spent nearly half of their total income on food; by 1963, they still spent just over a third of their income on this basic need. It was not until 1958 that average Germans began shifting their expenditures away from necessities.

Though consumers were drawn to goods like televisions, automobiles, and household labor-saving devices, what people initially desired was *Genußmittel.* A German term that does not translate easily into English, Genußmittel literally means "articles of pleasure" and includes items physically consumed expressly for pleasure, as opposed to items of necessity such as food. Included among the Genußmittel are spices, coffee, tea, chocolate, alcohol, and even narcotics such as opium.[4] The word *Genußmittel* implies, according to David Jacobson, "that these substances are luxuries for sybaritic enjoyment, means for creating Epicurean delights and, by extension, a state of sensual bliss."[5]

Between the founding of the republic and the middle of the sixties, rising consumption of Genußmittel far outstripped any other type of

3. See Wolfgang Schivelbusch's provocative book *Tastes of Paradise: A Social History of Spices, Stimulants, and Intoxicants* (New York: Pantheon, 1992), esp. 3–14.
4. On Genußmittel, see Thomas Hengartner and Christoph Maia Merki, eds., *Genußmittel: Ein kulturgeschichtliches Handbuch* (Frankfurt: Campus, 1999).
5. Schivelbusch, *Tastes of Paradise,* xiii.

expenditure. Spending on beer exceeded the rise in real income by a third.[6] In 1950, individuals spent over five million deutsche marks on alcohol and over four million deutsche marks on tobacco and consumed over thirty-eight liters of beer per capita. Consumption of these luxuries increased drastically in the late 1950s; by 1963, alcohol and tobacco purchases had risen more than threefold.[7] Three years later, alcohol consumption had reached the highest point in German history, and, per person, Germans drank more alcohol than milk.[8] The rise in Genußmittel consumption signaled Germans' rising willingness to spend money to buy intoxicants a decade before the drug wave of the late 1960s. An increasing consumption of tobacco, coffee, chocolate, beer, and wine became a sign of growing affluence. Though these ephemeral consumables did not change the basic rhythms of life, as did the television set or the automobile, they made everyday life more enjoyable. Germans valued them not so much as status symbols, though this certainly occurred, but as something akin to a fundamental right.[9]

Consumption and Addiction

Though adults dramatically increased their own alcohol and tobacco use, they worried about their children's consumption habits. To parents, government authorities, and youth welfare experts alike, youth consumption represented a risk to the moral fiber of the country. They feared that the ability to purchase pleasure threatened to remove children from the guiding hand of tradition and thrust them into a commercial world they had neither the wisdom nor the self-restraint to overcome. Rather than preparing for a life of industry and hard work, the new "teenagers" appeared to be content to revel in their youth and newfound purchasing power.

During the fifties, youth experts tended to conflate notions of consumption and addiction. Addiction was not a specific physical or psychological illness but rather any habit that threatened to confound or

6. "Bier: Sieg der Flasche," *Der Spiegel* 18, no. 43 (21 October 1964): 54.

7. Norber Mieck, "Entwicklung der Suchtgefahren," in *30 Jahre der Hamburg Landesstelle gegen die Suchtgefahren* (Hamburg, 1978), 9.

8. "Wohlstand: Über alles in der Welt," *Der Spiegel* 20, no. 1–2 (3 January 1966): 23.

9. "Bier: Sieg der Flasche," 54.

skew the moral compass of young people, turning them into hedonistic consumers rather than cultured citizens. One youth protection advocate warned that the consumerism of modern life threatened youth more than ever before and had specific consequences: "They surrender themselves to the two greatest of types of endangerment: all forms of addiction (eating sweets, tobacco, alcohol, light-weight reading, movies, dancing, pop music, games, etc.,) and all forms of aberrant sexual development."[10] Experts located youths' addiction on a spectrum based on their level of indulgence in consumer society. By preventing young people from entering into commercial relationships that endangered their development, youth protection advocates believed they could prevent the slide into the colonization of everyday life by the free market.

The idea that unbridled consumption represented the greatest menace to youth was not new. Attempts to control youth consumption grew with the development of modern youth welfare policy. As early as the Wilhelmine period, government officials and "youth savers" worried about the effects of industrialization on young unskilled workers between "primary school and the barracks," the period crucial in transforming young men into good citizens.[11] Often this meant guiding or controlling the behavior of young men with decidedly different ideas of propriety and thrift than those of reformers interested in curbing their youthful excesses. Indeed, middle-class reformers believed that young workers squandered their money on penny dreadfuls, movies, alcohol, cigarettes, and sex and used legislative action to attempt to impose their own set of values upon Germany's working-class youth.[12] As youth welfare expanded during the Weimar Republic, social workers focused on two types of "problem behavior": consumption and (mostly young women's) sexuality. Frequently the two were, at least in the eyes of the authorities, directly connected. Under the Nazis, the scientific rationalist tendencies of the Weimar welfare system became explicitly racialized. The novelty of Nazi policy rested not in the understanding of the roots of problem youth; like the policy of the Weimar period, it relied on psychological models. The Nazis, however, saw

10. Anton Strambowski, "Jugendgefährdung—ein Problem unserer Zeit," *Jugendschutz* 1, no. 1 (1956): 4.

11. Derek S. Linton, *"Who Has the Youth Has the Future": The Campaign to Save Young Workers in Imperial Germany* (Cambridge: Cambridge University Press, 1991), 227.

12. Linton, *"Who Has the Youth,"* 44.

outward deviance as a sign of genetic inferiority that should be purged from the body social.[13]

The collapse of the state at the end of the Second World War failed to lead to the reformation of youth welfare in the Western sectors. Though the occupation governments discarded certain laws, particularly those dealing with censorship, there was a marked continuity in youth welfare policy and personnel.[14] After the war, the National Youth Welfare Law still stood in its Nazi form.[15] While many of the more coercive measures instituted under the Third Reich were abandoned in favor of progressive, therapeutic policies that hearkened back to Weimar and favored preventative, consensual strategies,[16] the system retained the conservative ideology that placed "normal" and "deviant" youths in wholly separate categories. This meant that youth welfare policy in the postwar period focused on maintaining a (often artificial) division between problem youth and their peers to police the boundaries between "normality" and "waywardness."[17]

Although the public discourse about youth after the end of the war focused on controlling "criminal" youth, by the middle of the 1950s, the fears of mass unrest among the nation's youth rapidly gave way to a focus on "youth protection."[18] Indeed, by the late 1950s the youth protection movement dominated debates on problem youth. With the founding of the national organization Action Youth Protection (Aktion Jugendschutz) in 1951, which published its own influential journal beginning in 1956, youth protection became a significant force in youth advocacy and became an integral part of most state welfare departments.[19]

13. See Dickinson, *The Politics of German Child Welfare from the Empire to the Federal Republic* (Cambridge, MA: Harvard University Press, 1996), and Detlev J. K. Peukert, *Inside Nazi Germany: Conformity, Opposition and Racism in Everyday Life,* trans. Richard Deveson (New York: Penguin, 1987): 208–35.

14. Dickinson, *Politics of German Child Welfare,* 244–45.

15. Ibid., 245.

16. Ibid., 252.

17. On the coercive nature of youth protection in the 1950s, see Julia Ubbelohde, "Der Umgang mit jugendlichen Normverstößen," in *Wandlungsprozesse in Westdeutschland: Belastung, Integration, Liberalisierung, 1945–1980,* ed. Ulrich Herbert (Göttingen: Wallstein, 2002), 402–35.

18. Schildt, *Moderne Zeiten,* 153–54; Ubbelohde, "Der Umgang mit jugendlichen Normverstößen," 402–11.

19. For an admittedly biased review of the first ten years of youth protection work, see Bundesarbeitsstelle Aktion Jugendschutz, *Jugendschutz heute und morgen* (Hamm: Hoheneck, 1961).

During the 1950s, controlling consumerism became an increasingly significant priority for conservative youth welfare and youth protection advocates. They saw young consumers' habits as part of a spiritual decline dating back to industrialization and wished to mold youth into a morality based in a "mythical Christian-patriarchal golden age, which they located at the beginning of the nineteenth century, before the onset of the age of iron."[20] Though the occupation governments had rejected the Nazi Censorship Law of 1935 and the Youth Protection Law of 1943, reconstituting these types of protections became a primary goal of conservative youth welfare experts after the founding of the Federal Republic in 1949. In particular, conservative critics believed that the spread of consumer technologies such as radio, television, film, and phonographs threatened to destroy traditional social ties and to leave young people morally adrift, bereft of spiritual guidance.[21]

By the early 1950s, conservative reformers had turned to legislation—just as their Weimar counterparts had done—as a means to protect youth from the threat of the entertainment industry and perceived increases in youth crime and deviance. As early as 1949 the film industry, in order to ward off state intervention, began a voluntary system of self-censorship. Two years later the Law for the Protection of Youth in Public, the cornerstone of the youth protection movement in the Federal Republic, went into effect. The new law regulated the acceptable ages for moviegoing, dancing, drinking, smoking, and gambling, among other provisions. Then, in 1952 the Federal Republic passed a new law controlling objectionable literature that bore a striking resemblance to the 1926 law.[22] The purpose of these laws was to insulate youth from what critics saw as the penetration of the private sphere by the market economy. Rather than seeing capitalism as a boon to democratic citizenship, youth protection advocates saw consumerism as a threat to the underpinnings of the social contract. Though adults should certainly participate in the market, youth deserved a space free

---

20. Dickinson, *Politics of German Child Welfare*, 265.

21. Ibid., 266; Ubbelohde, "Der Umgang mit jugendlichen Normverstößen," 403–6.

22. Dickinson, *Politics of German Child Welfare*, 267. See also Germany (West), *Bundesgesetze zum Schutz der Jugend in der Öffentlichkeit und über die Verbreitung jugendgefährdender Schriften* (Munich: Beck, 1954); Bundesarbeitsstelle Aktion Jugendschutz, *Jugendschutz;* and Karl Hukeler, *Jugendschutz in öffentlich-rechtlicher Sicht* (Lucern: Fachgruppe Jugendschutz, Caritaszentrale, 1961).

of the force of modern consumer economy in which to grow not merely as economic actors but as moral individuals. "The topos of the youth endangerment acted as foil for a general discussion of values, norms and morals," Julia Ubbelohde concludes, "and intensified the pre-existing fears of cultural change in the Federal Republic."[23]

Patterns of Youth Consumption

Despite the concerns and legislative efforts of youth protection advocates, youth emerged as a distinct market for the first time at the end of the 1950s. New types of entertainment, new products, and new experiences beckoned, and by 1963 youth buying power had dramatically increased. According to market survey estimates, the total purchasing power of youths was around twelve billion deutsche marks. Seventy-two percent of young Germans owned their own bicycle, 44 percent a camera, and 29 percent a radio. The average university or high school student had a weekly disposable income of over ten deutsche marks, while young workers had over thirty-seven deutsche marks a week to spend as they saw fit.[24] Considering that the average adult male worker only earned around one thousand deutsche marks a month, this was a considerable sum.[25]

Much of this new disposable income went to small pleasures and Genußmittel. More than half of young men and fifteen percent of young women smoked. A third of young men drank beer often, and nearly half of young women drank coffee frequently (a statistic that in itself raises interesting questions about the gendering of intoxication).[26] In the late 1950s, it was drinking and smoking that often provoked outrage from the youth protection advocates. Otto Landt of Hamburg's state office of Action Youth Protection warned that "alcohol and tobacco are much more dangerous than morphine or cocaine."[27] Indeed, the way experts wrote about cigarettes and alcohol foreshadowed the way they would talk about drugs a decade later.

23. Ubbelohde, "Der Umgang mit jugendlichen Normverstößen," 411.
24. "Jugendbericht: Oben sitzt einer," *Der Spiegel* 19, no. 28 (7 July 1965): 22–23.
25. See Statistischen Landesamt Hamburg, ed., *Statistisches Jahrbuch für Hamburg, 1968/1969*, 346.
26. "Jugendbericht: Oben sitzt einer," 22–23.
27. Otto Landt, "Das Sucht-Gespräch mit Jugendlichen," *Jugendschutz* 3, no. 6 (1958): 15.

The first smoking experience is unpleasant and often arouses a strong defensive reaction from the body. Dependence takes place gradually. Yet soon—as with dependence on most alkaloids—a desire for another dose of nicotine begins. Without another dose of nicotine the body does not feel right. Out of this emerges a psychological addiction that only subsides after a couple of cigarettes. The youth needs nicotine. He has thus developed a real addiction that imperiously demands satisfaction. Pocket money is no longer enough; often other devious ways must be attempted. Thus the danger of sliding down the slippery slope has emerged.[28]

The moral was clear: smoking leads to addiction. Once addicted, the addict runs out of money to support his (in these stories it was always "his") addiction and is forced to turn to crime. This familiar progression, popularized first by nineteenth-century temperance movements, proved easily adaptable to most threatening forms of consumption. Philosophically grounded in the idea that senseless consumption signified moral failure, the theory of the "slippery slope" came to dominate twentieth-century thinking about all substance abuse.

For authorities threatened by youth consumption, the principal response was repression. In Hamburg during the late 1950s the state Youth Authority and the Women's Police created a new form of youth policing. Youth Protection Units (*Jugendschutztruppe*) made rounds to bars and public places where youth congregated, transporting those caught drinking or smoking home to their parents.[29] At the same time, however, authorities tried to co-opt youth rebellion and force it into an institutional framework, where, if they could not stop unwanted activities, they could at least tame them. In 1957, concerned about the growing popularity of rock-and-roll dancing, Hamburg's Action Youth Protection began holding dances with "modern dance music and modern dancing." Under the watchful eyes of adults, five hundred youths, "some of them so-called '*Halbstarken*',"[30] danced without the "intemperance" of the various commercial dance clubs.[31] Whether or not these efforts reformed their intended targets, they reflect the authori-

28. Gerhard Hüffmann, "Süchte bedrohen die Jugend," *Jugendschutz* 1, no. 2 (1956): 8.

29. Paula Karpinski, "Jugendschutz in einer Welt- und Hafenstadt," *Jugendschutz* 6 (1961): 33–35.

30. On Halbstarken, see Thomas Grotum, *Die Halbstarken: zur Geschichte einer Jugendkultur der 50er Jahre* (New York: Campus, 1994).

31. "'Treffpunkt Jugend' mit Rock 'n Roll," *Jugendschutz* 2, no. 6 (1957): 23. See also

ties' recognition of a new type of power wielded by youth: the power to consume as they chose.

A rise in expendable income and changes in patterns of consumption, as well as in the ideas of what it meant to consume, provided the preconditions for the massive rise in drug use by Germany's youth in the late 1960s. People earned more, and near the end of the 1950s they began spending more. While adults continued to remember the hunger years, they nonetheless began to increase their consumption. Youths, unburdened by memories of the hard winters of 1947 and 1948, developed new ideas of what it meant to consume. They learned from the media and from each other that consumption could and should be pleasurable. Without this basic change in the way people saw their economic roles, the enormous spending on recreational pharmaceuticals would not have occurred.

The Internationalization of Youth

Along with the growth of affluence and the welfare state in the industrial West, internationalization was one of the defining trends of the postwar period. Internationalization occurred in any number of areas: business, transportation, military cooperation, international government, nuclear regulation, and crime and policing, among others. An underappreciated aspect of this internationalization, though, was the unprecedented cooperation among youth beginning in the 1960s. The very success of capitalist economies in the industrial West opened the door for the formation of cross-cultural ties that brought youth from different national backgrounds closer together than ever before. Not only did young people share a cultural vocabulary dominated by rock and roll; they also had more individual contact with other nations due to massive increases in tourism and travel.[32] The identification of young people with a real or imagined international youth movement was not new. The "Swing Kids" of the Third Reich or the Halbstarken

Walter Becker, "Jugendtanz—eine Frage der Erziehung und des Jugendschutzes," *Jugend-schutz* 7 (1962): 11–15.

32. On the increase in tourism in Germany, see Hasso Spode, ed., *Goldstrand und Teutonengrill: Kultur- und Sozialgeschichte des Tourismus in Deutschland 1945 bis 1989* (Berlin: W. Moser, 1996), especially the contribution of Rainer Schönhammer, "Unabhängiger Jugendtourismus in der Nachkriegszeit," 117–28. For the fifties, see Schildt, *Moderne Zeiten,* 180–208, and Alon Confino, "Traveling as a Culture of Remembrance," *History and Memory* 12 (2000): 92–121.

of the 1950s certainly saw themselves as part of a larger cultural movement. What was new in the 1960s was that, while youths' interaction with cultural products became increasingly international as the youth market grew, young people also began to experience a new freedom of mobility. They began both to recognize and to exploit the contacts between like-minded people in other nations and used these connections to build international movements and markets.

The increasing number of youths traveling outside the borders of the Federal Republic, the emergence of new forms of international cultural production, the formation of youth groups that spanned borders and continents, as well as the explosion in the underground press created a new sense among young people that they could bridge the traditional boundaries of the nation and create new forms of politics and culture based on shared ideas. The expansion of drug use cannot be fully understood without taking this new form of internationalism into account; without these international contacts and youthful entrepreneurialism, the drug trade could not have become so pervasive and persistent. Yet the ways in which the new consumerism and internationalism converged differed from place to place, and the drug scenes that developed also showed a remarkable amount of variation. The remainder of this chapter will trace how these processes merged in Hamburg in the 1960s, creating new forms of youth culture and consumption.

Drug Scenes

Youth drug consumption flourished in the context of international exchange. Between 1964 and 1968, young people on both sides of the Atlantic developed a fairly sophisticated, international market in illicit drugs. Along with this market grew a distinct drug culture, with new forms of expression based on the use of drugs. Young people developed new rituals and created a distinct language to describe their experiences. It was an international language, dominated by Anglo-American slang adapted to serve distinct scenes. Yet expanding drug use was at once an international and a distinctly local phenomenon. Over the course of a decade, most of western Europe developed new and not necessarily homogenous patterns of drug consumption. Different cities developed distinct drug scenes, depending on location, supply, and local preferences.

The term *drug scene* deserves some clarification. I have chosen to use the term *drug scene* to characterize the specific patterns of youth drug consumption that emerged in the 1960s. The word *scene* used to describe the drug milieu was widespread in Germany by the end of the sixties. Young drug users usually referred to the drug trade and the participants as the scene; journalists wrote about the scene, and even officials thought of the organization of drug distribution and consumption as a scene. A drug scene is not merely a place where drug transactions take place, though that is certainly a part of any drug scene. Rather, it is a set of social relationships that develop around a market in illicit drugs. For practical purposes, a drug scene usually is limited geographically to a city or urban area, since the majority of individuals involved in the drug market have little to do with the international or domestic distribution of drugs. One's relationship to the scene is a product of one's role in that scene (consumer, dealer, trafficker, etc.) and, more important, of one's contacts.[33] Though there has long been a certain amount of street dealing, especially in the last two decades, the illegal nature of the drug market has meant that drug dealers tend to prefer to transact business with people they know. Therefore, the number and quality of contacts often define one's role and status in the scene. The end result of this is that individuals more involved with the drug scene have better access to drugs, but they also carry greater risk of coming to the attention of the police.

I take the term *drug culture,* as opposed to the term *drug scene,* to mean the cultural manifestations that developed as a result of the spread of drug use. Drug use in the 1960s and early 1970s profoundly affected certain established forms of popular culture: it spawned the psychedelic rock movement; writers both new and established wrote about drug use; filmmakers began to use drug themes in their work; fashion turned to the psychedelic movement for inspiration; and graphic artists illustrated the influence of drugs, especially in poster art and comic books. At the same time, drug consumption created a market for new items, such as drug paraphernalia, which became, in many cases, art forms of their own. Concomitant with rising drug use was the

33. Anthropologists and epidemiologists have shown that drug markets often act like kinship systems with certain groups tied to other groups through loose contacts, often dealers. See Martin A. Plant, *Drug Users in an English Town* (London: Tavistock, 1975).

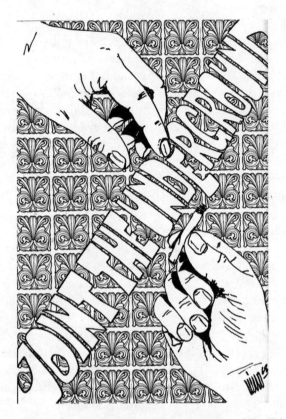

Fig. 1. Psychedelic art was a transatlantic phenomenon, and English drug termi-
nology was widely used. (*Peng,* no. 4 [1968]: 18, SSC, M613/12. Courtesy of Department of Special Collections, Stanford University Libraries.)

introduction of new cultural forms that, though not directly a result of
drug use, gained a certain popularity among drug users. These
included a fascination with Eastern religions, macrobiotic cooking,
and yoga, for example. As drug use expanded in the 1970s, entrepreneurs capitalized on the rising popularity of drug consumption and
created a secondary licit market based on this youth culture. Head
shops, ceramic bongs, psychedelic rock, posters, and T-shirts embla-
zoned with pot leaves or magic mushrooms arrived, at least in Germany, mostly after 1968. Indeed, many of the cultural forms associated
with drug use formed the basis of an alternative culture that took on a
life of its own over the course of the 1970s.

Despite the rapid rise in drug use throughout the industrial West, the development of local scenes was uneven and more rapid in some places than others. Germany lagged behind the United States, England, Scandinavia, and the Netherlands in drug consumption. Yet Germans did not look directly to the United States for instruction and encouragement, as is often assumed. America and Americans were certainly a major influence. But the American influence on the drug scene in Hamburg was, more often than not, mediated through larger and richer scenes in London, Copenhagen, and Amsterdam. Hamburg's drug scene looked to America but through a distinctly European lens.

Hamburg's Scene

Hamburg's own drug epidemic began quietly. In the mid-1960s, stock images of the sixties drug culture—youngsters clad in psychedelic clothing or black turtlenecks passing a joint or taking LSD—had yet to manifest themselves. In fact, hash and marijuana consumption came to Germany quite late. Instead, speed was the initial drug of choice in Hamburg.[34] Curious youths found it easy to buy diet pills and various stimulants, many of which were available over the counter. Taken as prescribed, these drugs did little; taken in large doses, they produced a sense of euphoria and excitement. Other widely prescribed stimulants such as Preludin, Ritalin, and Captagon, popular with prostitutes for some time, proved easy to find. Students used these stimulants to stay awake and study for exams; athletes took them to improve their performance; but more and more frequently, small groups of youths popped uppers to go to clubs and dance all night.[35]

The drug culture in Hamburg during the early years revolved around the numerous beat clubs. These clubs featured rock-and-roll bands and gave young people a space relatively free of adult supervision. In the first few years of the sixties certain clubs around the

34. Arthur Marwick, in *The Sixties: Cultural Revolution in Britain, France, Italy, and the United States, c. 1958–1974* (Oxford: Oxford University Press, 1998), 78, argues that the progression from speed to grass was also true of London.

35. Arthur Kreuzer, *Drogen und Delinquenz: eine jugendkriminologisch-empirische Untersuchung der Erscheinungsformen und Zusammenhänge* (Wiesbaden: Akademische, 1975), 82. On the history of Preludin, see "Preludin: Bomben auf St. Pauli," *Der Spiegel* 20, no. 8 (14 February 1966): 58.

Reeperbahn (Hamburg's red-light district), such as the Top Ten Club, the Kaiserkeller, and the Star Club on Hamburg's notorious Große Freiheit Straße, drew not only German beat bands but bands from England and the United States as well. The Beatles spent their formative years in Hamburg's Kaiserkeller and Star Club before moving on to Liverpool's famous Cave Club. Many lesser-known Liverpool bands also spent time in Hamburg, where the work was plentiful. The Star Club also brought in big-name touring shows. In the summer of 1963, for example, Ray Charles, Bill Haley and the Comets, the Searchers, and Chubby Checker all played the Star Club.[36] This constant flow of British and American bands into Hamburg kept the local scene abreast of the happenings in London and, to a certain extent, in America. The music also drew young people from Scandinavia to Hamburg and acted as a catalyst to the internationalization of Hamburg's youth.

The use of stimulants by club goers in these early years was identified not by the police but rather by the policing arm of the Youth Authority, the so-called Youth Protection Units. Originally formed as a joint venture between the Youth Protection Department and the Women's Police, the Youth Protection Units patrolled the streets of Hamburg looking for "wayward" youth. The focus of their work was twofold: they sought to control male youth consumption (smoking, drinking, and pornography) and youth sexuality (protecting the sexual purity of young women by keeping them from the sex trade and guarding young men from homosexual predators). This meant that officers spent most of their time patrolling areas where youth congregated: parks, train stations, and especially bars and music clubs. Indeed, the clubs near the university and in St. Pauli proved to be the most intractable problems for the Youth Protection Units.

Several of the earliest cases of youth drug consumption that came to the attention of the authorities implicated one club in particular. Early in 1964, Palette—a downtown club on ABC Straße near Gänsemarkt and not far north of city hall—became the popular hangout for the nascent youth drug scene.[37] One writer described Palette this way:

36. See Rüdger Articus et al., *Die Beatles in Harburg* (Hamburg: Hamburger Museum für Archäologie und die Geschichte Harburgs, 1996), 20–21.
37. Palette was the subject of an important modernist novel by Hubert Fichte.

The air in the bar was a stuffy haze of beer, hairspray, tobacco smoke and mothballs. The barmaid announced free rounds by ringing a ship's bell. In the room to the right of the entrance, a man momentarily stumbled over a half-empty *Green,* as bottles of a Hamburg export beer are called. In the niche at the entrance to the third room, called the *End,* the dropouts slept. From time to time, the bartender came and talked to one or another of them. Then the dropouts rummaged in their pockets and Captagon tablets, Prelus (Preludin) or Hash (marijuana cigarettes) changed hands.[38]

Palette received considerable attention from the police and the Youth Authority because of this type of drug trade as well as its reputation as a gay hangout. It was shut down in 1964 but later reopened under the name "Why not?" and remained popular with dropouts and young tourists.[39]

The case reports resulting from the Youth Protection Units are an invaluable resource in reconstructing the early drug scene in Hamburg. Their notes on the youth scene are the best direct evidence we have of the emergence of a drug scene in Hamburg until the "discovery" of drug consumption by the authorities at the end of the 1960s. For example, on 13 April 1964, during their normal rounds, Youth Protection Unit officers discovered a nineteen-year-old Austrian woman named Sonja. Since she was apparently homeless and without means, the officers took her into custody. Under questioning at the police station, Sonja claimed that she was staying with a twenty-two-year-old student named Lutz who worked at the Axel Springer publishing firm. She also admitted to having a "relationship" with a young Englishman named Mike. When she was searched before being sent to a young women's hostel (*Mädchenheim*), the investigators found a number of brown pills wrapped in blue paper and stuffed inside a matchbox. Sonja initially protested that she had no idea where the matchbox had come from but under further questioning admitted that Mike had given it to her two days earlier.[40]

---

38. Margret Kosel, *Gammler Beatniks Provos: Die schleichende Revolution* (Frankfurt am Main: Verlag Bärmeier & Nikel, 1967), 84.

39. Kosel, *Gammler Beatniks Provos,* 84–85.

40. StAH, 354-5 II, Jugendbehörde II, Abl. 11.11.1992, 356-04.04 Band 1, Report from Jugendschutztruppe -A-, 14 April 1964.

On 5 July 1964, a young Swedish woman named Ingrid arrived in Hamburg. That night she went to Palette and met Lutz, the man Sonja had stayed with. He offered her a place to stay. Two days later, in the evening, Ingrid returned to the club to drink a few beers. After a time, a young man introduced himself and handed her ten small, white pills. He told her that if she took all of them at once, she would feel wonderful. With little hesitation, Ingrid swallowed the bunch. Soon she became nauseous and bolted for the door. As she vomited violently outside the front door, Youth Protection Unit officers arrived. Before taking her to a doctor, they questioned a second, seventeen-year-old girl, who admitted to having been given two tablets of speed.[41]

In the middle of October 1964, a Youth Protection Unit patrol picked up a twenty-two-year-old woman named Gretchen. Gretchen had run away from home in December 1961. According to her statement, she and her mother had argued frequently because of Gretchen's regular visits to Palette. Gretchen's twin sister had long visited the club and had "gone downhill"; Gretchen's mother worried that she would do the same. Two months later Gretchen reported to the young women's hostel at Schwanewik, though she only slept there. Sometimes she stayed with a friend. During the day, she hung out with other dropouts at Palette or another club named Kaffeeklappe. She did not have a steady job, but she claimed the dropouts looked out for each other, sharing money or stealing money from other customers at Palette. According to her story, only once had she been involved with drugs. A young man named Mike had asked her for twenty deutsche marks. She gave him the money, and the two headed down to the Reeperbahn. At the corner of Herbertstraße, where prostitution was legal and regulated, they found a man who sold them thirty tablets of Preludin for eighteen deutsche marks. They could not sell the pills, so they turned them over to another dropout who claimed he could sell them. She never saw the man again and thought he had probably been arrested, since so many of the Palette regulars had been. "Those who 'drop out' too long all become criminals," Gretchen claimed, "and I don't want to."[42]

41. StAH, 354-5 II, Jugendbehörde II, Abl. 11.11.1992, 356-04.04 Band 1, Report from Jugendschutztruppe -C-, 8 July 1964.

42. StAH, 354-5 II, Jugendbehörde II, Abl. 11.11.1992, 356-04.04 Band 1, Report from Jugendschutztruppe, 16 October 1964. Walter Becker, Ltd. Regierungsdirektor in the Ham-

These reports and others like them illustrate the international character of the scene and the ways in which cultural change was slowly transforming youth consumption by the mid-1960s, fully half a decade before the drug problem became a public issue. New commercial spaces and new forms of consumerism promoted a youth culture geographically and ideologically distinct from the adult world: this was the physical and cultural space in which the drug scene would emerge as a major cultural force by the seventies.

Members of the Scene

These Youth Protection Unit cases, however, only illuminate a portion of the emergent drug scene. By the mid-1960s, drug users came from several segments of society. Though the scene was not as diverse as it would become, members of several marginal groups came together in the clubs around the Reeperbahn: sailors, bohemians, prostitutes, students, and dropouts.

One group that had always been prominent in the St. Pauli port district was sailors. Drug use and trade had long been part of the experience of the merchant seaman, and sailors from all over the world poured into Hamburg's notorious red-light district. Calling in ports in Morocco, South Africa, India, and Asia, where cannabis and opium consumption were the norm rather than the exception, many sailors smuggled drugs to the West for personal consumption and a quick profit.

Small circles of bohemians welcomed new experiences, including drugs. Students at the Art College, intellectuals, writers, and journalists proved willing to experiment. These were young, educated children of the 1950s German middle-class milieu that was fascinated with French existentialism and modern jazz. Though small in number, these "Exis," as they were called, represented the continental equivalent of the American beatniks. They borrowed from American and French intellectual currents, inhabiting loose groups that resented "their parents' material orientation, philistine lifestyles, and voluntary subjuga-

burg Youth Authority, used these three examples in his 1967 article "Die neue Rauschgiftwelle," *Zentralblatt für Jugendrecht und Jugendwohlfahrt* 54 (1967): 362. He misrepresents the cases as recent.

tion to stifling social norms."[43] It is difficult to gauge the extent of these groups or their effect on the emergence of more widespread drug consumption because they tended to keep to themselves and rarely came to the attention of the police.[44]

Speed use had long been a part of the sex trade in Hamburg. Pimps, bartenders, and porters in certain St. Pauli clubs carried on a lively trade selling speed to prostitutes, who routinely used the stimulants Captagon, Preludin, and Pervitin. The large supply of speed used in these circles came from drugs diverted from pharmaceutical companies, usually through an inside contact, or from Scandinavians who brought the drug down from Stockholm's drug scene.[45]

University students had a more ambivalent attitude toward drug use. In the first few years, some student protesters used speed as a means to keep working long into the night. Yet the dominant Marxist bent of the German New Left viewed drug consumption with suspicion. Though there was some initial interest in the "consciousness expansion" of cannabis and LSD, most Leftist students saw drugs as a diversion from the mission of overthrowing the political system. Drugs, so the argument went, were antirevolutionary; the way to an expanded consciousness lay not in achieving chemical alteration but in overcoming an oppressive capitalist economic system.

The Gammler

The group of youths most involved in the early spread of drug use was the so-called *Gammler,* or Dropouts. *Gammler,* a term with negative connotations, was a label placed on young bohemian types by the media but a label that they adopted and translated into a badge of honor. Sporting long hair and flaunting their rejection of the bourgeois values of industriousness and thrift, these young dropouts congregated in most of the large cities: near the Gedächtniskirche or on Kurfürstendamm in Berlin, on the Reeperbahn in Hamburg, and on Nikolaiplatz in Munich. Seeing themselves as part of a larger international movement, many of these young people traveled to Paris, Stockholm,

---

43. Sabina von Dirke, *All Power to the Imagination! The West German Counterculture from the Student Movement to the Greens* (Lincoln: University of Nebraska Press, 1997), 23.

44. Kreuzer, *Drogen und Delinquenz,* 138.

45. Ibid., 138–39.

Rome, Amsterdam, and London.[46] Though it is impossible to accurately report the number of Gammlers, one historian estimates that, at their high point, there were two hundred thousand full-time hippies in the United States and another two hundred thousand in Europe, and many more were sympathetic to the movement.[47] A contemporary journalist estimated only around one hundred thousand in Europe.[48]

In a 1966 cover article, *Der Spiegel* described the "typical" German Gammler:

> They move easily through the Old World and now and then also through the New World. With a sleeping bag under the arm, a few coins in the pocket, they hitch rides with the stream of tourist convoys and settle wherever the sun always shines or where they find companions who also proudly call themselves "*Wir Typen.*" Like migratory birds they tend to go south in the autumn or settle down by their mother's hearth when winter gets near.[49]

Though the German dropouts certainly remained cognizant of their Germanness, many of them felt they had more in common with *Provos* in Amsterdam, the "heads" and "freaks" in London, *Raggare* in Stockholm, or the hippies in San Francisco than with other groups in their own society.[50] Though these young people from various countries were often quite different, they shared a common core belief in the rejection of the values of their parents' generation, exacerbated in Germany by the rising awareness of the Nazi past.

Concomitant with the rejection of the past was a rejection of consumerism. The dropouts and the nascent student movements were, in fact, two sides of a coin. Both rejected the idea of the affluent society based on mass consumption. Yet while the student movement, inspired by Marxism, saw the imminent collapse of capitalism under the weight of its own internal contradictions, the Gammler youth simply rejected capitalistic society altogether. In a sense, the dropouts marked the cul-

46. Ibid., 139, 226–28. See also Kosel, *Gammler Beatniks Provos*, 9–15, 55–117.
47. Marwick, *The Sixties*, 480.
48. Walter Hollstein, "Gammler und Provos," *Frankfurter Hefte* 22 (1967): 410.
49. "Gammler: Schalom aleichem," *Der Spiegel* 20, no. 39 (19 September 1966): 72.
50. See Kosel, *Gammler Beatniks Provos*, 53–80; Marwick, *The Sixties*, 479–98. See also Walter Hollstein, "Hippies im Wandel," *Frankfurter Hefte* 23 (1968): 641, and Hollstein, "Gammler und Provos," 409–10.

mination of the Wirtschaftswunder. They took the promise of affluence for all and rising leisure time and stood it on its head, rejecting affluence and reversing the traditional relationship of work to leisure. Rather than working in order to be able to enjoy some leisure, they made leisure a profession in itself. As one dropout on Hamburg's Reeperbahn put it: "It [dropping out] is a hard job."[51]

Drugs fit perfectly into the "anti-ideology" ideology of the Gammler. Taking drugs represented, at heart, the consumption of pleasure in a tangible form. At the same time, the dropouts symbolically rejected traditional forms of consumption by smoking hashish, as opposed to their parents' ever-increasing consumption of alcohol. Rather than confronting the so-called alcohol generation, though, they simply ignored it, which was all the more infuriating to adults.[52] These young people took drugs not because their parents disapproved, though this was certainly an added benefit; they took drugs because they wanted to, because it was fun, and because they just did not care what their parents' generation thought.

Parents worried that their children would "tune in, turn on, and drop out." Drugs presented both a real and an imagined threat, as did the refusal of the dropouts to pursue a "normal" lifestyle. Walter Becker, the influential leader of Action Youth Protection, saw the Gammler as the heart of the danger posed by youth rebellion:

> An international phenomenon, most *Gammlers* here [in Germany] appear to be at risk. If we include other groups of youths under this heading, then most show signs of considerable instability. They rebel against the norms of middle-class society in indiscriminate ways but in a weak-willed manner, wishy-washy and feeble as it were. They are not true rebels who enthrall us and are able to lead to new destinations but rather tired mutineers more inclined to resignation than protest. In their circles they turn to marijuana cigarettes, small brown packets or—more recently—to LSD-25! The authorities must acknowledge and fight against this danger to our youth in a timely manner. *Due to the devastating effects of drugs, there can be no pardon.*[53]

51. "Gammler: Schalom aleichem," 76.
52. "Jugend: Übertriebene Generation," *Der Spiegel* 21, no. 41 (2 October 1967): 168.
53. Becker, "Die neue Rauschgiftwelle," 361.

Adults felt threatened by the dropouts because this motley crew publicly flaunted what their critics most desired: an orderly society. Their appearance, their refusal to work, their obtrusive begging, and their drug use put a public face on a much larger conflict. Drug use appeared to be a threat because many adults saw drugs as leading to this kind of behavior, when, in fact, the opposite was probably the case.

Yet Becker was right in that Gammlers played an important role in the early drug trade in Hamburg. As the popularity of speed use, predominantly Preludin, continued to spread between 1964 and 1966, police began to focus on these young dropouts. On 24 November 1965, police arrested eighteen-year-old Marion K. at a bar in Harburg, south of the Elbe. She had recently run away from a youth home and, despite already having gone through a withdrawal treatment at a local hospital a year before, had begun using Preludin again. She admitted to purchasing 250 tablets, using some and selling the rest.[54] In February 1966, police caught a nineteen-year-old Swede named Klaus, who had convinced a friend who worked in a doctor's office to steal a prescription book for him. He and his friend then carved a doctor's stamp. Klaus managed to fill two prescriptions for Preludin before being discovered.[55] In June authorities uncovered a group of young men at Rahlstedt Youth Home conspiring to sell Preludin.[56] In September, the Youth Authority questioned a dropout named Adolf, who claimed to be "unenthusiastic" about continuing his life as a Gammler and asserted that Preludin use was becoming more and more popular with the dropouts, many of whom were becoming addicts.[57]

The use of drugs in clubs spread after 1966 as the ranks of the long-time dropouts were swelled by an influx of new drug consumers drawn by the increasing visibility of drug consumption in both the media and the clubs. While in 1964 the number of clubs where drugs were prevalent was small, limited to Club 99 and a few of the clubs on the Reeper-

54. StAH, 354-5 II, Jugendbehörde II, Abl. 11.11.1992 356-04.04 Band 1, KM Tullius, Report, 29 November 1965.

55. StAH, 354-5 II, Jugendbehörde II, Abl. 11.11.1992 356-04.04 Band 1, KK 1 B 2, Report, 18 March 1966.

56. StAH, 354-5 II, Jugendbehörde II, Abl. 11.11.1992 356-04.04 Band 1, Amt für Jugendbeförderung, "Verkauf von Preludin-Tabletten im Jugendheim Rahlstedt," 1 June 1966.

57. StAH, 354-5 II, Jugendbehörde II, Abl. 11.11.1992 356-04.04 Band 1, Gehrcke, "Preludin," 20 September 1966.

bahn, by 1968 drugs could be had in any number of clubs. The Youth Protection Department considered nineteen clubs to be drug hangouts. Most were located within a twenty-block radius around the Reeperbahn. One block on Große Freiheit was home to three suspected clubs: Club 39, Salambo, and Imbißstube. Other St. Pauli clubs included Mambo-Schänke, Drei-Weisheiten, Rattenkeller, Top-ten, Past-Ten, as well as the Hotel Nobistor and the Sahara-Inn. Club 99, near the Dammtor train station and the university, remained a center of the drug trade, along with a club across from the main train station at first called Oblomoff but later changed to Augustenburg. Police found the spread of clubs to other parts of Hamburg more troubling. Authorities suspected the Casino Club in Harburg, as well as Cleopatra on Bramfelder Chaussee north of Barmbeck, of involvement in the drug trade. Even in the relatively middle-class western suburb of Groß Flottbek, a club called Big Ranch across from the horse-racing track fell under suspicion.[58]

Morocco, the Hash Trail, and International Distribution

After the middle of the decade an international culture based on a rejection of industrial society, an interest in Eastern spiritualism, and a penchant for drug use began to coalesce. Americans came to Europe in increasing numbers, while Britons and Swedes began to travel to Morocco along with their American compatriots. For the next few years, Morocco was the focus of the European hash trade, because of both its close proximity and its exotic appeal.[59] The international fascination with Tangier, home in the 1950s to prominent writers and drug users like William Burroughs and Paul Bowles, was rooted in the availability and cultural acceptance of cannabis. The rapid increase in

58. StAH, 354-5 II, Jugendbehörde II, Abl. 11.11.1992 356-04.04 Band 2, Regierungsoberinspektor Hinsch, "Abgabe von Rauschgiften in Gaststätten," 23 July 1968; StAH, 354-5 II, Jugendbehörde II, Abl. 11.11.1992 356-04.04 Band 2, Herman Brandt, "Bekämpfung von Rauschgiftgebrauch," 5 December 1968.

59. For examples, see UN, *Summary of Reports on Illicit Transactions and Seizures,* E/NS/1963/Summary 12, p. 11. E/NS/1964/Summary 3, pp. 8–9; E/NS/1964/Summary 4, pp. 10–11; E/NS/1964/Summary 12, pp. 6–7; E/NS/1966/Summary 8, p. 15; E/NS/1966/Summary 9, p. 8; E/NS/1966/Summary 10, p. 8; E/NS/1967/Summary 5, p. 9; E/NS/1967/Summary 6, p. 11. See also Richard Neville, *Play Power: Exploring the International Underground* (New York: Random House, 1970), 232–36.

arrests of young Americans and Europeans in both Morocco and Spain attested to a blossoming drug culture that crossed national boundaries.[60]

Cannabis increasingly found its way to West Germany in the mid-1960s. On 3 March 1965, police in Soltau arrested a young American man and a Swedish woman for stealing gasoline. Upon inspection of their car, the officers found slightly more than a kilogram of marijuana under the backseat. According to the report, these two had been employed by a drug trafficking group in Stockholm to purchase the drugs in Tangier. After driving through West Germany, France, and Spain, they traded a Moroccan some clothing for the marijuana. On the trip back to Sweden, they delivered a small quantity of the drug to a jazz musician in Paris and to a Turk in Cologne. The American admitted that he had made the journey to Morocco a number of times and had sold the drug in both Spain and the United States.[61]

In the summer of 1966, Christian B., only sixteen years old, stole three thousand deutsche marks and various valuables from his parents. Christian planned to drive to Morocco and buy some marijuana with his nineteen-year-old friend Ulrich B., who provided a car. On the way, they met Luis T., a twenty-five-year-old man from Peru. The three of them hit it off, so the Germans invited him to come along on their journey. Near Tetuan, Morocco, they purchased 8 kilograms of marijuana for eight hundred deutsche marks. They hid the contraband in the car and drove back across Spain and France. In Belgium they split 200 grams into small packages, which Luis tried to sell in several cities. Convinced that London was the place to sell the hash, Luis attempted to cajole his new friends into the journey across the English Channel. Christian and Ulrich wanted to go back to Germany instead and sell the stash there. Luis decided to part company with the Germans and went to stay with a friend in Antwerp. The two German teens then drove to Hamburg. Ulrich offered the marijuana to a porter at one of the clubs on the Reeperbahn for twenty thousand deutsche marks. The police were tipped off about the deal and waited for Ulrich to return with the contraband. Not long after, Ulrich returned, and the porter turned him down. The police followed Ulrich back to the car. Once he

60. E/NS/1965/Summary 4, p. 9; E/NS/1965/Summary 5, pp. 10–11.
61. E/NS/1966/Summary 5, p. 10.

realized he was being followed, Ulrich ran for the car and tried to pull away. The police rammed the car to keep the young men from escaping. The arresting officers found 7.8 kilograms of marijuana hidden under the trunk.[62]

While young Europeans traveled to foreign lands in search of hashish, immigrants from the developing world brought traditional forms of cannabis consumption to Europe: Algerians in France, Turks in Germany, and West Africans and West Indians in Britain. Among the Algerian workers in France, smoking kif—a North African cannabis product[63]—was a matter of tradition. Some young Algerians, though, took part in the burgeoning international youth networks, introducing hashish to young people in much of southern Europe and supplying much of the demand of the American troops stationed in southern Germany.[64] In Britain, Nigerians and other West Africans, as well as Jamaican immigrants, played a significant role in the trade.[65] In Germany, Munich and Frankfurt became the early centers of the marijuana trade, Munich because of its large number of Turkish guest workers and Frankfurt because of its proximity to large numbers of American soldiers.[66] At the same time, Spaniards and Moroccans played an important part in the traffic because of the increased interest in Moroccan hashish.[67]

As time wore on, young hippies began driving through the Balkans to Istanbul or Beirut, smuggling hashish back to Europe through Bulgaria, Yugoslavia, and Austria.[68] Turks bringing small shipments into

62. StAH, 354-5 II, Jugendbehörde II, Abl. 11.11.1992 356-04.04 Band 1, "Jahresbericht für die Rauschgiftkommission des Wirtschafts- und Sozialrates der Vereinten Nationen," 19 January 1967, BfI, Rgd. KK Westfal, Report, 1966; StAH, 354-5 II, Jugendbehörde II, Abl. 11.11.1992 356-04.04 Band 1, KM Rytlewski, Report, 28 July 1966; StAH, 354-5 II, Jugendbehörde II, Abl. 11.11.1992 356-04.04 Band 1, KM Rytlewski, "Vernehmegung," 28 July 1966.

63. Kif is a Moroccan cannabis preparation. The term became popular for most cannabis products and is still in use today.

64. See Kreuzer, *Drogen und Delinquenz,* 139, 212–13. E/NS/1964/Summary 3, pp. 6–8; E/NS/1965/Summary 4, p. 8; E/NS/1966/Summary 9, p. 10; E/NS/1968/Summary 2, p. 13; E/IT/1966/21; E/IT/1967/74.

65. See E/NS/1964/Summary 4, p. 10; E/NS/1966/Summary 5, p. 15.

66. See E/NS/1965/Summary 5, p. 12; E/NS/1966/Summary 5, p. 10; E/NS/1968/Summary 2, p. 12.

67. See E/NS/1965/Summary 5, p. 12; E/NS/1966/Summary 5, pp. 10, 14; E/NS/1967/Summary 10, p. 15.

68. See E/NS/1965/Summary 5, pp. 11, 14; E/NS/1966/Summary 7, pp. 11–13; E/NS/1966/Summary 8, p. 15; E/NS/196/Summary 8, pp. 22–23; E/NS/1967/Summary 10, p. 10; E/NS/1968/Summary pp. 2, 13.

southern Germany also traveled this route extensively. Occasionally Lebanese smugglers took advantage of this path, though they preferred to use shipping channels. In late March 1966, Mustafa T. was returning from Turkey to his job in Munich when he was arrested in Yugoslavia with 150 grams of hashish. A month later, Yugoslavian customs arrested Saim B. for trafficking 8 kilograms to Germany. Six days later, officers discovered 3.75 kilograms of hashish in a false-bottomed suitcase belonging to Sezaj B., who claimed to be delivering the drugs to Mehmed O. in Munich.[69] In August 1968, Bulgarian police arrested a German, a South African, and a Malaysian trying to smuggle 19 kilograms of hash into the Federal Republic. Two months later, they arrested a young Englishman seeking to smuggle 18 kilograms from Afghanistan to Australia. A few days thereafter, 14 kilograms of hashish were discovered in the gas tank of a car driven by an Iranian traveling to the Federal Republic.[70] As these cases exemplify, the traffic in hashish through the Balkans initially included both Europeans bringing drugs back from their travels and Turks, Lebanese, and Iranians delivering drugs to the Federal Republic and Scandinavia; most of this trade remained relatively small-scale.

Around 1966, the hippies who had caused such a stir in Morocco began to migrate toward the Middle East and South Asia. Seeking "enlightenment" in Eastern mysticism and ample supplies of cannabis, young dropouts headed down the hash trail.[71] For the first few years, over half the number traveling the hash trail were young Americans, but Europeans made up most of the remainder; in the early seventies this relationship was reversed. Many of those who made the trip did so in search of some "authentic experience" or to escape what they saw as the oppressiveness of the home countries. According to Lieschen Müller,

> you either stayed home and got into politics, the French Revolution of '68, the Vietnam demonstrations, Red Rudi Dutschke in Berlin, or you went East. A lot of people stayed for the politics, got disillusioned and then went East, because things hadn't changed overnight as expected.[72]

69. E/NS/1967/Summary 8, pp. 22–23.

70. E/NS/1968/Summary 3, p. 8.

71. Neville, *Play Power,* 207.

72. Lieschen Müller quoted in David Tomory, *A Season in Heaven: True Tales from the Road to Kathmandu* (London: Lonely Planet, 1998), 25.

The trip east, however, was normally only a temporary escape. A few stayed for years; most returned to their homes and a more normal life.[73]

Between 1968 and 1971, what had been a trickle of hashish mainly from Morocco became a flood from the Near and Middle East and Central Asia.[74] Hashish smuggling, which had been a way to supply oneself and one's friends, became a way to finance a life on the margins. As a result, young Europeans and North Americans attempted to smuggle ever-larger caches of contraband. Many of them ended up serving lengthy sentences in wretched conditions in countries like Turkey, Lebanon, Bulgaria, and Yugoslavia.

No one knows the number of young Westerners who made this journey, though the Indian and Nepalese government tourism statistics recorded about forty-seven thousand American visitors in 1966 and slightly fewer Europeans.[75] A much smaller estimate that probably gives a better idea of the traffic on the hippie trail counted two thousand hippies passing through Kabul in 1967 alone.[76] What was certain, however, was that more and more hippies were being arrested for trafficking hashish. In August 1967, for example, German police were on the trail of their first large-scale bust. Two British students sold ten kilograms of hashish in Munich and Frankfurt, after which they headed back toward the East. In December, they purchased eighty kilograms of hashish in Pakistan. The two then flew to Paris, rented a car, and drove to Frankfurt. On New Year's Day in 1968, Frankfurt police arrested them for attempting to sell the hashish.[77]

Hashish and LSD in Hamburg

How did this broadly international increase in hashish smuggling affect Hamburg? For the first few years (1964–66), Hamburg was sim-

---

73. See Tomory, *A Season in Heaven,* and Jonathon Green, *All Dressed Up: The Sixties and the Counter-culture* (London: Jonathan Cape, 1998), 224–36. For a more critical view of hippies in the East, see Vera Vuckovacki, *Endstation Kathmandu* (n.p.: blick + bild Verlag, 1972).

74. See Neville, *Play Power,* 203–50. On Kabul, see also Suzanne Labin, *Hippies, Drogues et Sexe* (Paris: La Table Ronde, 1970), 112–19.

75. Tomory, *A Season in Heaven,* 16.

76. Neville, *Play Power,* 207.

77. E/NS/1968/Summary, pp. 1, 3.

ply a way station for the larger drug scenes in Stockholm and Copen-hagen. Police repeatedly claimed that Hamburg served mainly as a "trans-shipment center."[78] Despite the reluctance of police to admit that Hamburg also hosted a growing internal market, the number of hashish consumers grew rapidly in 1966 and 1967. On 1 February 1967 during the annual press conference on crime, Hamburg senator Hans Ruhnau pointed for the first time to an alarming rise in drug con-sumption. In that year's annual narcotics summary to the Federal Criminal Office, the Hamburg police reported a rapid climb in the number of hashish cases: "The number of hashish/marijuana cases coming to light rose from 9 in 1966 to 70. Fifty-five of these were youth and teenagers, including 8 foreigners."[79]

Hamburg's Youth Protection Units uncovered much of the new hashish consumption. In 1967, they detained forty-three teens between the ages of fifteen and twenty for drug possession. Young men made up the bulk of the detainees, averaging nineteen years of age. The young women caught with drugs were just seventeen, on average. Most came from so-called orderly homes. Except for seven students attending a secondary modern school (*Realschule*), all attended a vocational school (*Volksschule*), implying that most came from working-class families. Most of the youths initially received drugs from friends, par-ticularly from friends who were dropouts. They usually bought drugs at clubs in St. Pauli, around the Reeperbahn, and on Große Freiheit Straße, but they preferred to smoke their hash in small groups, either in someone's home or in one of the parks.[80]

What linked these teens more than their shared sociological charac-teristics was their experience of drug use. Smoking hashish was pleas-ant for most, though the experience varied. One respondent declared,

---

78. See "Das Rauschgift Angebot in Hamburg wächst," *Die Welt,* 27 December 1967; Ulrich Mackensen, "Rauschgift am 'Tor zur Freude': Erfolgreiche Razzia der Hamburger Polizei," *Vorwärts,* 15 November 1967, in StAH, 354-5 II, Jugendbehörde II, Abl. 11.11.1992 356-04.04 Band 1; Helmut Locher, "Rauschgift kommt: Bundesrepublik wird Tummelplatz der Banden," *Vorwärts,* 20 April 1967, in StAH, 354-5 II, Jugendbehörde II, Abl. 11.11.1992 356-04.04 Band 1.

79. StAH, 354-5 II, Jugendbehörde II, Abl. 11.11.1992 356-04.04 Band 1, BfIH, Rgd, "Jahresbericht für die Rauschgiftkommission des Wirtschafts- und Sozialrates der Vereinten Nationen," 17 January 1968.

80. StAH, 354-5 II, Jugendbehörde II, Abl. 11.11.1992, 356-04.04 Band 1, Brandt, "Rauschgift unter Jugendlichen in Hamburg," 12 October 1967.

"I felt transported to another world." Another claimed, "My spirit was carried off somewhere." Some had a less spiritual and more common reaction: "I suddenly had to laugh, and I couldn't stop laughing," or "The music sounds entirely different. I could hear every mistake. If I haven't smoked any hashish, music isn't so important to me." At least one young man was not as convinced of the effects of hashish: "I couldn't feel anything."[81]

Along with hashish consumption, a market in LSD emerged in 1967. Though LSD had probably been available sporadically in Hamburg since 1966, Hamburg police criminal director Herbert Hoyer claimed at the end of 1967 that not a single case of LSD consumption had come to the attention of the police.[82] Despite police claims to the contrary, it is fairly clear that LSD was available in Hamburg's clubs in 1967–68. In a *Konkret* article that same month, Stefan Aust commented on the obliviousness exhibited by police to the rapid changes in drug consumption: "The naïveté of the official offices is simply fantastic. Everyone who doesn't look exactly like a police officer can buy LSD in every second beat club or hippie bar in the Federal Republic. In every big city, there are already several thousand young people taking LSD."[83] Aust was probably more correct than Hoyer, but the rapid spread of LSD, already a reality in American cities and in London, did not occur before 1969.

Drug Culture

Since the 1960s, the mythical year of 1968 has been seen as the pivotal moment in postwar history by both nostalgic '68ers and their critics. Although the political events of 1968 took center stage, other facets of youth culture grew substantially yet garnered less attention than the student protests. Drug use blossomed in 1968. What had been a fairly peripheral activity began to spread, as more and more young people experimented with drugs. This spread in drug use took place quietly; the authorities and the press were too busy dealing with the more explosive combination of war and protest to pay much attention to

81. Ibid.
82. "Das Rauschgift-Angebot in Hamburg wächst," *Die Welt,* 27 December 1967.
83. Stefan Aust, "LSD in Deutschland," *Konkret,* December 1967, 18.

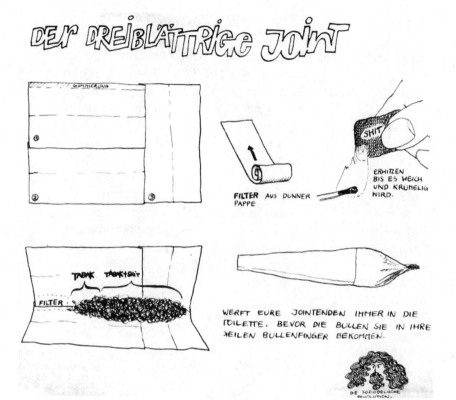

Fig. 2.   Though satirical, the instructions for a "three-paper joint" illustrate the ways in which the drug scene was created through peer networks that shared insider knowledge. (*Peng,* no. 4 [1968]: 16, SSC, M613/12. Courtesy of Department of Special Collections, Stanford University Libraries.)

drug use. But, unlike the massive protests, drug consumption occurred on the scale of everyday life. The drug scene quietly grew without directly challenging the power of the state.

A report by an anonymous social worker gives a certain insight into the everyday world of the drug scene. One of the members of the Hamburg Youth Department visited Club 99, on the Esplanade near city hall, and wrote a memorandum about those experiences. The report follows the format of an ethnography but often reads like the musings of a postmodern urban flaneur, fascinated and repulsed by a world that seemed exotic and threatening. This horrific captivation springs from the realization that the author has entered a completely foreign world within Hamburg, reminiscent of the flaneurs of "Outcast London" during the 1870s and 1880s.[84] The author opens the report with a foreboding description of the surroundings. "In the club the same atmosphere dominates the entire day. It turns out that the club is a long tunnel in which almost no daylight enters," the author claims. "The darkness is partially illuminated by dim lamps. This long crepuscular tunnel is confusingly arranged because of the many small niches, and because of this, the youth can go about their pleasure undisturbed."[85] Behind the bar, Günther or Wolfgang, the two bartenders, handed out beers and cokes to the ragged teens planted on bar stools. Beyond the packed bar area, visitors passed into the claustrophobic back room. Even darker than the bar area and incessantly smoky, the back room consisted of numerous small niches. These tight spaces, most large enough for only two or three people, were filled day and night with high school students skipping school, students from Hamburg's university, apprentices, hippies, street kids, and working-class toughs. Klatches of young men and women sat on benches or bar stools or stood, smoking cigarettes and talking about philosophy, the state of the student protests, the drudgeries of high school, or sex. Much of the conversation, however, focused on drugs: someone's recent trip to Istanbul and the best way to smuggle hash back to Germany; the place to score in Amsterdam; whom to contact in London for "Blue God" LSD; how to dry banana peels in the oven for smoking; or a friend of a friend who knew a nurse who could get pills.

The social worker claimed that it was not difficult to buy drugs at Club 99, attesting that, "In the meantime, I have often asked after stuff and have received something every time."[86] The small alcoves, hidden from the view of prying eyes, and the filthy bathrooms at the back of the bar offered ample opportunity to transact business. Yet the bargains made at Club 99 were not the kind of deals that particularly interested the police; this was all small-time trade: a gram of hashish, a few

84. See Judith Walkowitz, *City of Dreadful Delight: Narratives of Sexual Danger in Late-Victorian London* (Chicago: University of Chicago Press, 1992), esp. 15–39.

85. StAH, 354-5 II, Jugendbehörde II, Abl. 11.11.1992 356-04.04 Band 2, "Club 99," 1 March 1968.

86. Ibid.

uppers, or some barbiturates. Someone might trade a joint for a few pills or trade a few grams of hash for a stolen radio.[87]

This kind of ethnographic detail, however, was only part of the report; much of the report was given over to telling horror stories and warning of the dangers—real or imagined—of this new milieu. In the middle of the report, the author tells the story of a young girl:

> Late one afternoon as I came into the club, an approximately 16-year-old girl slept in a partially hidden niche. As she was awoken by the words of an older guest: She's taken too many birth control pills, she looks pretty wrecked. . . . Talking between them was out of the question at first, because she was hardly in the shape to talk rationally. When she had regained some of her senses, she disappeared for a few minutes and then returned. Her acquaintance told her as they were leaving that she shouldn't take so many tablets at the same time in the future. Of course she could have some anytime she wanted.[88]

This and the other stories reported by the author repeatedly highlight the sexual danger of this milieu. The author concludes that the place itself is a threat and must be closed: the fault is not placed on the youths but on the milieu itself. These new social spaces breed corruption and must be stamped out so that youths can regain their senses.

Despite the fears of the author and the tone of fascinated horror, this ethnographic report gives us a glimpse into the everyday experience of the drug scene: young people sharing a joint, passing around a bottle of schnapps someone had shoplifted, or taking a few pills. Bars like Club 99 played midwife to an emerging drug culture. The culture of drug use emerged at the intersection of popular culture, consumption, and rebellion. It developed among groups of friends who shared a set of values gleaned from popular culture, a widespread discontent with the affluent society, and a longing for some kind of meaning outside of the traditional passage from school to work. They craved "authentic" experience and sought ways to escape what they saw as a mundane, bourgeois existence. Drugs offered a means to this end. Rather than being a form of resistance to market mechanisms beyond

87. Ibid.
88. Ibid.

their control or the result of youth being swindled by the machinations of the culture industry, youth drug use marked a very real triumph of postwar youth consumer culture. Young people rejected consumption through consumption. Though they believed smoking hashish or dropping acid could release them from the vulgar materialism of modern capitalism, they were actually promoting the development of a global capitalist market in drugs.

The Meaning of Drugs for Youth

The emergence of an anticonsumerist ethos in the 1960s was not limited to illicit drug consumption; the student movement and, later, Leftist terrorism were at least partially motivated by similar concerns. Yet illicit drug consumers articulated their opposition to consumerism in novel ways. In order to understand what drugs meant to young Germans in the second half of the sixties, we must turn to different kinds of evidence. Opinion polls and other quantitative evidence do not exist for this period. Instead, we are forced to look for the answers in more qualitative sources: literature, memoirs, journalism, and oral histories.

The common thread that ties these sources together is a similar articulation of shared concerns. These young cultural radicals—and by the end of the sixties larger numbers drawn toward radical critiques— sought a *social* transformation. Though widespread disagreement on precisely how to reach this transformation proved the rule rather than the exception, student radicals, proto-terrorists, dropouts, and drug users tended to share an aversion to what they saw as the tyranny of consumer society. Political radicalism and drug consumption were not separate issues; the ideologies of the two overlapped and, at times, parted ways. When looking at the evidence from the "counterculture," what we find is an ambiguous mix of revolutionary socialism, of "consciousness expansion," and of the sheer refusal of the social dropout. In the German case, these three mixed freely, though perhaps leaning more heavily to socialist or communist radicalism than elsewhere. In the words of the cultural radicals involved in the drug scene we find an overlap between the politics of revolutionary action and the politics of personal transformation.

The German literary sources written by young drug consumers in the sixties are few in comparison to the larger literature in the United

States or Great Britain.[89] Even so, the few sources we do have give a glimpse into the specifically German context. Bernward Vesper's insightful book *Die Reise* (The Trip) winds together the story of three separate journeys: Vesper's trip around the Federal Republic, an LSD trip taken with a Jewish American artist in Munich's English Garden, and a journey into Vesper's past. After becoming disillusioned with the German student movement and breaking with Gudrun Ensslin, who left him and their child to form the Red Army Faction with Andreas Baader, Vesper turned to the counterculture in a search for authenticity. Vesper saw hashish and LSD as a way to escape the dreary conformism of the Federal Republic and to find a new consciousness that transcended the everyday. "Narcotics. Already this name alone, everything is connected with it: unconsciousness, anaesthetization, destruction of reality," Vesper wrote. "But we have been anaesthetized since our childhoods. Drugs tear the veil of reality, wake us, make us alive, and make us conscious of our situation for the first time."[90]

Vesper saw drugs as a way to "expand the consciousness," yet he also saw drug consumption as part of a larger rejection of his parents' generation. His drug consumption was part of a sustained attack against his parents' generation and against his father, a former Nazi Party member and one of Hitler's favorite poets.

> The revolt took place against those who made me into a pig, it is not a blind hate, not an urge, back to nirvana, before birth. But the rebellion against the twenty years in my parents' house, against the father, the manipulation, the seduction, the waste of youth, the enthusiasm, the élan, the hope—at that moment I grasped that it is singularly unrepeatable. I don't know when it became dark, but I know that it is the day and the time for clarification. For, like me, we have all been cheated, out of our dreams, out of love, spirit, merriment, out of fucking, of hash and trips (everyone will be cheated further).[91]

89. See, for example, Bernward Vesper, *Die Reise: Romanessay* (Jossa: März bei Zweitausandeins, 1977), as well as Hubert Fichte, *Die Palette* (Reinbeck bei Hamburg: Rowohlt, 1968) and *Detlevs Imitationen Grünspan* (Reinbeck bei Hamburg: Rowohlt, 1971).

90. Vesper, *Die Reise*, 64. Vesper is one of the truly fascinating stories of the sixties; on his life, see Gerd Koenen, *Vesper, Ensslin, Baader: Urszenen des deutschen Terrorismus* (Cologne: Verlag Kiepenheuer & Witsch, 2003).

91. Vesper, *Die Reise*, 55.

Vesper, like many of his contemporaries, felt cheated by the promises of the so-called affluent society. Drugs, for Vesper, could not replace the need for social transformation but could offer both insight into the human condition and an escape from it. Drugs might transform the self, though he had doubts about this, but nevertheless they did act as a potent symbol of the refusal to conform, to give in to the demands of consumer society.

This great refusal ethos did not always center, like Vesper's, on such an Oedipal object; often the generational conflict took on a much more political tone. The German political provocateur Klint Knorndel, in his story *Good Times,* claimed that the members of the drug scene could act as a revolutionary vanguard.

> One day, when there are enough dropouts, we will have finally grasped "Revolution." Then it won't involve ideologies or state forms. It will involve old and young. Spiritually old or young. And then no more of the old will make THEIR profit out of revolution. The old are the dead. Their spirit and their paradise are already dead. Alone through their existence and their maxims, alone through their glances, they infect us daily with their death, so that we will probably die at 30. When it is understood, all of the old will have to die mercilessly. Then what they *must* destroy, day for day, word for word, is our *paradise.*[92]

In 1971, Jost Hermand dismissed this kind of provocation, claiming it represented the "ideological salad" that had become widespread at the end of the sixties, one that focused on sex and drug consumption.[93] Yet despite the lack of ideological purity, this kind of mixing of the politically revolutionary and self-transformational was widespread in Germany at the end of the sixties and cannot or should not be simply dismissed. Drugs and revolution were not distinct but rather blended into an ideology based on the rejection of the affluent society, consumerism, and consumption.

Journalists and writers sympathetic to the new youth movements also focused on the rejection of consumption. Walter Hollstein, writing

92. Quoted in Jost Hermand, *Pop International: Eine kritische Analyse* (Frankfurt am Main: Athenäum, 1971), 141.
93. Ibid., 141.

in the *Frankfurter Heft,* pointed to the relationship between drug use and a rejection of bourgeois consumption:

As the Dutch Provo Constantin Nieuwenhuis has formulated programmatically, the dropouts [*Gammler*] want to free their comrades from work and turn life into a game. These revolutionaries of modern existence [*Dasein*] are not in agreement, however, with the kind of free time they are now presented with. The dropouts criticize the fact that today's leisure time has become stale and empty. Man has become a slave to consumption and, in his free time, turns to the suggestions of advertisements and illustrated newspapers, instead of doing what he wants and what corresponds to him. The dropout consciously removes himself from obligatory consumption, while he makes do and lives on the bare essentials.[94]

This metaphor that equates consumption with slavery became a central critique of consumer society and a widely shared sentiment. Adults, so the dropouts argued, were bound to their goods and to the social responsibility of buying and consuming commodities they did not need. This bondage to things created hollow men, who had lost the freedom of discernment and even individuality by being tied to an homogenizing consumer culture.

In memoirs and biographies, the themes, despite the distortions of memory, are presented in a similar manner, highlighting drug consumption as rebellion against bourgeois society.[95] In his memoir, Bommi Baumann, a self-proclaimed "urban guerrilla" and member of the 2 June Movement, recalled the period from 1967 to 1969 as a time of radical cultural experimentation. Baumann helped found the Central Committee of the Roaming Hash Rebels in West Berlin in 1969. In a leaflet entitled "It Is Time to Destroy," the Hash Rebels announced:

The Hash Rebels are the militant kernel of Berlin's counterculture. They fight against the modern monopoly capitalist system of slavery. They are fighting for their own free decisions over their bodies

---

94. Holstein, "Gammler und Provos," 417.

95. See, for example, Stefan Aust, *Der Pirat: Die Drogenkarriere des Jan C.* (Hamburg: Hoffmann und Campe, 1990); Christiana F., Kai Hermann, and Horst Rieck, *Wir Kinder vom Bahnhof Zoo* (Hamburg: Gruner und Jahr, 1979); Ursula Dechêne, *Der lange Tod des Fixers P.: Eine Dokumentarerzählung* (Munich: R. Piper, 1974).

and form of life. JOIN THIS STRUGGLE. Build militant cadres in towns and cities. Contact similar groups. Shit on the society of middle age and taboos. Become wild and do beautiful things. Have a joint. Whatever you see that you don't like, destroy. Dare to struggle, dare to win.[96]

Again, the trope of slavery comes to the fore as well as the call to action. This flyer calls for political struggle and for destruction but also for "beautiful" actions and for joints. The revolution is not only a call to arms but also a call to refusal and to unmediated pleasure signified by a joint. Drugs, in a tangible form, symbolize the revolution of the self that is coincident with drug consumption but not encompassed by it. Drugs become a tool to a larger purpose: the transformation of the self *and* the transformation of society.

When we turn to oral histories from the period, we find a similar set of issues motivating young drug consumers: a frustration with contemporary politics, a rejection of the affluent society, and a criticism of enforced consumerism and bourgeois morality. In his forward to a collection of oral histories from young, recovering junkies in Berlin, Eckhard Joite recalls the period around 1968 with a certain nostalgia:

Originally the "subculture" understood itself as a kind of "counter-culture" [*Gegengesellschaft*], whose faint whiff of oriental rituals was supposed to represent a deeply felt protest against the absurdity of consumer society. That was the time when they'd nearly hunt you to death in Hamburg just because you had long hair and looked a little more colorful than others. The "consciousness expanding" drugs became a membership card to a "new society," became an entrance ticket. I smoked hashish too, dropped LSD, and then made a huge deal of it. We wanted to infiltrate the military machinery with LSD; drugs in the tap water were supposed to finally bring paradise.[97]

Though Joite argued that that phase of the drug wave had ended and been replaced by the hard realities of intravenous opiate addiction, many of the stories taken from young drug addicts about the late sixties echo these notions of drugs as an invigorating force.

96. Bommi Bauman, *How It All Began* (Vancouver: Pulp Press, 1977), 56.
97. Eckhard Joite, ed., *Fixen, Opium fürs Volk, Konsumentenprotokolle* (Berlin: Wagenbach, 1972), 7.

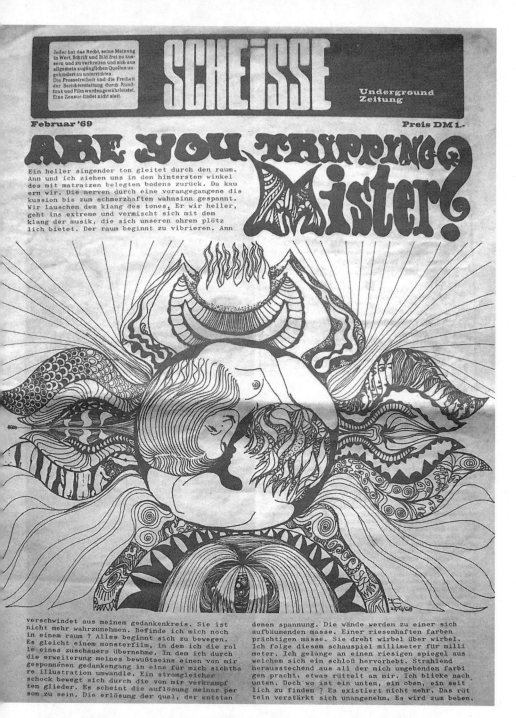

Fig. 3. LSD was a favorite topic of the underground press in the late 1960s, and with LSD came psychedelic art that was widely disseminated. (Klaus Nuß, "Are You Tripping Mister?" *Scheisse Underground Zeitung,* February 1969, 1–2, SSC, M613/1. Courtesy of Department of Special Collections, Stanford University Libraries.)

Dietmar, a school dropout who spent time in a youth home, remembered the end of the sixties as a time when an alternative to bourgeois society seemed possible.

The first time: I smoked shit then. That's after I left the [state] home. Then I went to a commune and spent the night there. They offered me joints. The first time I had a bad experience with it. Because I had been drinking before arriving, a half a bottle of schnapps. Although they told me that it didn't go well with shit, I smoked. Then I spent four or five hours laying on the toilette, half the night puking. After that I dropped LSD. I found that so amazing, so crazy, I experienced some weird things then that I had never experienced before. . . . At the beginning, when I left the youth home, so around three months, I believed that if everyone took acid or something we could really create an alternative to society. After that I noticed that not everything in the scene was like I had thought it was. That dealing was going on and such, and a lot of people went on a pretty rough trip. But a year before, I definitely would have gone through the fire for Mao Tse-tung, even though I didn't exactly know what was going on with him.[98]

The tie between drugs and Mao was not coincidental but rather points again to the widespread tendency among young people to link drug consumption and revolutionary politics.

Yet not all young drug users saw themselves as political revolutionaries. Many, in fact, rejected revolutionary politics and focused on the transformation of the self. Hubert, a skilled worker, put his feelings about the past in verse. His free verse iterates many of the clichés that helped young people at the end of the 1960s organize their opposition to consumer society and illustrates how those who were not professional writers, journalists, or politicians articulated their frustration with the affluent society and the promise offered by drug consumption.

I was insanely uptight.
I thought to myself, it can't continue this way and I let my hair
    grow.
Then I got to know how far people are tolerant.

98. Ibid., 17–18.

I am sick of these people. They don't want to have anything to do
   with me.
But I also found friends.
We all need each other.
I need you, you need me, we sit in the same boat.
I'm not interested in politics.
I'm not interested in anything.
I simply have no desire.
I would rather sit there and listen to music.
I feel good the way I am.
Since I am conscious.
Without kif I would have remained stupid.
I know the difference.
I have to say yes and no, I want to be myself.
I know myself.
I am I.
I am there.
It's all the same to me.
Everything I do is good.
I am an empty head with hair.
I am a piece of meat with eyes.
I am standing there and laughing myself to death.[99]

Hubert's refusal lacks the explicit political content of many of the others but retains that fundamental belief that drugs, and the "consciousness expansion" offered by drugs, were a method of transforming the self. His claim that "Without kif I would have remained stupid" echoes the popular vocabulary of consciousness expansion, and his addendum that he "knows the difference" implies that the tropes about consciousness expansion were a way to articulate rebellion or refusal appropriated by young drug consumers. This ideology of the transformation of the self acted as an organizing principle of the way in which they viewed the world. Given this, dismissing the ideological constructions of the drug culture—the rejection of consumerism, the transformation of the self, and the subsequent transformation of society—as the folly of youth should not be taken lightly. These principles, in a cer-

99. Joite, *Fixen*, 21–22.

tain time and place, meant something to many young people; it helped them make sense of their place in the world during a period of social transformation and offered them a way to understand and critique society.

Conclusion

Walter Becker, director of the national Action Youth Protection association and the most prominent voice warning of the dire consequences of rising drug consumption during the 1960s, saw drugs as a harbinger of things to come. "Addiction is the central problem of our times," Becker perceptively noted. "A universal addictive attitude is becoming, to a certain extent, the model of modern life and human needs."[100] Drug consumption was part and parcel of a larger revolution in consumption sweeping the Western world. People acquired things at an unprecedented rate. Particularly novel was the rising purchasing power of youth. During the 1960s, young people bought things they had never been able to before: radios, records, magazines, books, and bicycles. And they bought drugs. Over the course of the 1960s, young people became more and more disaffected with the society created by their elders. For many, discontent took the form of protests against the state, the war in Vietnam, control of the media, and the failing education system. Others simply rejected the status quo altogether. The flight into drugs was a flight from reality, but it was also a retreat from a society many youths felt no longer served their needs.

Within this context, young people created a space for themselves, out of the reach of the adult world. The birth of a drug scene was an international phenomenon. Not only did it take place in most Western countries, but it took place *because* large numbers of youths became more international in their influences and tastes. Though this emergence of an international youth culture took place most visibly in the world of popular culture, it also took place on the ground, with young people coming into direct contact with like-minded individuals from other countries.

Changes in consumption regimes and the internationalization of youth did not cause drug use. We cannot blame consumerism and

100. Becker, "Die neue Rauschgiftwelle," 363.

travel for drug consumption; to do so would not only be crudely simplistic but also parrot the laments of the sixties as the decade of permissiveness that led to the inevitable and destructive decline in morality. New patterns of consumer practice, new forms of production to meet those desires, and an increasingly international economic structure fundamentally changed the social structures of the industrial West. The new consumerism and the unprecedented prosperity improved the lives of many. Yet the consequences were complicated and often unforeseeable. The new social realities and globalization created the preconditions for the boom in drug consumption of the last thirty years. In this respect, drug consumption represents, ironically, the success of consumerism.

3. Transforming Production and Distribution

By the beginning of the 1970s, the drug scene in Hamburg had been "made"; that is, it had become a stable and growing part of youth culture with considerable staying power. While the creation of a drug scene in Hamburg was the product of changes in consumption and the internationalization of youth culture, the demand for drugs continually outstripped supply. By the early 1970s, the key to an expanding drug scene rested in the distribution system. While the popularity of pharmaceutical drugs continued into the early 1970s, the growth in the market increasingly relied on illicit and mostly international production. This market was actually a bifurcated market, split between cannabis and opiate products, although these two markets often overlapped. Understanding the transition of the distribution system from a largely improvised local system that relied on a patchwork of pharmacy burglaries, individual smuggling, and misuse of freely available substances to international distribution is key to understanding the persistence of drug consumption.

The path of many recreational drugs from production to consumption on the streets of Hamburg during the late sixties and early seventies often proved to be a circuitous and complicated one. Hashish might originate in Helmand province in eastern Afghanistan, grown and harvested by peasant families utilizing traditional, labor-intensive methods. That crop of resin would then be sold to a middleman who traveled from village to village buying up individual lots of hashish from impoverished farmers at a fairly low price, but a sum that was much more than farmers could earn from other staple crops. The middleman, who probably worked for a family-based smuggling operation, would then transport his collected goods to a depot near the Iranian border or perhaps on the Pakistani border, where the value of the hashish would increase manyfold. The collected wares of several of these middlemen would then be loaded onto donkey trains and then smuggled by armed groups across the porous Iranian border and delivered to a depot somewhere in the countryside, where it would be sold at a price several times higher than the price at the border. From there, the shipment likely would be shipped by truck to Beirut or Istanbul and sold to Turkish or Lebanese smugglers. If Beirut had been the destination, the shipment of hashish would travel next by ship to Italy before making its way north to the rest of Europe's hashish consumers. If the hashish had traveled to Istanbul, it would be packed onto trucks and shipped to Yugoslavia, where it would be split into smaller shipments and smuggled across the Austrian border in hidden compartments built into modified passenger cars. Once a shipment made it into Germany—by auto through the relatively porous borders, by plane through Frankfurt or Munich, or by ship in Bremen or Hamburg—it was generally sold in smaller lots of a few kilograms to young Germans who then sold it on the streets.

While this pattern of production and distribution became a commonplace in the 1970s, its emergence and its particular dimensions were not the inevitable result of the changes of the sixties. The path from the fields of the developing world to the streets of European cities contained seeds of traditional smuggling patterns and of new facets created or magnified by the great post–Second World War trade boom. Although the particular form of "modernization" that Germany experienced in the fifties and sixties may have been peculiar to the industrial West, this process of modernization had global reverberations and global consequences. The boom in consumerism and consumer desire, the growth of travel, the support for global free trade, and the resurgent international labor mobility all had aftershocks that mutated in the distorting prism of divergent needs and ideologies as the effects rippled out from the center toward the periphery.

At the time, the fact that youth drug consumption in Germany and changes in production and distribution in the Near and Middle East, in North Africa, and as far away as Southeast Asia were related was generally ignored.[1] Rather than seeing drug trafficking as part of a larger system of capitalist expansion, both police and politicians chose to offer a fairly simplistic portrait of the drug trade as the purview of "evil" traffickers. Ideologically, drug consumption and modernization were antithetical: the hedonistic and irresponsible pleasure of drug consumption and the slavery of addiction could not be reconciled with the promises of the affluent society and the expansion of the democratic spirit. But the hills of Asia and the streets of Hamburg by the seventies were not so far apart. The modernization of West Germany and the other industrial states prompted changes in other areas of the world that held unintended consequences.

While young people in Hamburg were smoking hashish, trying LSD for the first time, and hanging out in new clubs, larger changes were taking place in the global political economy of drugs. Over the course of the sixties and early seventies, traditional patterns of production and distribution, which had held sway since the 1920s, were transformed into a new modern drug trade. By *modern* drug trade I mean specifically the system of organized or semiorganized multinational drug trade that began in the 1960s and solidified by the mid-1970s, the drug trade that has now become an everyday part of the world we live in. The hallmarks of this trade include the concentration of cultivation and production in developing countries or areas with weak or nonexistent political control, the diversification of methods for distribution, and the utilization of multinational and often multiethnic supply networks to facilitate distribution in a wide area, such as Europe. This kind of drug trade was a product of drastic changes on a global scale during the 1960s and 1970s: the enormous growth in international trade; unprecedented population increase, urbanization, and industrialization in the developing world; the global migration of workers, primarily from the developing world to the labor-deficient countries of North America and western Europe; and an explosion in spending power and consumption habits of the population of the industrial West.[2]

1. There were exceptions to this. Perhaps the most perceptive book on drugs written in Germany during the seventies was Günter Amendt, *Sucht, Profit, Sucht: Politische Ökonomie des Drogenhandels* (Frankfurt am Main: März, 1972).

2. The prominent sociologist Manuel Castells has argued in his influential book, *End of Millennium*, that the rise of international crime is part and parcel of larger transformations in the modern information age; Castells, *End of Millennium*, vol. 3 of *The Information Age: Economy, Society, and Culture* (Oxford: Blackwell, 1998), 167–68.

In West Germany, and in most of the industrial West, the public understood the drug trade in terms of a dichotomy between consumers and distributors. Consumers, most of whom were young Germans, were seen as victims of malevolent pushers. Conventional thought on illicit drug consumption failed to understand drugs as a product located within circuits of commodities. Germans paid relatively little attention to drug production due to the international scale of the drug trade and especially the fact that drug production occurred in the so-called developing world. This oversight was compounded by the federal system, which limited the ability to police the drug traffic on a national scale, much less on an international one. This changed somewhat over the course of the 1970s as responsibility for policing the drug problem became more centralized and as the U.S. Drug Enforcement Administration began to export its own war on drugs. But the German authorities generally tended to understand the nation's drug problem in terms of consumption and distribution.[3]

In Germany beginning in the late 1960s, drug distributors bore the brunt of the antinarcotics campaigns, both by the police and in the press. The fact that many of these distributors were foreign increased the demonization. Indeed, invectives against drug trafficking that invoked Germany's "foreigner problem" became a respectable way to cast aspersions on Germany's immigrant population. The notion that foreigners sold poison to adolescent Germans brought into relief the deeply ambivalent relationship between the Federal Republic and her invited "guest workers." The belief that the rise in criminality in the 1960s and 1970s was the result of the guest workers' arrival was widespread in the early 1970s and served as a justification for the obviously flawed principle that the badly needed foreign workers were merely temporary guests who would eventually return to their home countries.[4]

While immigration policy, changes in agricultural and tax policy in the Middle East, new customs treaties between European and non-European countries, political corruption, and European immigration

---

3. See H. Richard Friman, *Narco-Diplomacy: Exporting the U.S. War on Drugs* (Ithaca: Cornell University Press, 1996), 87–112, and Ethan Nadelman, *Cops across Borders: The Internationalization of U.S. Criminal Law Enforcement* (University Park: Pennsylvania State University Press, 1993).

4. See Stephen Castles and Godula Kosack, *Immigrant Workers and Class Structure in Western Europe,* 2d ed. (Oxford: Oxford University Press, 1985), 341–55.

initially may appear as disparate topics, they were all products of the postwar economic modernization, and they all intersected in the drug trade. Unwinding the complicated cords that bind these trends and showing how drugs are embedded in the process of "normal" modernization can only be accomplished by delving into the development of the global drug trade.

The International Drug Economy in the Middle East

In 1965, looking back on twenty years of work, the United Nations Commission on Narcotic Drugs almost presciently pointed to the rise of the global drug problem in the coming decade. According to the commission,

> A number of factors have contributed to the evolution of the traffic: the commercial development of air transport; the movement of populations (e.g., the appearance of an illicit traffic of cannabis in countries in which it was hitherto unknown, due in particular to the influx of labourers from countries in which cannabis was consumed); the general internationalization of many forms of human activities which, in terms of traffic, has been reflected in the formation of international gangs powerfully organized; and the industrialization and technical evolution of those parts of the world in which the raw materials are produced (the idea of an illicit heroin factory in the more inaccessible parts of South East Asia would have seemed absurd 50 years ago). Social and economic changes also have created new markets: young people for whom parental supervision is less now than it used to be; and individuals leaving traditional rural societies with their strong organization to join a disorganized urban proletariat. Furthermore, the very success of international control has contributed to change the pattern of traffic: instead of diversions from the licit trade of the "white drugs" which now appears to be negligible, the illicit traffic relies almost wholly on illicit sources of supply.[5]

This description aimed presumably at the countries of North America and western Europe pointed to the future of the illicit drug trade.

---

5. United Nations, Commission on Narcotic Drugs, "Review of the Commission's Work during Its First Twenty Years," E/CN.7/471, 27 October 1965, 43–44.

Yet this trade was fundamentally tied to a much longer history of imperialism and exploitation. Though widespread drug use among young people in the West was new in the 1960s, the production, distribution, and consumption of drugs in the Near and Far East had been a constant factor since at least the nineteenth century. Indeed, the historian Carl Trocki has argued that imperialism "east of Suez" would have taken a much different shape or failed altogether without the drug trade.[6]

Any study of the rise of drug trafficking in western Europe during the 1960s and 1970s, then, must take into account the changing patterns of drug production and distribution outside the boundaries of Europe. Much of the opium and most all of the hashish entering Europe in the decade between 1965 and 1975 came from a handful of countries in the Near and Middle East: Turkey, Lebanon, Afghanistan, Pakistan, and Iran. Drug production in these countries was not new in the sixties; the international trade was widespread and thoroughly entrenched by the first decades of the twentieth century. Opium was a major cash crop in Turkey and Iran, both of which produced on a large scale for the Chinese market. With the collapse of this market after the communist victory in 1949, however, much of this production shifted toward internal markets in Iran and Egypt, and by the mid-1960s Iran had already developed a modern drug problem even earlier than the western European consuming countries.

The rise of demand in Europe during the late 1960s did not radically alter the traditional forms of production in the Near and Middle East but rather created new patterns of distribution. At the same time, the increasingly vigilant international "war on drugs" drove production into new areas largely outside any effective, centralized, national political control, such as the hinterlands of Afghanistan and Pakistan as well as the remote highlands of the so-called Golden Triangle of Burma, Laos, and Thailand. In order to understand the changes in production and distribution, one must first understand the dynamics of the drug trade before the rise of youth drug consumption in Europe. The key to understanding the drug trade in the Near and Middle East lies in the complicated history of drugs in Iran.

6. Carl Trocki, *Opium, Empire, and the Global Political Economy: A Study of the Asian Opium Trade, 1750–1950* (London: Routledge, 1999).

Iran

Iran had been deeply implicated in the international opium trade since the nineteenth century. Despite attempts in the 1920s and 1930s to reduce and then to end opium production and distribution, Iran remained, at the outbreak of the Second World War, a key opium-producing and opium-consuming state. While drug production and distribution sank worldwide in the first two decades of the postwar period, Iran's central role as a producing and consuming country allowed the expansion of drug production in neighboring countries and the establishment of durable distribution networks that proved elastic enough to expand for the European market when new demand beckoned in the 1960s.

The Second World War changed the face of the global drug trade. The traditional illicit trafficking routes and especially the lucrative American and Chinese markets were cut off, forcing traffickers to find new distribution routes and new markets. Opium and heroin smuggled to the United States from the Near and Middle East was "reduced to almost nothing."[7] Since the overland route through the Balkans was obviously untenable and the sea route around Italy equally dangerous, traffickers in the Middle East concentrated on the traditional Egyptian market. While Turkish and Syrian traffickers' access to their French contacts and the large American market had been closed off, shipping routes to the Persian Gulf remained open, and Iranian opium traffickers took over this lucrative commerce. American officials at the League of Nations complained that the amount of opium smuggled into U.S. ports in 1942 had increased 441 percent over the previous year and that three-fourths of that had been Iranian.[8] Further, they claimed that the traditional prominence of Turkey, China, Yugoslavia, and Italy in the North American market had been supplanted by imports from British ports, Iran, India, and Mexico.[9]

After the war, the Iranian Council of Ministers attempted to suppress the opium trade. In June 1946, they passed Decree Number 13138,

7. League of Nations, AC, 1945.XI.2, 16.
8. League of Nations, Secretariat of Traffic in Opium and Other Dangerous Drugs, AC, 1946.XI.4, 15.
9. United Nations, E/NR/1944/Summary, 23.

which established a department named the General Administration for the Prohibition of Cultivation of Opium Poppy and Use of Opium. The regulation called for the complete cessation of opium production and consumption and "involved great difficulties both for the government and landowners and farmers who were engaged in the cultivation and sale of opium over a long period." Prohibition cost the government 350 million rials annually, or almost eleven million U.S. dollars.[10] Initially, the monopoly continued to export its own opium stocks, earning 310 million rials, or 9.5 million U.S. dollars, in 1947 and 1948, while banning independent cultivation and burning fields sown in secret. In 1947, 187 hectares were destroyed, followed by 1,417 the next year.

The loss of opium tax revenue and an increase in smuggling from bordering countries led the Iranian Parliament in 1949 to repeal the prohibition instituted by the Council of Ministers, claiming that, since Iran already was recognized internationally as an opium-producing country, it had every right to continue growing the crop. The prime motivation for this about-face was the government's need for the large amounts of foreign currency the opium trade earned, "in order to assist the growers and improve the economic condition of the country."[11] Drastic increases in opium exports in 1950 and 1951 earned more than 200 million rials each year, or 20 percent of the entire Iranian budget.[12] Western exhortations to attempt crop substitution programs and to suppress traditional local practices were simply not practical in the context of Iran, a country facing real and pervasive agricultural problems and composed of many areas only loosely under government control.

Nevertheless, the Iranian Parliament's initial support for continuing the opium trade diminished as more ominous drugs began to appear. The rise of clandestine heroin manufacturing from morphine base smuggled from the USSR and Iraq in the mid-1950s along with the emergence of heroin consumption in urban areas was further compounded by pressure from the U.S. government and finally led the government to suppress the cultivation of opium.[13] On 15 November 1955,

10. United Nations, E/NR/1945/Summary, 29.
11. United Nations, E/NR/1949/Summary, 65–66.
12. United Nations, E/NR/1950/Summary, 52.
13. United Nations, E/NR/1954/Summary, 31.

the Senate and the Chamber of Deputies prohibited the production of the opium poppy throughout Iran. When this ban went into effect, the government of Iran estimated that there were at least 1.5 million opium addicts in Iran, out of a population of 20 million.

Banning production did not lead magically to widespread abstinence. The immediate effects of the prohibition included unrest in the countryside and widespread illicit cultivation, while drastic reduction in the availability of opium led prices to surge, hurting opium users among the urban poor and middle class.[14] The most important and enduring result, however, was the gradual rise of opium smuggling into the country. The suppression of opium production in Iran did not result in the gradual withering of opium consumption there. Instead, it disadvantaged Iranian farmers while opening the Iranian market to Turkish opium and stimulating opium production in both Afghanistan and Pakistan.

In the wake of the ban, illicit cultivation became a serious problem for officials. Clandestine cultivation spread in the mountainous provinces of Lorestan and Fars, as well as the eastern border province Khorasan. In 1959, for example, the Iranian Gendarmerie discovered and destroyed 13,972 fields covering 3,098 hectares.[15] By 1963, covert cultivation had expanded to remote areas of Khuzistan, Esfahan, Kerman, and Khozassan.[16]

If the difficulties the police faced in suppressing opium farming were daunting, stopping the flood of smuggled opium proved utterly impossible. Police throughout the Near and Middle East were woefully unprepared for the task of suppressing large-scale smuggling. Until the 1970s, Turkey was the only country with anything approximating a modern police force, and policing the opium traffic did not become a major priority for the Turkish government until the late 1960s, largely as a result of pressure and massive financial support from the United States. In major drug-producing and transit countries, such as Lebanon, Syria, and Iran, large geographical areas remained outside of any control whatsoever. For over a century, Iran had been both an

14. United Nations, E/NR/1955/Summary, 11, 32, 42; E/NR/1956/Summary, 62.

15. United Nations, Committee on Narcotics and Dangerous Drugs, *Review of the Illicit Traffic in Narcotic Drugs during 1959,* E/CN.7/387, 8.

16. United Nations, Committee on Narcotics and Dangerous Drugs, *Review of the Illicit Traffic in Narcotic Drugs during 1962.* E/CN.7/443, 4 April 1963, 10.

opium-producing and an opium-consuming country. For many, opium had become a part of everyday life, and opium addiction, more than most habits, proved difficult to defeat.

Much more ominous than the traditional trade in opium, however, was the increased traffic in refined narcotics. Before the war, the production of morphine base had been limited to trafficking centers like Beirut, Istanbul, or Marseilles. Yet government attempts to suppress opium smuggling in Iran and Turkey led traffickers to refine raw opium into morphine base in crude, illicit laboratories closer to producing areas. Refining the opium closer to the areas of production had real advantages for producers. The resulting morphine weighed only one-tenth of the opium used to produce it and lacked the pungent odor associated with raw opium. It was therefore much easier to smuggle. By the end of the 1950s, morphine refining was widespread in western Iran near the Turkish border as well as in the rural areas around Tehran.

The next sign of a major shift in production was the appearance of heroin factories in the opium-producing areas. The arrival of heroin factories in Turkey and Iran indicated Turkish traffickers' efforts to bypass their Corsican contacts in Marseilles and the emergence of a new illicit market in Iran.[17] In 1959, for instance, Iranian authorities seized 4.35 kilograms of heroin, a seventeenfold increase over the previous year. By the early sixties, the expansion of the heroin trade had reached alarming proportions; in 1963, Iranian police uncovered nine heroin laboratories and seized 15.47 kilograms of heroin.[18]

The drastic increase in heroin consumption among younger urban residents, especially in Teheran, and the persistent demand for opium among older addicts both in the cities and in rural areas provided an enormous incentive for smugglers. Prohibition stimulated production

17. For an excellent discussion of the famous French Connection in Marseilles, see Alfred W. McCoy, *The Politics of Heroin: CIA Complicity in the Global Drug Trade* (Brooklyn, NY: Lawrence Hill, 1991), chap. 2. An interesting if tawdry account of the circuitous route from the fields of Turkey to the heroin markets of New York in the later 1960s is Alvin Moscow, *Merchants of Heroin: An In-Depth Portrayal of Business in the Underworld* (New York: Dial Press, 1968). See also Catherine Lamour and Michel R. Lamberti, *The International Connection: Opium from Growers to Pushers,* trans. Peter and Betty Ross (New York: Pantheon, 1974), 17–35.

18. United Nations, Committee on Narcotics and Dangerous Drugs, *Review of the Illicit Traffic in Narcotic Drugs during 1962,* E/CN.7/443, 4 April 1963, 4.

in bordering countries, especially in Afghanistan and Pakistan, and opened up a cottage industry for domestic and foreign smugglers. The potential profit was enormous. In 1963, for example, a smuggler could buy a kilogram of opium at the Afghan border for between $38 and $55. That same kilogram would bring $150 to $163 wholesale in Teheran. At the Turkish frontier, a kilogram could be had for $32 to $38 but would earn $125 to $138 in Teheran. If refined into heroin, that same kilogram could bring as much as $1,500 in the retail market.[19] As the profit rose, so did the violence; government agents had frequent gun battles with smugglers on the Turkish and Afghani borders. By the mid-1960s, both smuggling and heroin production had reached epidemic proportions, as smuggling became more organized and the size of shipments rose dramatically. Authorities discovered seventeen heroin labs in 1964 and again in 1965. Further, there were reports of enormous shipments discovered hidden in oil tankers.[20] The estimated amount of smuggled opium that reached consumers was a staggering 140 tons.[21]

The rapid changes in drug consumption were fueled by social change in Iranian society during the 1960s: rapid urbanization and industrialization, social dislocation, and widespread unemployment, all of which led to an early and significant shift toward a modern drug problem. The rapid growth in the popularity of heroin among youth in Teheran coupled with the internal ban on opium production and the resulting surge in smuggling led to the proliferation of heroin labs in the 1960s. The profound increase in heroin consumption, according to the Iranian government, was "attributable to social and economic pressures, the ease with which the drug can be administered, and the higher stimulation it affords."[22] The traditional opium consumption of the rural population gradually gave way to a modern drug problem. In a matter of years this same pattern not only spread to the United States

19. United Nations, Committee on Narcotics and Dangerous Drugs, *Review of the Illicit Traffic in Narcotic Drugs during 1962*, E/CN.7/443, 4 April 1963, Annex III, 4.
20. United Nations, Committee on Narcotics and Dangerous Drugs, *Review of the Illicit Traffic in Narcotic Drugs during 1964*, E/CN.7/472, 15 November 1965, 15–16; United Nations, Committee on Narcotics and Dangerous Drugs, *Review of the Illicit Traffic in Narcotic Drugs during 1966/1967*, E/CN.7/506, 16 October 1967, 2.
21. United Nations, Committee on Narcotics and Dangerous Drugs, *Review of the Illicit Traffic in Narcotic Drugs during 1964*, E/CN.7/472, 15 November 1965, 15–16.
22. United Nations, *Summary of Annual Reports*, 1962, E/NR/1962/Summary, 31.

and western Europe but would become quite literally a global problem. Established patterns of substance abuse remained, but a global market for opium and cannabis products emerged as a significant factor in the global economy.

In 1969, after fourteen years of prohibition, Iran once again began to produce opium. Frustrated with his government's inability to stem the tide of drugs coming in from Turkey and Afghanistan and the loss of foreign currency, and in the face of harsh criticism from the international community, the shah decided to reintroduce the cultivation of the poppy. The shah stressed, however, that he would be willing to prohibit production again as soon as his neighbors did the same.[23] The resurgence of cultivation in Iran did not reduce smuggling into the country though. American investigators estimated that traffickers smuggled 170 tons of opium into Iran from Afghanistan and Pakistan in 1972 alone,[24] despite legislation passed in 1969 that imposed the death penalty for "trafficking in any amount of opium or heroin or for the possession of more than two kilograms of opium or ten grams of heroin, morphine, or cocaine."[25] To prove its commitment to halting smuggling, Iran executed 133 traffickers between 1969 and 1972, most believed to be Afghans.[26] This serious threat did not stop the traffic; the enormous profits to be had continued to lure people into the trade.

New to Iran in the early 1970s was the rise of hashish cultivation. Though hashish consumption had been traditional among certain groups such as the dervishes, cannabis use was not widespread in Iran.[27] Beginning in 1970, cultivation of cannabis in Iran skyrocketed. In 1969, police seized only 92 kilograms; two years later authorities confiscated 2,407 kilograms. The total reached 5,054 kilograms by 1973. Rising demand for the drug in Europe directly caused the large-scale cannabis cultivation in Iran. The high profits that the drug yielded, coupled with the fact that hashish smuggling, unlike opium,

23. Cabinet Committee on International Narcotics Control, *World Opium Survey* (Washington, DC: Cabinet Committee on International Narcotics Control, 1972), A12. See also Hasan-Ali Azarakhsh, "The Nature and Extent of Drug Abuse in Iran," in *CENTO Seminar on Public Health and Medical Problems Involved in Narcotics Drug Addiction,* ed. Central Treaty Organization (n.p.: Central Treaty Organization, 1972), 24–25.
24. Cabinet Committee on International Narcotics Control, *World Opium Survey,* A14.
25. Ibid., A15.
26. Ibid.
27. Azarakhsh, "Nature and Extent," 26.

did not carry the death penalty, transformed the traditional role of Iran in the drug trade. A country that for decades had been primarily a drug importer became an exporter.

Iran's place in the growth of the international drug trade cannot be overstated. The enormous global demand for drugs stimulated a thriving trade throughout the Middle East and provided a training ground for drug smuggling on a large scale. Turkish and Iranian traffickers got rich on the Iranian trade. When European demand for hashish, and later opium, appeared, these organized and semiorganized groups simply turned to the West and continued their trade with new clients.

Drug Trafficking and Political Control in Afghanistan, Pakistan, Lebanon, and Turkey

The rise in popularity of hashish among European youth coincided with an increase in worldwide smuggling. New developments in the Near and Middle East prompted increased cultivation of hashish and opium in more and more remote areas. While the reestablishment of opium production in Iran and the subsequent prohibition of cultivation in Turkey led to the emergence of a more organized traffic, the massive increases in hashish and opium production in the hinterlands of Afghanistan and Pakistan exacerbated the problems inherent in international control. Widespread corruption and political instability in the Middle Eastern countries only fueled the fire. Concurrent police successes in Europe only led to the development of new routes and strategies.

Part of the problem with international control was a fundamental misunderstanding of the drug trade on the part of the international diplomats who coordinated the "global war on drugs" in its infancy. They based international supply reduction efforts on an enlightenment vision of individuals as economically rational actors. They firmly believed that the illicit drug trade was based on the same kind of economic rationale as any other international industry and that opium and hashish cultivators, given training and increased infrastructure, would make a rational choice to halt the labor-intensive drug cultivation and substitute other, less socially harmful crops such as cotton. The solution proved to be fatally flawed. It failed to take into account the regional cultural differences and the evidence, such as we have seen in the case of Iran, that suppression of cultivation did not lead to the gradual withering of the drug trade but stimulated cultivation in more remote regions and promoted the rise of organized smuggling.

Iran's suppression of the opium trade after 1955, for example, stimulated production in Afghanistan and Pakistan and led to widespread smuggling, which the governments of these two countries were completely unable to suppress. Illustrating the sheer magnitude of the problem, officials estimated that Afghanistan produced one hundred tons of illicit opium in 1971.[28] The Afghan government admitted that opium "was traditionally produced in Badakhshan where it was the only cash crop, as well as in Nengarhar and the tribal areas. . . . In Badakhshan the law could not be enforced without creating economic difficulties possibly leading to unrest."[29] The Pashtun tribes likewise were largely autonomous and answered directly to the royal family. According to the study of an American delegation in 1971, "the king regards these tribes as an important pillar of support and will not want to antagonize them."[30] The free market economics of liberal international planners made little sense in the social and economic context of these remote drug-producing areas.

Hashish cultivation presented its own set of problems for the Afghan government. According to officials in Kabul, "wild [cannabis] growth covered very extensive areas especially in the north and south. It was clear that there were some people regularly at work to collect resin from this wild growth and this process had increased in response to foreign demand."[31] Widely consumed by men and women in both rural and urban areas, particularly by the lower and middle classes, hashish was cultivated as a supplementary crop because it provided a much higher rate of return than most crops. Though hashish production and consumption had been nominally illegal since 1957, Afghans mostly ignored the law. After undertaking field research between 1970 and 1973, the French anthropologist C-J. Charpentier wrote: "The

28. Cabinet Committee on International Narcotics Control, *World Opium Survey*, A7.
29. United Nations, Committee on Narcotics and Dangerous Drugs, *Report of the Ad Hoc Committee on the Illicit Traffic in the Near and Middle East, 1971–1972*, E/CN.7/550, 1 November 1972, 8–9.
30. Cabinet Committee on International Narcotics Control, *World Opium Survey*, A9.
31. Resin from the cannabis plant is used to make hashish. United Nations, Committee on Narcotics and Dangerous Drugs, *Report of the Ad Hoc Committee*, E/CN.7/550, 9.

anti-hashish act is more to be regarded as a cover for the government in order to avoid criticism on its policy from Europe and the U.S.A. Hashish can be bought in almost every bazaar but it is generally sold surreptitiously."[32] Charpentier claimed that local consumption of hashish had increased due to the stimulus of "the last few years' hippie invasion in Afghanistan."[33] In the early 1970s, Kabul had become a frequent stop of young Americans and Europeans on the hippie trail to Goa. Drug tourism became big business for the cash-starved areas of central Asia. According to both Charpentier and the Kabul government, the influx of drug tourists had, for the first time, made hashish consumption a "social problem."[34]

Young Western drug users often paid a high price after being caught with drugs in the Middle East. Drug laws, though only selectively enforced, carried long prison terms or even the death penalty in countries desperate to reduce the number of consumers, such as Iran, or countries attempting to stop the flow of drugs into the international traffic, such as Turkey. The lurid stories of Western youth in Middle Eastern prisons widely disseminated in the industrial West did not discuss the fact that the drug tourism of these youngsters was also the cause of social problems in Afghanistan and other drug-producing countries. Nevertheless, with the rise of the global drug problem in the 1970s, drug consumption was not simply an import to western Europe and North America from the developing world. Individuals from Europe and North America helped spread new forms of drug abuse to many areas of the globe.

Aggravating the hashish problem in Afghanistan was the fact that the government had no way to police the drug traffic.[35] They did not have a single policeman trained or equipped to police the drug traffic. For the smuggler the risk was small, while the profit to be had was enormous. In 1973, opium purchased in the Jalalabad region for seven

32. C-J. Charpentier, "The Use of Hashish and Opium in Afghanistan." *Anthropos* 68 (1973): 482–84.

33. Ibid., 484.

34. Ibid.; United Nations, Committee on Narcotics and Dangerous Drugs, *Report of the Ad Hoc Committee*, E/CN.7/550, 9.

35. United Nations, Committee on Narcotics and Dangerous Drugs, *Report of the Ad Hoc Committee*, E/CN.7/550, 10.

thousand afghanis could be sold in Iran for one hundred thousand afghanis, a fourteenfold profit.[36]

. Pakistan met similar difficulties while attempting to suppress the drug trade. Cultivation of opium was permitted in the North West Frontier Province, but in many of the tribal areas south of the Khyber Pass the government had no control whatsoever well into the 1970s. Pashtun tribesmen near the Afghan border offered farmers there three to four times the government monopoly's price and smuggled much of this into Iran.[37] The Pakistani government chose not to interfere in this trade, citing traditional tribal resistance to government intervention.[38] Likewise, cannabis grew wild in many of the mountainous regions of the northwest.[39] Mohammad Yousof Orakzai, the chairman of Pakistan's Narcotics Control Board, admitted in 1974 that "most of the cannabis was derived from plantations in inaccessible tribal areas where destruction of such crops was not thought feasible."[40]

Though the lack of centralized government control in remote areas proved to be a substantial stumbling block in policing drugs, the problem was compounded by political instability and governmental corruption. The profitability of the drug trade and the desire to reduce the inherent risks of smuggling led many traffickers to bribe public officials, from border guards to members of Parliament. In the worst cases, government officials were involved directly in smuggling. The most glaring national example of the relationship between political unrest, corruption, and the drug traffic was Lebanon. Lebanon had been a central distribution point of the Middle East drug traffic since the interwar period. With its open port (goods were not subject to customs inspections) and modern airport as well as its role as a primary financial center, by the 1950s Beirut had become the transit point of choice for traffickers in both opium and hashish. Turkish opium smuggled into Syria was converted into morphine base and then smuggled

36. Charpentier, "Use of Hashish," 487.
37. Cabinet Committee on International Narcotics Control, *World Opium Survey,* A19.
38. Ibid., A20.
39. Ibid., 4–8.
40. United Nations, Committee on Narcotics and Dangerous Drugs, *First Report of the Sub-Commission on Illicit Traffic and Related Matters in the Near and Middle East 1973–1974,* E/CN.7/566, 5.

through Beirut to the Corsican-run heroin labs of Marseilles before being sent on to New York and Montreal, the favored points of entry into North America.[41]

Cultivation of cannabis was rampant in the lush, fertile Bekaa Valley between the Lebanon and Anti-Lebanon mountain chains. During the 1950s and 1960s the majority of this hashish production was aimed at the large consumer market in Egypt. But with the rise of European demand during the later 1960s, Lebanese traffickers exported more of their product to this growing market. In 1966, the Lebanese government, prodded by the United States, began a crop substitution program in the Bekaa Valley and the Hermel Highlands aimed at a reduction in cannabis cultivation in a twenty-five-hundred-square-kilometer region around Baalbeck.[42] Despite the attempt to promote the cultivation of sunflowers as a source of seeds and oil, the cultivation of cannabis remained prevalent. Lebanon continued to produce more hashish than any other country, averaging roughly two hundred thousand kilograms a year. By the early 1970s much of the hashish reaching Europe came from this crop.[43]

September 1970 marked the beginning of a major shift in the Lebanese drug trade. Rising political instability resulting from the conflict between Israel and the Palestinians drove important changes in the Middle Eastern drug trade. Fearing that the Palestine Liberation Organization's (PLO) activities against Israel from bases inside his kingdom would bring the country into yet another war, King Hussein of Jordan unleashed his military against the group. The success of Hussein's operation drove many members of the PLO to cross through Syria into southern Lebanon. The presence of Palestinians waging war on Israel in refugee camps situated on the border, and their influence on rising factionalism within Lebanese society, wreaked havoc on an

41. See McCoy, *Politics of Heroin,* 46–76; Lamour and Lamberti, *International Connection,* 17–35; Paul B. Stares, *Global Habit: The Drug Problem in a Borderless World* (Washington, DC: Brookings Institution, 1996), 25–27; Cabinet Committee on International Narcotics Control, *World Opium Survey,* 18–25; and Alvin Moscow, *Merchants of Heroin,* 3–130.

42. United Nations, Committee on Narcotics and Dangerous Drugs, *Operations Financed by the United Nations Fund for Drug Abuse Control,* E/CN.7/574, 1 November 1974, 21.

43. U.S. Congress, House Committee on Foreign Affairs, *The International Narcotics Trade and Its Relation to the United States,* 92d Congress, 2d sess., 1972, H. Rept. 92–836, 55; O. Hänni, "Generalversammlung der INTERPOL 1968," *Kriminalistik* (1969): 5.

already unstable Lebanese government. As violence mounted in the south and in the major cities, Lebanon slid slowly into the chaos that culminated in civil war in 1975.[44] Plagued with internal strife, the Lebanese government was in no position to stamp out cannabis cultivation in the Bekaa. Crop substitution programs failed, and hashish production and distribution continued unabated.

To make matters worse, high-level government corruption almost guaranteed that illicit production would thrive. United States investigators implicated leading Lebanese legislators in the hashish traffic.[45] Though Lebanon provides the most extreme example, political instability and corruption also played a role in much of the rest of the Middle East, especially in Afghanistan, Pakistan, and Syria.

The politics of drug abatement, and particularly of the globalization of the war on drugs supported by the United States, was more successful north of Lebanon. In 1972, two separate events fundamentally altered Turkey's role in the international drug trade. The first was the demise of the famous French Connection.[46] Traditionally, Turkish opium had been smuggled by ship from Istanbul or Beirut to heroin labs around Marseilles. These labs, run by Corsican organized crime in collusion with the American mafia, provided the majority of the heroin for the North American market. Prodded by intense pressure from the United States and rising domestic heroin consumption, the French increased the number of agents in Marseilles from eight officers in 1969 to seventy-seven in 1971.[47] In a series of spectacular raids on heroin labs, six in 1972 alone, the French police effectively put an end to Marseilles's role as North America's heroin supplier.[48]

The other momentous event was Turkey's decision to halt the cultivation of opium throughout the country. Turkey had begun the slow suppression of opium in 1961 by outlawing cultivation near the frontiers. Before then, opium cultivation had been legal throughout the

44. See Charles Winslow, *Lebanon: War and Politics in a Fragmented Society* (London: Routledge, 1996), 155–200.

45. U.S. Congress, House Committee on Foreign Affairs, *International Narcotics Trade,* 56.

46. This subject has been exhaustively researched elsewhere. See, especially, McCoy, *Politics of Heroin,* chap. 2; Lamour and Lamberti, *International Connection,* chap. 2. For a more sensationalistic yet evocative account, see Alvin Moscow, *Merchants of Heroin.*

47. McCoy, *Politics of Heroin,* 69.

48. Lamour and Lamberti, *International Connection,* 31.

country.[49] In 1967, the United States, offering a carrot of three million dollars and a stick in the form of trade threats, convinced the Turkish government to begin reducing the area of cultivation with the goal of eventual suppression. U.S. funds supported the creation of a 750-man narcotics squad, crop substitution programs, and administrative modernization. In 1971, four years after the initial outlay of three million dollars, Nixon's global war on drugs provided Turkey with thirty-five million dollars in aid if it agreed to end cultivation once and for all.[50] The Turkish government used fifteen million dollars of the payment to finance indemnities to the opium farmers and the rest to finance antiopium initiatives. The push for the elimination of the opium trade created a "strong backlash among Turkish parliamentarians," forcing Prime Minister Süleyman Demirel to slow the eradication program.[51] It was only with the military coup of 1971 under the leadership of Prime Minister Nihat Erim that the pace of eradication was accelerated; the provinces producing opium had been reduced to seven and were further reduced to four the next year. It was agreed that cultivation would end after the 1972 harvest and that subsidies would be paid based on the amount of opium produced in the final year. Consequently, Turkey's cultivation in 1972 was enormous. This also meant that nearly twenty-eight thousand farmers were forced to find another source of income. In the short term, the government admitted, there would be severe hardship for the farmers, but they hoped that the economic support from the United States would promote industrial projects in the affected area.[52]

Although suppression of opium cultivation proved surprisingly effective due to an increase in policing and the use of modern technologies such as aerial surveillance, the cessation of opium production turned Turkey from a center of illegal cultivation and export to a transit country. Turkey's professional traffickers shifted from smuggling

49. United Nations, Committee on Narcotics and Dangerous Drugs, *Report of the Ad Hoc Committee,* E/CN.7/550, 15.

50. McCoy, *Politics of Heroin,* 72–73. See also U.S. Congress, House Committee on Foreign Affairs, *The International Narcotics Trade,* 58–66; U.S. Congress, House Committee of Foreign Affairs, *International Aspects of the Narcotics Problem: Hearings before the Subcommittee on Europe,* 92d, Cong., 1st sess., 1971.

51. George S. Harris, *Turkey: Coping with Crisis* (Boulder, CO: Westview, 1985), 191.

52. United Nations, Committee on Narcotics and Dangerous Drugs, *Report of the Ad Hoc Committee,* E/CN.7/550, 16–17.

opium produced in Turkey to Iran or France to transporting other nations' opium and hashish into Germany, Denmark, and the Netherlands through the Balkans. The shift of production from Turkey, where a relatively effective police force could control cultivation to some extent, to the hinter regions of Iran, Afghanistan, and Pakistan merely exacerbated the problem it was designed to solve. While the United States had believed that the suppression of opium production in Turkey and the destruction of the French Connection would reduce the traffic to North America, the result in the middle term was quite different. Heroin from Southeast Asia quickly filled the void, and the global situation drastically degenerated. Production moved to areas where diplomatic pressure and financial inducements would be useless. The apparent early success of the war on drugs proved to be a colossal failure. To add insult to injury, two years after the initial ban in 1972, the Turkish government reestablished opium production. The elimination of cultivation had stimulated production elsewhere, crop substitution had failed, and the Turkish government felt that the U.S. government had targeted it unjustly.

The Balkan Route and the German Drug Trade

The emergence of modern drug trafficking into the Federal Republic was driven by two very different transformations in the global illicit trade. The first significant change was the rise of the "Balkan route" in the early 1970s. Traditionally, traffickers transported opium from the Near and Middle East through Beirut and Istanbul to the ports of southern France or Italy, often via Egypt or North Africa. Increased policing of this traffic during the late 1960s led traffickers to find another route. The overland route via the Balkans proved the logical alternative.

By the early 1970s, the Balkan route overtook the sea route as the primary method of transporting opium or morphine base to the labs of southern France and hashish to the Federal Republic, the Netherlands, and Scandinavia. Following a path from Afghanistan, Iran, and Turkey across the Bosporus into Greece and through Bulgaria and Yugoslavia, cars and trucks brought their contraband to staging points in Yugoslavia and Austria. There, traffickers divided their loads into smaller parcels and transferred the contraband into cars with built-in, hidden compartments. In order to reduce suspicion, they employed Germans as mules, since citizens of Middle Eastern countries were much more likely to be searched. From Austria, transporters drove small shipments either through Salzburg and on to Munich or through Linz crossing the border at Passau to Nürnberg. From these locations, they were transported to Frankfurt, Berlin, the Ruhr cities, or Hamburg, as well as Amsterdam and Copenhagen.[53]

Smugglers also took advantage of the massive growth in legitimate trade from the Near and Middle East to western Europe. Western Europe's growing reliance on perishable products such as meats, fruits, and vegetables from the Near and Middle East encouraged the growth of large-scale drug smuggling. In particular, European authorities worried about the ramifications of a specific international customs agreement, the Transport International Routier (TIR), on the illicit traffic in drugs. The treaty was the result of increasing European consumer demand for perishable products that could be grown year-round in countries like Turkey. The terms of this treaty stipulated that trucks from member countries, such as Iran and Turkey, could be checked once by customs at the point of origin and sealed and then could pass through international borders without a customs inspection.[54] The amount of hashish or opium that could be smuggled in this way was enormous. For instance, over three million TIR trucks entered Bulgaria in 1975 alone. Over thirty trucks from Turkey entered the Federal Republic each day, and it was estimated that half of the morphine base

53. See, for example, United Nations, Committee on Narcotics and Dangerous Drugs, *Review of the Illicit Traffic in Narcotic Drugs and Psychotropic Substances during 1973,* E/CN.7/575, 6 December 1974, 6, 29; United Nations, Committee on Narcotics and Dangerous Drugs , *Review of the Illicit Traffic in Narcotic Drugs and Psychotropic Substances during 1968 and 1969,* E/CN.7/535, 12 July 1971, 23–24. StAH, Band II, Bundeskriminalamt Report, 31 October 1975. See also Werner Wegener, *"Balkan-Route" contra "Seidenstrasse": Die tödlichen Rauschgiftstraßen von Asien nach Westeuropa* (Berlin: Schmidt-Römhild, 1996), 13–21.

54. See Cabinet Committee on International Narcotics Control, *World Opium Survey,* A61; Lamour and Lamberti, *International Connection,* 25–26; United Nations, Committee on Narcotics and Dangerous Drugs, *Trends in Illicit Traffic during the First Six Months of 1972,* E/CN.7/548/Add.1, 12 December 1972, 5; Rebscher, "Interpol-Nachrichten: Die Entwicklung des internationalen Rauschgifthandels im Jahre 1972," *Kriminalistik* 27 (1973): 499–500; Eckart Kemmelmeier, "Die Stellung des Bundeskriminalamtes in der kriminalpolizeilichen Bekämpfung der Rauschmittelkriminalität," *Kriminalistik* 28 (1974): 68–73.

smuggled out of Turkey was loaded on TIR trucks.[55] The use of international trade agreements by smugglers highlighted one of the glaring problems faced by the German government: despite all its efforts, it could not halt the flow of drugs into the Federal Republic without seriously compromising legitimate trade. In the end, it was much more important to the Bonn government to protect legitimate trade than to quash the smuggling of illicit drugs.

The International Heroin Trade

The second major change driving the emergence of modern drug trafficking was the rapid influx of heroin from Southeast Asia beginning in 1973 and the concomitant emergence of Amsterdam as the center of the European drug traffic. The Balkan route was primarily used for transporting hashish and, to a lesser extent, raw opium. As a rule, heroin had little impact on northern Europe until the first few years of the seventies. Most intravenous drug users in Hamburg relied on local sources of pharmaceutical narcotics, most of which were stolen from pharmacies in Hamburg and outlying areas. This changed in autumn 1972, when police had more success in preventing pharmacy burglaries, largely due to new pharmacy regulations that required pharmacists to place all addictive drugs under lock and key and to reduce the amount in stock. While the amount of pharmaceutical narcotics on the market continued to drop, new illicitly produced narcotics began to appear in the Hamburg scene in late 1972.

In the first half of 1973, the Hamburg market was flooded with so-called Berliner Polamidon, a particularly powerful solution of the synthetic narcotic methadone. Produced by a young pharmacist named Ulrich K. in Berlin, Berliner Polamidon introduced the Hamburg drug scene to illicitly produced narcotics. When the Hamburg and Berlin police arrested Ulrich K. after a lengthy investigation, they seized 320 bottles of the methadone solution. When in September the supply of

55. United Nations, Committee on Narcotics and Dangerous Drugs, *Report of a Meeting of a Consultative Group on Illicit Drug Traffic in East and Central Europe,* E/CN.7/597/Add.1, 30 December 1976, 3–4; Robert Solomon and H. Versteeg, *A Review of the Development and Present State of the Illicit International Heroin Trade* (Ottawa: Non-Medical Use of Drugs Directorate, 1978), 236, 254.

methadone had run out, addicts turned to a new source of narcotics: heroin smuggled from Amsterdam. By the end of 1973, police warned that "the drug heroin will become in the near future the number one drug crime problem in Hamburg."[56]

Heroin began replacing pharmaceutical drugs in 1973 because of global changes in the heroin market. Over the course of the second half of the 1960s and the early 1970s, the Golden Triangle became the largest producer of heroin in the world. The increase in production in the Golden Triangle was directly tied to the American presence in Vietnam. By 1970, labs in Thailand, Cambodia, and Laos brought in Chinese chemists from Hong Kong, who began producing 80 to 99 percent pure Number 4 heroin and marketing it in South Vietnam. Heroin use spread quickly among U.S. servicemen. By mid-1971, the army estimated that 10 to 15 percent of all lower-ranking enlisted men were using heroin.[57] High-ranking members of the South Vietnamese military and government played important roles in the trade, further straining relationships with the U.S. administration—this despite the fact that the CIA was implicated as well.[58] As the U.S. military implemented their "Vietnamization" policy and pulled American troops out of the country in 1973 and 1974, the heroin labs of Southeast Asia did not go out of business. Instead, powerful organized crime groups in Hong Kong, the legendary triads, began to control the trade stimulated by American involvement in Vietnam and Laos. As these groups sought new markets, Europe's growing demand for narcotics appeared to be a virgin territory, and expatriate Chinese in Amsterdam provided a base for operations.

As early as 1972, large shipments of pure Number 4 heroin began to appear in Amsterdam. As a result, officials tightened security at Amsterdam's international airport, leading the traffickers to use European mules to transport the drugs from various European airports to Amsterdam; in particular, Frankfurt's busy international airport became an important transshipment point in the international trade. By late 1973, when heroin became a fixture in Hamburg's drug scene, the Chinese syndicates had a firm hold on the entire European heroin market.

56. HBfI, K245, "Jahresbericht 1973."
57. McCoy, *Politics of Heroin,* 222–23.
58. Ibid., 226–48.

In its annual report to the Federal Criminal Police (Bundeskriminalamt), the Hamburg drug squad lamented that "Hamburg has the largest demand for drugs and therefore the largest share of drug criminality in the Federal Republic."[59] Yet the drug squad continued to focus on breaking up international smuggler rings and targeting foreign smugglers rather than pursuing drug consumers. In 1973, the drug squad investigated 235 foreigners. Of the 262 indictments for drug crimes, 110 of those charged were foreigners, the majority of whom came from Turkey and Iran, while smaller numbers were from Ghana, Tunisia, the United Kingdom, and the United States. It was clear to the officers of the drug squad that the drug scene was qualitatively changing and that the influx of heroin would transform it even further.

In 1974 and 1975, a new pattern emerged in Hamburg. Police were faced with two quite distinct problems. On the one hand, the trade in hashish and LSD seemed to have stagnated after its initial rise in the early 1970s, while the number of young people using these drugs seemed to be slowly dropping. On the other hand, a new group of hard-core heroin users had become a permanent fixture. The police added on average ten new names to its list of known heroin users monthly. This was, in fact, the face of the modern European drug problem: a bifurcated trade of widespread hashish consumption and a smaller but more significant population of intravenous heroin users.[60]

The changing patterns of drug trafficking and drug abuse in Hamburg during the first half of the 1970s were a result of global changes in the distribution of drugs. The initial trade in hashish, speed, and LSD during the sixties, fueled by the general rejection of traditional norms and a new spirit of experimentation, did not disappear; it simply became normalized. Further, the growing threat posed by a new, global market in heroin made cannabis seem less important and less dangerous to the police and the general public. Though the sources of the hashish and heroin trade would change over the following thirty years, and though there might be temporary shortages, by the mid-1970s the global trade in drugs had become an intrinsic part of the global economy. What had been, from the 1930s to the 1960s, an American or an Asian problem had become a global problem.

59. HBfI, K245, "Jahresbericht 1973," 3.
60. HBfI, K245, "Rauschgiftkriminalität in Hamburg," 30 June 1975.

Foreign Labor in Germany

Understanding how drug markets worked—how production and distribution changed over time—is obviously significant. Yet it does not answer more qualitative questions. Why did police and the press focus on drugs as a foreign threat? Why did drug smuggling become associated so closely with foreign, and particularly Turkish and Iranian, traffickers? To answer these questions, one has to turn away from the global picture and focus on the changing relationship between foreign "guest workers" and Germans in the crucial period of the 1960s and early 1970s.

The history of foreigners in Germany has been well documented.[61] The long and often tragic history of labor in Germany before the founding of the Federal Republic in 1949 need not detain us here, although there are numerous continuities in foreign labor policy before, during, and after the Second World War. By the late 1950s, the German economy had recovered from the destruction of the war to such an extent that it faced a labor shortage. In order to alleviate the threat of an inflationary economy, German industry sought to supplement its workforce by recruiting low-wage laborers from other countries. The Bonn government began concluding agreements with a number of foreign governments to provide guest workers in 1955, a process that rapidly accelerated after 1961, when the erection of the Berlin Wall abruptly halted the influx of laborers from the German Democratic Republic. West Germany set up recruiting offices first in Italy, then in other southern European countries, and later extended the labor base to the southwest through the Balkans and Turkey.

The economic downturn of 1966–67 tested the planning of German

61. See, for instance, Ulrich Herbert, *A History of Foreign Labor in Germany, 1880–1980: Seasonal Workers/Forced Laborers/Guest Workers,* trans. William Templer (Ann Arbor: University of Michigan Press, 1990); Karen Schönwälder, *Einwanderung und ethnische Pluralität: Politische Entscheidungen und öffentliche Debatten in Großbritannien und der Bundesrepublik von der 1950er bis zu den 1970er Jahren* (Essen: Klartext, 2001); Klaus J. Bade, *Auswanderer—Wanderarbeiter—Gastarbeiter: Bevölkerung, Arbeitsmarkt und Wanderung in Deutschland seit der Mitte des 19. Jahrhunderts,* vol. 2 (Ostfildern: Scripta Mercaturae, 1984); Ray C. Rist, *Guestworkers in Germany: The Prospects for Pluralism* (New York: Praeger, 1978); and Harmut Berghoff, "Population Change and Its Repercussions on the Social History of the Federal Republic," in *The Federal Republic of Germany since 1949: Politics, Society, and Economy before and after Unification,* ed. Klaus Larres and Panikos Panayi (London: Longman, 1996), 35–73.

policymakers. For the first time, public opinion began to turn against guest workers. The press began running negative stories about guest workers, highlighting their criminal or sexual exploits.[62] The massive influx of foreign workers during the 1960s met rising German unemployment head-on and led to accusations that foreigners were taking "German" jobs.[63] Yet when the rapid economic recovery of 1968 dissipated much of the protest, demand for foreign workers skyrocketed.[64] In the three years between 1968 and 1971, German industry imported more foreign workers than in the eighteen-year period between the founding of the Federal Republic and 1967. Most notably, workers poured in from the untapped labor pool in Turkey. In Hamburg, for instance, the number of Turkish residents doubled in two years from 7,222 in 1969 to 14,762 in 1971; by 1974 that number had more than doubled again. By February 1972, Turkish nationals represented the largest foreign group in the Federal Republic.[65]

If 1961 had paved the way for foreign workers in Germany, 1973 proved to be a watershed in the history of guest laborers. The worldwide economic crisis that year had drastic effects on foreign workers in Germany. For the first time, German officials publicly questioned the wisdom of Germany's two-decade history of utilizing foreign workers. In January 1973 the Social Democratic chancellor, Willy Brandt, asserted the need to "carefully consider where the ability of our society to absorb has been exhausted, and where social common sense and responsibility dictate that the process be halted."[66] On 23 November 1973 the German government ended all recruitment from countries that did not belong to the European Economic Community.[67] The economic recovery of 1968 did not repeat itself. The economy failed to recover quickly, and inflation became a nagging problem. Even though the number of foreigners employed in the Federal Republic fell drastically—by half a million in two years—the number of foreigners residing in Germany continued to increase. German policymakers' twenty-

62. Herbert, *History of Foreign Labor,* 226; Schönwälder, *Einwanderung und ethnische Pluralität,* 186–88.

63. Herbert, *History of Foreign Labor,* 226–27; Schönwälder, *Einwanderung und ethnische Pluralität,* 178–86.

64. Herbert, *History of Foreign Labor,* 228–29.

65. Ibid., 230.

66. Willy Brandt, quoted in Herbert, *History of Foreign Labor,* 234.

67. Ibid., 234.

year vision of a reserve army of labor underwent a silent metamorphosis. The fact that the Federal Republic, quite by accident, had become a de facto country of immigration bewildered German officials.[68] The guest workers of the 1960s had become the immigrants of the 1970s.

The legacy of the recruitment policies of the 1950s and 1960s proved complex and often difficult. Immigrants' decisions to stay in Germany coupled with their role as a semipermanent underclass led to a number of social problems: housing deficiencies, unemployment, and rising social welfare costs. These new postindustrial realities prompted the government to take a Janus-faced approach to dealing with the large numbers of foreign immigrants, seeing them as necessary and expendable at the same time.[69] The new government policy further exacerbated the situation of Germany's guest workers. The policy became a justification for right-wing polemicists to target foreign residents and a foundation for a rising climate of *Ausländerfeindlichkeit* (hostility toward foreigners).

It was an unfortunate coincidence that the increase in organized drug smuggling corresponded with the rapid influx of foreign workers in the early 1970s. Though foreign and especially Turkish guest workers often were blamed for the increase in crime, and especially for violent and sexual crimes, the connection between Turkish residents and drug dealing had a powerful effect on the public image of foreigners.[70] Though some Turkish and Iranian residents did traffic in drugs, the vast majority of guest workers were law-abiding citizens. The public conception of Turkish and Iranian residents as drug dealers had less to do with the number of individuals involved in the trade than it did with a larger climate of xenophobia and a general fear of being overrun by foreigners (*Überfremdung*). The press, in particular, was fascinated by the spectacular combination of drugs, crime, and ethnicity. The tabloid press in particular never tired of running sensational stories about drugs. It specialized in three types of drug stories, all equally dramatic: young Germans overdosing, celebrities being caught with drugs, and police arresting drug smugglers. All three of these offered the chance for large-print, hot-selling headlines.

68. Ibid., 235.

69. Ibid., 247.

70. On the creation in the press of Turks as criminals, see Schönwälder, *Einwanderung und ethnische Pluralität,* 186–88.

Fig. 4. "Last night I sold two cops ten kilos of camel shit." By 1973, the wide-spread image of Middle Easterners as drug traffickers drew satiric comments from underground newspapers. (*ELDA,* no. 3 [1973]: 5, SSC, M613/12. Courtesy of Department of Special Collections, Stanford University Libraries.)

Bild—one of the most popular and most tawdry German newspapers—tended to run the most sensational articles. In July 1972, for instance, the editors ran a story entitled "He Knew Everything about the International Drug-Mafia—But He Had Wild Fears: Opium Smuggler Hangs Himself from His Cell Window." The story describes a St. Pauli waiter named Gerd Marotzke, who had been arrested by Danish police with a kilogram of raw opium. Marotzke, according to the article, had instructions to deliver the drugs to a middleman in Sweden. After his arrest, Hamburg police cut a deal with the waiter, and he was transported to Hamburg. He told the drug squad what they wanted to know in return for a reduced sentence. "Marotzke was enormously afraid that his Turkish bosses would take revenge," an officer told the reporter. "They threatened to kill him when he got out." The article ended by quoting the police officer: "Now some of the bosses can breathe a sigh of relief. Marotzke knew everything."[71]

The image of threatening, conspiratorial foreign drug kingpins and shadowy international drug rings was established and iterated in the press, always in conjunction with Turkish, Iranian, or Afghani citizens. In November 1972, Mohammed H., an Afghani taxi driver in Hamburg, was arrested with 360 kilograms of hashish after police raided his apartment. "He had disguised himself perfectly as a taxi driver," *Bild* reported, as if he could not possibly be a drug trafficker and a taxi driver at the same time. The *Hamburger Abendblatt* echoed this sentiment and added, "No one knew that he was the middleman in the service of an extensive international drug ring."[72]

Though the press undoubtedly played the most important role in disseminating the notion that drug smuggling was the exclusive domain of conspiratorial foreigners, the idea permeated German public culture. By the seventies, the police certainly began to see international organized crime as public enemy number one. In 1971, for instance, more than a hundred high-ranking officers in the various state police agencies met for a seminar on the drug problem at the Police Institute at Hiltrup. Organized by Hans Zühlsdorf from the Hamburg Criminal Police, the focus of the meeting was an exchange of information on the differing experiences of the drug traffic at the state level. In the opening keynote speech, Zühlsdorf warned of rapid changes in the international traffic within Germany. Before 1971, he asserted, the majority of the hashish traffic had involved sundry hippies and dropouts, but the traffic was becoming more organized and more threatening. He claimed that gangs of Turks and Iranians had based their organizations on the model of government intelligence agencies and increasingly dominated the trade. Zühlsdorf argued that the police should use all possible methods against these foreign criminals and at the same time end their "small war" against drug con-

71. Ernst Lutcke and Walter Weber, "Opium-Schmuggler erhängte sich am Zellenfenster," *Bild*, 17 July 1972.
72. "Sieben Zentner Haschisch sichergestellt," *Hamburger Abendblatt*, 29 November 1972; "Taxifahrer lagerte Hasch in der Wohnung," *Bild*, 30 November 1972.

sumers.[73] Zühlsdorf perceived Germans as the victims of foreign con-
spirators, who were intent on preying on the weak.

Over the next three years police refined and disseminated this profile
of the drug trade: drug traffickers were almost exclusively foreigners,
especially from Turkey and Iran.[74] Drug traffickers were a serious
threat to the state and as such had to be investigated thoroughly, tried,
convicted, and deported after serving their sentence. Some officials did
acknowledge the structural features of the trade that determined this
scenario: drug traffickers tended to be foreign because the distribution
of drugs was organized at the point of production, and few Germans
possessed the contacts that would make large-scale drug smuggling
possible. Yet it is clear from criminal statistics that German police were
more likely to investigate Turks and Iranians for drug crimes; they in
turn were much more likely than other ethnic groups to be convicted of
drug crimes.[75]

By 1974, the economic downturn had placed foreign workers in a
precarious position, and Turks in particular were blamed for Germany's social and economic problems. In October 1974, at a convention held by the Federal Criminal Police in Wiesbaden, Otto Boettcher,
the head of police in West Berlin, painted a grim picture of the future
of ethnic relations in Germany:

> When I speak about the foreigner problem, I cannot avoid glancing
> at America. There are now more than two and a half million foreign
> workers employed in the Federal Republic. But now add to this
> number the foreign family members of those living here legally as
> well as foreigners living here illegally—whose number is unknown—

73. Theo Segbers, "Das jüngste Kind der Kripo: Bericht und Gedanken über die Arbeitstagung Rauschgift des Polizei-Instituts Hiltrup," *Kriminalistik* 25 (1971): 337–38. See also
StAH, 351-10 II, Sozialbehörde II, Abl.3 135.27-0 Band 2, Polizei-Instituts Hiltrup, "Die
Bekämpfung der Rauschmittelkriminalität," 24–28 April 1972; Jürgen Wohldorf, "Kripo ist
gegen die Rauschgift-Welle nur kümmerlich gerüstet," *Hamburger Abendblatt,* 5 May 1971.

74. See, for example, Gerhard Kürbis and Günther Müller, "Im Sondereinsatz gegen
Rauschgifthändler," *Kriminalistik* 25 (1971): 449–52; Theo Segbers, "Bitteres Tagungsergeb-
nis: Bericht über die Norddeutschen Kriminalistentage," *Kriminalistik* 25 (1971): 613–15;
Hans Zühlsdorf, "Die Rauschgiftkriminalität in der Bundesrepublik," *Kriminalistik* 28
(1974): 349–55. Karl-Heinz Gemmer, "Organisiertes Verbrechen—eine Gefahr für die innere
Sicherheit?" *Kriminalistik* 28 (1974): 529–33.

75. See 351-10 II, Sozialbehörde II, Abl.3 135.01-1 Band 1, K245, "Monatlichen
Berichten," 1973–75.

and the sum foreshadows the problems that will open up in this field. Irrespective of the tensions and difficulties that arise from the tendency of the majority of foreigners living here to ghettoize themselves, the danger exists that large numbers of the second generation of guest workers will turn to crime, and that they will adapt forms of crime and will be less capable of integration than their parents' generation.[76]

This was not an isolated view. By the middle of the 1970s, police officials had accepted a stereotype of foreigners, their role in organized crime, and the severity of the threat they posed to the German state. Despite changes in the ethnicity of drug smugglers in the following years, from Turks in the 1970s to Kurds in the 1980s to Ghanaians and Nigerians in the 1990s, the drug problem has remained inextricably linked to the "foreigner problem."

Conclusion

The emergence of a drug scene in Hamburg in the late 1960s cannot be understood without taking into account the complicated history of drugs in the twentieth century. Drug cultivation and distribution did not begin in the sixties and was not simply a product of rising demand in the industrial West. Global drug economies had been a crucial part of international commerce since at least the seventeenth century. European empires were largely built on drugs, and this legacy of our imperial past continues to cast its shadow across the developing world.

It was in the twentieth century, however, that the modern drug trade emerged. Changing patterns of drug distribution and the growth of a modern global drug market mirrored rising licit global trade. The success of smuggling worldwide, and the inability of Western countries to halt the flow of drugs across their borders in particular, relied as much on the desire of Western governments to create and participate in a global capitalist market economy as it did on the skill of the traffickers.

76. Otto Boettcher, "Definition and Entwicklung des organisierten Verbrechens in der Bundesrepublik—Konsequenzen für die Bekämpfung," in *Organisiertes Verbrechen: Arbeitstagung des Bundeskriminalamtes Wiesbaden vom 21. Oktober bis 25. Oktober 1974*, ed. Bundeskriminalamt (Wiesbaden: Bundeskriminalamt, 1975), 183.

Furthermore, despite a seemingly insatiable demand for drugs in Europe and North America, changing patterns of the international distribution of drugs did not entail a unidirectional flow of drugs from the developing world to the West. Trade in the Near and Middle East, as well as in Southeast Asia, long antedated the drug culture of the 1960s. The transformation of drug markets in this region was a response to two interrelated developments: rising demand in the West, and Europe and the United States in particular, and the concomitant pressure that government officials in the West brought to bear on drug-producing countries with few resources to control, much less eliminate, the international trade in hashish and opium. In particular, the American-led war on drugs began to put pressure on the governments of producer countries in the late sixties and early seventies, and drug production was forced into ever-more remote areas where political control was either unfeasible or impossible. Faced with financial incentive packages on the one hand and economic sanctions on the other, countries such as Iran and Turkey attempted to crack down on illicit cultivation and distribution within their borders. But drug production and trafficking provided financial inducements that appealed not only to organized crime groups but also to small farmers thrust into a global market they could not control.

Political and social unrest was endemic in much of the developing world throughout the postwar period, and it also played a role in transforming the drug trade. Social upheaval caused by population increases, urbanization, and industrialization in countries such as Iran and Lebanon transformed widely practiced traditional forms of drug cultivation and use, while the disastrous effects of American involvement in Southeast Asia promoted the development of the global heroin trade. This was exacerbated by drug tourism, as young people from Europe and the United States traveled east in search of enlightenment and "authentic experience" in the 1960s and 1970s.

Despite young Europeans' involvement in the drug market as both traffickers and consumers, foreigners often bore the brunt of the blame for the "drug problem" in the Western world. Though the majority of the drug trade in Hamburg involved ethnic Germans, government officials and the police were convinced that malevolent *foreign* pushers victimized innocent *German* consumers; this image also pervaded popular perceptions of the drug trade. As a result, German policing practices targeted drug distributors and left drug consumers in relative peace. Though some immigrants took part in the drug trade in Europe, most were simply law-abiding "guests." But the rapid influx of Turkish workers after 1961 made these *Ausländer* an easy target for right-wing conservatives and the tabloid press, especially after the economic downturn of 1973 made them less crucial to the German economy. The image of guest workers as temporary partners in economic prosperity, prevalent in the 1960s, gave way over the course of the 1970s and 1980s to the reality of Germany as a de facto multicultural society. Citizenship law and long-held ideas about German culture promoted a static ethnic hierarchy. This structural inequality coupled with economic uncertainty and an atmosphere of distrust cultivated stereotypes of foreign residents as incapable of integration and prone to crime. Foremost among the fears of foreign crime was the drug trade. By the mid-seventies, perceptions of the drug market in Hamburg, as in much of Germany, had become closely linked to Germany's foreigner problem.

4. The Politics of Drugs

As winter set in and the tumultuous year 1968 lurched awkwardly toward its inconclusive end, the *Hamburger Morgenpost* ran a prominent story entitled "She Became Addicted to the Devil's Happiness!"[1] The sensational article began:

> Midnight on the Große Freiheit in St. Pauli. Standing in the entrance to the Star Club: Kids in their twenties [Twens], Teenagers, Hippies and Dropouts. Pounding rhythms of a band. Miniskirts bobbing up and down, laughter, small groups, shouting. Suddenly men with wide shoulders among them. At the same time, squealing brakes, paddy wagons, blue uniforms, and more broad-shouldered men.

According to the article, the Hamburg drug squad arrested seven people and took them to the Davidwache, the infamous police station on the Reeperbahn. The cells in the basement filled. People shouted and cursed, demanding that their rights be respected. The drug squad interviewed the young men and women. Among those questioned was Petra: eighteen years old, blond, and an addict. The detectives asked Petra the usual questions. She in turn furnished the usual answers: "I was only standing with the group by accident. Shooting up? I don't know what shooting up means. I didn't know they were dealing. I certainly don't know any of them." But, the article continued, Petra was beginning to feel the pains of withdrawal; she needed her next shot. The female detective walked over to Petra and grabbed her arm—needle tracks. A few hours later, Petra's mother picked her up.

Later the reporter sat in Petra's room. She and her friend Bernhard

---

1. "Sie verfiel dem Glück des Teufels!" *Hamburger Morgenpost,* 28 October 1968; StAH, 354-5 II, Jugendbehörde II, Abl. 11.11.1992 356-04.04 Band 2.

were high on morphine. Bernhard claimed his father was a drunk and beat him. The reporter felt less than sympathetic. Petra told her story:

> I ran away at 16. Four months at Ochsenzoll.[2] I was thin as a rail. I beat the insanity. I screamed, raged, got on my knees and wanted to kiss the nurses' feet. Give me a full CANNON! Come on, give me at least a little SHOT! The others in the room slugged me. I was too loud, too crazy. Then I was tied to the bed. After 120 days, they said I was cured.

As a postscript, the reporter noted that four months was, in fact, not enough. Petra was not cured and soon returned to the local drug scene.

Petra's story still held the power to shock in the autumn of 1968. Five years later it would be an all too common part of the urban land-scape. In the intervening period, drugs moved from the periphery of German society toward the center. On television and in the press, images of flower children high on hashish and LSD gave way to pho-tos of junkies dying in public toilets and darkened doorsteps, needles still dangling from disfigured arms. Not that hashish and LSD some-how disappeared. In fact, drug consumption of all kinds exploded between 1968 and 1970, while the average age of drug users sank. What had been seen as a distinctly un-German phenomenon became a visible daily reminder of how wrong that idea of exceptionalism had been. In Germany, much as in the rest of the industrialized world, drugs became a normal part of daily urban life, despite drastic attempts to stem the tide.

Though drug use was already widespread in Hamburg by the end of the 1960s, drugs did not become a public problem until 1969. Before that time, discussion of drug use among Germany's youth had been largely limited to small circles of experts: youth protection advocates, physicians, and police. The relatively small amount of attention drugs received in the press tended to focus on the much more visible patterns of drug use in the United States, London, and Stockholm or on iso-lated groups of bohemian drug users in Germany. Yet with the rapid rise in drug arrests, pharmacy burglaries, and media coverage after 1968, drugs became a central issue and provoked intense media specu-lation, legislative action, and scientific interest.

---

2. Allgemeine Krankenhaus Ochsenzoll was the primary hospital for the detoxification of addicts in the 1960s.

The period 1969–75 proved to be a time of crisis in the understanding of the drug problem in Germany. The traditional youth protection
ethos broke down over the course of the sixties and was challenged by
a new therapeutic ethos.[3] While the champions of the youth protection
mind-set believed that modern society, and particularly modern consumer culture, was a danger to social cohesion, the proponents of the
therapeutic ethos saw drug consumption as a reaction to the challenges
of modernization. For the older model, drugs were a sign of individual
failure; for the new model, drugs were a logical outcome of bewildering
change.

The rapid rise of drug consumption by German youth challenged
the traditional belief that drug abuse was a manifestation of underlying
psychiatric problems. During the early seventies, the initial fascination
with drugs as a means to expand the consciousness among young people gave way to largely class-based patterns of drug use. Though
hashish and LSD consumption continued to rise, the spread of drug
injection and a concomitant junkie culture led to a new popular understanding of drug consumption. "Soft" drug consumption—mostly
hashish and LSD—became accepted as an unfortunate side effect of
modernity, while "hard" drug consumption and especially opiate
abuse became a new form of deviance. The divide between these two
quite different forms of drug consumption was based largely on class.
Middle- and upper-class youth continued to use soft drugs, while hard
drugs remained largely the domain of young people from working-
class backgrounds who had significant problems before they began
using drugs. By the middle of the seventies, a new understanding of
drug abuse had solidified, at least for a time. Though the authorities
condemned drug consumption in all its forms, most of the energies of
both the police and social agencies were aimed at the new "problem"
drug users.

This path, however, was not inevitable. During the early seventies,
there were a number of options open to policymakers and experts. The
events of 1968 and the proliferation of "alternative" groups in the after-
math had a profound effect on the politics of Germany and marked a
significant shift away from the more conservative policies of the fifties
and early sixties. The debates over drug consumption in the early seventies tested this transformation. How could politicians deal with what

3. On this important transformation, see Ubbelohde, "Der Umgang," 425–35.

was more and more obviously a public problem without the resort to massive force? How could the federal and state governments deal with the widespread lawlessness that widespread drug consumption represented? While conservatives tended to hone arguments long practiced by the youth protection movement, many liberals believed that soft drug use should be decriminalized, if not completely legalized. This debate, although nominally about public health or law and order, became enmeshed within a larger debate over the legacy of 1968. For those who lamented the loss of the values of sober orderliness of the fifties, drugs represented a most vivid symbol of what the libertinage that had emerged out of 1968 had wrought. For the Left, drugs merely represented an externalization of a legitimate dissatisfaction with West German society.

Yet by the midseventies, the more controversial demands coming out of 1960s radicalism had fallen into disrepute. The changing face of addiction and the economic collapse in the wake of the oil crisis of 1973 led to the collapse of the political space in which alternative conceptions of drug consumption had thrived. Drug addiction had become a part of daily life in Hamburg, and drug policy had reached a sort of equilibrium. Drug addicts were to be treated within a medical model that stressed abstinence, and drug trafficking and dealing were to be punished to the full extent of the law. In the span of half a decade, drug abuse took its place as a potent symbol of the dark side of modern life.

This change, however, had been unimaginable in the late sixties. At the end of 1968, Hamburg was woefully unprepared for the massive rise in drug consumption. Hamburg's drug squad had been formed on 1 July 1967, with five members, who were also responsible for policing pornography. The next year, two more officers were added, bringing the number to seven, three of whom were assigned to controlling pornography.[4] The Youth Authority had begun to discuss the problem, had held a number of lectures for concerned groups, and had printed five thousand copies of an "improvised" pamphlet on the theme "drugs and intoxication."[5] At the University Hospital at Eppendorf and the General Hospital at Ochsenzoll, a few young drug users

4. See Bürgerschaft HH, Drucksache VII/1115, 5. StAH, 136.1, BfI, 1108, Hoyer, "Rauschgiftdelikte."

5. StAH, 351-10 II, Sozialbehörde II, Abl.3 135.20-0 Band 2, Eckard Günther, "Bisher im Bereich der Hamburger Verwaltung getroffene Maßnahmen gegen den Rauschmittel Mißbrauch junger Menschen," 3 March 1971. See also Bürgerschaft HH, Drucksache

were treated for withdrawal symptoms or hepatitis in the closed psy-
·chiatric departments. In 1968, that was the entirety of Hamburg's public response to drug use.[6]

As the number of young drug users coming to the attention of the
authorities began to rise rapidly in 1969, members of the state bureaucracy, public health advocates, welfare agencies, and the police all
knew that something more had to be done. The responsibility for dealing with drugs, however, cut across both bureaucratic and conceptual
boundaries. Drugs fell under the jurisdiction of at least five of Hamburg's state authorities (*Behörden*). The Youth Authority had responsibility for youth protection and youth welfare, including state youth
custodial care (*Fürsorgeerziehung*). The Department of the Interior
was responsible for the police. The Authority for Work and Social
Welfare dealt with adult welfare and handled addicts over the age of
twenty-one (and later over eighteen), while the School Authority was
charged with the task of implementing an antidrug education program.
Finally, the Health Authority claimed responsibility for both treatment within the hospitals and the control of pharmacies and physicians. During the course of 1969, all these state organs attempted to
begin to deal with the rise in drug consumption. Their efforts were,
however, largely uncoordinated and improvised.

Drug policy in Hamburg was not merely state imposed but rather
arose from complex negotiations between public and private organizations, between politicians and the public, and between experts and
drug users. Not all of these negotiations, however, took place on an
equal footing; some groups had more sway than others, and much of
the debate relied on polemics, recriminations, poor information, or
disinformation. Even so, in the first few years of the 1970s, public and
private groups poured an enormous amount of energy into dealing
with drugs and produced a flood of new ideas about the nature of
addiction and the means with which to treat it.

VII/1115, 5. The quickly assembled pamphlet "Droge und Rausch: Eine Arbeitshilfe für die
Praxis" was aimed not at young users but rather at those taking an active role in dealing with
the drug problem, including youth workers and teachers. See StAH, 351-10 II, Sozialbehörde
II, Abl. 3 135.22-1 Band 1, Jugendbehörde, "Droge und Rausch: Eine Arbeitshilfe für die
Praxis," 1968.

6. See StAH, 351-10 II, Sozialbehörde II, Abl.3 135.20-0 Band 2, Eckhard Günther,
"Bisher im Bereich der Hamburger Verwaltung getroffene Maßnahmen gegen den
Rauschmittel Mißbrauch junger Menschen," 3 March 1971.

Private Welfare Organizations and the Subsidiary Principle

Addiction was not new in Hamburg; alcoholism had long been an enormous problem in German society. Care of addicts in Hamburg had been delegated since the Weimar Republic to private welfare organizations. This "subsidiary principle" (*Subsidiaritätsprinzip*) "gave precedence to private over public welfare agencies."[7] In the case of substance abuse, this had generally meant that the state had depended on the churches to deal with alcohol abuse. The same subsidiary principle included youth welfare services as well; the Protestant and Catholic welfare organizations ran many of the youth homes. Yet the novelty of drug abuse and the seemingly intractable nature of youth drug addiction posed new problems for private organizations, most of which proved slow to rise to the challenges.

The established youth homes not administered by the state, for example, did not want drug users admitted to their facilities. In April 1969, a member of the Education (*Erziehung*) Department of the Youth Authority met with members of the private youth homes, run mostly by the Evangelical Church, to discuss the possibility of placing drug-addicted or "endangered" youth. Representatives of the youth homes refused to consider taking in young people involved with drugs. They believed that incorporating these adolescents would compromise discipline and expose their charges to bad influences. Furthermore, they believed that drug-addicted youths needed special facilities they could not offer, such as a locked-down unit and psychiatric help. The members suggested that the Youth Department found a home specifically for these troubled youth that would include a closed wing, psychiatric and psychological services, and a flexible approach to dealing with the special problems of this population.[8]

These youth homes were not the only private organizations unwilling or unable to deal with new forms of youth drug consumption. For most of the established private initiatives involved with addiction, drug abuse among young people and especially the alarming increase in

7. David Crew, *Germans on Welfare* (Oxford: Oxford University Press, 1998), 19. Young-Sun Hong, *Welfare, Modernity, and the Weimar State: 1919–1933* (Princeton: Princeton University Press, 1998), 82–84.

8. StAH, 354-5 II, Jugendbehörde II, Abl. 11.11.1992 356-04.04 Band 3, Fuchs, "Unterbringung von "Rauschgiftsüchtigen' Jugendlichen in Heimen fremder Träger," 30 April 1969.

intravenous drug addiction caught them unaware and unable to find meaningful solutions to the challenges posed by new forms of addiction. Until the late sixties, dealing with substance abuse had meant dealing with alcoholism. There was an elaborate system of state and private organizations that focused on this problem: Caritasverband, the Catholic welfare organization, ran a counseling center for addicts (Beratungsstelle für Suchtkranke); Diakonisches Werk, the Evangelical welfare organization, had an "addiction help" department; and the Order of the Good Templars was active in Hamburg. The work of these groups and others was organized through the Hamburg Landesstelle gegen die Suchtgefahren (Hamburg State Office against the Threat of Addiction), a semiautonomous branch of the national Deutsche Hauptstelle gegen die Suchtgefahren (German Main Office against the Threat of Addiction). Founded in 1949, the Landesstelle membership included the Good Templars, the German Women's Association for an Alcohol-Free Culture (Deutscher Frauenbund für alkoholfreie Kultur), the Evangelical State Consortium for Resistance to the Threat of Addiction (Evangelische Landesarbeitsgemeinschaft zur Abwehr der Suchtgefahren), the Blue Cross (Blaues Kreuz), as well as the Protestant and Catholic welfare organizations.[9]

The responsibility for dealing with addiction was shared between these private welfare organizations and the state until the late sixties. The drug wave changed this relationship. Most of the private organizations, with the notable exception of the Protestant welfare organization, were unable to adapt to the rapidly changing face of addiction. Leaders, such as Otto Landt of the Landesstelle gegen die Suchtgefahren, failed to recognize the writing on the wall until it was much too late, despite the frequent prodding of younger individuals involved in searching for answers to the drug problem, such as Dieter Maul, a representative of the Hamburger Jugendring e.V. and future director of the Landesstelle. When these organizations finally understood the import of the changing nature of addiction, they were reticent to become involved. Much of this was due to the fact that they were accustomed to dealing with middle-aged men and women with drinking problems. Based on temperance ideology, their conceptual model

9. Hamburg Landesstelle gegen die Suchtgefahren, *25 Jahre der Hamburg Landesstelle gegen die Suchtgefahren 1949/1974* (Hamburg: Krause-Druck-Stade, 1974), 16–21.

perceived addiction as a threat to the family and stressed the need for abstinence; this fit awkwardly, if at all, with the new forms of drug consumption. Adolescents smoking hashish or injecting narcotics simply did not adhere to this worldview.[10]

Public Drug Treatment and Social Welfare

If the private organizations dealing with addiction were unprepared to deal with the startling rise in addiction, the state public health authorities were in an even worse state. In 1969, the only places available to treat addicts in Hamburg were the closed psychiatric wards of the General Hospital at Ochsenzoll and the University Hospital at Eppendorf. Both of these hospitals, however, were accustomed to dealing with severe cases of mental illness, were badly understaffed, and were unable to provide the kind of attention drug users needed.

At the General Hospital at Ochsenzoll, the number of drug users treated quadrupled between 1968 and 1969. Dr. Wunnenberg, head of the psychiatric department, considered the situation dire.

In Hamburg, we are in a very bad situation—especially in our hospital. First, we have too few beds. Second, the stations, which presently must take in addicted patients along with others, are not doing enough to protect against the supply of refined illegal narcotics for and through these young people, who have only one interest: their narcotics! . . . In addition, we have too few doctors to allow all the addicts in need to receive sufficient, proper psychotherapy. Finally, in this area it is obvious that Hamburg has a regrettable lack of social-psychiatric facilities.[11]

Most of the young people sent for "treatment" at the hospitals did not go willingly but instead were committed by the courts or by a

10. The most significant exception was the Evangelical Church. Diakonisches Werk attempted to play a major role but found the road difficult. After early attempts to treat young drug users, the welfare organization chose to focus on other areas of youth social welfare. This shift is covered later in the chapter. See StAH, 315-10 II, Sozialbehörde II, 012.71-4-1 Band 1, Caritasverband, "Beratungsstelle für Suchtkranke," 1971, and "Beratungstelle für Suchtkranke," 1972.

11. StAH, 354-5 II, Jugendbehörde II, Abt. 29.10.86, 356.03.01-1 Band 8, Wunnenberg, "Therapeutische Möglichkeiten beim Rauschmittelgebrauch junger Menschen," speech given at the IX Interbehördliche Arbeitstagung: "Praxis des Jugendschutzes," 9 January 1970.

court-appointed guardian. The relapse rate after such treatment in Hamburg's hospitals was nearly 100 percent.[12] Instead of curing addicts, the psychiatric departments had become revolving doors, treating the same individuals again and again. Among drug users, they provoked fear and animosity. "You can't keep yourself busy," one user complained. "There aren't any books. You get to see the doctor only once a day, for only a short time. It is like being in prison; you feel so confined; everything is locked. The desire to get away from drugs is lost because of this."[13]

Another possible avenue of help for drug users was the State Social Welfare Office (Landessozialamt), which traditionally claimed responsibly for supervising adult alcoholics and drug addicts. A special office for at-risk adults (Gefährdeten) dealt separately with male and female substance abusers, most of whom were alcoholics. Compared to the number of alcoholics supervised—over a thousand men and over three hundred women at any given time—the number of drug addicts remained negligible. Before the late sixties, the State Social Welfare Office did supervise a few drug addicts, but most of these were between the ages of forty and fifty, were addicted to morphine during medical treatment, or were themselves medical personnel. Some of them were placed under the guardianship of the State Social Welfare Office. Others were addicted to sleeping pills, painkillers, or other pills and were supervised by the department. The women's section of the State Social Welfare Office dealt with a wider range of problems but also supervised a number of women addicted to pills.[14]

The profile of drug addicts changed rapidly during 1969, when a

12. StAH, 351-10 II, Sozialbehörde II, Abl.3 135.22-1 Band 1, Sierakowsky and Brandt, "Niederschrift über die Besprechung des Koordinierungsausschußes in Hamburg am 24. März 1969 im Jugendheim Hamburg 13, Abteistr. 36," 26 March 1969.

13. Quoted in Ute von Hirschheydt, "Erfahrungen mit jungen Rauschmittelkonsumenten: Deskriptiv phänomenologische Darstellung der Drogenszene eines Hamburger Kollektivs" (PhD diss., Fachbereich Medizin der Universität Hamburg, 1972), 62. See also Paul Wendiggensen, "Hamburger Drogenkonsumenten in Kliniken, Haftanstalten und der Drogenscene: Ergebnisse einer deskriptiv-statistischen Untersuchung" (PhD diss., Fachbereich Medizin der Universität Hamburg, 1972), 41–42.

14. StAH, 315-10 II, Sozialbehörde II, 135.22-1 Band 1, Menold, "Bericht über die Betreuung rauschmittel-bezw. rauschgiftsüchtiger junger Männer und Frauen in der Gefährdetenhilfe," 18 June 1970. StAH, 351-10 II, Sozialbehörde II, Abl.3 135.20-0 Band 3, Mieck, "Zuordnung der beiden neuen Sozialarbeiterstellen für die Arbeit an Rauschmittelabhängigen im Bereich SH 30/31," 22 October 1970, and Mieck, "Hilfe für Suchtgefährdete," 10 February 1972.

number of young people between the ages of twenty and twenty-three who were addicted to various intravenous drugs began requesting aid at the at-risk office. The amount of time and effort needed to deal with these new drug addicts overwhelmed the social workers. In addition to the young addicts seeking help, the office was inundated with parents, friends, doctors, and social workers, not to mention representatives of the Youth Authority and the Health Authority, all seeking advice on how to deal with addicted young people. By mid-1970, the social workers at the at-risk office had handled approximately fifty young addicts.

The work of the at-risk department's staff was divided by gender. The men's section was inundated with "fixers," young men deeply involved in the drug scene who injected various opiates or stimulants and who were for the most part physically addicted to drugs. The women's section, on the other hand, dealt with a much smaller number of cases. Most of these women were younger than their male counterparts, and most only used hashish and LSD. Because of this, young women who had begun injecting drugs were transferred to the men's section.[15]

It was difficult, if not impossible, to get a treatment bed for the addicts, even if they desperately wanted to quit using drugs. The state-run social welfare or pedagogical homes (*sozial-pädagogische Heime*) lacked the expertise to deal with detoxification. The psychiatric departments in the hospitals had proved to be quite unsuccessful, and patients there were often able to continue their drug habits even in the locked-down departments. In some cases, the state welfare authorities sent young people to a private clinic in the nearby city of Bremen-Oberneuland, though only two of these patients managed to remain for the entire six-month program; most abandoned the program and returned to the drug scene.

15. StAH, 315-10 II, Sozialbehörde II, 135.22-1 Band 1, Menold, "Bericht über die Betreuung rauschmittel-bezw. rauschgiftsüchtiger junger Männer und Frauen in der Gefärdetenhilfe," 18 June 1970. StAH, 351-10 II, Sozialbehörde II, Abl.3 135.20-0 Band 3, Mieck, "Zuordnung der beiden neuen Sozialarbeiterstellen für die Arbeit an Rauschmittelabhängigen im Bereich SH 30/31," 22 October 1970. The practice of transferring female hard drug users to the men's section (SH31) ended in January 1972, when the responsibility for women returned to the women's section (SH30); StAH, 351-10 II, Sozialbehörde II, Abl.3 135.20-0 Band 4, Müller-Dieckert, "Betreuung Rauschmittelabhängiger in SH 3," 31 January 1972.

The Police

Much like the social welfare agencies, the police were unprepared for the rapid spread of drug consumption. During 1969, they desperately tried to keep up with a rapidly changing drug trade. That year, the police arrested 272 individuals for cannabis consumption, 25 for cannabis and opiate consumption, and 2 for cannabis and LSD consumption. Two hundred of these were under the age of twenty-one. But the police believed that the actual number of cannabis users was in fact much higher.[16] The most alarming problem police faced, however, was not consumption but a rapid increase in the number of pharmacy burglaries. In 1968, there had been only eight pharmacy burglaries; in 1969, that number rose to seventy-four. Most of these burglaries involved small groups of young people attempting to find a steady source of opiates. More than half of the burglaries were solved, and thirty-four individuals were prosecuted. The police actively pursued a preventative policy, which focused on making pharmacy burglaries more difficult and less profitable. They ordered pharmacies to keep dangerous drugs under lock and key in a secure cabinet.[17] Police also asked pharmacists to keep no more than a one-day supply of narcotics on hand, to have an alarm installed, to leave the lights on, and to remove all visual obstructions from the windows. In addition to these self-policing directives, the police increased patrols of pharmacies.[18]

Combating smuggling remained the top priority for police. In particular, police worried about the organized smuggling of amphetamines, particularly Preludin and Pervitin, from Hungary and Italy to Scandinavia, much of which passed through Hamburg. In 1969, the police investigated 161 individuals for smuggling or dealing drugs. Of these, 58 were foreigners. The police complained bitterly that foreign smugglers could bring their wares into the Federal Republic with impunity, since the penalties were so light; the largest sentence allowable under the Opium Law was three years in prison. Most of those convicted, however, served much less than the maximum. In 1968, the

16. HBfI, K245, "Jahresbericht 1969."
17. This was articulated in the Apothekenbetriebsverordnung from 7 August 1968.
18. HBfI, K245, "Jahresbericht 1968," "Jahresbericht 1969." StAH, 136.1, BfI, 1145, Timmerman, "Betäubungsmittel-Diebstähle bei Apothekeneinbrüchen, Besprechung 22. Aug. 1969," 22 August 1969. StAH, 136.1, BfI, 1145, Reuter, "Diebstähle von Betäubungsmittel in Apotheken," 27 November 1970.

longest sentence was seven months in prison; in 1969, one smuggler received two years in prison, but most received relatively light sentences.[19]

Another shocking increase was the amount of drugs confiscated by the police. Much of this was due to the increase in the number of pharmacy burglaries, but the amount of cannabis seized also exploded. For example, in 1968 Hamburg police seized 133 ampoules of morphine; the next year they confiscated 35.5 grams of powdered morphine, 1,097 ampoules, and 1,060 milliliters of morphine solution. In 1968, they seized two trips (individual doses) of LSD; the next year it was eighty-five. Most startling, though, in 1968 they seized 21 kilograms of cannabis; the next year they confiscated 377 kilograms. Much of this increase was due to increased policing, though the police were still severely understaffed. The main reason was the rapid increase in drug use among young people and the concomitant increase in smuggling.[20]

The police were acutely aware of the difficulties involved in policing the drug problem from the outset. Arresting large numbers of young people for drug consumption was unpopular, especially if they were children of Hamburg's more prominent citizens. On the other hand, policing smuggling was difficult and time-consuming. Most of all, policing appeared to be futile. Despite rapid increases in the number of arrests and the size of seizures, drugs continued to pour into Hamburg; more young people seemed to be using drugs, and prices continued to drop. The trade in drugs no longer took place among small groups of initiates. Indeed, a broad market in illicit drugs was beginning to form. Demand continued to rise exponentially, and the incredible profits arising from the trade encouraged the growth in organized smuggling. Under these circumstances, Hamburg's police attempted to disown the responsibility for dealing with drug consumers. Drug consumption, they claimed, ought to be a social welfare rather than a police matter. Instead, they would focus their energies on bringing drug dealers and drug smugglers to justice. Though Hamburg's police continued to

19. HBfI, K243, "Jahresbericht 1968," "Jahresbericht 1969." StAH, 136.1, BfI 1108, Hoyer, "Jugend und Rauschgift," 15 August 1969. StAH, 351-10 II, Sozialbehörde II, Abl. 3 135.00-3 Band 1, "Rauschgiftgenuß Jugendlicher," 3 February 1970.

20. HBfI, K245, "Jahresbericht 1968," "Jahresbericht 1969." StAH, 136.1, BfI 1108, Hoyer, "Jugend und Rauschgift," 15 August 1969. StAH, 351-10 II, Sozialbehörde II, Abl. 3 135.00-3 Band 1, "Rauschgiftgenuß Jugendlicher," 3 February 1970.

arrest consumers, they chose to distance themselves from the specter of mass arrests of Hamburg's young and to focus on the already demonized dealers and smugglers.[21]

The Politics of Drug Consumption

It was in this context that the Hamburg legislature first took up the question of rising drug abuse. On 30 October 1968, five members of the Hamburg Bürgerschaft (City Council) requested that the Senate (the administrative body of the Bürgerschaft) report on the development of addiction in Hamburg, the sociological reasons behind this growth, the possible therapeutic measures to combat addiction, as well as "the Senate's plans for dealing with this task with particular consideration of the necessary expansion of the relevant hospital departments."[22] More than a year later, after considerable consultation with various state agencies and outside experts, the Senate finally reported its findings on 4 November 1969.

The report noted a sharp increase in the number of young people using drugs. The Youth Authority reported that in the first half of 1969 around 150 young drug users were known by name. Approximately the same number of users had sought anonymous counseling, most of whom were eighteen or nineteen years old, though the officials warned that the age was showing a marked tendency to decrease. Similarly, the hospital psychiatric departments reported a rapid rise in the number of young drug addicts in treatment. Of the young people receiving treatment at the hospitals, some reported using drugs for only a few months while others claimed to have been using for much longer periods of up to four years. Despite the concrete figures provided by the Youth Authority and the hospitals, the Senate acknowledged that the number of young drug consumers was undoubtedly much higher and estimated that around two thousand of Hamburg's youth were involved in the

---

21. See, for example, StAH, 136.1, BfI, 1108, Bochert, "Rauschgift Kriminalität in Hamburg," 19 March 1970. StAH, 351-10 II, Sozialbehörde II, Abl.3 135.22-1 Band 1, Günther, "Niederschrift über eine Besprechung bei der Behörde für Inneres am 28. Sept. 1970," 16 October 1970, and "Niederschrift über eine Besprechung bei der Behörde für Inneres am 4 September 1970."

22. Drucksache der Bürgerschaft HH, VI/1641; Antrag der Abg. Plattner, Christiansen, Kirst, Nicolaysen, Phillipp, Betr.: Suchtkrankheiten, 30 October 1968.

drug scene. The rapid rise in hashish consumption during 1968 troubled the Senate. They blamed the increased supply and drop in price on
foreign guest workers, whom they accused of smuggling the drugs into
Hamburg; they attributed young people's willingness to experiment on
the press and popular culture. After hashish consumption, intravenous
opiate use seemed to be the largest problem, followed closely by stimulants, such as Preludin and Captagon. LSD, the report claimed, was
used only infrequently.

The Senate's report was not, however, particularly conservative.
Rather than demonizing drugs in morally imperative terms, the report
painted drugs as a societal problem. The report pointed out that alcoholism was still a much greater problem than drug use and that the
abuse of prescribed drugs such as tranquilizers and barbiturates was
also rampant.[23] Drug abuse, the report argued, was not just a problem
of youth but rather part of a larger trend among both young and old
toward the use of chemicals to elude the problems of modern life; it
was, in fact, an unintended consequence of modernization.

The Senate believed that the cause of drug consumption could be
traced back to the challenges posed by the protests of the sixties. Drug
consumption was indeed a part of the protest against the establishment, a means of group identification, and a rejection of traditional
societal values. Yet drug use as a part of a larger protest movement,
according to the report, was a form of "collective psychosis." Groups
of dropouts and hippies used drugs to set themselves apart from the
"society of their fathers" and to distance themselves from the "existing
order." Young people believed that what the Senate termed the "com-
puter society" had failed them and protested against it through "broken relationships, promiscuity, contempt for middle-class values such
as property, profession and success." The report claimed that the
"Flower-power-and-happy-pills-Period"[24] was only a transitional
phase. Significantly, the Senate elided the implications of social class
on drug use, preferring to portray drug consumption as an equal
opportunity social ill. The report claimed that drug users came from

23. Drucksache der Bürgerschaft HH, VI/2474; Mitteilung des Senats an die Bürgerschaft, Suchtkrankheiten, 4 November 1969, 2–3.
24. This is yet another excellent example of how prevalent English was in the drug milieu.
Though this seems like a translation, it is a direct quote, easily noted as such because of the
use of hyphens.

"school children, apprentices, university students, office workers and the unemployed" and that the overwhelming majority came from respectable (*gutbürgerliche*) families. Yet if they traveled too far down the path of drug abuse, they would likely drop out of school, lose their jobs, stop caring about their families or the future, and become obsessed with obtaining drugs.[25] This belief, which appears to have been widespread both in politics and among the polity, played a particularly important role in the direction of drug policy. Had Hamburg's elite determined early on that drug abuse was mostly a problem of working-class youth, the path toward a more punitive policy would have been much more attractive; however, since drug addiction was perceived as a threat to *all* of Hamburg's youth, a harsh route toward increased criminal penalties for consumers proved politically unappealing.

The Senate acknowledged that, since drug use was rapidly becoming specifically a youth problem, the therapeutic responses required the cooperation of parents, teachers, psychologists, and welfare workers, as well as the professional support of physicians. The Senate outlined three critical areas: administration, social psychology, and medicine. Administrative measures included preventing the flow of prescription pharmaceuticals into the black market and halting the import of illegal drugs, particularly cannabis products from Turkey, Afghanistan, Pakistan, and Nepal. In the area of pedagogy and social psychology, counseling and oversight by youth authorities needed to be strengthened, and the cooperation between parents and schools needed to be augmented. Social workers needed more direct contact with at-risk youth and their social environment; therefore, welfare workers from the state and from religious groups must be better educated about drug issues. Hashish and marijuana should be their primary concern, with total abstinence the goal, while the information provided to young people should be factual and clear rather than sensational and emotional. The responsibility for dealing with young people, the Senate stressed, must fall to both the state and private organizations. In the worst cases, the state should turn to juridical measures, including making young drug users wards of the state.[26] Despite this ambitious plan, the report was

25. Drucksache der Bürgerschaft HH, VI/2474, 4.
26. Young drug users, so the report stated, could be brought under the control of the state by invoking § 1837 of the Bürgerliches Gesetzbuch before the Vormundschaftsgericht.

deeply pessimistic about the chances for the rehabilitation of young addicts. The possibility of recovery appeared slim and required long-term stationary care of up to six months in a closed psychiatric facility where psychotherapy and group therapy should be made available.[27]

Beyond those recommendations, the Senate proposed a number of specific measures to combat the rise in drug consumption. First, in March 1969, the Coordination Committee for Questions of Narcotic and Pharmaceutical Use by Young People was formed. Made up of members of the Justice Authority, the School Authority, the Work and Social Welfare Authority, the Health Authority, the State Criminal Police, as well as hospital doctors and a judge from the Guardianship Court, the committee was mandated to "provide the opportunity to discuss the situation and serve as the coordinator on specific measures." The Senate also planned to expand the dissemination of information and to provide expanded counseling opportunities by creating a network of information and counseling centers. The Senate placed the greatest responsibility for combating the drug problem, however, in the hands of the psychiatric institutions and the Health Authority. Since experience had shown that successful rehabilitation of drug addicts depended on the intensity of counseling in an institutional setting, it instructed the Health Authority to expand the number of places available and to provide the necessary personnel. The end result, the Senate declared, must be a major increase in the number of beds available to treat drug addicts, though the exact method of this expansion was not specified.[28]

This report provoked heated discussion in the Bürgerschaft. The debate was a significant one in that it laid out the basic positions that guided the thinking of Hamburg's politicians in the realm of drug policy. On the political Right, drug abuse was seen as a danger to the very fabric of society entangled in a larger field of protest. Drug abuse was just another example, though a particularly threatening example, of the waywardness of youth. Something had gone terribly wrong with the nation's youth, and what they needed was order and discipline; they must be drawn back into the fold and made to believe in the promise of welfare for all. The political Right acknowledged the need

27. Drucksache der Bürgerschaft HH, VI/2474, 4–5.
28. Drucksache der Bürgerschaft HH, VI/2474, 5–6.

for medical treatment but perceived drug use and addiction as an individual moral failing. Not only did drug use lead to a destruction of one's character, but it probably grew out of some personal defect as well. In a sense, the conservatives in Hamburg were still fighting a rearguard action against the changes of the sixties and particularly 1968. They conjured up images, real or imagined, of an earlier time when children behaved in an orderly manner; they believed in the same ethos that motivated the youth protection movement, which after 1968 was in eclipse.

According to the political Left, society was to blame. Children—innocent children—were overwhelmed by the burdens of a new post-industrial society and sought, quite understandably, to escape the turmoil of a troubled world. It was this side of the political spectrum from which the therapeutic mind-set sprang. This therapeutic conception stressed the exigencies of modern life and the psychological roots of problem behaviors. Whereas the Right saw addiction as a moral problem wrapped in a medical package, the therapeutic Left saw addiction as a medical problem, a psychiatric problem to be exact, rooted in societal failure.

Leonhardt's Hashish Report, *Liberalism, and the Drug Problem*

In 1970, Societäts published Rudolf Walter Leonhardt's popular liberal polemic against German drug policy, *Hashish Report*. Born in 1921 in Altenburg, Leonhardt studied philosophy during the 1940s and 1950s in Leipzig, Bonn, and Cambridge, England. After receiving his doctorate from the University of Bonn in 1950, he worked as a BBC correspondent. In 1953, he began work in Hamburg as a correspondent and political editor of *Die Zeit*. Two years later he became editor of the feuilleton section of *Die Zeit*. During the late fifties and first half of the sixties, Leonhardt published several books on modern literature, German studies, and the German Democratic Republic.[29] By the late sixties, he turned his interest toward the social margins, including drug users. This change in focus led to the 1969 publication of *Who Will Throw the First Stone?*—a study of "drunk driving, divorce, sex crime,

29. "Rudolf Walter Leonhardt," in *Wer ist Wer? Das Deutsche Who's Who*, ed. Walter Habel, vol. 17 (Frankfurt am Main: Societäts, 1973), 639.

incest, prostitution, homosexuality, abortion and murder" as well as hashish consumption.[30]

The next year he turned his considerable talents to the question of hashish consumption. The resulting book, *Hashish Report,* was a collection of essays written by Leonhardt and translations of a number of important government commissions on the question of cannabis consumption, including excerpts from the seven-volume study "Report of the Indian Hemp Drug Commission," published in 1894 by the British government; "The Marihuana Problem in the City of New York," the so-called LaGuardia Report published in 1944; the 1969 "Cannabis Report by the Advisory Committee on Drug Dependence," published by the British government; and "Clinical and Psychological Effects of Marihuana in Man," written by A. T. Weil, N. E. Zinberg, and J. M. Nelsen and published in the American periodical *Science* in 1969.

Leonhardt's book was important because it was the most conspicuous example of the liberal argument for the decriminalization of soft drugs. Far from being some long-haired advocate of the countercultural lifestyle, Leonhardt was a forty-nine-year-old editor of the prominent and well-respected weekly *Die Zeit.* Heavily influenced by Bertrand Russell, Leonhardt carried on the tradition of a long line of liberal reformers who attempted to mix compassion with an empirical pragmatism. "I could certainly imagine myself in the role of a hashish propagandist," he wrote. "Radical liberal convictions want to drag me in this direction as well as an arduously earned pacifism."[31] Of course, not every liberal-minded reformer wanted to be a propagandist for drug consumption—indeed, Leonhardt was more of an apologist than a propagandist. Yet Leonhardt's argument that the criminalization of hashish caused more problems than it solved struck a chord with like-minded individuals. The very prominence of this type of middle-aged liberalism became the strongest counterweight to the law-and-order conservative response and found sympathetic minds in the Hamburg Social Democratic Party (SPD).

Leonhardt argued that the threat posed by hashish consumption was minimal. He compared the effects of hashish smoking to those of

30. Rudolf Walter Leonhardt, *Haschisch-Report: Dokumente und Fakten zur Beurteilung eines sogenannten Rauschgifts* (Munich: R. Piper, 1970), 7–8. See also idem, *Wer wirft den ersten Stein?—Minoritäten in einer züchtigen Gesellschaft* (Munich: R. Piper, 1969).

31. Leonhardt, *Haschisch-Report,* 9.

certain legal drugs such as alcohol and tobacco and found hashish to be comparatively harmless. "The discussion over hashish/marijuana is in full swing," claimed Leonhardt. "And it will continue. It will, if I see it correctly, end in the legalization of hashish. But until it reaches that point, many more harmless hashish smokers and not so harmless hashish dealers must serve as scapegoats."[32] For Leonhardt the harm done by drug prohibition far outweighed the risk posed by decriminalizing drugs.[33] Most of all, Leonhardt wanted to be sure that the Federal Republic did not carelessly follow the American hard line against drug use. Though he did not go so far as to propose that hashish should be freely available to everyone, he did think that the indiscriminate punishment of drug offenders was dangerous and that many otherwise quite normal young people were being sentenced to terms in prison or psychiatric units unjustly.

Leonhardt took issue with the idea that hashish consumption should be treated as an addiction. Hashish, he claimed, was neither physically nor psychologically addictive if used in moderation. Yet the widespread ignorance about drug use led most to believe that hash smoking led necessarily to "illness, helplessness, addiction, and even criminality."[34] Leonhardt vehemently denied this. He argued, instead, that hashish consumption, rather than being a cause of illness, was merely an indicator of some other deeper problem. Young people did not "drop out" because they smoked hashish, he argued; they smoked hashish because they had already "dropped out." The campaign against hashish he decried as just another witch hunt: "We would like to know: Are women with red hair really witches? Does masturbation make you ill? Is hashish especially harmful?"[35]

Leonhardt understood that the most potent argument against hashish was that it led to heroin use. He attacked this position from two sides. First, he maintained that the scientific evidence was as yet inconclusive. Second, he pointed to the example of the United States, where statistical studies had shown that hashish consumption continued to increase while the number of junkies remained fairly constant. He believed that the only real connection between hashish and heroin

32. Ibid., 7.
33. Ibid., 9–10.
34. Ibid., 15.
35. Ibid., 16.

was that they were both illegal: "As long as hashish is criminalized, wherever there is hashish, opium will be available as well."[36] Criminalization failed to reduce consumption and led to unwarranted mistreatment of harmless hashish consumers in the form of prison and psychiatric wards. Even more preposterous to Leonhardt was the system of law that placed heroin, cocaine, and hashish on the same level. "Any legislation that believes it can subsume an injection of cocaine and a marijuana cigarette under the same category—whether 'narcotic' or 'drugs'—can only be unjust and for that reason must . . . one day be judged a failure."[37]

Leonhardt anticipated the criticism of his position. Conservative critics, he argued, when faced with the decriminalization of a behavior, whether it be homosexuality, abortion, or drugs, would automatically react as if the sky were falling and accuse proponents of decriminalization of fostering social disintegration: "Whoever supports the decriminalization of a behavior will always expose himself to the suspicion that he wants to propagate the behavior: Smoke hashish! Get a divorce! Love your own sex!"[38] Leonhardt insisted that this was not his purpose and that he did not recommend that anyone smoke hashish. Even so, he was convinced that "either hashish is a criminal act or it is not. The great majority of the sufficiently enlightened are in agreement that it is not."[39] This was, in fact, the key to the liberal position on hashish. Liberals claimed to expound the "enlightened" response, while accusing conservatives of floundering in moralistic and unscientific suppositions about the drug problem.

Leonhardt's liberalism stressed the freedom of the individual to make choices about his or her own body. He argued that any state that allows the water and air to be polluted and that prohibits neither the use of alcohol and nicotine nor the consumption of cyanide had no right to punish drug users who were aware of the dangers of their actions. This argument emphasized the arbitrary nature of the drug laws and pointed out the hypocrisy of the public health argument against drug consumption. For Leonhardt, freedom superceded the importance of protecting the commonweal or social order: "Though intoxication may result in a certain obstruction of the gears of a per-

36. Ibid., 34.
37. Ibid., 57.
38. Ibid., 35.
39. Ibid.

fected consumer society, this may not lead to an individual loss of freedom in any system that wants to be founded on 'freedom.'"[40] The only time when intoxication voided the right to freedom, Leonhardt claimed, was when it led directly to the commission of a crime. This idea of drug consumption as a victimless crime came to dominate liberal thinking about the drug problem.

The response of members of the psychiatric discipline was swift and sure. In an open letter to *Die Zeit,* Dr. Kleiner, a Berlin neurologist and psychotherapist, chastised Leonhardt as "hash apologist Nr. 1" and *Die Zeit* as his mouthpiece.[41] Kleiner argued that Leonhardt's careless declamations that hashish was not addictive had led countless youths astray. Kleiner called on the chief editor of the periodical, Marion Gräfin Dönhoff, to publish more scientifically sound information and to halt Leonhardt's dangerous polemics.[42]

The book was widely read and prompted a flurry of responses during the next few years.[43] The liberal tendency, shared by many of these publications, to treat hashish as no more harmful than alcohol and tobacco was not popular with the government, which tended to see this kind of argument as a trivialization of the "real" dangers of hashish consumption. Indeed, the parliamentary state secretary of the Federal Ministry for Youth, Family, and Health, Heinz Westfal, wrote to the chairman of the Trade Association of German Book Dealers (Börsenverein des deutschen Buchhandels) in July 1972, complaining that polemics such as Leonhardt's had led a large number of young people, who otherwise would not have tried drugs, to drug use. Westfal urged book publishers to take their duties seriously and urged the association to "resolve and recommend" to its members that they show care in publishing books that trivialized the dangers of drug consumption.[44] The chairman of the association rebuked Westfal's request, noting that

40. Ibid., 68.

41. Kleiner, "Offener Brief an 'Die Zeit' in Sache Rudolf Walter Leonhardt und seine Haschisch-Apologetik," *Suchtgefahren* 18, no. 1 (1972): 30.

42. Ibid., 30–31.

43. For example, see Ulf Homann, *Das Haschischverbot: Gesellschaftliche Funktion und Wirkung* (Frankfurt am Main: Fischer-Taschenbuch, 1972), and Ulli Olvedi, *LSD-Report* (Frankfurt am Main: Suhrkamp, 1972). Another influential work was the Marxist interpretation of the drug trade by Amendt and Stiehler, *Sucht Profit Sucht:* an updated version is Günter Amendt, *Sucht Profit Sucht* (Frankfurt am Main: Zweitausendeins, 1984).

44. Letter published in Bundesministerium für Jugend, Familie und Gesundheit, *Dokumente zum Drogenproblem mit Information für Eltern und Erzieher* (Düsseldorf: Econ, 1972), 169–70.

such an action fell outside of the responsibility of the association and conflicted with the absolute freedom of the press.[45]

The Federal Government's Action Program and the New Narcotics Law

As can be seen from the positions taken by the Hamburg Bürgerschaft and Senate and by the publications of the liberal popular press, consumption and distribution of drugs were widely perceived as separate issues. As a result the federal government committed itself to a strategy that increased the pressure applied to drug traffickers and dealers while strengthening the possibilities for consumers to receive help for their drug problems. Though the intricacies of the German federal system left it in a weak legislative position to have much of an effect on the drug problem, it could both pour money on the problem and provide coordination of state and federal, as well as public and private, drug abatement strategies. On 12 November 1970, Federal Minister for Youth, Family, and Health Käte Strobel announced the federal government's Action Program for Combating Drug and Narcotic Abuse (Aktionsprogramm der Bundesregierung zur Bekämpfung des Drogen- und Rauschmittelmißbrauchs). The Action Program called for federal government intervention in three areas: preventative education programs, therapeutic services for drug users, and legislative measures.

First, and of great importance to the federal government, was the need to organize preventative measures against the further spread of drug addiction. The Action Program called for a national education campaign to be created by the Federal Center for Health Education (Bundeszentrale für gesundheitliche Aufklärung) in Cologne. This campaign was to include brochures, posters, and advertisements in the press, on radio and television, and at the movies. The campaign focused on a single slogan: "Hashish ruins you, while the dealer makes money." On the posters, this phrase was placed next to a picture of a tragic figure smoking a large joint. At the same time, teachers, counselors, youth leaders, and social workers attended seminars about the dangers of drug addiction, in order to be able to recognize young people with drug problems and point them toward help. Finally, the federal government committed itself to financial support of private orga-

45. Ibid., 170–71.

nizations, such as Action Youth Protection and the Deutsche Hauptstelle gegen die Suchtgefahren.[46]

Second, the federal government agreed to provide financial assistance for therapeutic initiatives. It promised to fund model programs
in the various states, especially in the larger cities. These were to
include counseling centers, ambulant care, and stationary therapeutic
centers, both public and private. The federal government stated that
the current care of drug-addicted youth in psychiatric wards of local
hospitals was unacceptable and promised aid for clinics devoted
specifically to treating these troubled youth.[47]

Finally, the federal government vowed to increase the pressure on
the illegal trade in drugs through legislation. The constitution of the
Federal Republic limited the government, however, in the force it
could bring to bear: fighting crime was the responsibility of the individual states.[48] Before 1972, the Federal Criminal Police held little
direct policing power, acting instead as an information clearinghouse.
On the other hand, the federal government did have the power to
amend the list of controlled substances. The Action Program included
a number of measures to include new designer drugs, such as LSD, in
the list of controlled substances[49] and to tighten the control over nar-

---

46. Ibid., 106–7.

47. Ibid., 107–8.

48. This is set out in Article 30, 83 of the Basic Law.

49. The process of including new controlled drugs under the Opium Law, and later under
the Narcotics Law, was ongoing, prompted by new patterns of youth drug consumption and
international agreements, especially the Single Convention of 1961, to which the Federal
Republic was a signatory. The Single Convention was not ratified, however, until 2 February
1973; see Bundestag Drucksache 7/126, 7/638, and 7/2557. There were a number of additions
to the list of controlled substances between 1967 and 1975, including LSD, mescalin, psilocy-
bin, and DOM (STP). By 1974, the number of drugs that could not be prescribed within the
Federal Republic had reached 102. See "Verordnung über die den Betäubungsmitteln gleichgestellten Stoffe vom 21. Februar 1967," *Bundesgesetzblatt*, 1967, pt. 1, 197–98; "Verordnung zur Änderung der Verordnung über das Verschreiben Betäubungsmittel enthaltender
Arzneien und ihre Abgabe in den Apotheken vom 23. Februar 1967," *Bundesgesetzblatt*,
1967, pt. 1, 227–31; "Fünfte Verordnung über die den Betäubungsmitteln gleichgestellten
Stoffe vom 6. April 1971," *Bundesgesetzblatt*, 1971, pt. 1, 315–16; "Verordnung zur Änderung
der Verordnung über das Verschreiben Betäubungsmittel enthaltender Arzneien und ihre
Abgabe in den Apotheken vom 6. April 1971," *Bundesgesetzblatt*, 1971, pt. 1, 317–19; "Sechste
Verordnung über die den Betäubungsmitteln gleichgestellten Stoffe vom 17. Januar 1974,"
Bundesgesetzblatt, 1974, pt. 1, 97–98; "Verordnung über das Verschreiben, die Abgabe und
den Nachweis des Verbleibs von Betäubungsmitteln vom 24. Januar 1974," *Bundesgesetzblatt*, 1974, pt. 1, 110–18.

cotics in pharmacies, including requiring special prescription forms for controlled substances.[50] Further, it could change the amended Weimar-era Opium Law, which many believed to be antiquated and unsuited for the realities of the new drug trade. The proposal for a new Narcotics Law (Gesetz über den Verkehr mit Betäubungsmitteln) strengthened penalties for drug traffickers and dealers, while reducing the penalties for drug consumers. Under the 1929 Opium Law, the maximum penalty for any transgression was three years in prison and a fine. The new proposal raised the maximum for "especially serious cases"—which included delivery of drugs to a minor under age eighteen, as well as drug crimes committed as part of an organized gang— to a minimum of one year and a maximum of ten years in prison.[51] It also criminalized possession of a controlled substance (not expressly considered a crime under the old Opium Law), punishable by up to three years in prison; this cleared up some confusion in the courts.[52] At the same time, however, judges were given more leeway in deciding whom to prosecute; for example, charges against an individual accused of possessing or acquiring drugs "for personal consumption in small amounts" could be dismissed. It took more than two years for the new Narcotics Law to work its way through the legislative process, but when it was finally promulgated on 1 December 1972, the new law had changed little from the proposals of the Action Program.

In addition to the legal changes, the federal government sought to increase the cooperation between different levels of policing. Though the Federal Criminal Police was designed to act mainly as a collection point for information, the Action Program called for their intervention in cases of international smuggling. In cases of dispute between different states over jurisdiction, the Federal Criminal Police were empowered to decide which state retained jurisdiction. In addition to their

50. Bundesministerium für Jugend, Familie und Gesundheit, *Dokumente zum Drogenproblem,* 104.

51. "Novellierung des Opiumgesetzes: Härtere Strafen beim Handel mit Suchtstoffen," in Bundesministerium für Jugend, Familie und Gesundheit, *Dokumente zum Drogenproblem,* 113–14. See also "Gesetz zur Änderung des Gesetzes über den Verkehr mit Betäubungsmitteln (Opiumgesetz) vom 22. Dezember 1971," *Bundesgesetzblatt,* 1971, pt. 1, 2092–97. An excellent commentary on the new Betäubungsmittelgesetz is Walter Becker, ed., *Betäubungsmittelgesetz: Möglichkeiten und Grenzen* (Hamm: Hoheneck, 1972).

52. Walter Becker cites two cases in particular: Amtsgericht in Mönchengladbach AZ 10 Ds 78/70 and OLG Stuttgart vom 3.6.1971 AZ 2ss 181/71; Becker, *Betäubungsmittelgesetz,* 29.

duties within Germany, they were charged with coordinating international cooperation, including contact with Interpol, bordering states, and the American Bureau of Narcotics and Dangerous Drugs (after 1973 renamed the Drug Enforcement Administration), which had an office at the U.S. embassy in Bonn.[53] Finally, due to the widespread belief that foreigners and particularly Turkish and Iranian guest workers were deeply involved in drug smuggling, the Action Program called for a change to the Foreigner Law that would allow the immediate deportation of foreigners convicted of drug offenses after the completion of their prison sentences.[54]

The Action Program set out in detail the role the federal government would play in the coming years in combating the drug problem. The loose federal system prevented the national government from playing much of a direct role in the day-to-day fight against the drug trade. Though they retained control of the customs agency, which played a crucial role in interdiction at the nation's borders, and though the strength and reach of the Federal Criminal Police would grow in the coming years due in no small part to the growing problem of policing the international drug trade, the federal government was relegated to funding local projects and coordinating local efforts. The everyday job of dealing with drug abuse fell to the various states.

Policy in Hamburg

While the federal government attempted to foster new approaches to drug policy and abuse prevention, the bulk of the work of drug policy-making fell to the states. In Hamburg, it was not until 1971 that new programs received necessary organizational and fiscal support. On 16 March 1971, the Hamburg Senate made its first comprehensive statement on the drug problem. "The possibility that the psychic stability of a considerable portion of the maturing generation will be endangered can no longer be ruled out," the Senate declared. "The Senate has keenly followed the development in Hamburg and has instituted a

53. On the influence of the American drug enforcement establishment in Germany, see H. Richard Friman's excellent comparative book, *Narcodiplomacy: Exporting the U.S. War on Drugs* (Ithaca: Cornell University Press, 1996), 87–112.

54. Bundesministerium für Jugend, Familie und Gesundheit, *Dokumente zum Drogenproblem*, 106.

series of necessary measures. It is of the opinion, that these coordinating efforts must be considerably strengthened."[55] The report laid out a number of reasons for the increased awareness of the need to do something and the need to do it immediately. Between 1967 and 1970, the number of drug offenses had mushroomed 1,800 percent, from 235 in 1968 to 1,878 in 1970. Some of this increase, the Senate report noted, could be traced to the increase in police activity, yet the numbers were still shocking. Pharmacy break-ins in Hamburg continued to increase, from none in 1967 to 134 in 1970; this number did not include the 85 break-ins in the surrounding countryside during 1969. Furthermore, since 1967 eight young people had died as a result of drug use.

The number of schoolchildren using drugs had increased drastically. A study of 497 Hamburg teens from the three highest academic high school grades by Professor J. M. Burchard of the University Hospital at Eppendorf concluded that 31.6 percent of young men and 17.6 percent of young women had tried drugs and that only 56 percent claimed to be disinterested in taking drugs. Taking into account the number of Hamburg youth born between 1945 and 1957, the Senate surmised that between five thousand and fifteen thousand young people frequently consumed drugs. Of the underage consumers, the Authority for Schools, Youth, and Vocational Training reported that the bulk attended academic high schools (*Gymnasium*) but warned that the number of users in Hamburg's vocational schools (*Berufsschulen*) and secondary modern schools (*Realschulen*) was on the rise. Though most of the young people limited their drug use to hashish or marijuana, the use of hard drugs was also on the rise. They estimated the core of intravenous drug users to number at least one thousand, with the number undoubtedly rising.

The Senate's view of the existing trends and prognostications about the future of drug abuse was far from rosy. As they did in 1969, members of the Senate in 1971 did not simply dismiss drug use as criminal activity or as an exceptional illness. Senators placed the blame for this trend in a number of areas. First, they argued that modern industrial society saw drug use as an acceptable way to produce a "desired physical or psychological 'normal state.'" Self-medication for almost any

der Bürgerschaft HH, VII/1115; Mitteilung des Senats an die Bürger-
des Mißbrauchs von Rauschmitteln, 16 March 1971, 1.

ailment had become a reflex. Second, they observed that many young people, particularly young intellectuals, were rejecting the demands of the "productive society." What had been perceived as a normal generational conflict had transformed into widespread protest. The desire to protest often led to radical political activity, but it also produced a youth subculture that used drugs to "lift the 'hostility' of the world through altering their consciousness, if only for a short while." This basic mistrust of the adult world by young drug users, according to the Senate report, was the main difficulty in attempting to steer children and teens away from drug use.[56]

The Senate emphatically argued that hashish was a "gateway" drug that opened the door to hard drug use.[57] The Senate found the widespread belief that hashish and marijuana were less harmful than other drugs to be specious and unscientific. They argued that the spread of these ideas led young people to question whether the dangers of hard drugs, such as opium, were also exaggerated. Hashish acted as a sort of barrier. If young people crossed one barrier, they were more likely to believe that all barriers were artificial. Furthermore, the Senate stressed that hashish was psychologically addictive and could lead to passivity and alteration of one's personality. In certain predisposed individuals, the first joint could lead to addiction and a loss of personal freedom. "It is certainly proper that the trade in hemp drugs not be legalized," the Senate concluded. "Whether, on the other hand, it is appropriate to do without any differentiation between hemp drugs and other narcotics, the future must prove."[58]

In order to combat the rising rates of drug consumption, the Senate proposed three types of measures: repressive, therapeutic, and prophylactic. In the area of repression, the Senate saw little to make them hopeful. Despite some success in fighting the organized trade in drugs, little had been or could be done about the continued proliferation of young people smuggling small amounts of various drugs into the country for their own use or to share with friends. Nor could much be done to stifle the trade within Hamburg itself. Effectively combating the

56. Ibid., 2.
57. The term for this in German is usually either *Umsteigeeffekt* or *Schrittmacherfunktion*.
58. Drucksache der Bürgerschaft HH, VII/1115; Mitteilung des Senats an die Bürgerschaft, Bekämpfung des Mißbrauchs von Rauschmitteln, 16 March 1971, 2–3.

internal trade would require instituting an extensive net of informants in Hamburg's schools at the very least, and this for practical and political reasons would be far less than ideal. Due to their inability to repress consumers, the Senate decided that the police should focus on breaking the organized trade in drugs. To facilitate the fight against drug dealers, the Senate authorized a doubling of Hamburg's drug squad.[59] Other measures proposed by the Senate were an increase in the Youth Protection Units, an increase in the personnel assigned to drug crimes at the district attorney's office, an increase in the laboratory capacity for testing confiscated drugs and urine samples, and a reduction in the amount of narcotics held in pharmacies.[60]

If the range of repressive measures available seemed grim, therapeutic solutions appeared moribund, despite the plans first articulated in 1969. According to the Senate, young addicts were not seeking help, and when they did, they were often in a very bad state of physical and mental health. Even when they sought and received medical attention, such as a medically supervised withdrawal, the rate of success was dismal, and they practically all soon returned to drug use. The Senate placed at least part of the blame on the inadequate facilities. The General Hospital at Ochsenzoll, where most young addicts were sent for withdrawal treatment, only provided emergency stationary care and lacked any social services or psychotherapy. The lack of proper facilities dedicated to young drug users had led Hamburg judges to sentence offenders to long terms in reformatories, which only exacerbated the problem because these facilities also lacked any counseling or psychotherapeutic services.

With all this in mind, the Senate proclaimed that "without intensive psychotherapy and social therapy in addition to withdrawal cures a long-lasting success is not attainable" and proposed that new forms of private long-term care, such as therapeutic living communities, should receive state financial support.[61] Though other larger-scale initiatives were not immediately possible, the Senate planned to open a public

59. Ibid., 3–4.
60. Ibid., 6.
61. When the report was promulgated two *Wohngemeinschaften* were operative (Reitbrook, run by Jugendhilfe e.V., and Graumannsweg, run by Jugend hilft Jugend e.V.), and two others were in the planning stages (to be run by Release Hamburg and Verein zur Bekämpfung der Rauschgiftgefahr).

institution for at-risk drug users by the first half of 1972; it would include twenty-five beds and a full staff complement. To deal with the rise in the number of young drug addicts in Hamburg's prisons, the Senate planned to transfer all drug-addicted inmates to the Vierlande juvenile detention institution and to provide medical personnel from the Health Authority.

The difficulties at the General Hospital at Ochsenzoll also prompted the Senate to call for the hiring of social therapeutic and social pedagogic professionals. It instructed each of the regional health offices to hire a full-time youth psychiatrist and a full-time welfare worker to deal with the increasing number of intravenous drug users. Likewise, the Senate called on the Youth Department to offer counseling to every young drug user and to institute a new program of "street work," in which social workers would do outreach work and try to bring drug users into contact with social services. Since young drug users should also have a place to seek counseling, the Senate proposed a walk-in counseling center to be paid for by the state. Finally, because the number of young drug users had increased at a substantial rate in comparison with adults, the age of maturity would, in the case of drug abuse, be lowered from age twenty-one to eighteen; this would allow the Work and Social Welfare Authority to shoulder part of the burden by taking over the cases of eighteen- to twenty-one-year-olds from the Youth Authority.[62]

Because of the difficulties in treating drug addiction once it began to run its course, the Senate declared that the key to fighting addiction must rest with prophylactic measures. The goal of these educational programs must be to convince younger children not to begin using drugs, to reduce the number of hashish users who moved on to hard drug consumption, and to convince not yet addicted hashish users to give up drug use altogether. Since many young people were skeptical about antidrug messages, which they often saw as simplistic scare tactics, the Senate stressed that educational programs must be based on scientifically indisputable arguments. The challenge was to convince young people that adults and the state were telling the truth about drugs.

62. Drucksache der Bürgerschaft HH, VII/1115; Mitteilung des Senats an die Bürgerschaft, Bekämpfung des Mißbrauchs von Rauschmitteln, 16 March 1971, 6–7.

The Senate proposed a number of prophylactic measures. First, in order to gauge the success of prophylactic programs, it demanded regular surveys of drug consumption in Hamburg.[63] The Senate proposed support for three programs undertaken by the psychiatric clinic at the University Hospital at Eppendorf: a representative survey of Hamburg's students, a study of long-term drug users, and a double-blind experiment with pure cannabinol (liquid THC). Further, each school should have a teacher educated in the drug problem who could run classes on the dangers of drug abuse as well as counsel students, parents, and other teachers with questions about drug abuse.[64]

Finally, the Senate provided for the institution of a Coordination, Information, and Documentation Center, which would be charged with a number of tasks: providing overall planning, monitoring progress, collecting and archiving information about drug abuse, disseminating information to those involved in the drug abuse field, making professional literature available in a library, writing press reports, and publishing brochures and posters, among many other duties.

The measures proposed by the Senate in this first comprehensive report on drug addiction were wide-ranging and expensive. The total projected cost for these programs reached well over two million deutsche marks, of which the vast majority went to personnel salaries. Despite the emphasis in the report on prophylaxis, most of the money went to policing and therapeutic measures. The police were allocated over DM 800,000, while the therapeutic measures received more than twice that amount. Prevention accounted for only DM 360,000, and the bulk of that went to the Coordination, Information, and Documentation Center.

Despite the obvious urgency of the issue, the Senate's report was shunted off into a special committee made up of the sociopolitical and health committees of the Bürgerschaft. The joint committee met a number of times during the spring of 1971 and called a large number of experts and interested parties to comment on the state of the problem and the Senate plan.[65] The experts who testified before the committee stressed preventative measures and counseling. They saw dissemina-

63. Ibid., 4–5.

64. Ibid., 7.

65. The transcripts for these meetings can be found in StAH, 351-10 II, Sozialbehörde II, Abl.3 135.22-8-1 Band 1.

tion of information and drug education as the keys to dealing with the drug problem, but only if the information was scientific and irrefutable rather than simply an attempt to scare young people. Many of the experts were psychiatric professionals, and most of these believed that counseling centers staffed with knowledgeable professionals were necessary because drug use was merely an outward sign of the preexisting psychiatric problems of the young users. At the same time, counseling could only succeed if the family was involved; therefore, drug therapy also meant family therapy.[66]

As to the ever-present question of hashish as a gateway drug, the committee reported that, although hashish consumption did not automatically lead to hard drug use, this was a real and present danger. Despite this belief that drug use was in fact a slippery slope, the committee stressed that drug abuse was first and foremost a medical problem and that drug users were ill and deserving of a humane response. As a result, the committee recommended that "The conventional, traditional withdrawal treatment within clinics must be replaced by a psychotherapeutic or a social-therapeutic treatment." They saw little hope of undertaking this type of treatment within state-run institutions since young people tended to see the authorities as tools of a repressive regime. Much of this resentment was justified, because the lack of dedicated facilities had meant that young people with drug problems had been incarcerated in closed psychiatric units with the general psychiatric population without a specific program and with little or no aftercare.[67] As a result of the lack of proper facilities, counseling, and aftercare, the experts predicted that the failure rate was somewhere close to 100 percent. They hoped that new private therapeutic communities would play a key role by offering the kind of aftercare unavailable in public hospitals.[68]

66. Drucksache der Bürgerschaft HH, VII/1448; Gemeinsamer Bericht des Sozialpolitischen Ausschußes und des Gesundheitsausschußes, 29 September 1971, 1–2.

67. A series of articles in the *Frankfurter Rundschau* between February and June 1971 led to a debate in the Bürgerschaft over the treatment of patients in the General Hospital at Ochsenzoll, which housed most of the young drug addicts during their withdrawal treatment. See Stenographische Berichten der Bürgerschaft HH, VII, 35. Sitzung am 2. Juni 1971, 1841–1847. On this issue, see also Valentin Schiedek, "Zur Drogensituation in Hamburg," *hjr info: Information des Hamburger Jugendringes* (February 1971): 14.

68. Drucksache der Bürgerschaft HH, VII/1448; Gemeinsamer Bericht des Sozialpolitischen Ausschußes und des Gesundheitsausschußes, 29 September 1971, 2–3.

The committee reported its findings to the Bürgerschaft on 9 September 1971. The final recommendations were a strange blend of pragmatism and denial. The committee sought to place youth drug consumption within the scope of normal behavior. "A sign of every generation is the break from defined societal norms, especially by young people," they argued. "Similar examples one could think of are alcoholism and youth criminality. Drug consumption, in any case, must be seen in this context."[69] Yet the committee failed to take into account the quickly changing nature of the drug trade and the emergence of class and ethnic difference in drug consumption and distribution: "The special danger to youth from socially underprivileged classes observed in the USA cannot, in general, be confirmed in the Federal Republic because the exceptional social problems such as racial prejudice and unemployment do not exist."[70] This, of course, was patently untrue. The rapid increase of the number of Turkish guest workers in Germany, though solving an urgent need for labor, had begun to exacerbate feelings of ethnicity and racial difference, especially in relationship to the issue of drug trafficking. And the shortage of labor that led to the rapid increase in the number of foreign citizens in Germany was coming to an end; two years later, with the onset of the global energy crisis set off by the Organization of Petroleum Exporting Countries (OPEC) oil embargo, the labor market would slump and the issue of race and ethnicity would be further aggravated.

Ultimately, the committee's recommendations closely followed the program laid out by the Senate. The committee believed that "the drug problem should be taken very seriously and that the consumption of hashish should not be seen as harmless." The committee argued that the chances of healing drug addicts were slim, even with the proper treatment. Therefore, they proposed that prophylaxis should be the main aim of the drug response.[71] On 3 November 1971, the Bürgerschaft agreed to fund the measures included in the revised plan, budgeting approximately 2.5 million marks.[72] This sweeping plan built the

69. Ibid., 1.

70. Ibid.

71. Ibid., 3.

72. Drucksache der Bürgerschaft HH, VII/1498; Dringlicher Antrag! Sofortmaßnahmen zur Bekämpfung des Mißbrauchs von Rauschmitteln, 19 October 1971. For the debate, see Stenographische Bericht der Bürgerschaft HH, 7. Wahlperiode, 46. Sitzung am 3. Nov. 1971, 2295–2309. See also BfI, Referat Drogen und Sucht, Eckhard Günther, "Die Maßnahmen Hamburgs gegen den Rauschmittelmißbrauch," n.d., 5.

foundation of Hamburg's response to drug addiction, and its basic outline changed little until the onset of the AIDS crisis in the mid-1980s.

The Jasinsky Survey and Public Opinion

While Hamburg's plan was being considered by the joint committee, new information came to light about the extent of drug consumption. The release of the first representative survey of drug consumption by Hamburg's schoolchildren, the so-called Jasinsky Report, on 30 August 1971 marked a turning point in the public understanding of the drug problem. The following day the *Hamburger Abendblatt* ran a front-page story on the report. The headlines outlined the study's findings in bold print:

The first Hamburg drug report is a shock!
An alarming number of children smoke hash
3,000 students sell narcotics
14,600 of Hamburg students over 14 years of age take drugs regularly. Therefore every eighth [student].
A further 10,600 have already had contact with drugs, consuming them occasionally.
Around half of Hamburg students maintain that they can get hashish within 24 hours.
The largest number of drug consumers are between 14 and 16.
Around 3,000 students occasionally or regularly deal drugs.

The *Abendblatt* concluded: "The drug wave splashes higher than many have heretofore suspected."[73]

Michael Jasinsky, a sociologist at the Seminar for Social Sciences at the University of Hamburg, carried out the survey of 4,797 students.[74] The results contradicted a widely held image of the academic high schools as the center of drug consumption.[75] Once the prerogative of

73. "Erster Hamburger Drogen-report ist ein Schock!" *Hamburger Abendblatt,* 31 August 1971. Also located in StAH, 351-10 II, Sozialbehörde II, Abl.3 135.20-0 Band 3.

74. Staatliche Pressestelle Hamburg, "Drogenkonsum Hamburger Schüler: Ergebnisse einer im Auftrag der Behörde für Schule, Jugend und Berufsbildung durchgeführten Untersuchung," 30 August 1971, 1–2. For an extended discussion of the methodology and problems of the survey, see Arthur Kreuzer, *Drogen und Delinquenz,* 55–66.

75. StAH, 136.1, BfI, 1108, Lamprecht, "Kleine Anfrage des abgeordneten Bergmann," 22 September 1969. StAH, 351-10 II, Sozialbehörde II, Abl.3 135.20-0 Band 1, Ruhnau and

relatively well-off children, drug use had quickly spread throughout the Hamburg school system. The highest percentage of consumers attended vocational schools, where one-third of those students had used drugs at least once; one-fifth claimed to be regular drug consumers, and a further one-fifth displayed some interest in trying drugs. In the academic high schools, only slightly more than 15 percent admitted to using drugs, and less than 8 percent used drugs frequently. The percentages in the secondary normal schools were only slightly higher than those in the academic high schools. In all, Jasinsky projected that 25,289 Hamburg students had used drugs at least once, 14,642 took drugs regularly, and a further 22,301 expressed interest in trying drugs.[76]

The survey also proved what policymakers, politicians, and the police had long feared: the age of drug consumers was dropping rapidly. Over half of all drug consumers were under the age of sixteen, while almost 10 percent were under fourteen. The percentage of those questioned who admitted using drugs at least once increased with age. Approximately 16 percent under the age of fourteen had at least tried drugs, while the percentage of seventeen- to twenty-year-olds rose to 39 percent. The age of first drug use also varied by sex. Though less likely to try drugs in the first place, girls were more likely than boys to try drugs at an early age. Until age sixteen, the percentage of girls who tried drugs for the first time was higher than the percentage of boys. After age sixteen, the opposite was true. Indeed, almost 65 percent of female consumers tried drugs before their sixteenth birthday, while only 53 percent of male consumers did the same. Yet in the long run, more young men than young women tried drugs.[77]

For the vast majority of consumers, hashish was the drug they consumed first. For nearly half of those surveyed, hashish was the only drug they had tried. One-quarter had used at least three drugs, and another one-eighth had tried at least four. In all, 82 percent of consumers had tried hashish, 50 percent stimulants, 19 percent hallucinogens, and 7 percent opiates. Far fewer had injected drugs; only 2.2 per-

Birckholz, "Kleine Anfrage des Abgeordneten Bergmann an den Senat, betreffenend," 23 September 1969. Drucksache der Bürgerschaft HH, VII/1115; Mitteilung des Senats an die Bürgerschaft, Bekämpfung des Mißbrauchs von Rauschmitteln, 16 March 1971, 2.

76. Staatliche Pressestelle Hamburg, "Drogenkonsum Hamburger Schüler": 3–4.

77. Ibid., 4–5.

cent admitted to injecting opiates, and only 1.8 percent had tried amphetamines.[78]

Social class played a role in determining who tried drugs. Jasinsky found that the upper and upper middle classes were overrepresented. The middle and lower middle classes were only slightly underrepresented, and the lower class was heavily underrepresented. Although Jasinsky recognized that class was a factor, he gave no reason for this discrepancy.[79]

The survey also included a number of questions designed to determine the social causes of drug use. Many of the questions focused on factors associated with delinquency. Jasinsky found that drug consumers were more likely to come from single-parent families than nonconsumers. They were much more likely to have an unhappy home life and more likely to have alcoholic or drug-addicted family members. Young drug users skipped school and ran away from home much more frequently than nonconsumers. Affluence also correlated with drug consumption. Students who had more than thirty deutsche marks of pocket money a week were two and a half times more likely to try drugs than those with less. Likewise, students whose father had finished an academic diploma (*Abitur*) tried drugs more often than others. Drug use also correlated with other substance abuse. Students who admitted to being drunk in the previous two months were twice as likely to try drugs. And smokers were three times as likely to have at least experimented with drugs. The strongest correlation, however, proved to be the drug consumption of friends. Students were more than six times as likely to try drugs if their best friend used drugs. The final question asked whether students agreed with the statement "This society can be changed only through revolution." Less than 10 percent of nonconsumers agreed with this statement, while 22 percent of consumers answered in the affirmative.[80]

Jasinsky also wanted to know how easy it was for students to purchase drugs. He asked each student whether they could find drugs within twenty-four hours. Nearly half answered that they could purchase hashish in the allotted amount of time. More than one-quarter

78. Ibid., 6.
79. Ibid., 7–8.
80. Ibid., 9.

could find stimulants, and fifteen percent could buy opiates. Even more shocking, nearly 10 percent of students admitted to having sold drugs in order to pay for their own consumption. A little less than half of these claimed to be selling drugs at the time that the survey was given.[81]

At the same time the Jasinsky survey was under way, the Institute for Applied Social Science carried out a survey of public opinion in Hamburg about the drug problem.[82] The surveyors asked a representative sample of 1,009 Hamburg citizens over the age of eighteen their opinions about the increase in drug abuse in the metropolitan region. In addition to their opinions, respondents were asked their age, gender, and educational level, as well as their reading habits. The assumption of the surveyors was that this information would give a clear indication about the relationship between different social groups and their opinions on drug consumption.[83]

The results of the survey were striking in some respects and predictable in others. The most conspicuous finding of the surveyors concluded that the vast majority of Hamburg's residents knew little if anything about drugs. Though most Hamburg citizens claimed to know what hashish was, only 35 percent had ever heard of heroin. The survey also highlighted very real generational and class-based opinions about drug use. Older people tended to see drugs as a great threat to society and to believe that all drugs were roughly equivalent. Individuals under the age of thirty thought of drugs as less dangerous and believed that hashish posed much less of a threat than heroin and other hard drugs. Members of the middle and upper classes and the better educated tended to be more liberal toward drug consumption than the working class. Yet taken as a whole, the survey showed that Hamburg's residents did not perceive the drug wave as a great priority in comparison with housing, unemployment, and education. The poll, however, was not widely published and failed to have the same impact as the Jasinsky Report and its much more sensational conclusions.

81. Ibid., 10.
82. Institut für angewandte Sozialwissenschaften, "Meinungen in Hamburg zum Rauschgiftproblem," April 1971.
83. Ibid., 1–8.

Conclusion

The first three years of the 1970s was a crucial period in the development of Germany's drug problems and solutions. In those three years, a window of opportunity was opened; traditional understandings of drug use and addiction, social structures and deviance, and welfare and consumption could be questioned. The problem of drug use by young people became a public problem, and the public understanding of drugs, and in particular the distinction between hard and soft drugs, was still a matter of intense disagreement in the early seventies.

The politics of drugs went through an ambivalent transformation between 1969 and 1973. The psychiatric model that dominated the understanding and treatment of addiction came under a concerted attack, not by young drug consumers but by liberals like Rudolf Walter Leonhardt and even members of the SPD and the Free Democratic Party (FDP). The debates over drugs were discussions about the real problems associated with drug abuse, but they were also, at the same time, conflicts over the legacies of 1968. In many ways, it was a debate over the process of modernization and what it did to young people.

Rather than merely a technical debate over the relative merits of abatement and treatment strategies, the debate became a locus for a debate over the limits of protest, the extent of youth anomie in post-industrial society, and the "success" of the affluent society. At the same time, it was a debate about two sets of values, one in decline and the other ascendant. These two sets of values did not track directly with political parties, though there was certainly a correlation between party and the approach to drugs. But in a larger sense these sets of values—the youth protection paradigm versus the therapeutic mind-set—were part of a larger conflict over the path of modernization in the Federal Republic.

The debates over drugs, along with larger debates over sexuality and gender, pornography, and deviance, severely tested the dominance of the youth protection paradigm that had emerged under the Kaiserreich to deal with the effects of industrialization, that thrived both under the Weimar Republic and Nazi dictatorship, and that reemerged largely unscathed after the Second World War. This youth protection ethos perceived modern society as a threat to traditional relationships, particularly gender relationships and class relationships. In particular, consumer culture threatened traditional forms of socialization. For those who still held to this position in the early seventies, drugs were only the most glaring example of the harm of consumer society on the nation's youth. This mind-set, under attack by a changing culture since the midsixties, survived the debates over drugs, but with the power of its ideas and the power to implement policy almost obliterated. In the end, the Youth Protection ethos could not survive the transformation of the Federal Republic into a more democratic state after 1968. Its static image of an idyllic, orderly national community could not easily coexist with the triumph of consumer capitalism, with its extravagant claims to the primacy of personal choice, over the course of the sixties.

The ascendant ethos—the therapeutic mind-set—fit much more comfortably into the new Germany. It was, in many respects, the much-subdued remnants of the revolutionary spirit of 1968. This therapeutic mind-set, though associated with the political Left, proved to be more individualistic than that of the youth protectionists. It saw individuals as victims of society, usually capitalist society. It saw protest as a quite reasonable response to the state and to the inequities in the economy, and it focused on the psychological damage perpetrated on individuals by society. In the debates over drugs, this therapeutic mind-set won a partial victory. The psychiatric model of drug use as an individual pathology that had dominated the treatment of drug addiction in most of the twentieth century was challenged and changed by the democratic sentiments of the therapeutic ethos. In a sense, the therapeutic ethos managed to transform the understanding of the causes of addiction, replacing the view that drug addiction was an outward sign of individual failure with a model that saw drug addiction as a reaction to the anomie created by modernization.

Yet this victory was ephemeral and contained certain compromises. While the individual drug consumer became "normal" and understandable, the same graciousness did not apply to dealers and traffickers. Drug policy became bifurcated: consumers deserved therapy while dealers deserved prison, a policy that proved to be remarkably unsuccessful in both respects. Yet this was the exhausted compromise reached by 1974. Policing remained a central focus of drug policy, but consumers became a social problem rather than strictly a criminal problem. This compromise, despite its contradictions, lasted for over a decade until the spread of AIDS in the mideighties and the emergence of an international "harm reduction" movement led to a fundamental shift in thinking.

The therapeutic ethos was, in many respects, energetic and innovative. The idea that drug consumption was not merely an external sign of personal failure, along with the collapse of the political will to use the state's full coercive power against young people after 1968, allowed the space for radical experiments in how to actually deal with drug addiction on the level of everyday life. It is to these new models that we shift next.

5. Treating Addicts

While politicians and the press debated drugs in the early 1970s, attempting to apportion blame and define the lines between victims and perpetrators, public and private groups attempted to find some way to deal with the new drug problem. The intensity of interest in drug treatment and the wide variety of approaches to the problem grew rapidly at the very end of the sixties as traditional addiction treatment organizations and new groups coming out of the drug scene sought new forms for dealing with the drug wave. The number of treatment options for young addicts exploded in the first two years of the seventies throughout the Federal Republic. By 1971, the Federal Ministry for Youth, Family, and Health counted 118 organizations that offered help to drug users. These included both traditional medical and welfare organizations and new associations founded for the express purpose of treating drug misuse. The kinds of treatment available included five withdrawal clinics, over fifty counseling centers, and over forty therapeutic communities.[1]

The breadth of experimentation in drug treatment reached its peak in the first few years of the seventies as the state and traditional welfare organizations attempted to adapt to the rise of drug addiction and new groups formed to offer alternative drug therapy, all in an attempt to stem the tide of drug addiction. The types of organizations involved ranged from traditional religious welfare organizations to radical groups formed from ex-users or students imbued with the radicalism of 1968 and interested in working with marginal groups (*Randgruppen*).

Both the state and the new private associations looked to international models to find new ways to deal with what was perceived as a

---

1. Martin Schmid, *Drogenhilfe in Deutschland: Entstehung und Entwicklung 1970–2000* (Frankfurt am Main: Campus, 2003), 135.

new problem. Methods of treatment came from American models as well as from the United Kingdom and Scandinavia. Indeed, the rise of a new treatment regime was an international undertaking. Yet while Germans looked abroad for models, the resulting groups and approaches were inflected by local traditions and the events of the previous half decade.

While the medical profession focused on the immediate problem of drug withdrawal and stabilization, the traditional welfare groups and new associations attempted to deal with the everyday problems of drug users on the street and the desperate need for long-term care. The boundaries between older welfare groups, the state, and the new, more radical associations were both real and porous. Perhaps the most striking aspect of the profusion of new treatment models in the early seventies was the interaction between the state and private associations. Hamburg, along with other states, proved to be remarkably willing to fund experimentation, even when the goals of the groups involved seemed to clash with the goals of the state. The reasons for this willingness to carve out a space for experimentation are complex. They include both a sense of the overwhelming mass of the problem that threatened to break the traditional forms of addiction treatment and even the psychiatric departments of major hospitals; the intervention of state bureaucrats like Eckhard Günther who proved willing to give considerable space to radical groups with the hope that they might be effective; and, not least, the substantial cost differential between traditional modes of treatment and the new groups. Yet the most powerful impetus to allow radical experimentation was the sheer scale of the problem; for a time, the state was willing to give almost anyone a chance to help.

The experiments in Hamburg took a number of forms: therapeutic communities, counseling centers, street workers, and a new drug treatment hospital. Some were public, some private, and some a collaboration between the two. Some were consummately staid and professional, and some were so loosely organized and radical that drug treatment served part of a larger vision of transforming society. Yet this period of experimentation only lasted a few years. With the economic downturn in 1974, the social and economic space that allowed for radical experimentation collapsed. While the state's coffers were full in the early seventies, the state saw drug treatment as a valuable investment. With the collapse of the golden age, drug treatment became expendable, radical experimentation became too expensive, and drug users seemed less worthy of state spending. This led to a reformation of the drug treatment regime as groups either managed to stabilize and adopt standards of professionalization or failed.

The story of drug treatment in the early seventies highlights the remarkable creativity of the post-1968 period. Even though the dreams of revolution that had motivated the '68ers had collapsed into fragmentation, many young people took Rudi Dutschke's advice and began their "long march through the institutions," while others began to carve out new dreams, shifting their focus from revolution to the transformation of everyday life. But, significantly, this path was paved with the help of the state. Instead of trying to impose order, to control the response to the drug problem, the state proved willing to allow experimentation, even when it clashed with its own interests.

Therapeutic Communities

While the Bürgerschaft heard from expert witnesses and debated the comprehensive plan for dealing with the increase in drug consumption in 1969 and as pollsters spread out to determine the extent of drug use, private groups began organizing various programs to deal with the rise in drug abuse and lack of treatment options. Most important among these groups were the therapeutic communities. These therapeutic communities sought to offer young drug users a stable environment for long-term or at least longer-term care in a communal setting. Over the first half of the 1970s, the therapeutic communities served as a locus for experimentation in drug treatment. Several organizations from the more traditional social welfare organizations to radical groups coming out of the counterculture set up long-term treatment regimes funded, at least in part, by the state government. Most of these proved unstable. Few survived for more than a handful of years, and those that did managed to do so by either adopting or creating a therapeutic framework that adhered to a professional therapeutic model. Even so, these organizations were significant because they sought to bring new ideas to what was perceived of as a new problem, and they point to the radical possibilities that still seemed plausible at the beginning of the seventies.

The idea for therapeutic communities came from American models, specifically Synanon and Daytop Village. Charles E. Dederich founded Synanon in 1958 in Santa Monica, California. Based on the idea of creating a "total institution" of ex–drug users, Synanon used unorthodox forms of group therapy that emphasized direct confrontation and catharsis to create a sense of group identification. The treatment regime was not a professional one, but one created by the ex-users themselves. It emphasized strict discipline and dismissed anyone who refused to follow the rules. Dederich believed that "junkies need Synanon, we don't need them."[2]

This concept of a voluntary community of ex–drug users that demanded a commitment to the group and complete abstinence was widely copied in the sixties. In 1963, the Probation Department of the Kings County Supreme Court of New York state formed a pilot program named Daytop to deal with the increasing number of drug violations. Once the board of the new organization visited Synanon, they decided to attempt to create a similar community for New York's drug-using population. After a shaky start, Daytop moved to Staten Island in 1965, changed its name to Daytop Village, and formed a nonprofit organization, which had mixed success. Two years later, the board hired David Deitch, a former member of Synanon, to run Daytop. Deitch immediately introduced changes to create a stronger sense of community. Yet by 1968, Deitch's thinking about the role of the group had become much more radical; instead of merely seeing the group as a means for treating addiction, Deitch began to believe that the Daytop community offered a better model for society at large—a model in which altruism and responsibility played a crucial role. The more conservative board members disagreed with Deitch's new political stance (and with his poster of Che Guevera) and, after a lengthy battle, wrested control of Daytop from him in 1969.[3]

The success of Synanon and Daytop was internationally recognized and provided a model for new forms of therapeutic communities in

2. Quoted in Barry Sugarman, *Daytop Village: A Therapeutic Community* (New York: Holt, Rinehart, and Winston, 1974), 8. On Synanon, see also Lewis Yablonsky, *The Tunnel Back* (New York: Macmillan, 1965), and Guy Endore, *Synanon* (Garden City, NY: Doubleday, 1968).

3. Sugarman, *Daytop Village,* 8–10, 119–32. On Daytop, see also Daniel Casriel, *Daytop: Three Addicts and Their Cure* (New York: Hill and Wang, 1971).

Germany. The philosophy of these new groups differed widely. Some emerged from the counterculture and hoped to reproduce Daytop's radical critique of "normal" society; others came out of the German religious social welfare tradition. In either case, the goal was similar: to provide young drug users with long-term stationary therapy away from the pressures of the urban drug scene. Yet the means and the results varied widely from group to group.

Diakonisches Werk, the Evangelical welfare organization, frustrated with the radical political or utopian mind-set of some of the experimental therapeutic communities, made a short-lived attempt at setting up a therapeutic community in Harburg in 1971. The house on Großmoordamm Straße had places for ten drug addicts between the ages of fifteen and nineteen, though the community was rarely, if ever, filled to capacity. The Großmoordamm collective received by far the most money from the state, over seventy marks per child per day. Yet this experiment quickly proved a failure. By the end of March 1972, Großmoordamm was forced to shut its doors when the two therapists left to take other jobs. The difficulties of dealing with young drug addicts seemed overwhelming. The lessons of Diakonisches Werk's brief attempt at creating a proper therapeutic community, according to Rolf Siebrecht, the head of Diakonisches Werk's antidrug efforts, were quite negative. Siebrecht bemoaned the difficulties of treating young addicts and claimed that "young junkies, who through unsuccessful upbringing have never been properly socialized, cannot be resocialized."

After the closing of the Großmoordam experiment, Diakonisches Werk planned to open another, more heavily regulated therapeutic community, but this project never came to fruition.[4] Instead, the Martha Foundation, a partner in Diakonisches Werk, created the Social-Therapeutic Center at Hamburg-Hummelsbüttel, which opened on 1 July 1972. This center was different from the project at Großmoordam. It was modeled on traditional institutions for alcoholism, offering stationary and ambulant treatment for both alcoholics and

4. StAH, 351-10 II, Sozialbehörde II, Abl.3 135.04-5, Band 1, Siebrecht, "Die Arbeit an Drogengefährdeten in Hamburg aus der Sicht der Evang. luth. Landeskirche," n.d.; StAH, 351-10 II, Sozialbehörde II, Abl.3 135.21-2 Band 1, Mieck, "Wohngemeinschaften für Drogenabhängige," 9 June 1972; StAH, 351-10 II, Sozialbehörde II, Abl.3 135.21-2 Band 1, Mieck, "Therapeutische Wohngemeinschaften," 12 January 1972.

drug users.[5] It lacked the novel character of the therapeutic communities and represented much more of a traditional institution and eventually catered mostly to older alcoholics.[6]

During 1971, the Youth Department of the Authority for Schools, Youth, and Vocational Education transformed the former girls' home at Maschen into a therapeutic community for young men. This public institution differed substantially from the private initiatives and served more as a way to provide special care to the young drug addicts in state custodial care (*Fürsorgeerziehung* or *freiwillige Fürsorgeerziehung*). The home at Maschen offered young drug users some specialized attention that would otherwise be unavailable. They were expected to follow the house rules, and repeated infractions resulted in transfer to the reformatory at Wolfsdorf, the threat of which apparently was enough to keep most in line. In any case, the fact that participation was not entirely voluntary meant that this public institution had more in common with other public youth homes than with most of the private therapeutic communities.[7]

Another well-respected, private social welfare group, the Youth Help Association (Jugendhilfe e.V.), founded a therapeutic community in January 1971 named Project Reitbrook. Members of Hamburg's Youth and Justice Authorities had formed Jugendhilfe in 1957. Dedicated to youth welfare, it ran a retreat for at-risk youth on the Elbe, aimed at removing troubled children from the negative influences of the city. Several social workers approached the group in early 1971 with the idea of opening an experimental therapeutic community. The association agreed to support the program and purchased an old village schoolhouse at Reitbrook, in far southeast Hamburg. The therapeutic concept of the project hinged on offering young drug addicts an alternative to life in the drug scene.

Initially, the staff was inspired by the antiauthoritarian child psy-

5. StAH, 351-10 II, Sozialbehörde II, Abl.3 135.20-7 Band 1, Martha-Stiftung, "Sozialtherapeutisches Zentrum Hamburg-Hummelsbüttel," 1972.

6. See R. Müller, "Sozialtherapeutisches Zentrum für Suchtkranke in Hamburg—Versuch einer Darstellung der Konzeption und erste Erfahrungen," *Suchtgefahren* 19 (1973): 92–99.

7. StAH, 351-10 II, Sozialbehörde II, Abl.3 135.21-2 Band 1, S. Mieck, Amt für Soziales und Rehabilitation der Arbeits- und Sozialbehörde, "Therapeutische Wohngemeinschaften Maschen," 8 November 1972; StAH, 351-10 II, Sozialbehörde II, Abl.3 135.20-7 Band 1, E. Guenther, "Vermerk," 10 March 1972.

chology that had become popular in social work circles during the late sixties and sought to create a permissive atmosphere. After the home experienced a number of organizational and financial difficulties, a member of the Youth Authority agreed to head the project. The new leader brought a firm hand to the organization, changing the focus to a much more orderly therapeutic regime. As a result, during the winter of that first year most of the original staff was replaced. The new program was based on discipline and adherence to group norms.

The change was so successful that during the summer of 1972 the group opened a second house at Billwerder Billdeich named Dependence. This second house allowed for a two-step program. The first intensive phase took place at Reitbrook. In order to be accepted into the group, an applicant first had to fill out a lengthy application. If the applicant fit the strict criteria, he or she had to sign an agreement to obey all the house rules, of which there were many. If a resident repeatedly broke the rules, especially the rules against drug consumption, they could be expelled. Residents in this first phase could not leave the premises without a chaperone. They lived within a strictly regimented schedule, waking early, working, and going to bed early. In addition to assigned chores, such as cooking and cleaning, they took part in daily group therapy sessions and scheduled individual therapy. In the evenings there were planned activities that kept the residents busy and active. After the first phase was completed, the residents transferred to the Dependence house. The second phase focused on reintegrating residents into society. This included attending public school. In the afternoons, residents were required to complete their homework, and in the evenings, they took part in group therapy. After completing the second phase, residents were reintegrated into society. The entire program lasted approximately eighteen months.[8] This kind of professionalized

8. StAH, 351-10 II, Sozialbehörde II, Abl.3 135.04-1 Band 6, Eckhard Günther, "Bericht über die Arbeit der von Hamburg aus geförderten therapeutischen Wohngemeinschaften für Drogenabhängige," 2 August, 1973, 4–7; StAH, Sozialbehörde II, Abl.3 135.21-2-10 Band 1, Harald Kruse, "Tatigkeitsbericht," summer 1972; StAH, 315-10 II, Sozialbehörde II, Abl. 3, 135.21-2-1 Band 1, Christensen, "Zum Leiter des Makerenko-Kollektivs Herrn Strassmann," 15 October 1971. BfIH, Referat Drogen und Sucht, "Konzept einer forschungsoffenen, strukturell gegliederten, durchgehenden Therapiekette für Drogenabhängige in Hamburg," [1973]. See also Werner Sillescu, "Wer 'gammelt', greift viel eher zur Droge: Berichte aus der Wohnkommune Reitbrook," *Hamburger Abendblatt*, 4 January 1972.

structure based on the goal of social reintegration of young addicts became the norm for long-term treatment facilities.

While the experimental forms of treatment pursued by these established groups adhered to an emerging therapeutic model, new groups emerged at the beginning of the seventies in an attempt to do something about the growing incidence of youth addiction. On 8 June 1970, another group, headed by Paul Schulz, a progressive Evangelical pastor at St. Jacobi, formed an association named Release Hamburg.[9] A year later, the association opened a therapeutic community in Geesthacht, in the Schleswig-Holstein countryside southeast of Hamburg, in a house that had served as a residence for guest workers. The staff was made up of a psychologist, a social worker, a law student, as well as a graphic artist and his wife. For the first few months, the staff attempted to counsel young ex-junkies alongside other troubled youth who had no experience with drugs. This experiment met with little success; within six weeks the non–drug users were removed from the group. By the beginning of 1972, the social worker had resigned and been replaced by a younger psychologist. The internal disagreements continued, and by April the entire professional staff had resigned. Soon thereafter, the association reformed under the leadership of a medical student, a social worker, and an ex-addict. The new leadership planned to increase the number of residents to twenty, though this proved to be impractical. Due to the expense of renting such a large house when they were only treating five to nine residents, the Geesthacht collective was dissolved in the fall of 1972. Four of the members who were judged stable moved back to Hamburg, while the remaining five youths moved with the medical student into a farmhouse in Müssen.

In 1975, the work of Release Hamburg was taken over by a new association, Therapiehilfe e.V., founded the previous year by Eckhard Günther, Hamburg's coordinator for drug problems. The farmhouse in Müssen was integrated into a larger group of therapeutic communities around Hamburg. Therapiehilfe differed from the previous organi-

9. On Schulz, see "Tätige Hilfe: Pastor holte Experten vor den Altar," *Hamburger Morgenpost,* 17 March 1972; "Ohne Fachwissen ist Hilfe nicht viel wert," *Hamburger Morgenpost,* 12 March 1972.

zations in certain respects; instead of separating different steps of treatment in different locations, this organization created a consolidated three-step hierarchy within each location.[10]

While Jugendhilfe and Release Hamburg had a number of internal problems in the first few years of their existence, they were, for the most part, a welcome addition to the therapeutic regime in Hamburg. The two other major associations, Jugend hilft Jugend e.V. (Youth Helps Youth) and the Verein zur Bekämpfung der Rauschgiftgefahr (Association for the Struggle Against the Narcotics Threat), were much more controversial. Both of these groups emerged from the political Left and sought to create a radical alternative to traditional therapeutic methods. As a result, they were often at odds with the state authorities, who nonetheless supported their efforts, though often only with great reservations.

A trade school teacher named Günter Strassmann founded Jugend hilft Jugend in October 1970. The original group lived in a farmhouse near Kaltenkirchen, Schleswig-Holstein. In February 1972, the group moved into a house in Hamburg on Graumannsweg, added a student to the staff, and increased the number of residents. At the house on Graumannsweg, Jugend hilft Jugend developed a particularly coherent and sophisticated critique of the relationship between drug addiction and postindustrial capitalism, which merits quoting at length:

10. StAH, 351-10 II, Sozialbehörde II, Abl.3 135.04-1 Band 6, Eckhard Günther, "Bericht über die Arbeit der von Hamburg aus geförderten therapeutischen Wohngemeinschaften für Drogenabhängige," 2 August 1973, 11–13. StAH, 351-10 II, Sozialbehörde II, Abl.3 135.21-2-3 Band 1, Release Hamburg e.V., "Modell einer Therapeutischen WG für Rauschmittelgefährdete Jugendliche," 29 October 1970; StAH, 351-10 II, Sozialbehörde II, Abl.3 135.20-0 Band 2, Release Hamburg e.V., "Release Hamburg," 1970; StAH, 351-10 II, Sozialbehörde II, Abl.3 135.21-2 Band 1, Mueller-Dieckert, "Therapeutische WG," 8 October 1971; StAH, 351-10 II, Sozialbehörde II, Abl.3 135.20-7 Band 1, E. Günther, "Wohngemeinschaft," 14 July 1972; StAH, 351-10 II, Sozialbehörde II, Abl.3 135.21-2-3 Band 2, E. Günther, "Übersiedlung der Therapiegruppe des Vereins 'Release Hamburg e.V.' nach Müssen, Krs. Lauenburg," 3 November 1972; StAH, 351-10 II, Sozialbehörde II, Abl.3 135.21-2-3 Band 2, Release Hamburg e.V. and Wendiggensen, "Information über Aufgabe des Hauses Kronsberg 35, Trennung der Geesthachter Gruppe in zwei kleinere Gruppen. Anmietung eines Bauernhauses zum 1.11.72," 23 October 1972; StAH, 351-10 II, Sozialbehörde II, Abl.3 135.20-0 Band 7, Gronwaldt, "Situationsbericht Sachgebiet Drogenabhängiger," 11 January 1973; StAH, 351-10 II, Sozialbehörde II, Abl.3 135.21-2 Band 1, S. Mieck, "Sozialtherapeutische Wohngemeinschaften für Drogenabhängige," 21 February 1973; BfI, Referat Drogen und Sucht, Eckhard Günter, "Zur Lage in Hamburg—Rauschmittelmißbrauch und Gegenmaßnahmen," [1976]. Letter given to the author by Kurt-Jürgen Lange, Referat Drogen und Sucht.

The development of our society produces in increasing numbers marginalized, degraded, criminal, and flipped out individuals. They drift outside of legal norms. Why? Are they still members of this society? We have the choice to ignore them or to engage with them. We engage them and the source of their predicament, especially because they are almost exclusively youth who are beginning an independent life and must adapt to defined norms. We do not want to simply "patch them up"; therefore, we must question these norms, which wear you down. . . .

Rivalry and greed cultivate acquisitiveness and the celebration of ownership. Everyone wants to be an owner, be it an owner of money, of autos, of a house, of a wife—be it of your own clothing, of a room, or a toy. Whoever owns, owns alone; he isolates himself from the community; he guards something that has been produced by many and should be used by many. Many young people have recognized this isolation machine and because of this "community understanding" have flipped out. It doesn't matter whether one has broken out of a stifling family situation, out of a narrow-minded educational system, or out of a state institution. The flight usually ends in total isolation and resignation, in unsolvable personal conflicts and in confusion. From there it is a small step to drugs, to illegality, to brutal criminality.[11]

Whether one agreed with this analysis or not, and most members of Hamburg's government certainly did not, the message carried a powerful resonance for those who had already "flipped out" and those young people involved with the protest movements of '68. The members of Jugend hilft Jugend wanted to recreate a lost sense of community. But the community they sought to build was both physically and ideologically separate from society at large.

This search for a new form of antiauthoritarian community led to internal divisions. The lack of stable members and the problems related to living in the city, much closer to the drug scene, led to an increase in the number of relapses and conflicts between the members. When a new student member was accused of taking part in pharmacy burglaries in the countryside around Hamburg, the group split into

---

11. StAH, 351-10 II, Sozialbehörde II, Abl.3 135.21-2-1 Band 1, Jugend hilft Jugend, "Konzeption Drogenkollektiv Graumannsweg."

factions. One faction returned to the countryside, renting a farmhouse in Hattstedt near Husum, Schleswig-Holstein, while the other remained in the house on Graumannsweg. The Hattstedt group soon moved to another house in Hardebek near Neumünster. Meanwhile, the Graumannsweg collective continued to have internal problems and split again in 1971. A group of social pedagogy students took over the leadership of the Graumannsweg home and eventually joined the Verein zur Bekämpfung der Rauschgiftgefahr organization.

The other group, headed by Jugend hilft Jugend founder Günter Strassmann, left with several members and moved into a garden house on Johann-Meyer-Straße in Bergedorf and then to an eight-room house in Bergedorf in July 1972. This group renamed itself Makarenko-Kollektiv after the great Russian pedagogue A. S. Makarenko, who was widely popular among educational reformers on the Left in the late sixties and early seventies.[12] Their group philosophy was based on the idea that modern society caused drug addiction; only by showing young drug users a positive example of an alternative to exploitative capitalist society could they hope to prevent their self-destructive behavior. "We try to create the possibility for the flipped out, those on the margins of society, or the outcasts to find an alternative to their wretched lives, for which they are more or less innocent."[13] Members of the local government were far less than certain about the motives and methods of the group. In October 1971, a member of the social welfare staff in Bergedorf visited the Makarenko-Kollektiv and reported, "The first impression of the house was almost shocking. In all of the rooms an enormous mess like a Bohemian's lodgings. In the first room on the only wall a very large bookcase! In Strassmann's room a poster on the wall: 'Three Shots at Rudi Dutschke'.[14] On the floor evidently a double bed, unmade, to the right a typewriter with a lot of paper."[15] Along with conflict with local authorities, the group

12. StAH, 315-10 II, Sozialbehörde II, Abl. 3, 135.21-2-1 Band 1, E. Wolgast and G. Strassmann, "Entstehungsgeschichte des 'Makarenko-Kollektivs,'" 23 November 1971.

13. StAH, 315-10 II, Sozialbehörde II, Abl. 3, 135.21-2-1 Band 1, E. Wolgast and G. Strassmann, "Entstehungsgeschichte des 'Makarenko-Kollektivs,'" 23 November 1971.

14. StAH, 315-10 II, Sozialbehörde II, Abl. 3, 135.21-2-1 Band 1, Christensen, "Zum Leiter des Makerenko-Kollektivs Herrn Strassmann," 15 October 1971.

15. Ibid.

had frequent internal problems, and Strassmann left the group with his wife in order to finish their educations in January 1973.[16]

In late 1971 and early 1972, after the founding of the Makarenko group and the defection of the Graumannsweg group to the Verein zur Bekämpfung der Rauschgiftgefahr, another therapeutic community was organized in a house at Sander Damm that was associated with Jugend hilft Jugend. This collective focused not on drug users per se but rather on young people released from prison on parole. Despite the differences in objectives, however, the two groups worked closely together and created a workable partnership.[17]

Meanwhile, the group that had split from the Graumannsweg collective and moved to Hardebek in the summer of 1971 formed a new association that winter called Projekt aktive Umweltgestaltung (Project Active Environment Molding). They lived in an uncompleted seventeen-room farmhouse, where they worked the land, ran a small offset printer, and had a photography darkroom. There was no organized therapy to speak of. They saw themselves, instead, as a collective, working together to overcome their problems, problems caused by a consumer society totally bereft of community.[18]

The final group, the Verein zur Bekämpfung der Rauschgiftgefahr, was the most radical. Despite its early success, the radical approach championed by the group led to attacks from the outside and internal conflict. While the group flourished between 1971 and 1973, by 1975 it had dissolved. Their story is an interesting and instructive one, which

16. StAH, 351-10 II, Sozialbehörde II, Abl.3 135.04-1 Band 6, Eckhard Günther, "Bericht über die Arbeit der von Hamburg aus geförderten therapeutischen Wohngemeinschaften für Drogenabhängige," 2 August, 1973, 7–9; StAH, 315-10 II, Sozialbehörde II, Abl. 3, 135.21-2-1 Band 1, E. Wolgast and G. Strassmann, "Entstehungsgeschichte des 'Makarenko-Kollektivs,'" 23 November 1971.

17. StAH, 351-10 II, Sozialbehörde II, Abl.3 135.04-1 Band 6, Eckhard Günther, "Bericht über die Arbeit der von Hamburg aus geförderten therapeutischen Wohngemeinschaften für Drogenabhängige," 2 August 1973, 9; StAH, 351-10 II, Sozialbehörde II, Abl.3 135.20-0 Band 7, Gronwaldt, "Situationsbericht Sachgebiet Drogenabhängiger," 11 January 1973.

18. StAH, 351-10 II, Sozialbehörde II, Abl.3 135.04-1 Band 6, Eckhard Günther, "Bericht über die Arbeit der von Hamburg aus geförderten therapeutischen Wohngemeinschaften für Drogenabhängige," 2 August 1973, 10–11. StAH, 351-10 II, Sozialbehörde II, Abl.3 135.21-2 Band 1, S. Mieck, "Therapeutische Wohngemeinschaften," 12 January 1972; StAH, 351-10 II, Sozialbehörde II, Abl.3 135.21-2 Band 1, S. Mieck, "Sozialtherapeutische. Wohngemeinschaften für Drogenabhängige," 21 February 1973.

will be taken up in the next chapter. But for the time being, it can be said that the Verein zur Bekämpfung der Rauschgiftgefahr grew out of the radicalism of the 1960s and died with the onset of economic collapse after the oil embargo of 1973 and the subsequent drastic cutbacks in state funding.

It was this trajectory that marked the course of most of the early experiments in therapeutic communities—Release Hamburg, Jugend hilft Jugend, as well as the Verein zur Bekämpfung der Rauschgiftgefahr. Emerging from the desire to create a radical alternative to traditional psychiatric models of addiction and therapy, either the groups developed into a more structured, professionalized, and traditional form of therapy, as did Jugend hilft Jugend and Release Hamburg when it was taken over by Therapiehilfe, or they died. The reasons for this are complicated. First, the economic crisis had a direct effect on the therapeutic communities; the state had less money to spend on experiments and less will to do so. Second, the radical therapeutic communities emerged during the crisis years, when local officials were willing to try almost anything to stem the tide of drug addiction. The therapeutic communities certainly had only a mixed success rate, but it was, in any case, higher than the traditional revolving door of the city hospitals' psychiatric departments. Furthermore, when the move toward therapeutic communities began, Germany had an extreme dearth of trained professionals in the field of drug addiction. Had they wanted to create state institutions with traditional methods, they could not; there simply were not enough people to staff them, and the cost would have been enormous. By farming the work of long-term care for young drug addicts out to private organizations and paying a daily stipend from the social welfare disability budget, the government both supported the traditional subsidiary principle and created a more cost-effective system. Yet by the midseventies, there were more trained professionals, and politicians demanded a less radical approach to drug addiction. In addition, the radical therapeutic communities fell out of favor as the social understanding of drug abuse changed. In 1970 and 1971, officials and experts still saw drugs in terms of a wave, some implacable social force that could only be stopped through drastic measures. And in this conception, all drugs were the same and every child was liable to be swept away by the tide.

By 1973, however, the conception of drug addiction began to

change, due to the social makeup of drug users and the changing market. As the number of drug users seemed to be leveling off after the initial explosion in 1970, experts began to accept the fact that drug use was not going to go away and that the problem they needed to focus on was not hashish consumption but a specific "hard kernel" of problem drug users.[19] This sense of denouement meant that groups that were seen as troubling during the crisis period became extraneous. Finally, the radicalism that created these organizations and the feeling that individuals could make a difference in the drug problem crashed head-on with the intractability of the problem. As the young radicals began to age, the struggles of the late sixties and early seventies lost at least a part of their allure. Many of the individuals involved in the various projects drifted off to start a career or a family, left to find another cause, or just faded into the background.

The Growth of State Services for Drug Users

The therapeutic communities were the most peculiar of the responses to rising drug use; the fact that they were privately run certainly made possible the variety of approaches and particularly the unorthodox means of some groups. The responses organized by the state were perhaps less adventurous. Nonetheless, they represented a distinct turn away from the conservative medical approach to dependence that had dominated the understanding of addiction since the 1920s. They also marked a willingness of the state to take responsibility for dealing directly with young drug users. Rather than permitting private and ecumenical welfare organizations to dominate the therapeutic regime, Hamburg's government determined that the state had a fundamental responsibility to take the lead in dealing with the drug problem. Much of the reason for this was that private organizations were either unwilling or unable to launch and sustain a concerted effort. Yet many members of Hamburg's government and its bureaucracy believed that only the state could organize and support an adequate response to the new drug market. As a result, the Hamburg bureaucracies set up a number

---

19. See, for example, Eckhard Günther, "Der harte Kern der Drogenszene," *Berichte und Dokumente aus der Freien und Hansestadt Hamburg,* No. 402, Staatliche Pressestelle Hamburg, 18 April 1974.

of specific initiatives to deal with the increasing number of problem drug users. The Youth Department organized a state-run counseling center, which included a number of outreach workers, while the Health Authority set up the Therapy Center at Altona (Therapiezentrum Altona, or TZA), which was to act as a stationary and ambulant clinic and the center of Hamburg's "therapy chain."

The Youth Department had played a central role in the fight against addiction since the midsixties. Its counseling center, founded in 1969, was one of the first organized responses to youth drug use and served as a model for much of the rest of the Federal Republic. Soon, though, members of the Youth Department realized that the counseling center was not enough. Because the center was closely associated with the Youth Department and was housed in a state building, young drug users were reticent about taking their problems—their illegal problems—to the state authorities, the very people in charge of dealing with delinquent youth. Meanwhile, members of the Youth Department involved with the issue of drug use took a number of study trips to other European countries and were impressed with the idea of street workers as practiced in Sweden.[20] The planning for a new counseling center, one physically separate from the Youth Department, continued for quite some time and became an integral part of the Senate's 1971 comprehensive plan.

At the beginning of April 1972, six social workers and two student interns moved into eight rooms on the third floor of a former bank building in Altona on Königstraße. The center was commonly known by its address, Königstraße 16A, or simply KÖ 16A. The location was ideal. It was close to the drug scene in St. Pauli, and the rest of the building was empty, which reduced the possibility of disagreements with neighbors. This latter blessing, however, did not last long. Soon, a portion of the Department for Fishing Research moved in on the second floor, and a small grocers shop rented the first floor. The shop sold alcohol, which made it less than the ideal downstairs neighbor for an addiction-counseling clinic. After renovating their new office, the group began their work in early May. The center's hours were lim-

20. StAH, 136.1, BfI, 1108, Brandt, "Studienreise nach Dänemark vom 20. bis 23.11.68," 1968; StAH, 315-10 II, Sozialbehörde II, Abl. 3, 135.21-2-15 Band 1, J315, "Anforderung eines Berichtes über die Arbeit im Beratungszentrum," [1973].

ited—8:00 a.m. to 8:00 p.m. on Monday through Friday and 3:00 p.m. to 8:00 p.m. on Saturday—but with only six to ten employees it meant long hours for everyone.

The plan for KÖ 16A was simple, at least on paper. The street workers were to venture out in pairs into the clubs, bars, and parks that made up Hamburg's drug scene and make direct contact with drug users. When a drug user expressed a desire to receive help with his or her problem, the street workers would send that person to KÖ 16A. Once the drug user made contact with the counseling center, the counselors would determine the best course for dealing with the individual, whether this meant sending him or her to a hospital for withdrawal, arranging for a place in one of the therapeutic communities, providing long-term ambulant counseling, or simply providing the user with a drug-free place to loiter and a sympathetic ear.

All of this, however, was based on two key concepts: anonymity and free will. The only chance for the success of KÖ 16A lay in convincing the members of Hamburg's drug scene that a state institution would and could actually serve their interests. Street workers were the key to making drug users aware of the possibility and convincing them that the counseling center was not a trap that could land them in the hands of the police. The founders of KÖ 16A were quite aware of this fact and the widespread feeling within the scene that the state could not be trusted. In order to try and manage this perception, KÖ 16A guaranteed that individuals would be treated anonymously as long as they wished, though it was necessary to give up that anonymity in order to receive intensive treatment and referrals to the hospital or the therapeutic communities. The information given to the counselors, likewise, would not be handed over to the police under any circumstances. Nor could the police enter the premises of the counseling center; the staff actually discouraged the police from coming near the center, as it tended to scare off users who might otherwise seek help.

Besides anonymity, the other major premise was that all contact with the center must be based on the free will of the client. Indeed, this was one of the key ideas that came out of the drug wave of the late sixties and early seventies. The argument was that addiction, particularly in the case of intravenous drug users, was difficult, if not impossible, to cure and that relapses were the rule rather than the exception. Therefore, drug users in seek of help must be absolutely dedicated to the prospect of leading an abstinent life before drug treatment was worthwhile. Any coercion, whether parental or state, would almost certainly doom any prospect of success. Furthermore, if the counseling center were required to deal with a large number of clients ordered by the courts to seek help but personally uninterested in treatment, the center's staff would be too overwhelmed to help those who actually wished to change their lives. On a more practical level, long-term care, such as the therapeutic communities, required that their clients be willing to change, and they were quick to send away those who did not show a deep desire to alter their life's path.

The intensive counseling had a clear set of objectives. First, the counselors sought to deal with the immediate problems. In the case of intravenous drug users this meant getting the client into a withdrawal program at one of the local hospitals; other drug users were encouraged to remove themselves from the daily pressures of the drug scene. Second, they sought to place the clients in a stable atmosphere by securing housing and placing them in a school or a job. Third, clients were encouraged to break off contact with other drug users, and especially drug dealers, while building new relationships that did not center on drug consumption. Fourth, the staff sought to return the drug users to the family unit; this often meant including the family in counseling. Finally, the clients received psychological counseling; this included strengthening the drug users' sense of self-worth and teaching them how to deal with conflict without resorting to self-destructive behavior.

If the objectives for the counseling center and street work were sensible and well planned, the day-to-day reality of dealing with Hamburg's rapidly changing drug scene challenged and often frustrated the expectations of the workers. Soon after the counseling center's opening it became a place for young people with drug problems to congregate. At KÖ 16A, they could relax, "drink tea, listen to music, play games such as table tennis," and have a social worker there in case they needed someone to listen to their problems.[21] Often young people would visit almost daily for weeks before seeking substantial help from the social workers. Indeed, the social workers quickly learned to wait more or less patiently for clients to ask for help. During the first few

21. StAH, 315-10 II, Sozialbehörde II, Abl. 3, 135.21-2-15 Band 1, J315, "Anforderung eines Berichtes über die Arbeit im Beratungszentrum," [1973], 8.

months, due to inadequate staffing, the counselors could not meet the demand for aid. It took a full year for KÖ 16A to reach its full staff complement. Nevertheless, during the first year of operation, the center undertook the intensive counseling of twenty-six young women and forty-nine young men between the ages of fifteen and twenty-one. About half of these clients were considered "fixers," while the other half tended to use hashish, LSD, speed, or various prescription drugs. Though the counselors had a few notable successes, most of their clients continued to use drugs, and relapses were the rule rather than the exception.[22]

From the beginning of the planning stages of KÖ 16A, it was clear that street work would be the key to its success. Officials in Hamburg had been impressed with the achievements of street work in the United States and Sweden in the late sixties. Before KÖ 16A opened, the Youth Department hired a young social worker named Klaus-Günther Struck to test whether street work would prove an effective method with which to make contact with young drug users. After a ten-week trial period, Struck reported on the difficulties he met in his work.[23] In order to gain access to the scene, Struck believed that one had to present oneself as a "cool type," someone who knew the intricacies of the drug scene and who could be trusted not to turn drug users in to the authorities. Most difficult but of utmost importance, Struck argued, was establishing regular contact with drug dealers. Naturally, they were reticent to speak with a state employee, but once contact and trust were established, they could provide valuable information about the scene and day-to-day changes in the makeup of users and drug availability. Despite the difficulties encountered by Struck, the Youth Department saw the immediate benefit in establishing direct contacts with the drug scene. Not only could street workers offer drug users help and advice, but they were in a better position to gather information on the day-to-day changes within the scene.

The street workers began their work soon after KÖ 16A opened its doors. Working mostly in pairs, the street workers regularly visited "discos, bars, train stations, parks and restaurants." Initially, drug

22. Ibid., 14–18.

23. Quoted in Axel Peters, "Streetwork in der Drogenscene," *Neue Praxis: Kritische Zeitschrift für Sozialarbeit und Sozialpädagogik* 3 (1973): 33. See also Homann, *Das Haschischverbot.*

users met them with considerable resistance. Only by returning again and again to the scene did the street workers gain some acceptance. Often this meant hiding their identity as state employees for some time, waiting to be accepted before offering help out of the drug scene. Street workers also faced a quickly changing scene. While the drug scene had been largely confined to the bars and discos of St. Pauli and St. Georg during the late sixties, by the time street work really got under way, drug use had spread to clubs throughout Hamburg. As the scene changed rapidly, the incubators of the early drug scene—the Star Club, Palette, and Club 99—were long gone, and other clubs—Das EI, Tam-Tam, Fucktory, Flesh, Gibi, Blue 2000, and Madhouse—had taken their place. Likewise, the original ideological motivation of drug users had changed. Instead of being intrigued by "consciousness expansion" or simply acting out of curiosity, the drug users encountered by the street workers seemed to be attempting to escape their problems through drug use. Though hashish and LSD consumption were ubiquitous, the real problem facing the street workers was a rapid increase in the number of opiate junkies as well as amphetamine and barbiturate abusers.[24]

The final link in Hamburg's therapy chain and the centerpiece of its efforts against drug use was the TZA. This center acted as the initial intake point for problem drug users and, after detoxification, attempted to place addicts in long-term care, usually in the various therapeutic living communities. After considerable renovation, the TZA finally opened in two buildings of the former Altona General Hospital in May 1973. The center included twelve beds for detoxification and a program for long-term therapy for another twelve patients.

From the outset, the new institution was plagued by internal problems. The staff of fifteen, most of whom were recent graduates and only two of whom had previous experience with drug addiction, clashed with Dr. Hasse, the director hired to oversee the operation. According to Hasse, the young academics mistrusted traditional psychiatric understandings of drug addiction as a sign of psychological

24. StAH, 315-10 II, Sozialbehörde II, Abl. 3, 135.21-2-15 Band 1, J315, "Anforderung eines Berichtes über die Arbeit im Beratungszentrum," [1973], 20–24.

pathology and resented the power of the director as final policy arbiter. The conflict was generational. Hasse preferred to institute traditional psychiatric models of treatment, while the younger members of the staff had been influenced by new ideas about addiction and treatment, preferring group therapy that, Hasse argued, "took on the character of a therapeutic living community."[25] Despite the internal power struggles, the center admitted over two hundred addicts in its first two years of operation. The center had no problem attracting addicts desperate for help, though it did have a serious problem keeping them in therapy once admitted. Part of the difficulty rested in the initial policy of allowing clients to leave at any time. The staff soon found that addicts in detoxification often decided that addiction was better than withdrawal and left soon after admission. Turning the detoxification building into a lockdown unit modeled on closed psychiatric wards solved this dilemma. Yet half of the center's clients chose to leave the center after detoxification instead of pursing long-term care and presumably returned to the drug scene.[26]

The conflict between the staff and the directors continued to plague the center throughout the rest of its short lifetime. In 1975, one of the medical directors, Dr. Alexander Frater, wrote to officials in the Health Department, complaining that the situation at the TZA was "completely chaotic." He claimed that the staff had adopted an "anti-psychiatry" view of patient treatment and that patients were not even receiving basic physical examinations.[27] In the end, the constant internal fighting and the high cost of the institution meant that when the Hamburg Senate demanded that the Health Authority cut its budget during the financial crisis in 1974 the TZA was scheduled for closure. In 1976, the center shut its doors and a smaller detoxification program was instituted at General Hospital at Ochsenzoll.[28]

25. StAH, 351-10 II, Sozialbehörde II, Abl.3 135.04-1 Band 8, Hasse, "Stellungnahme des Leiters zur Krisensituation der Mitarbeiter im TZA," 4 June 1974.

26. E. Braunschweig et al., "Die klinische Einrichtung innerhalb der Therapiekette für Drogenabhängige in Hamburg," *Öffentliche Gesundheitswesen* 40 (1978): 670.

27. StAH, 351-10 II, Sozialbehörde II, Abl.3 135.04-1 Band 8, Alexander Frater, "Vermerk zur Arbeitssituation im TZA," 17 September 1975.

28. Braunschweig et al., "Die klinische Einrichtung," 671.

Conclusion

A new consensus about the drug problem emerged around 1974. While politicians and policymakers between 1968 and 1972 had been mainly concerned with the spread of the drug problem and the perceived threat to all of Hamburg's youth, the growth of the heroin market and the apparent stagnation in the number of new young drug users led policymakers to reshape their views. Eckhard Günther, the able coordinator for the drug problem in Hamburg, led the move toward a new understanding of the drug problem. In a 1974 report, Günther argued that the real problem in Hamburg was not the occasional hashish smoker but rather the relatively small group of habitual drug users. This "hard kernel" of drug users was responsible for the vast majority of drugs purchased in Hamburg, as well as for the property crime associated with drug addiction. Therefore, the therapeutic and policing resources, Günther argued, ought to be concentrated on this group.[29] This understanding of the drug problem as a hard kernel was widely held, though the response was perhaps not what Günther had envisioned. Rather than promoting treatment on demand and an increase in the number of beds available for long-term care of addicts, the hard kernel argument strengthened the hand of those in favor of a law-and-order approach to the drug problem. By the middle of the 1970s, drug policy in Hamburg had shifted toward a police response and away from a therapeutic response, a trend that would last until the AIDS crisis of the 1980s and the rising death overdose rate in the late 1980s forced a reexamination of drug policy all over Europe.[30]

The changing understanding of the drug problem in Hamburg may have helped the move away from treatment as a major focus of drug policy, but the decisive blow was fiscal rather than cognitive. The OPEC embargo of 1973 brought the postwar golden age to an end. A quarter century of economic expansion and seemingly endless possibilities crashed against the hard realities of recession and unemployment. By 1974, unemployment was on the rise and tax revenues had failed to

29. Eckhardt Günther, "Der harte Kern der Drogenszene." See also StAH, 351-10 II, Sozialbehörde II, Abl.3 135.27-0 Band 3, P/Ps4, "Rauschmittelkriminalität," 4 January 1974; StAH, 351-10 II, Sozialbehörde II, Abl.3 135.27-0 Band 3, Kurt-Jürgen Lange, "Bericht Rauschmittelkriminalität," 1 July 1974.

30. Michael Massing has argued that a similar process took place in the United States during the early 1970s; see Massing, *The Fix* (New York: Simon & Schuster, 1998).

meet expectations. As a result, in late 1974, the Hamburg Senate announced a general savings plan. This plan slashed budgets across the board. Drug treatment was particularly hard hit; the TZA was scheduled for closure and Eckhard Günther's Coordination Office was likewise reduced to a much smaller role. The only area of drug policy that did not experience large cuts was policing, though the police remained overwhelmed despite an almost yearly expansion in personnel.[31]

By the middle of the decade the space for radical alternatives had begun to collapse. The ideas about drug use that grew out of the radicalism of the sixties fell, for the most part, into disrepute. Hashish, once the consummate symbol of consciousness expansion, had become a gateway drug that led, almost inevitably, to hard drug use, crime, or death. The even more radical idea that drug use was a result of the consumer excesses of the welfare society and the commodification of individuals no longer convinced many. The meaning of drugs had stabilized, at least for a time. Drugs were simply commodities, an unfortunate but inevitable part of the urban landscape.

There were several reasons for this thinking. First, the ideas that motivated the rise of youth drug consumption in the first place had fallen from grace. The unbending faith in political, economic, and spiritual revolution as the duty and obligation of youth had lost much of its popularity. The enormous task of overturning society had given way to factionalism and other, more local projects, most of which were more reformist in sentiment. Likewise, the belief that the transformation of society could be achieved through an expansion of consciousness—a nebulous concept in the first place—had lost its mystique. Spiritual seekers moved on to greener fields, such as transcendental meditation, yoga, macrobiotic diets, and environmentalism, to name just a few.

Yet it was not merely ideas and sentiments that had evolved over the first half of the seventies. The market in drugs had changed drastically, as had the social makeup of drug users. The initial drug wave of the late sixties spawned an organized international traffic in drugs, dominated by hierarchical crime groups. Though these groups were not the

---

31. Eckhard Günter, "Zur Lage in Hamburg—Rauschmittelmißbrauch und Gegenmaßnahmen," paper given at the ICAA-Kongress, Hamburg, 1976, provided to the author by Kurt-Jürgen Lange of the Referat Drogen und Sucht der Behörde für Arbeits-, Gesundheit-, und Soziales Hamburg.

monolithic cartels of the eighties, they were able to secure a relatively stable supply of drugs to eager consumers. Meanwhile, the image of students smoking joints as a symbolic protest, driving their Volkswagens to Morocco, or getting stoned to a Beatles album had been replaced by the specter of younger and younger working-class youths sticking needles into their arms, turning to crime, and dying in the streets. This image actually veiled the continuing market for soft drugs; there seems to have been little reduction in the amount of hashish coming into the country. Yet the perception that the German drug problem described the drug consumption of a hard kernel of drug users had come to dominate the discussion by the midseventies.

Finally, this radical period collapsed under the enormous weight of the economic recession that dominated the second half of the seventies. When state coffers were flush during the first few years of the seventies, the idea of finding a solution to the drug problem could muster a considerable amount of support. Much of the reason why marginal groups with radical ideas could take part in searching for a workable solution to the drug problem was that representatives of the state were willing to fund them, often despite profound reservations. When the state's funds dried up after the 1973 economic crisis, experimentation could no longer garner much support. As the Hamburg government tightened its collective belt in 1974, results mattered. The effect was that the Coordination Office, which had played a central role in the implementation of Hamburg's therapy chain, closed its doors. The new TZA, the crown jewel in Hamburg's response, was scheduled for closure in 1976, despite protestations. Though much of the work of the TZA was moved to General Hospital at Ochsenzoll, the original concept was seriously compromised. The therapeutic communities, which had struggled for their first few years, had either stabilized or failed. The original antiauthoritarian ideology that had been the foundation of several of the groups had disintegrated. The Verein zur Bekämpfung der Rauschgiftgefahr imploded due to its own internal contradictions and a lack of funding; Jugend hilft Jugend abandoned much of its original Marxist critique and focused on creating a more traditional therapeutic regime; and Release Hamburg handed over its reigns to Therapiehilfe, which was consummately professional in outlook. In short, dealing with drugs became the realm of professionals.

In a larger sense, 1973 marked a turning point in German history.

The economic collapse buried the revolutionary ideals of the 1960s. Though many of the aims of radical protesters were carried on by specific causes—the environmental movement, the women's rights movement, gay liberation—or more radically by anarchists or, later, the squatters' movement, the idea that society could and should be radically transformed foundered on the economic uncertainty that came to define the second half of the seventies. The emancipatory fervor of youth faded as former radicals began the long march through the institutions.

6. Release Yourself!

The death of Benno Ohnesorg at a demonstration against the shah of Iran's visit to Berlin on 2 June 1967 has been recognized widely as a turning point in the West German student movement.[1] This event provided a focus around which the Left could organize and draw larger and larger numbers of young people into the "Movement." In a period of less than a year, the student movement brought together a large group of young people of various political proclivities and coalesced into a powerful expression of the widespread disaffection of large numbers of young Germans. Yet with the shooting of Rudi Dutschke in April 1968, the brutal repression of the Prague Spring, the failure of the May revolts in France, and the passage of the Emergency Laws in the Bundestag with the cooperation of the SPD, the student movement lost its coherence. The disillusionment caused by these political defeats caused a splintering of the Left. The ways out of the student movement were varied. The women's movement, the environmental movement, the alternative press, and, of course, terrorism have all been traced back to the fragmentation of the Left.[2] Another route out of the student movement was the so-called counterculture or underground, which organized or disorganized itself around a variety of themes and activities: yoga and various Eastern spiritualities, macrobiotic cooking

1. See, for example, Richard McCormick, *Politics of the Self: Feminism and the Postmodern in West German Literature and Film* (Princeton: Princeton University Press, 1991), 38.

2. See Sabine von Dirke, *"All Power to the Imagination!" The West German Counterculture from the Student Movement to the Greens* (Lincoln: University of Nebraska Press, 1997), esp. 29–104; McCormick, *Politics of the Self,* 21–42; Jost Hermand, *Die Kultur der Bundesrepublik Deutschland 1965–85* (Munich: Nymphenburger, 1988), 399–431, 508–22; Uta Frevert, *Women in German History: From Bourgeois Emancipation to Sexual Liberation,* trans. Stuart McKinnon-Evans (New York: Berg, 1989), 287–303; Mary Fullbrook, *The Divided Nation: A History of Germany 1918–1990* (New York: Oxford University Press, 1991), 283–87; Hermann Glaser, *Deutsche Kultur, 1945–2000* (Munich: Carl Hanser, 1997), 307–26.

Fig. 5.   Release, *Release: von den Anfängen 1970 in Hamburg bis zum Sommer 1973* (Hamburg: Release-Verlag, 1973). (Reproduced by permission of Herman Prigann.)

and free sexuality, communes and alternative child-rearing practices, and drug consumption.

There has been a tendency among scholars to treat the Movement and the counterculture as distinct entities, as two halves of the personal/political divide.[3] The student protests and subsequent terrorist movements are seen as inherently political, while cultural changes such as popular culture, drugs, and new spiritualities have been shunted aside as inherently apolitical. This dichotomy obfuscates more than it clarifies; the political challenges posed by youth at the end of the sixties and thereafter were inextricable from the larger cultural changes sweeping the Western world. In his memoir *Wie alles Anfing,* Bommi Baumann, a member of the 2 June Movement, argues that the overtly political and the cultural should be seen as a single entity. "Everyone

3. See McCormick, *Politics of the Self,* 34.

who has experiences and translates them makes his contribution on whatever level," Baumann writes. "If one works in a daycare center, the other stands on the barricades with his gun, the third brings back a pound of hashish from India, or some Mick Jagger dances so wildly on the stage that everyone goes crazy; everyone has a part in this process. I see it as a total story."[4] If one begins to approach the Movement not just as a political movement, or, more accurately, political movements, but rather as a specific aspect of a larger cultural transformation, then the barriers between public and private, personal and political, Movement and counterculture break down. Certainly there were, in every group, sentries manning the barricades and attempting to keep the barbarians from the gates of political purity. But the lines between the political and the personal, between the student movement, terrorism, and the counterculture, were blurred. Throughout the late sixties and early seventies, the ideas and practices of different groups converged and diverged, and organizations with quite different ends used similar means to realize their goals.

One such group that emerged out of the drug underground of the late sixties dedicated itself to the task of helping young people involved in the drug scene. Release, as the movement was called, was founded by young people, mostly former drug users, who sought to create an alternative solution to the explosion of drug consumption in the early seventies. The Release movement was a microcosm of the larger changes within the German countercultural Left in the early seventies. Not only did the founders of Release want to aid young drug users, but they also sought to create an alternative culture, to carve out a cultural and economic space within which they could create a radically anti-authoritarian *Gegenkultur*. This meant, for them, the formation of back-to-the-land communes, alternative presses, macrobiotic restaurants, hippy boutiques, film workshops, and rock bands. They did not, however, see the creation of an alternative culture as separate from the desires of the political Left for social revolution. Although the participants were suspicious of the political Left, often seeing the political radicalism of the early seventies as mere lip service rather than action, they were, at the very least, active sympathizers of even the far Left. In some cases, as in Heidelberg, there was considerable overlap between the Release movement and the most radical wings of political activists.

4. Michael Baumann, *How It All Began* (Vancouver: Pulp Press, 1981).

More important, however, they saw social transformation toward a future socialist society as the goal of their work. Though they believed that social revolution was predicated on the transformation of the self, they nevertheless believed that revolution was the goal. In many ways, then, the Release movement is emblematic of the more general changes in the German New Left in the early 1970s. As the coherence of the student movement disintegrated and many young people abandoned orthodox politics, they went on to found new movements and new projects but carried with them the goal of building a better society and revolutionizing everyday life.

The Establishment of an Alternative, 1969–70

The first Release organization was formed in Hamburg at the end of 1969 by a small group of young men and women who lived in an apartment on Bornstraße, just north of the university. These young people, many of whom had once been drug users, decided to try to do something to help the increasing number of young people who had "flipped out," had been arrested, or simply had nowhere to go. On 10 December 1969, they applied for registration as a legal association under the name Association for the Struggle against the Narcotics Threat (Verein zur Bekämpfung der Rauschgiftgefahr e.V.).[5] The unwieldy title, however, was only used formally. Everyone knew them simply as Release. The group's stated purpose was clearly laid out in the municipal registration forms. They sought to make contact with groups of endangered youth, with other organizations in the Federal Republic and outside it, and with the state authorities. They planned to carry out educational campaigns, utilizing posters, films, lectures, and the publication of educational material. The center of their organization, however, was to be a counseling center, where they could offer medical and legal aid to drug addicts, and a number of therapeutic living communities, in which addicts could receive long-term rehabilitation.[6]

Release was modeled on an organization of the same name in Lon-

5. The application was not formally registered until July 1970. See StAH, 351-10 II, Sozialbehörde II, Abl.3 135.04-1 Band 6, Koordinierungs- und Informationszentrale für Rauschmittelfragen, "Bericht über die Arbeit der von Hamburg aus geförderten therapeutischen Wohngemeinschaften für Drogenabhängige," 2 August 1973, 13.

6. Verein zur Bekämpfung der Rauschgiftgefahr e.V. will be hereafter referred to as VBR. 351-10 II, Sozialbehörde II, Abl.3 135.21-2-3 Band 1, VBR, "Satzung," 10 December 1969.

don. One of the founding members, Herman Prigann, had spent some time in London and had witnessed the work of Caroline Coon and the other members of Release London. The London group had been founded by Coon and a few others from the London scene in 1967 in an attempt to provide advice and legal aid to drug users arrested by the London police. The group soon became a central facet of the youth scene in London, tending to women with unwanted pregnancies and runaways, in addition to those involved with the drug scene. Release London represented a genuine effort to create a caring institution within the sizable London underground. One historian has called it "one of the most significant legacies of the alternative society."[7]

Armed with the knowledge that the London group had made a tangible difference in the London drug scene, the Hamburg group began its work in earnest in the summer of 1970. In September, the group held its first press conference at its office on Bornstraße and announced a comprehensive strategy to get young drug users off the street.

> In Hamburg the number of "fixers" or "shooters" is growing inexorably. We know the "scene," and we know that already more than a thousand young Hamburgers have reached for the needle instead of the "joint" and have found themselves on a path, from which they can no longer return. The police cannot prevent this. Prohibition, punishment, or threats of punishment don't help anything. . . .
>
> Therefore, we have founded the Association for the Struggle against the Narcotics Threat. Because we insert ourselves into the "scene," because we know how young people destroy themselves on opium, because we know that these people do not trust the police or other state authorities, because we know that the number of endangered youth grows daily, we have resolved to do everything we can to halt the threat to society posed by narcotics.[8]

Their strategy included a Release Center, which consisted of a phone bank and a drop-in center; a number of therapeutic living communities in the countryside surrounding Hamburg; and an education program designed to inform the public about the drug problem. Soon after the press conference they set up the phone bank, and by the end of September the group had received over two hundred calls.

7. Green, *All Dressed Up*, 190–91.
8. 351-10 II, Sozialbehörde II, Abl.3 135.21-2 Band 1, VBR, announcement, [1970].

The group's membership grew quickly. Within a few weeks of the press conference, it already had a dozen members. By the end of the year, around thirty-five people were living, on and off, in the apartment on Bornstraße, even though the apartment had room for only eight. It was an uncomfortable situation. "An uncanny number of guys rushing around the apartment . . . and junk . . . junk wherever you looked . . . and fucked up situations, and always overflowing," one member recalled.[9] Although the group believed in the power of individual self-transformation and proved reluctant to turn away active drug users, it was eventually forced to distance itself from addicts who preferred to see it as a drug connection rather than as a way out of the scene.

Though the group was becoming quite popular, it was still in desperate need of funding. Release began the long process of trying to obtain funding from the state, which up to that point had done almost nothing to deal with the growing number of young people strung out on drugs other than to arrest them. The chaotic environment on Bornstraße and the ragged appearance of the members no doubt did little to endear them to the authorities. Even so, they continued to have frequent discussions with members of the Hamburg Youth Authority and the Work and Social Welfare Authorities. The negotiations, however, often degenerated into impassioned arguments. The members of Release saw their role as helping young people help themselves; they also had little problem with young people using soft drugs, such as hashish and LSD, in moderation. Neither of these principles meshed well with the state bureaucrats' understanding of the drug problem. The notion of giving young people a radically antiauthoritarian space in which to express themselves and to free themselves from their addictions seemed to the representatives of the state as nothing more than a pipe dream. Indeed, many of the state representatives thought of the Release group as a "camouflaged drug ring."[10]

In October, the group published its first pamphlet and distributed it among Hamburg's drug users. Entitled "The Cool User," the pamphlet was a practical attempt to reduce the risks of drug use. It listed the things the cool user does and does not do.

9. VBR, *Der Release Trip* ([Hamburg]: [VBR], n.d.).
10. *Der Release Trip.*

The Cool User

Doesn't inject (and if he does, he makes sure that his works are clean and that there is no air inside the syringe).

Doesn't experiment with unknown drugs.

Puts high stock on the quality of the drugs and the trustworthiness of the dealer.

Doesn't use just any combination of drugs (life threatening: sleeping pills and alcohol or amphetamines).

Smokes and Trips only in trustworthy company and in a relaxed environment.

Only allows himself one trip a day.

Makes sure that Librium tablets are available. If a trip is bad, when you "flip out," take 100 mg Librium (it works after an hour) and an ice-cold drink, and if possible one with sugar in it.

Waits a couple of weeks after a bad trip before he tries to undertake a new journey.

Remembers that he will eventually come back from a bad trip without any drugs (or after a joint). Then he takes another 100 mg Librium (repeat if necessary).

Calls a psychiatrist (if possible, one that is familiar with the scene), if fear, emptiness, or loneliness repeatedly surfaces after drug use.

Knows, before he takes a drug, that the particular experiences he has wear off normally, after the drug has lost its effectiveness (normally after at most 24 hours.) Knows that drugs belong to reality, but also that reality is more than just drugs.[11]

Needless to say, the dissemination of this kind of practical information did not go over well with the state authorities, most of whom believed that it only encouraged more drug use. Yet it was exactly the kind of information that the scene desperately needed, since the number of injecting drug users was increasing rapidly and hepatitis was rampant.

The members of Release did not see themselves purely as a drug rehabilitation group that could "fix" drug users and return them to "normal" society. Rather, they sought to act as an advocate for drug

11. Private collection, Kurt-Jürgen Lange, Referat Drogen und Sucht, Hamburg; reproduced in Rolv Heuer et al., *Helft Euch selbst! Der Release-Report gegen die Sucht* (Reinbek bei Hamburg: Rowohlt, 1971), 85–87.

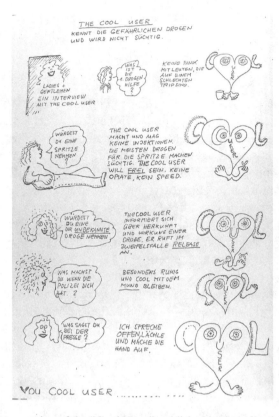

Fig. 6.   A later version of the "Cool User," published in the collective's 1973 book chronicling Release's activities. (Release, *Release: von den Anfängen 1970 in Hamburg bis zum Sommer 1973* [Hamburg: Release-Verlag, 1973]. Reproduced by permission of Herman Prigann.)

users, usually against the state. They had little interest in reintegrating the "flipped out" back into normal society. They wanted, instead, to remove drug users from the negative aspects of the drug scene, while building a community of individuals who could attempt to create a space within which to practice their own form of alternative communal life. The formation of communes would represent the seeds of a future socialist, utopian society, and the reason to treat drug addiction—which they understood as opiate or amphetamine addiction, not hashish or LSD use—was because it was inherently antirevolutionary and only acted to hinder the creation of a new, enlightened consciousness.

Earning the Trust of the State, 1970–71

By November, the group had begun building credibility by soliciting the help of professionals who donated their time, particularly doctors to whom they felt they could turn for solid advice. They enlisted a number of physicians, including Dr. Hans Wilhelm Beil, who wrote a weekly column for the *Hamburger Abendblatt* on youth issues and became a staunch advocate for young drug users. They also managed to find three lawyers who agreed to advocate for young people arrested for drug crimes.[12] This push to enhance their credibility with the state authorities paid off. On 5 November, the mayor of Hamburg, Peter Schulz, granted the group a meeting.[13]

The group's decision to turn to professionals for help improved their work, though it was also in many respects a ploy. In order to continue their work with the drug-addicted, they needed funding from the state. Until November 1970, they had received little encouragement. By involving "respectable" members of society, though, Release gained at least some legitimacy from the state's perspective, while retaining its own autonomy. Release was not simply manipulating the state youth and welfare bureaucracies, however. The state was also reliant on groups coming out of the political Left to try to deal with the drug problem. Release had contact with the scene and also had the trust of the drug users. The government bureaucracies had neither. This ambivalent, often antagonistic reliance upon one another was an important characteristic of the relationship between Release and the local agencies over the next four years.

An early example of the arrangement between the state and Release was the outreach work and group therapy that Release members

12. It should be noted that the list was proofed by a member of the Sozialbehörde, who found a number of the doctors listed were not actually actively working with the group. This sort of surveillance of the group was a hallmark of the relationship between the Behörden and the group; the members of the bureaucracy were quite suspicious of the group throughout its lifetime. 351-10 II, Sozialbehörde II, Abl. 2 251-50-166 Band 1, VBR, "Mitarbeiterliste," 4 November 1970. See also 354-5 II, Jugendbehörde II, Abl. 29.10.1986 356.04.06-7 Band 1, VBR, "Pressekonferenz 28.1.1971," 28 January 1971.

13. Heuer et al., *Helft Euch selbst!* 70.

undertook at the General Hospital at Barmbeck and at the youth detention center in Vierlande. Herman Prigann and Hans Meister approached the director of the youth detention center with an idea to work with the young prisoners convicted of drug crimes. The two were then sent to Dr. Ulrich Ehebald, the director of the psychoanalytic department at the General Hospital at Barmbeck. Ehebald reported back that Hans Meister was not suitable for the task but that Herman Prigann should be allowed to undertake the project. By the end of October, Prigann held weekly sessions with ten to thirty young inmates. His efforts were so successful that by January he was also counseling a group of ten young inmates in Hamburg's pretrial detention center (*Untersuchungshaft*).

Building a National Movement, 1970–71

Members of Release did not view the group merely as a local institution, providing services the state could or would not; they wanted to build an international movement. To this end, members visited similar groups in Helsinki, Copenhagen, Amsterdam, London, Oslo, and Stockholm that November. They also contacted another Release organization recently organized in Germany. Unlike the Hamburg group, the Heidelberg group was funded by the city from the outset. The city placed a large house at the group's disposal, which also had a medical staff, so they could actually detoxify young people there, saving them the unpleasant, and often horrifying, experience of detoxification in a public hospital.[14] Despite the differences in funding and facilities, however, both groups wanted to build a national network of Release groups. They did not want the group to be a national organization with a hierarchical structure, however. Instead, they conceived Germany's Release movement as a loose confederation of groups, each of which would make its own decisions and chart its own path.

With this plan in mind, several members of the Hamburg group began a tour of various cities in the Federal Republic in December, visiting groups that shared a similar agenda and government leaders who

14. 354-5 II, Jugendbehörde II, Abl. 29.10.1986 356.04.06-7 Band 1,VBR, "Pressekonferenz 28.1.1971," 28 January 1971. Heuer et al., *Helft Euch selbst!* 70. On the horrors of detoxification, see, esp., Joite, ed., 86–112.

could help fund the organization. They began by meeting with the Heidelberg group, between 5 and 9 December. Next, they met with a group of young people who had been working with wards of the state (*Fürsorgezöglinge*) in Cologne. On 12 December, they traveled to Bonn and met with Hamburg Bundestag member Alfons Pawelczyk, who arranged for three days of meetings with the federal officials overseeing drug policy. At the end of the meetings, the group members were optimistic about the possibility that these federal officials were serious about increasing funding for drug treatment. After their return to Hamburg, group members met with local officials in an attempt to secure daily payments from the state that were earmarked for private organizations that took in, and cared for, Hamburg youth.[15]

The Release Philosophy, 1971

As word spread through Hamburg about Release's work, more and more young people dropped by. In December alone, an estimated 450 young people visited the new office on Bundesstraße, while another 300 phoned its help line. Yet its serious financial predicament continued to escalate. The city prolonged the dispute over financial contributions. Release also faced having to move once again to a new location, since its Bundesstraße landlord intended to sell its office there.

In January, Release rented a farmhouse in Hattstedt bei Husum, to the northwest of Hamburg in Schleswig-Holstein, with the intention of taking at least four and possibly up to twelve Hamburg youth out of the urban environment.[16] On this property they could set up their own therapeutic community in which people would be free to help themselves overcome their addiction. Indeed, this was the battle cry of the entire movement—*Helft Euch selbst!* (Help Yourself!). They envisioned these rural living communities as a sort of Fourierist phalange, where everyone would be able to "do their own thing." The ex-users

15. 354–5 II, Jugendbehörde II, Abl. 29.10.1986 356.04.06-7 Band 1,Verein zur Bekämpfung der Rauschgiftgefahr, "Pressekonferenz 28.1.1971," 28 January 1971. Heuer et al., *Helft Euch selbst!* 70–71.

16. 354–5 II, Jugendbehörde II, Abl. 29.10.1986 356.04.06-7 Band 1, VBR, "Pressekonferenz 28.1.1971," 28 January 1971. Heuer et al., *Helft Euch selbst!* 71.351-10 II, Sozialbehörde II, Abl.3 135.04-1 Band 6, Koordinierungs- und Informationszentrale für Rauschmittelfragen, "Bericht über die Arbeit der von Hamburg aus geförderten therapeutischen Wohngemeinschaften für Drogenabhängige," 2 August 1973, 13.

would help those still kicking their habit, but there would be no authority, no demands, no rules.

The philosophical backing for this kind of project was published at the end of January in the group's first working paper, signed by Herman Prigann. The text begins by declaring, if in a rather obtuse way, the meaning of the organization.

> "Release" = Emancipation from every form of addiction. . . .
> "Release" is an emancipation process within social reality.
> Excursus: addiction = consumption = broken home situation
> = youth rebellion = refusal to learn = refusal to work.

Prigann presented the group's work as a mixture of drug therapy and alternative culture. Indeed, he saw the two as intrinsically bound: the therapy would consist of "creative production." By giving young addicts the tools with which to create an alternative to bourgeois life, he believed they would willingly give up the escape that drugs offered. In practice, this meant creating an alternative economy, an entrepreneurial underground that encompassed a tearoom, rock groups, concerts, film production, and an alternative press. Allowing young addicts to create their own culture would not reintegrate them into society but give them a space to build their own society.[17]

This was not a novel idea. The desire to create an alternative society was widespread in the early seventies in the wake of the disillusionment caused by the perceived failures of 1968. Yet Release did not make the turn exclusively toward the "politics of the self" or a "new subjectivity." They saw their work as an inherently public project, one that was obviously political. But they also proclaimed the need of the individuals to transform themselves; their interest in psychology and addiction meant that they leaned more toward Leary and Reich than toward Mao and Guevara.[18]

By the end of January 1971, the group's financial problems had reached a crisis point. On 28 January they held a press conference at which they announced that they were eight thousand deutsche marks in debt, being forced to vacate their offices on Bundesstraße, and to

17. Reprinted in Heuer et al., *Helft Euch selbst!* 98–99.

18. On the "politics of the self," see McCormick, *Politics of the Self,* esp. the introduction, and Sabine von Dirke, *"All Power to the Imagination!"* 67–104.

Fig. 7.   Release members at work. (Release, *Release: von den Anfängen 1970 in Hamburg bis zum Sommer 1973* [Hamburg: Release-Verlag, 1973]. Reproduced by permission of Herman Prigann.)

give up their living quarters on Bornstraße. The members had agreed among themselves to give up their Release work for two weeks in order to earn some money with which to continue. Eckhard Günther, the newly appointed coordinator for drug problems in Hamburg, observed the press conference and stayed for several hours afterward to observe the work of the group. Günther, a senior government official who had been the personal assistant to Helmut Schmidt while he was a senator in Hamburg, was less than impressed with the cleanliness of the office. But he was struck by the volume of visitors and phone calls and the way in which the members of the group knew those that stopped in by name. "My total impression has grown more positive," Günther wrote. "The people definitely do not see the goal as fully reintegrating their clients into bourgeois society. The will to bring them to abstinence, however, appears unmistakable." Though Günther's instincts told him that, in the long run, Release was definitely not the way to deal with drug addiction, on a practical level he was willing to lend them his support because they were actually having a positive effect on the drug scene.[19]

Despite Günther's growing admiration, or at least tolerance, of the group, they still received no funding from the state. In any case, working with representatives of the state tended to frustrate both parties: they spent much of their time talking past one another. Release members often felt that the two sides did not even speak the same language. One of their leaflets played on the problem.

We tried the hard way.
Until we found out that we had tried it at the wrong end again.
Behind us—months of fucked up negotiations with the authorities.
Result: *Nothing!!*
The idea was crazy enough, and we should have been able to foresee the result, but we were crazy (and still are) to believe that we could pay them to liberate power in order to release our generation (the part that we can reach with our message).
The idea:
To produce independence through "receipt of money for the medical care and healing of consumers of hard drugs" (officialdom-speak version) for the potential heads of our generation and through it to give them and us a chance to realize our vision of society.
Further: these heads were (and believe me, brother, they *are* . . .) multiplying.
Why multiplying????
In order to get enough power to end such things as: supervision by Big Brother's handmaiden, the pigs and the bureaucrats,
Jail . . .
The Nut-house . . .

19. 351-10 II, Sozialbehörde II, Abl.3 135.21-2-3 Band 1, Eckhard Günther, "Pressekonferenz des Vereins zur Bekämpfung der Rauschgiftgefahr, e.V. am 28.1.71," 1 February 1971.

Work Camp (horrible vision of the future) . . .
And finally Big Brother himself
. . . (you can certainly fill in a couple of things that occur to you)
We all row the same boat.
Find your *own* alternative.
DO IT!!!![20]

The brash sense of humor and the fanciful play on bureaucratic language demonstrate the chasm that existed between the perspective of the group and the official state view on addiction, but they also show the exuberance with which Release approached its work in the early seventies. They believed they could make a difference and that they could transform society.

During the spring of 1971, the group's finances received a much-needed infusion of cash. In March, the Association for the Support of Youth Initiatives agreed to assume the rent for the Hamburg office. Then in May the Hamburg Youth Authority finally agreed to pay a daily stipend of fourteen deutsche marks for each young drug user living in the group's therapeutic living community.[21]

Though the group still lacked the outright support of the various local authorities, they began to receive vocal support from some unlikely sources. Most helpful was the support of one of the leading experts in Hamburg on drug addiction, Dr. Ulrich Ehebald. Ehebald was a member of the psychoanalytic department at the General Hospital at Barmbeck and cosponsor of Herman Prigann's outreach program there. In April, when the director of a private drug clinic in Bremen-Oberneuland complained to the Hamburg Bürgerschaft about the work of Release and the entire ex-user treatment model, Dr. Ehebald was the only person to come to the group's defense. He argued that traditional treatment methods had failed and that "science must now learn from the ex-users."[22] Then in June Ehebald wrote a letter supporting the Release group. He wrote that, though they had approached each other with apprehension, they had been able to find a workable

---

20. Heuer et al., *Helft Euch selbst!* 96.
21. 354-5 II, Jugendbehörde II, Abl. 29.10.1986 356.04.06-7 Band 1, Garbe, "Stellungnahme zu dem erneuten Alternativmodell, bezogen auf die geplante Arbeit auf dem 'Jugendhof' in Otterndorf des VBR vom 22.4.71," 13 May 1971. Heuer et al., *Helft Euch selbst!* 72.
22. Heuer et al., *Helft Euch selbst!* 73.

solution. He claimed that the Hamburg Release group was, to his knowledge, the only group in Europe that had come up with a sensible plan that promised some measure of success in the fight against addiction.

Dr. Ehebald exemplified the general willingness among liberals to give young people the freedom to experiment with new, if radical, treatments. Whether or not liberals liked what these more radical organizations were attempting, they were curious to see whether their projects would work. "You speak of the reintegration of drug addicts," Ehebald wrote. "I believe that we ought to be very liberal on this point. As a doctor, I'm interested in rescuing youth from addiction. Whether they then integrate themselves into society in the way in which many of us would perhaps wish, or whether they go their own way, perhaps through the founding of communes, etc., this is then, to be sure, no longer a medical problem. Certainly a new model of human collaboration is being practiced here, which I personally observe with great interest and also with a certain curiosity."[23] This kind of tolerance was integral to the success of Release, and when it waned, the group's future was less secure.

On 13 June 1971, the group took part in a seminar on drugs at the Social Pedagogic Center at the University of Hamburg, along with several other groups forming their own alternative drug treatments. Out of the meeting came a new organization. Release joined with the members of the Social Pedagogic Center's drug seminar and another radical group, Jugend hilft Jugend, to form the Syndicate for the Support of Youth Collectives. Though the syndicate remained a loose confederation of the three organizations at best, the membership of a group from the university gave all the member groups a better base from which to deal with the government. The unification of three groups amplified their message and legitimized the creation of youth collectives as the dominant way to deal with long-term care for recovering drug addicts.

Soon after, the state began to take more active notice of the Release group. At the end of June, the commune in Otterndorf received several visits from members of the Hamburg Youth Authority. During the first visit, on 25 June, the chaotic life of the group shocked the visiting

23. 354-5 II, Jugendbehörde II, Abl. 29.10.1986 356.04.06-7 Band 1, Dr. Ulrich Ehebald, "Release-Zenter Otterndorf," 18 June 1971.

representatives: "The members were very unkempt; their clothing was disorderly, partially primitive. The members that I was able to see were unwashed and reeked terribly; I dare say that they have not bathed in quite some time." The members tried to explain to the visitors that life at the home was based on voluntarism, that no one was coerced into doing anything against his or her will. The gentlemen from the Youth Authority were not quite sure how to deal with this kind of experiment, and their opinions were conflicted. They certainly could not dream of placing a young person from an "orderly home" in this kind of atmosphere. Yet they saw very little chance of dealing with young drug addicts through normal channels. They decided, therefore, that if this group was willing to deal with these difficult cases, then their work should be supported.[24]

Three days later, Axel Peters and Hans Albers, the two men in the Youth Authority responsible for dealing with various private drug treatment organizations across the city, paid a visit to the house. The meeting was amiable, and the two left with a good impression of the group. Their report noted, however, that the group was not quite as radically egalitarian as they would like to think themselves. "Part of the group took part in an animated discussion," Peters recorded. "Several young women were working in the kitchen, a young girl caulked a window, and Herr Prigann, Herr Meister and two other young men were building in the 'Barn.'"[25] Apparently, the wish to create a new alternative to bourgeois life did not quite do away with the gendered division of labor. They noted another kind of hierarchy within the group; they believed that "Herr Meister is the 'manual head' of the collective, while Herr Prigann obviously appears to be the more praxis oriented planner and Herr Witecka the ideologue."[26] Certainly it was the case that some members shouldered more responsibility than others. But the 'group prided itself on consensus building as a means of decision making.

While part of the group continued to get the farmhouse in Otterndorf in order throughout July, several members traveled to Cologne to set up a new Release association. A group of ex-users in Cologne had convinced the city to provide them with a Release office, but they had

24. Heuer et al., *Helft Euch selbst!* 73.

25. 354-5 II, Jugendbehörde II, Abl. 29.10.1986 356.04.06-7 Band 1, Peters, "Projekt Jugendhof Otterndorf," 8 July 1971.

26. 354-5 II, Jugendbehörde II, Abl. 29.10.1986 356.04.06-7 Band 1, Peters, "Projekt Jugendhof Otterndorf," 8 July 1971.

fallen out with the city over the issue of oversight. The members of the Hamburg group helped them register as an official association, so that they could act independently. The Cologne members opened a new office and organized their group around a rural collective, much like the one in Otterndorf. With chapters of Release opening in several cities around West Germany, it seemed as if the Release concept might soon become a leading force in drug treatment.

Crisis in Release Heidelberg and the Limits of Tolerance, 1970–71

The political climate in Germany was growing tense by 1971 as terrorism continued to plague the government; the Release movement soon became embroiled in the attempts to suppress Leftist armed struggle. Just as the group in Cologne was getting on its feet, Release Heidelberg was wracked by internal crises. Dietmar Höhne had founded the organization in November 1970. After talks with the mayor, the city agreed to furnish the group with a house from which they could work. In the middle of November, the mayor asked to meet with Höhne, and another member named Henky went along. The mayor explained that he had received an anonymous tip that Höhne was a member of the Socialist Patients' Collective (Sozialistische Patientenkollektiv, or SPK). The SPK was a radical group formed by Dr. Wolfgang Huber at the University of Heidelberg. Huber believed that mental illness was the direct result of capitalism and that the mentally ill should band together against the system. He insisted that mental illness was in fact a sane response to an insane and oppressive world. The university attempted to dismiss Huber, leading the members of the collective to occupy one of the university buildings. The standoff ended nonviolently with compromises on both sides. Yet by early 1971, several members of the collective, inspired by the Red Army Faction, had moved toward terrorism. In mid-February two members of the collective, Sigfried Hausner and Carmen Roll, hatched a plan to blow up West German president Gustav Heinemann's train. The attempt failed, but it brought the SPK in direct conflict with the government and spawned the so-called second generation of the Red Army Faction.[27]

27. For a more detailed discussion of the SPK see Cornelia Brink, "Radikale Psychiatriekritik in der BRD. Zum Sozialistischen Patientenkollektiv in Heidelberg," in *Psychiatriereform als Gesellschaftsreform: die Hypothek des Nationalsozialismus und der Aufbruch der sechziger Jahre,* ed. Franz-Werner Kersting (Paderborn: Schöningh, 2003).

Höhne was indeed a member of the SPK, having joined in March after the bombing attempt, and firmly believed in their radical critique of capitalism. "Release-fight for peace: free yourself, fight for your freedom!" he demanded.

That means direct mobilization of the scene, the youth in prisons, youth homes and psychiatric institutions, in schools and in training. . . . The Black Power-speak of Stockeley [*sic*] Carmichael: trust your own experiences, proceed from the assumption that in capitalism there is nothing that makes one depressed, tortured, hampered, burdened, sick that doesn't originate in the capitalist means of production or in the contradiction between wage-labor and capital, that every oppressor, in whatever form he takes is a representative of the interests of capital, in the same way that every representative of the interests of capital, even if he is unaware, is an oppressor, that is to say: our enemy. . . . Between us and our enemies we must draw a clear line in the sand![28]

Höhne's radicalism almost certainly conflicted with the political views of Heidelberg's mayor. At the meeting Höhne admitted belonging to the SPK, though he assured the mayor that Release and the SPK were quite separate organizations. The mayor warned Höhne and Henky that, if he discovered that Release and the SPK were working together, he would promptly eliminate all financial aid from the city. The two assured him that there would be no need for such a rash measure; they would keep the two groups quite separate.

After the meeting with the mayor, the group settled down to the booming business of nursing the substantial Heidelberg drug scene. Six months later, in May 1971, two junkies, Ingo and Irene Warnke, joined the group. Ingo had been shooting junk since 1967 and was still on the needle. When they arrived at the house in Heidelberg, "there were 35 people in the house, of whom 10 were still shooting up and the rest smoked a lot of hashish."[29] He and Höhne fought constantly. The members who were still injecting attempted a group detoxification, but after three days they were back to old habits. Henky flipped out and left for Spain. Another member of the group, Mitsu, followed later.

28. Heuer et al., *Helft Euch selbst!* 124.
29. Joite, *Fixen*, 116.

Soon Ingo and Irene left to get clean. They went to a small farm-house in the Oldenwald that Dietmar Höhne had rented. After a week, they returned clean. Ingo, Irene, and Dietmar decided to clean up the house. Those who chose to continue to shoot up were kicked out of the group. Not long after, Dieter, one of the members who had chosen not to give up the needle, went to the farmhouse in the Oldenwald, hoping to repeat the success of Ingo and Irene. He had taken some morphine with him, however, and died of an overdose.

On 24 June, the police stopped two members of the SPK at a check-point. The two tried to outrun the police and in the process shot an officer in the arm. That night the police raided the SPK headquarters, and twelve members were arrested. Höhne was still a member of the group, though he was not among those arrested.

The tense atmosphere in Heidelberg due to the broadening campaign against terrorism compounded the problems within Release. In the following weeks, a struggle ensued over control of the group. Mitsu returned from Spain and accused Höhne and Ingo Warnke of being murderers because they had refused to take in addicts who continued injecting narcotics. On 13 July, the mayor requested a meeting with Höhne. Irene and Ingo accompanied him. When they arrived, they were surprised to see Mitsu and Henky already in attendance. That night, Henky returned to the Release house, packed his bags, and announced that he was quitting the group. Mitsu and Henky wanted to take over the group, so they complained to the authorities. In the ensuing struggle for control, Henky and Mitsu had the upper hand. Höhne's membership in the SPK had guaranteed that he would not be popular with the mayor. He was given a choice: either he could leave the Release group or the entire group's funding would be taken away. Ingo and Irene left with several members to found a new group in Berlin, while Höhne attempted to return to a normal life.[30]

Before the Heidelberg association spun out of control, several members of the Hamburg group visited Heidelberg. The members from Hamburg chastised the Heidelbergers for the way their operation was run, calling it a "voluntary ghetto." They commiserated with the problems the Heidelberg group was experiencing; at first, they too had had problems with junkies seeing Release as a place to find and take drugs.

30. Heuer et al., *Helft Euch selbst!* 120–22; Joite, *Fixen,* 116.

But they insisted that this was not the point of Release as a movement. Release, to them, meant creating a space within which members could begin the process of forming a stable alternative culture. Forming a counterculture was imperative, they argued, because the relatively liberal attitude the state was taking toward drugs would not last forever. "We must begin to build a scene now," Prigann argued. "So that in five, six years there is a solidarity there, if the nationalistic terror begins again. . . . History has shown us that such societies, like the one that still exists today, always need minorities to come down on when everything goes to hell. . . . And the next minority is, without a doubt, the drug minority."[31] The infighting in Heidelberg seemed pointless to the Hamburg members. Prigann was prescient about the limits of state tolerance. The state, lacking an infrastructure of its own, needed groups like Release in the early seventies. And since it appeared that they were having a positive effect, the state tolerated their eccentricities. When the seemingly unlimited finances began to dry up in the midseventies, though, the state proved less willing to be indulgent.

Building a Counterculture, 1971–72

Back in Hamburg in September, Release moved into a spacious new office on Karolinenstraße. The building—a former print shop—stood off the street in a courtyard. It was perfect for their purposes. Karolinenstraße lay just to the north of the St. Pauli red-light district, where most of the drug trade took place and where drug users would have easy access to their services. Release saw it as "an alternative-scene for the pleasure district."[32] The building itself was a large five-story brick edifice with tall French doors and far more space than the group had ever had before. On the first floor, they planned a workshop where handmade goods could be sold to the public—a kind of work project for the flipped out. Directly above the workshop would be an inexpensive hostel. On the next floor, the group would have its own office and offer space to other groups concerned with the drug problem, such as the Syndicate for the Support of Youth Collectives. From this urban Release center, they could offer a wide variety of services to the Ham-

31. Heuer et al., *Helft Euch selbst!* 114.
32. Ibid., 74.

burg scene: educational programs, medical counseling, legal help, telephone counseling, and group therapy. The center also acted as a central organ for the coordination of the therapeutic living communities, in which the long-term counseling of young drug users took place.

From the outset, the group had wanted to set up its own alternative printing press. They saw the ability to publish underground literature as a key part of building an alternative culture within Germany. This was in no way a new idea; underground papers were a hallmark of the countercultural Left from the midsixties. Purchasing an offset press, however, was a step toward their desire to create an alternative economy, through which they could fund their experiments in lifestyle. They purchased the press in September and immediately began publishing their own work as well as books on drugs and popular culture.

Release's first project was a brochure entitled "Release Info 2." The cover had a Robert Crumb–inspired cartoon, complete with letters made of clouds reading "beautiful new world" and exotic anthropomorphic automobiles devouring headless people. Above the title, the words *fight for peace*—in English—were encircled by a half moon and the word *Release*.[33] After publishing "Release Info 2," they put out a new version of Ronald Steckel's *Consciousness Expanding Drugs: An Invitation to Discussion,* which had first been published in Berlin in 1969.[34] By their own admission, the quality of these first publications was less than stellar, though it was at least a start.

Their work with the press and their contact with the scene in 1971 focused on raising awareness. A set of daily reports from September gives some insight into the day-to-day workings of the group. Early on 20 September, several of the members left the commune at Otterndorf for Hamburg. Once back in the city, they made contact with radio and television stations and sent a letter to the Rowohlt publishing house about the possibility of producing a book. Two men representing the landlord of the Karolinenstraße center came by to check on repairs. "One of them, a shithead," according to the report, "told me that he wouldn't give anything to people who mutilate themselves. He said he

33. *Der Release Trip.*

34. 354-5 II, Jugendbehörde II, Abl. 29.10.1986 356.04.06-7 Band 1, R. V. Hamburg, "Release Verlag Hamburg/Velgen," entered by Jugendbehörde 26 February 1973. See also Ronald Steckel, *Bewußtseinserweiternde Drogen; eine Aufforderung zur Diskussion* (Berlin: Edition Voltaire, 1969).

wasn't an alcoholic. I pointed out to him that this was a societal problem. What he meant was that National Socialism also started out with good intentions, and he admired our idealism."[35] Later they cooked pizzas and planned the press conference scheduled for the following week. The next day Thomas Struck, one of the members of the group, patrolled the area in the quarter, trying to make contact with the scene. Later the police barged into the center; apparently a neighbor had called the police and claimed to have heard a scream. On 23 September, Struck described a normal day at the center on Karolinenstraße: "We unloaded two deliveries of wood today. . . . I wrote 7 letters to the press. In the afternoon a guy dropped by in the company of two students. They took him in and are now trying to get him a bed in the Altona hospital. He's coming again today. Perhaps he'll say more then. The newspapers are full of stuff. Everybody is stoned." The day-to-day work at Release was not glamorous or well appreciated or even well paid, but the group provided a focal point for many young people who had no place else to turn.

While the members continued to work on the center and the printing activities were getting under way, the group received unexpected and unlikely support from *Bild,* the mouthpiece of the Springer publishing empire. "For exactly a year, Hamburg has had Release-people," *Bild* reported. "For an entire year, the founders—first and foremost Herman Prigann (29)—have had to struggle against the mistrust of the population and the Authorities. No one believed that the people, who at one time had been a slave to drugs, could manage to help addicts. Today it is certain: only they are in the position to bring back the 'flipped out.'"[36] The article even called for individuals to donate to the group, noting that the center lacked sufficient coal for the winter. The article concluded with a warning to parents: they should invest in Release because their children could be the next to fall prey to drug addiction and need someone to whom they could turn.

In October and November 1971, Release finally found a way out of its financial bind. With the kind of entrepreneurial spirit that marked the underground throughout Europe and North America, they went in

---

35. *Der Release Trip.*
36. "Hasch-Helfer im Hinterhof," *Bild,* 9 September 1971. See also Walter Weber, "Zwölf Jugendliche kämpfen gegen die Sucht," *Bild,* 22 April 1970.

search of something to sell to young people.[37] They found their savior in an unlikely place, a major record company. Kinney Music, the German subsidiary of Atlantic Records, agreed to produce an album and donate a sizable portion of each record sale to the group. A number of big-name bands—Led Zeppelin; Frank Zappa; Crosby, Stills, Nash, and Young; and James Taylor, to name a few—donated songs for an album entitled, in English, *Let It Rock for Release.* For each sale, Kinney Music donated DM 2 to Release. In addition to the album, Kinney Music sponsored a bus tour of the Federal Republic for members of the Release group. They spread the message against the use of hard drugs and, of course, promoted the album. The "Let It Rock" bus left Hamburg in the middle of November and traveled around the country for a month. If the success of the trip was measured by record sales, then it was a smashing success. Already by the end of the journey, the royalty checks began arriving. The next year, the Rolling Stones donated a live album that was published under the title *Let It Rock— Live at Leeds.* In the end, Release made around DM 250,000 from the venture.[38]

The Konkret *Antidrug Congress*

In early spring 1972, Klaus Ranier Röhl, publisher of the German New Left magazine *Konkret,* announced a national meeting of the Left to discuss the drug problem and make a unified statement on drugs. Röhl had been a powerful figure in New Left politics since the late 1950s. *Konkret* had been one of the major Leftist publications during the 1960s; by the late 1960s, it had a wide circulation and a loyal base. With *Konkret*'s backing, the antidrug congress was sure to be well attended.

Röhl had made his own statement about drugs two years earlier on the editorial page of his magazine. He condemned all drug use as inherently antirevolutionary. "Hash makes you stupid," he argued. Since the goal of the Left should be to hasten the inevitable revolution and

37. Arthur Marwick, *The Sixties,* 17, argues that this "entrepreneurial spirit" of the counterculture was one of the most important and most overlooked facets of change in popular culture.

38. 351-10 II, Sozialbehörde II, Abl.3 135.21-2-3 Band 1, S. E. Loch and A. R. Kinney Music GMBH, "Verein zur Bekämpfung der Rauschgiftgefahr, e.V. Record," 15 November 1971, and "Mick Jagger hilft Rauschgift-Süchtigen," *Bild,* 4 January 1972.

establish the foundation for a socialist state, drug use was only a distraction. Röhl denounced the idea of consciousness expansion, which had been so popular in the last two years of the sixties, as heretical. Material conditions determined consciousness, and altering one's consciousness could and would do nothing whatsoever to change material realities and bring in a new era of socialism. The idea that society could be transformed by turning on, tuning in, and dropping out seemed to Röhl to be ludicrous. Therefore. it was every good Leftist's duty to shun drugs and focus on politics. In the same vein as more conservative critics, Röhl sought to push drug consumption and drug users away from the realm of the political, to paint it as inherently apolitical.[39]

The congress was planned for 18 and 19 March in Hamburg. The highly fractured nature of the political Left[40] after 1968 guaranteed that the congress would be colorful and almost certainly confrontational. The choice of invited speakers also guaranteed that the venue would be lively. In addition to speakers from various leftist groups, Röhl invited Eckhard Günter and a representative of the Hamburg police to address the audience. He also invited members of the Hamburg Release group to speak about their work in the Hamburg scene.

The members of Release showed some trepidation about taking part in the congress. They had a healthy distrust of the dogmatic Marxists and feared that the congress might degenerate into a battle over the minutia of socialist doctrine. Release debated the merits of participating in the congress, and this discussion demonstrates their understanding of the relationship between the Left and the counterculture and between politics and violence. This dialogue expressed how the group saw itself fitting into the larger constellation of political and cultural change in the early seventies.

Release saw the antidrug congress as a forum in which to convince the political Left that drug users were not merely a breeding ground for the extreme Left and potential terrorists but rather members of the proletariat. They believed that the political Left saw drug users as essentially apolitical. Release saw drug use as a political act, but not one that could be conflated with the political violence perpetrated by groups like the Red Army Faction. "The Red Army Faction assumes

39. K. R. Röhl, "Hasch macht dumm!" *Konkret,* 26 February 1970, 8.
40. See McCormick, *Politics of the Self,* 41–42.

that it will not be possible to change the existing capitalist system through democratic reforms, through democratic machinations," one member argued, "because the power relationships that have existed for hundreds of years and still exist will not let themselves be questioned. . . . For them, there is no reformist perspective to changing society, only the revolutionary. Given that, we are in a difficult situation. We see that our own praxis is revolutionary. . . . The political groups, which have taken the hard revolutionary line, won't admit that. They say that we must make a clear differentiation between the enemy and us." Release saw their work as revolutionary, but they believed it was essential to work with the system, to be able to meet face to face with members of the government who could either hinder or help their cause. They rejected the strict revolutionary line that agitation and transformation must come from outside the halls of political power, and they dismissed the idea that socialism had to be instituted through violent means.

The members of Release believed that socialism had to be built, that transforming the world meant first transforming private life, that the personal was political, and that only by transforming the basic units of society could socialism triumph over capitalism. Prigann argued, "They will only understand us if we make it clear to them, o.k. you want socialism as the future form of society; you are working on this today and drawing up written conceptions? Each one sits in his hang-out and then one meets with whatever working group in a neutral place, but your life is not collectivized. You have never tried among yourselves to answer the economic question. . . . That is a concrete demand, build collectives here and now!" This sentiment, that the revolution meant transformation of the self as much as transformation of society, was one of the most important ideas to come out of the radicalism of the sixties, and it came as much from the counterculture as from the overtly political realm of student politics. Release saw its goal as a revolution in everyday life and a building of new forms of consciousness that would someday, somehow, spread and lead to a general transformation of society at large.[41]

When the congress met in March, over a thousand people crowded the Audi-max, the largest auditorium at the University of Hamburg.

41. *Der Release Trip.* See also Heuer et al., *Helft Euch selbst!*

The congress proceeded much as the Release group had feared. Groups on the political Left squabbled among themselves and attempted to involve Release in debates they would rather have avoided. According to a member of Hamburg's Social Welfare Authority who attended the conference:

> The course of the congress was impaired significantly throughout because members of the German Communist Party [DKP] and other "Leftist" organizations constantly changed the function of the work groups and embarked on their own radical political agendas. Frequently it led to arguments between the representatives of various theories. Members of the Release movement occasionally found themselves in an unpleasant situation because DKP representatives wanted to use them for their own political aims. The Release members, however, only wanted to present their therapy conception and advertise it.[42]

Despite their inability to avoid questions from the political Left about their political commitment, Release capitalized on the antidrug congress. They were able to stake out a claim as a Leftist response to the drug problem that seemed to work.

The Search for Stability, 1972–73

After the antidrug congress, Release attempted to continue building their therapy conception. Despite their successes, they faced challenges from several sides: the police, the community, and the state authorities. As was perhaps inevitable given the nature of their project, Release constantly had run-ins with the police. In May 1972, the police raided the group's clothing boutique, Mescal, located just north of the university. The police believed that opium was being dealt out of the storefront but failed to find any evidence.[43] In June, Youth Protection Police confiscated a copy of one of Release's comic books—a transla-

---

42. 351-10 II, Sozialbehörde II, Abl.3 135.20-0 Band 4, S. Mieck, Amt für Soziales und Rehabilitation der Arbeits- und Sozialbehörde, "Antidrogen-kongress der Zeitschrift Konkret am 18. und 19.3.1972 in Hamburg," 1972.

43. 354-5 II, Jugendbehörde II, Abl. 29.10.1986 356.04.06-7 Band 1, P. E. Dienstgruppe Jugendschutz, "Hamburg 19, Henriettenstrasse 45–47 und Hamburg 13, Schlüterstr./Hartungstr.," 26 May 1972.

tion of Robert Crumb's *Homegrown Comics*—at a rock concert in the park, believing that it transgressed Hamburg's Youth Protection Laws. This occasion allowed Release to show off their sense of humor and thumb their collective nose at the police at the same time. They reprinted the confiscation receipt with the following caption:

> what can you do when you're a policeman, like to read comics, but are so poor that you can't come up with 60 pfennigs?
>
> You simply confiscate the comic book (not all of them, no, but just one to read). You can always find a reason here: publishing obscene writings. now honestly, what is more obscene: our amusing comics or the naked, wounded Andreas Baader on the front page of today's BILD-Zeitung (next to it is "exclusive: the best pictures are in BILD")?????????[44]

Later that month, police arrested one of the young charges of the Graumannsweg collective in front of the Bonaparte dance club for possession of narcotics and paraphernalia. Needless to say, these incidents were quickly reported to the funding authorities and did little to further the group's cause.

The authorities also received complaints from parents of Release's young charges. In June, Eckhard Günther received a letter from a mother of one of the young patients at the Velgen collective. She had visited the Velgen house in early May and was aghast at the conditions. Not only were all the individuals unclean and the house a mess, but they looked hungry to her. Furthermore, she suspected that they were all on drugs. "As I came into the house," she complained, "one of the members was dozing naked on the sofa. I got the impression that they had 'group sex' there."[45] Whether or not there actually was "group sex" being practiced in Velgen, the permissive atmosphere of the living communities and their lack of adherence to bourgeois values of cleanliness and sexual propriety brought them into conflict with those who did not or could not understand their motivations.

More devastating, however, was an article published in *Die Welt* on

44. 354-5 II, Jugendbehörde II, Abl. 29.10.1986 356.04.06-7 Band 1, VBR, "Home grown comix!" June 1972.

45. 354-5 II, Jugendbehörde II, Abl. 29.10.1986 356.04.06-7 Band 1, Kraack and P. M. D. Jugendschutz, "Angelika B. K.," 16 June 1972. 354-5 II, Jugendbehörde II, Abl. 29.10.1986 356.04.06-7 Band 1, E. Prapucki, "Protokoll," 8 June 1972.

19 June. The Springer newspaper accused the Hamburg Release collectives of harboring deserters from the army. The charge of harboring deserters, which the group vigorously denied, was exacerbated by the ongoing police actions against the Red Army Faction. By implicating the group in aiding and abetting deserters, the Springer press also insinuated that they were open to harboring terrorists. Whether they were open to this idea is a matter of conjecture; however, the taint of terrorism would haunt the group through the remainder of its short lifetime.[46]

In August and September 1972, the group underwent another trial by fire, this time from the community. The group applied to open a macrobiotic restaurant in the Karolinenstraße Release Center. The community around the center vigorously protested their application to anyone who would listen. Misinformed, the citizens believed that Release had applied for a liquor permit and drew up a petition to halt the granting of a license, complaining that young people (of both sexes!) traipsed in and out of the center at all hours of the night and that rock music blared from the windows. Surprisingly, Eckhard Günther came to their defense, shielding them from the wrath of the Bürgerschaft, and the group received its food service permit despite the objections of the neighbors.[47]

In spite of all the setbacks, the group pressed on with its outreach and treatment and in November held an enormous rock concert at the Petrikirche. A stage was set up below the altar under the gigantic crucifix, and hundreds of people filled the church to hear the bands and watch an experimental film entitled *Tantra*. The group billed the occasion as an "educational" event, though it was much more of a happening than a dry colloquium on the evils of drugs. "The information was

46. "Ist 'Release e.V.' ein Verein, der Deserteuren Zuflucht bietet?" *Die Welt,* 19 June 1972. "Release-Zentren sollen ihre Arbeit offenlegen," *Die Welt,* 22 June 1972. 351-10 II, Sozialbehörde II, Abl. 2 251-50-166 Band 1, Mieck and S. 34, "Artikel in der Welt vom 19.6.72," 20 June 1972.

47. 351-10 II, Sozialbehörde II, Abl.3 135.21-2-3 Band 2, Kleist, Report, 9 August 1972. 351-10 II, Sozialbehörde II, Abl.3 135.21-2-3 Band 2, B. Rehders, Hamburg-Mitte and Wohnungs- und Ordnungsamt, Release restaurant permit, 14 August 1972. 351-10 II, Sozialbehörde II, Abl.3 135.21-2-3 Band 2, W. Baumann, Vorsitzender der Schutzgemeinschaft Karolinenviertel e.V., "Release-Center," 27 August 1972. 351-10 II, Sozialbehörde II, Abl. 3 135.21-2-3 Band 2, Graupner and others, "Release-Center," 19 September 1972. 351-10 II, Sozialbehörde II, Abl.3 135.21-2-3 Band 2, E. Günther, "Release-Center," September 1972.

drowned out by three rock bands and the consumer attitude of most of the young guests, who would rather hear music than pose questions," the *Hamburger Abendblatt* editorialized. Yet in terms of getting their message out to a larger audience, the evening could only have been judged a success by the members of Release.[48]

The next year proved even more trying for the group. In March, it again ran afoul of the police. An internal memo from the Hamburg Department of the Interior claimed that Release was an "agitation center of the extreme left." It accused the group of spreading radical propaganda through its printing press and noted that Herman Prigann had "come to light" due to his "anarchist contacts." Of course, this was merely a veiled accusation that Release was at least too sympathetic to terrorists and perhaps actively complicit. In any case, it hints that the political police involved in hunting down the terrorists were watching the group.[49]

The police and the neighboring community, however, were not the only groups Release had trouble with. The so-called Rockers—the German equivalent of North American biker gangs such as the Hell's Angels—disliked the group intensely. These working-class toughs harbored a great animosity toward the hippy set, which they considered effeminate, and though they themselves were prone to alcohol abuse, they saw drug use as degenerate. In May, a group of Rockers ransacked the center on Karolinenstaße, beating some of the members and forcing them out of the house. The next morning the police raided the building and found seventeen Rockers. Apparently, after they had run off the Release workers, they got drunk and passed out.[50]

Though the group faced pressures from within and without, they proved loyal to their charges. In early 1973, two of the young members, a twenty-five-year-old student named Monika and a twenty-year-old worker named Frank, left Germany to travel down the hippie trail to

48. *Hamburger Abendblatt,* "'Release' wollte informieren, doch man erfuhr wenig," 25–26 November 1972.

49. 351-10 II, Sozialbehörde II, Abl. 3 135.21-2-3 Band 2, "'Release'—Agitationszentrum der extremen Linken," 1 March 1973; 351-10 II, Sozialbehörde II, Abl.3 135.21-2-3 Band 2, VBR, "Den Zeitpunkt des Wandelns zu verpassen, nennt ihr die ding sich entwickeln lassen," [1973].

50. W. Weber and C. Gottwaldt, "17 Rocker überfielen die Drogen-Helfer," *Bild,* 11 May 1973. "Die U-Bahn-Rocker von Berne sind festgenommen: Jugendliche überfielen Release-Center in St. Pauli," *Die Welt,* 11 May 1973.

India. During a drug raid in Kabul, the two were arrested. They were released, but the police held their passports until they paid a sizable fine. In April one of the Release leaders, Thomas Witecka, raised money and drove to Kabul in an old *Morgenpost* newspaper delivery van to return the two home to West Germany.[51]

In June, the group received a crushing blow: a seventeen-year-old resident of the Otterndorf collective had died of an overdose. The young man had been an addict since the age of fourteen. In May, he had decided he had had enough and turned to Release for help. After detoxification, he went to the land collective in Otterndorf and had been doing quite well, holding down a job in nearby Cuxhaven. After six weeks, however, he received his first paycheck and went on a drug binge. He purchased around forty sleeping pills and Valium. When the group left for the city, the young man injected himself alone. Three hours later another member found him dead.[52] The fact that the young man died at the collective reflected poorly on the group and, for many within the state government, simply verified their long-held belief that the group was a cover for drug use and failed to serve its clients in an orderly and scientific manner.

The Denouement, 1974–75

Over the next six months, Release Hamburg slowly began to fall apart. In November, a young ex-resident of the land collective in Velgen wrote a scathing letter to the senator for health and social welfare. The woman had moved to Velgen in August with her two children. She claimed that serious cannabis use was rampant within the group (at a cost of three to four thousand deutsche marks per month) and that they neglected the children then living at the commune. She also alleged that several members of the group were planning to break with Release but not before they "stuff their pockets." Eckhard Günther responded to her letter quite sympathetically, and his letter gives us an insight into the complex relationship between the state and the group.

Three years ago, as the first attempts at reform in the therapeutic area began, no one could have known how the individual experi-

51. Ilsa Luksche, "Der Retter startet," *Hamburger Morgenpost,* 16 April 1973.
52. "Junge spritzte sich zu Tode," *Hamburger Morgenpost,* 23 June 1973.

ments would look. Consequently, in Hamburg we took the stand-point that all models should be given the same chances and the same support. In the meantime, we have come far enough that we are able to begin sorting. But there are also limitations that lay within the nature of the issue. For one thing, the gap between demand for drug treatment and its availability is extraordinarily great; second not every drug addict is suited for every type of facility, and third, facilities with professional staff constantly have to deal with the lack of personnel. Unfortunately, as long as there is a general lack of social workers, it is almost impossible to attract labor for stationary drug treatment facilities, because trained workers normally prefer easier jobs such as family welfare, for instance.[53]

From the beginning the state had needed groups like Release to deal with the enormous increase in drug abuse. As the state welfare agencies built up their own infrastructure, however, they would be able to weed out groups that did not adhere to what it considered a proper thera-peutic model.

In a larger sense, Günther's statement is important because it high-lights the fact that the state did not just use its repressive power to quash alternative lifestyles, even when those included illegal acts such as drug consumption. The state's liberal attitude and its symbiotic rela-tionship with private groups like Release were key aspects of the con-nection between the counterculture and the state into the midseventies. Local authorities were willing to support experiments because the problems they had traditionally dealt with had changed drastically over the course of the sixties.

By January 1974, Release was beginning to spin out of control. A young electrician who took over leadership appeared to be trying to bring some kind of order to a chaotic situation. The hostel was still open, though, and the press continued its work. In the two communes in Velgen and Otterndorf, the group was still treating sixteen youths. In all, approximately eighty young people lived, on and off, in the two farmhouses.[54] The macrobiotic restaurant had been forced to shut its doors, at least temporarily, because of a lack of funds. The funds from

53. 351-10 II, Sozialbehörde II, Abl. 3 135.21-2-3 Band 2, E. Günther, "Frau Renzi-Hub-schmid," 23 November 1973.

54. 351-10 II, Sozialbehörde II, Abl. 2 251-50-166 Band 1, Seyer-Sonderheimer, "Besuch Karolinenstr. 7-9," 15 January 1974.

the record sales had long ago run dry, and the state was not forthcoming with more aid.[55]

The second half of 1974 witnessed the slow death of Release Hamburg. The authorities had become more hostile to the group, while the city, wracked by its own financial crisis, demanded huge cutbacks in every department. In October, Axel Peters, a member of the Youth Authority, visited the collective at Otterndorf and came away with the opinion that the group was no longer serious about helping young addicts but instead expended most of their energy on the Release Orchestra rock band. Therefore, he recommended that their funding be suspended.[56]

The final blow occurred in November 1974. On 9 November, Günter von Drenkmann, the president of Germany's Superior Court of Justice, was killed in a botched kidnapping attempt, setting off a nationwide search for terrorists. The police action, named *Winterreise,* struck the Release group. The police raided the collective at Otterndorf in the belief that the group was harboring terrorists. Though they found no evidence that the group had in fact helped the terrorists, they reintroduced some previous drug charges against the group in order to justify their actions.[57]

In early December, the group met with representatives of the Work and Social Welfare Authority, which was still funding five "patients" at Otterndorf. Since its dissolution in September, the group from Velgen had also moved into the house in Otterndorf. In all, twenty-one people were living in the old farmhouse. The representatives from the Work and Social Welfare Authority were less than pleased with the situation and proposed that the group be denied any further funding from the Hamburg government. Their main concern was that the group was doing nothing to reintegrate the young people back into society, nor did they intend to do so. Furthermore, they believed that

55. 351-10 II, Sozialbehörde II, Abl. 3 135.21-2-3 Band 3, H. Prigann, "Grundsatzerklärung der Selbsthilfeorganisation Release zur Frage der finanziellen Unterstützung," 4 June 1974.

56. 351-10 II, Sozialbehörde II, Abl. 3 135.21-2-3 Band 2, Axel Peters, Report on visit to Otterndorf, 10 October 1974.

57. 351-10 II, Sozialbehörde II, Abl. 2 251-50-166 Band 2, Seyer-Sondheimer and S. 34, "Bericht über den Besuch der Tagessatzkommission in der WG 'Otterndorf' am 27.11.1974," 6 December 1974.

the young people who were receiving payments from the state had chosen to stay not for a cure but rather because they preferred the communal living offered by the group to reentering "normal" society.[58]

By April of the next year, the funding for the group had run out, and the city's counseling center no longer had any interest in placing individuals in the group's collectives.[59] The group members faded away, and the center on Karolinenstraße was transformed into a New Age center, complete with a ballet studio, a Guru Ram Ashram, a yoga room, a tea shop, a work shop, multimedia shows, and a bookstore.[60]

Conclusion

Though the Release group in Hamburg dissolved in early 1975, several of the other groups were able to adapt to the changed circumstances. More important, many of the ideas Release championed—practical information for drug users, the use of therapeutic communities to treat young addicts, and the decriminalization of soft drugs—have become a reality. It took the AIDS scare of the late 1980s to force the drug treatment community in Germany to look for new solutions. Now, in Hamburg, possession of small amounts of drugs has been, for all practical purposes, decriminalized; injecting drug users now have state-run "clean rooms" in which they can inject themselves in sterile conditions; and drug treatment is more widely available than ever before. Release was, in many ways, ahead of its time.

But Release was also a product of its time. The Release movement gives us a certain insight into why alternative cultures were able to gain a foothold in Germany in the first half of the seventies and became a major presence in the latter half. Although the emergence of new problems such as drug addiction and terrorism led to an expansion of state

---

58. 351-10 II, Sozialbehörde II, Abl. 2 251-50-166 Band 2, Seyer-Sondheimer and S. 34, "Bericht über den Besuch der Tagessatzkommission in der WG 'Otterndorf' am 27.11.1974," 6 December 1974.

59. 351-10 II, Sozialbehörde II, Abl. 2 251-50-166 Band 2, Seyer-Sondheimer, "Tagessatz für die therapeutische WG Otterndorf," 13 January 1975; 354-5 II, Jugendbehörde II, Abl. 29.10.1986 356.04.06-7 Band 2, Axel Peters, "Kostenförder VBR," 23 April 1975.

60. 354-5 II, Jugendbehörde II, Abl. 29.10.1986 356.04.06-7 Band 2, "Lorien: Programm für März-April 1976," 1976.

repression, it also created a certain cultural space in which groups could experiment with new ideas and new projects. The political revolution championed by the Left in the late sixties certainly did not occur. Yet, as Arthur Marwick has noted, the culture as a whole was dramatically transformed by the drastic changes of the sixties and early seventies.[61]

61. Marwick, *The Sixties,* 12–13.

7. Gendering Drugs

In 1972, a young woman named Irina drew a cartoon published under the title "Wahre Comiks" (fig. 8). The comic strip's format is unexceptional: six frames with images and text bubbles. The story itself is also standard drug tragedy. Framed as an epistle from a young girl to her parents, who presumably live in some small town in the provinces, each frame contains a text bubble with part of the letter about her life in the big city. While the texts paint a rosy picture about her progress, the images show a horrific descent into despair.

In the first frame, the letter begins: "At my new job, I get plenty of fresh air and am meeting a bunch of interesting people." In the image, a man gazes at a suited woman standing in front of a brick wall. Her tight-fitting suit caricatures business attire, drawing further attention to the business in which she is engaged. Her face seems hollow, more doll-like than human. The second frame opens in a spartan room: "You don't have to worry any more about me getting enough sleep," the letter continues. "Lately I've been spending lots of time in bed." The girl lies on her back staring at the ceiling while a naked man lies on top of her. "You would hardly recognize your formerly plump daughter," she writes next. "I've lost weight and now have gotten pretty thin." She stands naked in front of a mirror. Her ribs show through her flesh; her face is gaunt, and dark circles ring her eyes. In the fourth frame the text reads, "You would definitely like my friends. Most of the time we sit around together and listen to music," while the image depicts her sitting in a room with two young men and a record player. A young man in the corner has sunken cheeks and holds his knees next to his chest. The junkie reclining on the bed next to her has tied his upper arm and holds a needle in his hand. She sits leaning forward, her face becoming more abstract, less recognizable as distinctly human. "Thanks for the beautiful pearl necklace," she writes in the penulti-

Fig. 8. (Irina, "Wahre Comiks," *Hundert Blumen,* no. 4 [1972]: 16, SSC, M613/10. Courtesy of Department of Special Collections, Stanford University Libraries.)

mate frame. "It goes great with my new mauve dress." In the image, though, she sells her necklace to a pawnbroker. In the final frame, she sits alone in a room with a single bulb hanging from the ceiling. The frame catches her at the precise moment when she injects herself, the tie held tight in her mouth, the veins in her arm bulging. Though some external markers of gender are still there—breasts, a dress, long hair— her arm is grossly misshapen, almost manly. Her letter pleads, "By the way . . . could you send me 100 marks? I suddenly have to pay for a few unexpected things. If you don't have the money, 50 or even 20 marks would be enough." At the bottom of the frame is the benediction: "A loving daughter . . ."[1]

Over the past two decades, gender has become one of the primary categories of analysis within the historical field, but the same cannot be said about the history of drugs. Although there have been a number of works, particularly from anthropology and public policy, that have posited feminist critiques of institutional structures, of the media, and of the relationship between drugs and sex work, most of these works have been interested not in the construction of gender but rather in the relationship between discourses of addiction and women.[2] If we take seriously the notion that regimes of gender are socially and culturally constructed *and* that gender must include both femininity and masculinity, then these models only offer us so much. Gendering drugs includes not only constructing notions of femininity and masculinity but also inscribing those meanings on both the spectral category of drugs and the actual substances themselves. The anthropologist Maryon McDonald argues quite rightly that "a substance has no reality external to perceptions of it, or to the context of its use. . . . The substance is always the cultural values invested in it, and this applies

---

1. SSC, M613/10, Irina, "Wahre Comiks," *Hundert Blumen,* no. 4, [1972], 16.

2. See, for example, Nancy D. Campbell, *Using Women: Gender, Drug Policy, and Social Justice* (New York: Routledge, 2000); Lisa Maher, *Sexed Work: Gender, Race, and Resistance in a Brooklyn Drug Market* (Oxford: Clarendon Press, 1997); Jennifer Friedman and Marixsa Alicea, *Surviving Heroin: Interviews with Women in Methadone Clinics* (Gainesville: University of Florida Press, 2001); Laura E. Gomez, *Misconceiving Mothers: Legislators, Prosecutors, and the Politics of Prenatal Drug Exposure* (Philadelphia: Temple University Press, 1997); Assata Zerai and Rae Banks, *Dehumanizing Discourse, Anti-Drug Law, and Policy in America: A "Crack Mother's" Nightmare* (Burlington, VT: Ashgate, 2002); Susan C. Boyd, *Mothers and Illicit Drugs: Transcending the Myths* (Toronto: University of Toronto Press, 1999).

whether the values be those of the police, the pharmacologist or the user, for example."[3] This rejection of pharmacological determinism is important in thinking about drugs in general, but it proves even more important when thinking about gendering drugs. If these are not innocent substances that affect the *sexes* in different ways, then the *gendered* reactions to the consumption of illicit substances and, more significant, the reactions of individuals far removed from the drug trade must be explained and cannot be simply taken at face value.

The manner in which notions about the gender of drugs emerge is itself a complicated question. Certainly poststructuralism offers some ways to begin thinking about how power and knowledge work to create meaning and the role of institutions in solidifying that meaning.[4] In order to have a comprehensive picture of the shifts in the gendered understandings of drug consumption, then, one would need to understand the discourses recreating the meaning of specific drugs and constructing "the addict," such as criminology, psychiatry, and pharmacology; the institutional creation of meaning, such as hospitals, the police, and state bureaucracies; and the narratives recounted by the press.

The first few years of the seventies produced an enormous amount of interest in the drug problem from professionals and from the press. While there had been some interest in drugs in the sixties, particularly among the traditional agencies and associations associated with youth, the early seventies saw an explosion in both the scientific literature on drug consumption and the amount of coverage in the press. While the drug problem was most often seen as a monolithic problem of the category of "youth," there were significant gender aspects to the scientific interest in the drug problem and the press coverage.

In the late sixties and the early seventies, notions of gender were in crisis. The collapse of the organized student movement, the emergence of an organized feminist movement, the gay rights movement, the campaign for the legalization of abortion, as well as the proliferation of

3. Maryon McDonald, "Introduction: A Social-Anthropological View of Gender, Drink, and Drugs," in *Gender, Drink, and Drugs,* ed. Maryon McDonald (Oxford and New York: Berg, 1994), 18–19. For another example of an anthropological approach to the history of gender and drug consumption, see Marek Kohn, *Dope Girls.*

4. On poststructuralism and gender, see Kathleen Canning, *Gender History in Practice: Historical Perspectives on Bodies, Class, and Citizenship* (Ithaca: Cornell University Press, 2006).

alternative culture groups contributed to a sense that the fundamental rules of gender were under attack. If there had been a stable image of bourgeois femininity to which West German women were to aspire in the Wirtschaftswunder period, and if that image had not collapsed, it had been at least directly challenged by new models of identity politics based on exposing that model as inherently repressive.

This direct challenge to traditional notions of gender became wrapped up in the debates over drugs. In both the scientific discourses about drug users and the press, young male drug users were portrayed as either dangerously masculine or pathologically effete, while young women in the drug scene were ignored or their drug use was seen as a danger to the reproduction of the family or, more insidious, as a slippery slope into prostitution. These ideas were often contradictory, but they show the real ambivalence about the larger changes in society brought on by both the "sex wave" and the emergence of the women's movement. Drug use became a particularly stark example of the ways in which social and gender roles had shifted over the course of the sixties. And even in the most progressive corners, the ideas about drug use tended to reinforce traditional notions of gender. Drugs were a danger to society not only because of the spread of addiction but also because drug use distorted "normal" gender relationships. In the end, even though the drug culture was deeply embedded in a progressive political culture, seeking an alternative to the vapidity of consumer culture and the repressiveness of traditional mores, its existence served to defend traditional gender relationships and even the most conservative utopian notions of the traditional nuclear family. This was true in two quite different ways. On the one hand, drug abuse and the hard drug scene proved to be a limiting example; it drew a line that served as a real and imagined border between acceptable behavior and dangerous excess. This limiting function—seen most vividly in the widespread acceptance that drug use led almost inexorably to prostitution and the belief that drug abuse was the result of broken families and working mothers—served as ammunition for those stringently opposed to the changes in gender relationships championed by the women's movement. On the other hand, within the drug scene, the changes that were taking place as a result of the women's movement were stymied by a misogynistic culture that saw gender as sex and sex as power.

The Scientists

Before the late sixties, there was comparatively little research on drug consumption outside of basic pharmacological research. What little research there was on the social effects of drug consumption came from the traditional professions with a direct interest in addiction and substance abuse: the police, social welfare agencies, and the medical profession.[5] As drug consumption soared at the end of the sixties, it became the subject of intense interest in medical and social science publications. While there had been a number of surveys of youth drug consumption in the sixties, the first few years of the seventies saw an enormous increase in the number and quality of studies of drug consumption.[6] With the rise in drug consumption and, especially, the sharp rise in the number of young people being treated in large public hospitals for addiction and associated diseases (e.g., hepatitis), drug use became a topic of particular interest to medical students interested in epidemiology and substance abuse. Several prominent psychiatrists at medical schools in Germany's large cities supervised dissertations on the topic at the end of the sixties and in the early seventies. At the same time, criminologists became interested in the topic as arrests increased and delinquent youth of various forms (drug users, Rockers, communards, etc.) became the focus of intense interest in both the press and academic journals. These two fields, criminology and medical epidemi-

---

5. The medical and criminological literature on drug consumption during this period is vast. For an excellent bibliography of this literature, see Bernhard Hefele, *Drogenbibliographie: Verzeichnis der deutschsprachigen Literatur über Rauschmittel und Drogen von 1800 bis 1984: mit einer Übersicht über internationale Bibliographien,* 2 vols. (Munich: K. G. Saur, 1988).

6. The most important of the early investigators of drug consumption include Friedrich Bschor in Berlin, Klaus Wanke in Frankfurt, and J. M. Burchard in Hamburg. See Friedrich Bschor, "Jugend und Drogenkonsum," *Zeitschrift für Allgemeinmedizin* 48 (1972): 100–109; "Jugend und Drogenkonsum. Erfahrungen, Eindrücke und vorläufige Schlußfolgerungen aus einer Feldstudie in Berlin," *Soziale Arbeit* 19 (1970): 525–39; Friedrich Bschor, N. Dennemark, and J. Herha, "Junge Rauschmittelkonsumenten. Ergebnisse der Feldstudie 1969/1970 in Berlin," *Beiträge zur gerichtlichen Medizin* 28 (1971): 16–28. Klaus Wanke, "Neue Aspekte zum Suchtproblem: multifaktorielle Analysen klinischer Erfahrungen mit jungen Drogenkonsumenten" (PhD diss., Universität Frankfurt, 1971). J. M. Burchard, "Erfahr-ungsbericht über die Entwicklung der Rauschmittelproblematik in Hamburg seit 1968," in *Kongress der Deutsche Gesellschaft für Psychiatrie und Nervenheilkunde* (Bad Neuheim, 23–25 October 1970). Paul Kielholz and D. Ladewig, *Die Drogenabhängigkeit des modernen Menschen* (Munich: Lehmann, 1972).

ology, became the authoritative sources for information on the drug problem, and their scientific, quantitative approach helped create a picture of the average youth drug addict for consumption by politicians and the press.[7]

Hamburg became a particularly important node in the nationwide web of social science on drug addiction in the early seventies. The reasons for Hamburg's central role are complicated: Hamburg's drug scene was fairly large and accessible for researchers; the state government was willing to support research; the large number of addicts committed to Hamburg's public and university hospitals, youth homes, and correctional facilities offered a large sample of available subjects; and there was a certain critical mass of interest in the subject, particularly at the university. Many of the younger scientists who undertook work on drug consumption in the late sixties had some interest in the drug scene, and the explosion in progressive social work at the end of the sixties certainly played into this rapid expansion of research. Thus, in the first few years of the seventies several medical dissertations and criminological books and articles dissected the Hamburg scene and created both qualitative and quantitative outlines of the drug milieu. The results of these studies produced a normative framework to explain the casual drug consumer and the addict, gender differences in consumption practices, and the relationship between sexuality and drug consumption. The underlying assumptions that remain unsaid in these works tell us a great deal about the underlying gender politics of the early seventies.

Beginning in 1969, a group of young medical students under Professor Jan Gross at the psychiatric clinic at the University Hospital began a large study of drug users.[8] Eventually, this project produced three

7. For an excellent example of how medical discourses "create" addicts, see Caroline Jean Acker, *Creating the American Junkie* (Baltimore, MD: Johns Hopkins University Press, 2002).

8. Jörn-Uwe Behrendt, "Drogengebrauch unter Hamburger Gymnasiasten: Eine repräsentative empirische Untersuchung des Konsumverhaltens, der Einstellung zu Drogen und einiger Variablen des sozialen Hintergrundes" (MD diss., Universität Hamburg, 1971), 63; Ute von Hirschheydt, "Erfahrungen mit jungen Rauschmittelkonsumenten: Deskriptiv phänomenologische Darstellung der Drogenszene eines Hamburger Kollektivs" (MD diss., Universität Hamburg, 1972), 74; Paul Wendiggensen, "Hamburger Drogenkonsumenten in Kliniken, Haftanstalten und der Drogenscene: Ergebnisse einer deskriptiv-statistischen Untersuchung" (MD diss., Universität Hamburg, 1972), 52.

dissertations, while research at the Institute for Hygiene in the Hamburg bureaucracy led to another completed dissertation at the university.[9] The dissertations all attempted to understand the root causes of drug consumption through statistical and qualitative epidemiological research. Since these studies came out of the psychiatric program, it is not surprising that the resulting works tend to look for psychological roots for drug use. Yet the dissertations are a product of their time, and their results tend to stress environmental factors that fall much more comfortably into the therapeutic mind-set than a youth protection model.

In addition to these epidemiological studies, a young criminologist at the university, Arthur Kreuzer, undertook another large study of Hamburg's drug scene that led to a number of prominent articles and a book that stands as the most significant work on drug use in Germany from the seventies. Kreuzer's book and his articles played a prominent role in shaping the idea of the drug scene as a bifurcated social organization made up of large numbers of casual users and a core group of problem drug abusers.

Even with the quite visible rise of the women's movement in the first years of the seventies, gender as a concept—as opposed to sex as a biological fact—failed to serve as an important category in the studies of the drug scene. And while the medical and criminological studies were interested in differentiating between male and female consumers or addicts, there was little interest in the differing experiences of young men and women. Yet the choices made by the researchers in their search for origins show a certain model of deviance, popular in the early seventies, which interpreted drug consumption as a part of a larger crisis in gender and the family. Not that these studies were unsophisticated critiques of the libertinage unleashed by the cultural change of the sixties. In fact, in many ways, they challenged commonsense notions about the relationships between drug use and gender. Even so, in many ways, the results of these studies reinforced a wider worldview that a crisis in traditional gender relationships and the destruction of the nuclear family had led to a host of woes.

The studies all attempted to substantiate one of the key hypotheses

9. Bärbel Seelisch, "Untersuchung über die Rauschmittelgefährdung Jugendlicher in Hamburg" (MD diss., Universität Hamburg, 1972), 77.

raised earlier by psychiatrists and youth protection advocates: that drug use was a result of the breakdown of the nuclear family. In all of the dissertations, the authors confirmed that drug users came more often from broken homes. The authors' interpretations of the statistical data, however, proved to be more complicated. Both Wendiggensen and Hirschheydt found, for example, that although many young drug users came from divorced households, a significant number of those from broken homes in fact had spent time in Hamburg's social welfare system and had been remanded to a youth home. Indeed, they found that over 25 percent of the hard drug users in their study had spent time in the youth home system.[10] Indeed, Wendiggensen questioned whether the broken home thesis could explain drug use patterns, arguing that "one cannot characterize it as a necessary precondition for drug addiction given that a smaller portion of the consumers come from an at least outwardly intact home."[11] And while divorce and the death of a parent tended to occur more frequently in the homes of drug users than non–drug users, other factors associated with the broken home hypothesis played insignificant roles. For instance, youth protection advocates had long bemoaned the damage caused by working mothers. Seelisch asked the question, "Because an employed mother has less time to focus on the children, would it be possible that the children would have a feeling of neglect that could strengthen the curiosity about drug use?"[12] Yet Seelisch found that drug users were just as likely to come from homes with working mothers as nonusers. In both cases, 44 percent of mothers were employed outside of the home.[13] By the time Kreuzer undertook his study, the "structural broken home" thesis had fallen into disrepute among sociologists. Instead, Kreuzer argued that much more significant was the existence of a "functional broken home."[14] While earlier studies had been preoccupied with the idea of the collapse of the nuclear family, Kreuzer saw that the relationships within the family were a more

10. Hirschheydt, "Erfahrungen mit jungen Rauschmittelkonsumenten," 16–17; Wendiggensen, "Hamburger Drogenkonsumenten," 19–21. See also Seelisch, "Untersuchung über die Rauschmittelgefährdung Jugendlicher," 29–30.

11. Wendiggensen, "Hamburger Drogenkonsumenten," 20.

12. Seelisch, "Untersuchung über die Rauschmittelgefährdung Jugendlicher," 34.

13. Ibid., 34–35.

14. Kreuzer, *Drogen und Delinquenz,* 105.

significant marker of drug use and especially of hard drug use and immersion in the drug scene.[15]

The fact that the breakdown of the family was such a central question for the early researchers of the drug wave is significant. Although they found that there was a statistical correlation between broken families and drug consumption, there were important qualifications to that thesis. Indeed, the question of the broken home was both a reaction to a real change in demographic patterns and a political argument. The number of women rejecting traditional notions of femininity and motherhood led critics to complain loudly about the breakdown of the family—in particular the rising rates of divorce and of working mothers. Even though the social science tended to downplay the role of the breakdown of the family, as a political argument it had a lasting significance and continued to shape the debates over the family and wayward youth. The statistics proved that drug users came from broken homes, and the qualifications tended to be easily forgotten.

Another significant concern in studies of drug consumption was the relationship between "normal" masculinity and drug consumption, though the question was not couched in these terms. This set of questions cut two ways. On the one hand, social scientists were interested in whether some correlation between drug consumption and early sexual activity and promiscuity existed; on the other hand, there was a widespread interest in the relationship between drug consumption and gender roles. In all cases, an underlying assumption existed that "normal" masculinity meant monogamous heterosexuality. In attempting to explain why there were so many more male drug users than female, for example, Paul Wendiggensen turned to an earlier study to posit the notion that the reason rested in a tendency "by male subjects in comparison to non-consumers to have significantly lower aspirations to dominate, lower masculinity, and a tendency to compliancy in social situations, thus an absent identification with the behavioral stereotypes that are typically regarded as masculine."[16] Rather than drug use leading to a lack of masculinity, Wendiggensen, among others, posited that a weak masculinity might lead to drug use as a way of dealing with "normal" codes of masculinity.

---

15. Ibid., 105–14.
16. Wendiggensen, "Hamburger Drogenkonsumenten," 13.

All of the studies focused on the question of sexual habits. All found that drug users tended to have sex earlier and to change partners more frequently. Seelisch suggested that the reason for this might be that "the renunciation of still customary 'moral norms' is more widely distributed in this group than in the rest of the youth."[17] Kreuzer concluded that early and frequent sexual contact correlated with more intensive drug use, which he attributed to a lack of social control within the drug scene.[18] He also hypothesized that for some addicts drug consumption, and in particular injecting, might act as "a masochistic coitus surrogate that extracts a type of orgasm."[19] Hirschheydt went so far as to argue that drug consumption might act for some young drug users as a way to deal with the difficulties in discovering their sex role, that is, their homosexuality.[20]

For the most part, these medical students were not interested in treating young women as a specific group. They were most of all interested in studying youth as a category rather than uncovering gender differences. When they did differentiate women from their male counterparts, it was generally in opposition to young men rather than as a distinct group with distinct characteristics. Behrendt, for instance, noted that LSD and mescaline consumption remained an almost exclusively male domain, while young women were more likely to take tablets and stimulants, presumably because young women were "more cautious" than young men.[21]

The criminologist Kreuzer, on the other hand, paid close attention to the difference in gendered drug "life histories." In his intensive interviews with heavy drug users in Hamburg, he uncovered a number of significant and troubling patterns. While there seemed to be little difference in drug consumption among larger surveys of secondary students, members of the smaller fixer scene tended to show recognizable patterns. In particular, the women tended to be younger than the men. Indeed, Kreuzer argued that most young women became involved in the scene through a boyfriend. "A young girl, in the course of her intensive first sexual relationship," Kreuzer claimed, "is more likely

17. Seelisch, "Untersuchung über die Rauschmittelgefährdung Jugendlicher," 61.
18. Kreuzer, *Drogen und Delinquenz*, 125.
19. Ibid., 127.
20. Hirschheydt, "Erfahrungen mit jungen Rauschmittelkonsumenten," 20.
21. Behrendt, "Drogengebrauch unter Hamburger Gymnasiasten," 17.

prepared to adopt the behavioral patterns of her partner—such as contact with drugs. . . . Girls are indeed more strongly imprisoned by 'bourgeois beliefs' than young men."[22] Girls in the drug scene were, according to Kreuzer, victims of older fixers who preyed on their youth and naïveté and brought them into the lifestyle. Indeed, girls passed back and forth between quite different subcultures with ease. One of his subjects reported that she joined a Rocker gang at thirteen, spent several months with the group, and had her first sexual experience within that group. When the bar they hung out in turned into a meeting point for hash users, she joined their group, traded her leather outfits for jeans, and soon had sex with all the members of the hash clique.[23] For Kreuzer, this kind of malleability of identity seemed to be the reserve of young women.

Kreuzer also broached the subject that obsessed the press and the public imagination of drug usage: the connection between drug use and prostitution. Kreuzer saw prostitution as the most prevalent form of delinquency for young women in the scene. "It is a meaningful symptom of waywardness [*Verwahrlosung*]," he claimed in the language of the earlier youth protection activists, "namely of early sexual waywardness. . . . The stark proliferation of prostitution and prostitution-like relationships among young extreme drug users has to do with the widely observable growing sexual promiscuity by young people, with the particularly wayward disposition of the fixer population, and with the demoralization that derives from the drug career."[24] Prostitution was not limited to young women in the scene. Kreuzer, however, differentiated between two kinds of prostitution within the drug scene: trading sex for drugs within the scene and having sex for money. While women tended to take part in an active barter economy within the drug scene, they were unlikely to take part in strictly commercial prostitution. The so-called *Strichjungen*—the young men who turned to homosexual prostitution to feed their habits—on the other hand, usually undertook sexual work outside the scene for cash.[25] Active prostitution for money remained a minority activity within the scene, yet the slippery slope from drug consumption to prostitution, as we shall see, held the power to fascinate the

22. Kreuzer, *Drogen und Delinquenz*, 125.
23. Ibid., 145.
24. Ibid., 287.
25. Ibid., 289–90.

public and served a social control function. Authorities still perceived prostitution in the seventies as a form of delinquency. It was not until the 1980s and the arrival of AIDS that drug-addicted prostitutes began to demand public recognition and social services.

In the social science of the early years of the drug wave, sex differences proved more important than gender differences. Men were seen as the "normal" drug user, and women were relegated to a lesser position. While drug use for young men might point to gender identity problems, women were inherently tied to their sexual life. When differences were singled out between men and women, it almost invariably had to do with their sexual practices, such as prostitution. For the remainder, men were the subjects and women were merely a subcategory. Although these young scientists disproved some outdated notions, such as the broken home thesis, ultimately, their methods and the very framework of their studies acted to reinforce traditional notions of gender roles. The science was measured and willing to discard old notions when they proved false. Yet those stereotypical ideas survived in the public. It is fair to say that few read the new social science about drug consumers and that the press painted a quite different picture of the relationship between drugs and gender.

The Press

The vast majority of Germans during the late sixties and early seventies knew very little about drugs.[26] The press played a dominant role in constructing the gender of the category of drugs for ordinary Germans. For most Germans, their distance from the world in which drugs were bought, sold, and consumed meant that they thought about drugs in the abstract: drugs belonged in a single category; there could be little differentiation between different kinds of drugs; and since some illicit drugs were obviously bad (because the press told them so), then all drugs must be stopped. Still, it is fair to say that between approximately 1969 and 1973, largely because of the intense media scrutiny of the topic, public notions of what "drugs" were underwent a profound transformation.

26. See, for example, StAH, 135-1 VI, Staatliche Pressestelle VI, Institut für angewandte Sozialwissenschaften, "Meinungen in Hamburg zum Rauschgiftproblem," April 1971.

The German papers, though different in tone and political view-point, all tended to range fairly closely on the basic issues of drugs, though the more conservative newspapers were predisposed toward a law-and-order stance, while the more liberal ones favored a more medical approach to drug use. But they tended to tell similar narratives. More surprising was that alternative papers, which proliferated after 1968, also tended to perpetuate gendered notions of drug use. Although many of the papers were associated with the political Left (K-Gruppen, for example), many were also linked with the cultural underground, that segment of the population experimenting with new lifestyles at the end of the sixties and into the seventies.[27] Although one might expect an acceptance or even celebration of drug use in alternative magazines, their attitudes varied significantly and often were openly hostile to drug consumption.

In the press, drugs acted as a negative example, a way to solidify traditional gender relationships by providing extreme examples of the consequences of deviation from given norms. While narratives of women's drug use tended to reinforce traditional notions of gender rooted in biology, drug consumption and addiction posed significant problems to traditional ideas about masculinity; therefore, the masculinity of drugs failed to stabilize into an easily identifiable pattern: young male drug users could be either ruggedly masculine or effete, depending on the circumstances.

Biological Moralizing: Drugs and Femininity

An examination of how femininity was construed in both the mainstream press and the alternative press shows a surprising continuity of content, though the form differed somewhat. In both cases, the print press portrayed women as defined almost wholly by their reproductive life and sexuality. The two main objects of stories, and particularly of sensational stories, about women were the bond between drug consumption and deviant sexuality, particularly the cash nexus, and the

27. Underground newspapers I examined include *Roter Punkt, Agit 883, Zero, Floh, Humus, Song, Underground, Love, Germania, Pot, Scheisse, Päng, Radikalinski, Hundert Blumen,* and *Bambule.*

dangers of drug use to reproduction. In relationship to drugs, as in so many other areas of life, women were objects of the recurring tropes about prostitution and motherhood.

In the mainstream press, these conclusions tended to be drawn quite explicitly. Although a considerable breadth of opinion existed within the mainstream press about the origins and threats of the drug problem, the use of drugs seemed to set off a cultural alarm. Women's drug use in particular tended to be portrayed as purely deviant and threatening to the fabric of society. The demonization of women users played more prominently in the tabloid press and in *Bild* in particular. Yet these stories should not be dismissed as the figments or ravings of a lewd and shrill press. More people read *Bild* than the more "respectable" papers, and the same ideologies may be found in both conservative and liberal papers in a different vernacular. Furthermore, in most cases, the prose of the stories only played one part in constructing the "truth" about drugs; photographs and other visual sources created another powerful narrative that established or magnified powerful messages about what drugs meant to gender.

Take, for example, a story from *Bild* in July 1972. Wolfgang Fricke's article "I'm Afraid for My Baby" was part of a series run during the summer of 1972 entitled "Narcotics in Germany: Reports from Hell."[28] The article begins:

> When Beate T. sees a baby, she takes on the expressive eyes of a Madonna. An unhappy Madonna: Desire rests in her glance, ill-fated, trembling, and uncertain. Beate, the 19-year-old milliner, is pregnant, in her eighth month, and—she is addicted.
>
> So addicted that she hasn't once been able to quit shooting opiates for the sake of the tiny human growing inside her. "What do you think?" she asks, and she has certainly already asked this question a hundred times. "Will I have a healthy child?"
>
> She has probably also received no answer or self-conscious or elusive answers a hundred times. But Beate doesn't expect any reply at all.

28. All the mainstream press articles mentioned are part of a private *Presseausschnitte* collection that Dieter Maul, former director of the Hamburg Landesstelle gegen die Suchtgefahren, made available. Wolfgang Fricke, "Ich habe Angst um mein Baby," *Bild,* 13 July 1971.

She stares intensely at the strange child, as if she wants to photograph every detail: the dark tuft, the round eyes, the fat cheeks and the fidgety small hands.

After a discussion of Beate, her problems with her family, and her relationship with Kai, the child's father, Fricke continues, "Beate and Kai have been inseparable for years. The 'bad influence' that he is said to have had on the girl is seen not only by her father but by the police and the Youth Authority as well." Fricke's conception of women addicts as victims of men recurs in most stories. And although the relationship between women becoming addicted and their contact with young male users may be sociologically verifiable, not only does the narrative expunge women of their responsibility for their own behavior, but, in a much more negative light, it places them in the constant and irrevocable role of victim, eradicating any agency and, ultimately, making them slaves to their anatomy.

Fricke concludes with the moral of Beate's predicament. "For those who collect the 'experiences' that appear to have become today's fashionable sickness, addiction, unfitness for work, the slide into criminality or—customarily the 'easier way' for girls—into prostitution (and indeed into the cheapest) follow relatively quickly." Fricke then tells the story of Lucie—who began shooting up, fell into prostitution, and was degraded so far as to live with "an Oriental, who had had his nose eaten away by a disease"—as an exemplar of the cost of addiction for girls. "Lucie is the radical example for the collapse of character [*Verfall von Persönlichkeit*]," Fricke warns. "Lucie is a human wreck. She became one in little more than three years. 'For women, there is an express elevator to Hell,' the experienced junkies say."

All of the tropes used to mark women drug users as outside of the bounds of social life, as self-made pariahs, emerge in this fairly short article. But the text itself is only part of the story; the two images that accompany the article reinforce the message. The first is in a box that announces the series, "Reports from Hell." It shows one of the most common and powerful images used in stories with drug users: a tied-off arm being pierced by a needle.[29] The second image plays on the com-

29. For other examples, see Jürgen W. Wohldorf, "Kripo ist gegen die Rauschgift-Welle nur kümmerlich gerüstet," *Hamburger Abendblatt,* 5 May 1971; Dinah Otto, "Drogenszene Deutschland '71," *Deutsches Monatsblatt,* September 1971, 12–13; Peter Krukow, "Viele

mon image of women as mothers.[30] Beate stands over a baby carriage, looking at an infant. The caption reads: "A stranger's healthy child. Beate has only one thought: will my baby also be healthy?" The pregnant woman, not yet a mother, is already indicted as a bad mother.

Although a stigma against all drug use predominated in the mainstream press, the use of drugs by girls continually cropped up as an extreme example of the degradation brought on by drug abuse. Almost all of these stories portrayed these girls as victims of uncaring, even malevolent, men. In March 1972, *Bild* ran another article entitled "12-year-old Narcotics Addict!"[31] It told the story of two young girls: a student in Mülheim who was found unconscious on the street from an overdose and another thirteen-year-old girl who was brought to the police by her mother, who found tracks on her arm. According to the story, a fifteen-year-old boy had provided them with hashish and morphine. Another story from the *Hamburger Morgenpost* focused on the spread of hepatitis among young junkies.[32] The story stressed the dangers of the emergence of a community of hard drug users. The author, Edith Unger, argued that the real danger rested in the fact that these junkies actively spread their "disease." "Among these lived the diseased [*Kranken*] who also partly gave away the stuff—in order to drag others along with them," she warned. "A 20-year-old from Bremen is said to have used nasty beatings and torture to force his girlfriend to shoot herself up!"[33] Yet this kind of spectacular story was also supported by much more authoritative sources. In an article in the *Frankfurter Allgemeine Zeitung*, Arthur Kreuzer echoed the notion that women were victims of their male counterparts: "Female drug perpetrators stand out to the police less because they don't take part in dealing as much, because they hang out less frequently in conspicuous places, and mostly because they come to drugs through their

---

wollen jetzt los von der Droge," *Hamburger Abendblatt,* 15–16 March 1972; "Drogen-Alarm," *Die Welt,* 4 November 1972; Walter Weber, "Rauschgift? Dann können Sie bei uns nicht Mutter werden!" *Bild,* 17 May 1972.

30. This was not a new theme in 1972 and, in fact, had provided a leitmotif since the beginning of the drug wave. See, for instance, "Lsd-Rausch in der Schwangerschaft: Das Baby kam als Krüppel zur Welt," *Bild,* 18 November 1967.

31. "12jährige Rauschgiftsüchtig!" *Bild,* 20 March 1972.

32. Edith Unger, "Scharfe Schüsse gegen 'Schießer,'" *Hamburger Morgenpost,* 19 May 1971.

33. Ibid.

boyfriends."[34] Yet even in cases where women were arrested as drug couriers, they were portrayed as victims of both men and their own biology.[35]

The theme of women's victimhood almost certainly had some empirical basis. Yet for most Germans, who had little or no actual relationship to drugs or the drug scene, it created a narrative that focused on women's vulnerability. Although it shielded women from the harsher aspects of the war on drugs, it also reinforced a wider discourse of women's dependence on men. Even more troubling, women were portrayed as victims of both men and their own biology. The cultural import of these stories reinforced the idea that women's role in society essentially rested in their reproductive capacity. By using drugs, young women threatened their unborn children and thus the stability of society at large. Even more threatening, women who used drugs slid down the slippery slope to prostitution. Even girls from "good homes" could become diseased prostitutes if they failed to resist the call of drugs and the pressure from men, if they failed to follow the right path to marriage and family. In short, the discourse surrounding the issue of women and drugs ultimately helped to reinforce quite traditional notions of women's role in society at the very time when those ideals were under concerted attack from the emergence of organized feminism.

This kind of story is not unexpected. The nexus of sex and drugs makes for sensational journalism. Yet, more surprising, the alternative press echoed many of these same tropes. Gone for the most part were the fascination with motherhood and, to a certain extent, the morbid fascination with prostitution. Instead, the underground press tended to focus on "sexual freedom," though that notion was defined almost exclusively by men and in many cases was overtly misogynistic.

One of the more interesting and complicated tropes that showed up repeatedly was the notion of a "drug orgy." In many cases, writers in the alternative scene pilloried the notion, echoed repeatedly in the

34. Arthur Kreuzer, "Hält Opium, was Haschisch verspricht?" *Frankfurter Allgemeine Zeitung,* 30 June 1972.

35. See, for instance, "Urgroßmutter schickte sie mit Hasch auf Reisen," *Hamburger Morgenpost,* 20 June 1974, and Heinz Fischer, "Türken-Mädel weinten—Richter flohen," *Hamburger Morgenpost,* 3 February 1974. Both of these stories about Turkish drug mules have not only gendered aspects but racist overtones as well.

Fig. 9. The top half of a poster created by the underground newspaper *Pot* and disseminated by the Underground Press Syndicate that provides an example of the frequent and often misogynistic connections made by users between drug consumption and sexuality. ("The Acid Facts," SSC, M613/1. Courtesy of Department of Special Collections, Stanford University Libraries.)

mainstream press, that drug consumption led to wild sex orgies. In the fourth edition of *Pot* in a one-page poster entitled "The Acid Facts," the authors explain that "the psychedelic revolution is also a sexual revolution."[36] They contend that LSD does not create sexual demand but instead intensifies the sexual experience. Yet the poster is filled with images that reinforce traditional male fantasies. All the women on the poster are naked. A woman is taken from behind near the center of the image; another floats in space in a pinup pose with the word *Wow* above her head. The largest image is a woman's face with the visage of an angry caveman between her eyes. And at the bottom, two naked women tend to the fallen Icarus. It is hard not to surmise that the authors' belief that "the psychedelic revolution is also a sexual revolution" meant a peculiarly masculine sexual revolution, in which male fantasies were given free reign.

The widespread voyeuristic interest in drug orgies in the press drew criticism from the alternative magazines. In the first edition of *ELDA,* the authors of an article on the Release movement criticized the media and its role in creating negative attitudes toward drug users. "After Baader-Meinhof slowly took the rap for itself, new stories are expected about all forms of 'narcotics-orgies,' which sell so well," they write. "Why? Well, in spite of moralistic finger-pointing, in spite of damned lies, Otto-Normal-Consumer gets a report of how a world could be without sexual deformity but rather full of happiness and colors. The illustrated papers are becoming the opium of the bourgeoisie [*Spießbürger*] who, on top of that, can still bask in their own decency."[37]

Many of the stories about drugs and the drug culture written by the alternative press tended to be as misogynistic as those of the mainstream press. In an article about land communes in *Floh* in the summer of 1972, the author recommends the use of hashish and LSD and living together as "brother and sister." Yet he also criticizes women in the commune movement. "One experiences a great feeling of freedom in a gladdening sea of love," he argues. "But there is also a symptom that appears quite often, and it's the lack of women. Far too few women participate in the communes. For the most part, they don't have the need to make themselves independent. Many even have a mechanized

36. SSC, M613/1, *Pot,* No. 4, "The Acid Facts."
37. SSC, M613/14, "Release," *ELDA,* No. 3, 5.

household with a washing machine in mind! Perhaps they are also afraid of the commune's reputed unbridled sex. But no one can be forced to screw!"[38] Another communard and a founder of *Päng* magazine inserted a comment at the end of a letter from a young woman supporting the redevelopment of the urban guerrilla warfare movement after the setbacks to the Red Army Faction; the quote from the editor Raymond reads: "If I understand the primary women's problem, then it is the fact that almost all girls that I know never or only rarely have orgasms while fucking."[39] This kind of overt hostility toward women seems to have been, at least in the press, fairly uncommon. Even so, the evidence seems to suggest that even in the alternative press and on the left, women and drugs did not necessarily mix. Or to put it another way, "consciousness expansion" did not seem to necessarily entail an expanded consciousness about gender roles. Within the pro-drug movement, if one may call it that, women were often also defined by their biology and their sex.

Untangling Masculinity

Men, on the other hand, proved to be both the primary object of concern and, in a certain way, nonentities. The vast majority of stories in the mainstream press as well as in the alternative press were, at least at first glance, gender neutral. The overriding category of concern in most stories was generation rather than gender. The press continually portrayed drug consumption, and the drug trade, as a danger to youth. Yet, when reading these stories with an eye toward the sculpting of gendered understandings, it quickly becomes clear that, when newspaper authors wrote about youth, what they meant was young men. Stories about youth drug consumption often employed gender-neutral terms, but then raised the specter of the growing danger to girls specifically.[40] In many respects, the press coverage mirrored the social science discourse, which conceived of drugs as an almost peculiarly masculine vice. Consequently, this masculine branding of drugs forced

38. SSC, M613/16, "Landkommunarden," *Floh,* No. 2 [summer 1972], 8–9.
39. SSC, M613/1 *Päng,* No. 8–9 (1974), 7.
40. See, for example, "60000 drogengeschädigte Jungrentner in der Bundesrepublik," *Die Welt,* 20 June 1972, and Arthur Kreuzer, "Hält Opium."

women even further into the margins of drug consumption, making them the limit case.

While drugs were overwhelmingly coded as masculine, within this masculinity there was considerable room for interpretation. In the mainstream press, there were at least two prominent gendered characterizations of young masculinity. One was similar to the construction of women's drug consumption: boys were victims of their anatomy or often of their deviant psychology. Yet by the early seventies, particularly after the introduction of heroin into the drug scene in 1972, there was also considerable reporting on a threatening masculinity associated with drug use and particularly with drug dealers.

The dichotomy between masculine power and self-control versus feminine weakness and neuroses became a framing device for a certain genre of newspaper stories about young male addicts, in particular for the increasing number of stories after 1970 about drug overdose deaths.[41] For example, several stories appeared in various newspapers about the overdose death in March 1972 of eighteen-year-old Norbert Harmsen, whose death marked the twelfth drug-related death since 1967 and was seen widely as a wake-up call by the press. *Hamburger Abendblatt* reporter Peter Krukow approached Harmsen's case as a warning about the danger to all young men. "In addition, Hamburg is a city with a high percentage of flipped out, ruined boys [*Jugendlicher*] and teens [*Heranwachsender*], of young men on disability due to drugs [*Drogen-Frührentner*], of wrecks who can't be rehabilitated," he wrote. "Of children, who, for a joint, a hashish cigarette, are prepared to prostitute themselves."[42] The specter of young men prostituting themselves was provocative but unusual, while the tone, the idea that these young

---

41. See, for instance, "Tod durch Rauschgift," *Hamburger Morgenpost,* 12 March 1972; "Bonner Studentin im Meskalin-Rausch getötet," *Die Welt,* 14 April 1972; Alfred Heiden, "Ich sah Bonn in Flammen," *Hamburger Morgenpost,* 14 April 1972; "Hamburg: 19jähriger starb an Rauschgift," *Hamburger Abendblatt,* 5 July 1972; Edith Unger, "Ein Mann starb an Rauschgift," *Hamburger Morgenpost,* 18 July 1972; "Junge spritzte sich zu Tode," *Hamburger Morgenpost,* 23 June 1973; "Junger Mann starb an einer Überdosis Polamidon," *Hamburger Abendblatt,* 18 June 1973; "Das Rauschgift machte ihn kaputt," *Hamburger Abendblatt,* 12 June 1974; "Wahnsinnsdroge in Hamburg verkauft: Im LSD-Rausch nackt von der Brücke: Tot!" *Hamburger Morgenpost,* 9 January 1975.

42. Peter Krukow, "Viele wollen jetzt los von der Droge," *Hamburger Abendblatt,* 15–16 March 1972.

men had lost all control and were irredeemable, proved to be remarkably resilient.

A few months later, *Bild* ran a similar story about a young junkie who was sentenced to two years in prison for stealing a doctor's prescription book and forging prescriptions for Ritalin. Dr. Jessel, an "expert," testified to the young man's loss of self-control:

> A real addict. Although he is highly intelligent—at one time he wanted to become a graphic artist—he can no longer steer himself. He is a danger to the public security. Outside of a locked-down institution he soon will become a victim of the narcotics dealers.[43]

This notion of addicts as victims—of dealers, of their lack of self-control, of their addictions—had a powerful resonance throughout not only the press but the social science and medical discourses as well.

Even stories that focused on so-called drug-related crime [*Beschaffungskriminalität*] often portrayed the young perpetrators as effete victims of their own weakness. One story with the sensational headline "Addict Threatens Wife and Child" tells of the arrest of Helmut Kreipi, an addict who in desperation during withdrawal tried to force his wife to buy him drugs. After Kreipi discharged his pistol once, his wife fled with the child and called the police. The police sent *"Kriminalhauptmeister* C." to negotiate with Kreipi. The detective apparently knew that Kreipi did not pose a real threat and approached the door.

> "Helmut, it's me! Cut the crap! We have some 'stuff' for you. We're coming in now." Then he turned the key. Helmut Kreipi lay on the bed. A trembling, apathetic bundle of a man. Naked and bare [*Nackt und bloß*].[44]

Though such a story would normally have played out as a typical crime story about a man with a gun threatening a woman, the fact that Hel-

---

43. Richard Plagemann, "Süchtiger fälschte Rezepte," *Bild,* 6 July 1972.

44. Jurgen W. Wohldorf, "Süchtiger bedrohte Frau und Kinder," *Hamburger Morgenpost,* 30 September 1974. On the same incident, see also Volkhard Menke, "Mit Heroin aus der Wohnung gelockt," *Die Welt,* 1 October 1974. For similar stories, see Edith Unger and Walter Fischer, "Süchtiger schoß auf Polizisten," *Hamburger Morgenpost,* 13 December 1972, and Peter Leibing, "Helft uns—wir werden wahnsinnig: Drogenparty in der Wohnung eines Diakons," *Hamburger Abendblatt,* n.d.; B. Rudolph, "Amok-Schütze in Eppendorf: Rauschgiftsüchtiger verschanzte sich in der Wohnung," *Bild,* 30 September 1974.

mut was an addict meant that the detective did not have to fear him and that he could be characterized as a "trembling, apathetic bundle of a man" rather than as a violent criminal. Helmut, because he was an addict, could be described not in the masculine terms of a criminal but rather in the language of victimhood.

The many stories about drug dealers and traffickers tapped into a very different notion of masculinity. If the consumers and addicts were seen as victims, the press painted dealers with a threatening masculinity based on violence. In August 1972, Walter Weber wrote a story for *Bild* entitled "700 Marks Collected for a Murder," in which young dealers placed a contract on a seventeen-year-old student who they believed had "sung" to the police. The boy was pushed onto the U-Bahn tracks in an attempt to kill him, but passersby pulled him to safety. The story ends by quoting the young man: "Whoever gets in the dealers' way will be eliminated. They also want to conceal by any means necessary that there have already been heroin-deaths in Hamburg."[45] This kind of quite traditional narrative lends the category of dealer a certain violent masculinity, though one that did not fit comfortably with notions of bourgeois masculinity.

Stories about violent dealers often entailed discussions of ethnicity as well as gender. *Bild* ran a story about a prison suicide in the summer of 1972 that focused on the violence of drug dealers. A barkeep in St. Pauli named Gerd Marotzke had been arrested by Danish police trying to smuggle a kilogram of opium across the border. Marotzke had agreed to help the Hamburg Criminal Police in their investigation of the smuggling ring. The author quoted the Hamburg detective as saying, "Marotzke was incredibly afraid of the vengeance of his Turkish bosses. They threatened that they would kill him if he talked."[46] This kind of story about the violence associated in particular with foreign smugglers became a powerful theme in the press. Yet most of these stories did not have the same tone as those about young German consumers. Part of this had to do with the confluence of notions about criminals and foreigners, but much of it had to do with a conventional

45. Walter Weber, "700 Mark für einen Mord gesammelt," *Bild,* 14 August 1972.
46. Ernst Lütcke and Walter Weber, "Opium-Schmuggler erhängte sich am Zellenfenster," *Bild,* 17 July 1972.

narrative of cops and robbers, in which competing masculinities battle in the streets.[47]

The stories about men in the mainstream newspapers reflected a wider consensus that emerged in the early seventies about drugs. By the middle of 1972, the press, the government, and the "experts" had come to an agreement that the days of "consciousness expansion" had ended and that a new, more ominous drug trade had taken its place. According to this new consensus, although there continued to be widespread experimentation, most drug consumption now took place among a hard kernel of addicts; these addicts were ill, victims of addiction, of the lack of self-control, or of aberrant psychology. Yet the other half of the consensus placed drug dealers and traffickers at the apex of a pyramid of social ills, as poisoners of youth and a fundamental danger to the social order. After the emergence of this consensus, the stories about drugs stabilized: young addicts were effete victims, while dealers were masculine perpetrators in battle with the equivalent, or superior, masculinity of the police.

Though this binary opposition shows considerably more nuance than the equation of all women as victims of biology, the mainstream press's construction of addicts as effete victims met with resistance within the drug community and in the alternative press. In contradistinction, the alternative press championed their own version of the rugged masculinity of drug users. In an article about the problems with criminalization, the editors of *Germania* quoted Antonin Artaud to criticize the state: "I am the only judge of what is *in me*. What I do with my consciousness in private, as long as I don't commit a crime against

---

47. See, for instance, "Sieben Zentner Haschisch sichergestellt," *Hamburger Abendblatt,* 29 November 1972; "Internationaler Ring von Rauschgifthändlern in Hamburg aufgeflogen," *Die Welt,* 17 February 1973; Jürgen Brockmann, "5 Grenzen passiert—dann kam die Pleite," *Hamburger Morgenpost,* 19 February 1973; "Kripo ist jetzt dem Verteilerring der Haschisch-Bande auf der Spur," *Die Welt,* 19 February 1973; "IRA droht Hamburger Jugendrichtern: Mitglieder der irischen Terroristen-Organisation wegen Rauschgifthandels verurteilt," *Die Welt,* 10 May 1974; "Fünf Geiseln für den Hasch-König aus Hamburg," *Hamburger Morgenpost,* 21 May 1974; "Der Handel mit Heroin ist ein Mordversuch," *Frankfurter Rundschau,* 6 July 1974; "Rauschgifthändler im Friedhof verhaftet," *Süddeutsche Zeitung,* 25 July 1974; "Tasche des Türken enthielt 19 Kilo Hasch," *Hamburger Morgenpost,* 24 July 1974; Birgit-Ingeborg Loff, "Die Vertreibung aus dem Herrngarten: Scharfe Polizeikontrollen und Schnellverfahren gegen Drogenhändler," *Frankfurter Rundschau,* 9 October 1974.

Fig. 10.   The title page of a hashish cookbook written and illustrated by Hans-
Georg Behr in 1969 and published in 1970; the beautifully illustrated book is replete
with images of drugs and explicitly phallic sexuality. (Hans-Georg Behr, *Das
Haschish-Kochbuch* [Darmstadt: Joseph Melzer, 1970], title page, SSC, M613/12.
Courtesy of Department of Special Collections, Stanford University Libraries.)

someone else, is my personal business and not that of the State." This
kind of libertarian sentiment is then followed by a condemnation of the
image portrayed in the press of the addict as a sick, effeminate victim.

> Therefore a junkie is also a conscious human, just as much a master
> of his fate as you and I, just as free to decide for himself. He is not
> an unfortunate weakling, nor a pile of filth, nor a diseased person
> one must pity, nor a pervert or an immoral human. He has simply
> decided to experience other things with his consciousness than the
> others, and if he sometimes must suffer considerable doubt and con-

siderable pain for it, it is nothing exceptional: many of those who don't shoot up also do the same in different ways.[48]

Instead of portraying junkies as victims, this ex-user sees junkies as free actors. The article ends with a quote from Aleister Crowley advocating drugs as a test of free will. In this formulation, those who choose to use drugs exhibit a superior masculinity by proving their fundamental freedom: from government constraint, from morality, and ultimately from the body. The critique of the notion that drug consumers were weak, diseased, or immoral was even, on occasion, turned against the "straight world." In early 1974, the editor of *Päng* wrote an article about the law and hashish in which a former district attorney was quoted as calling his former colleagues "pathetic, diseased creatures, who as a result spend their entire lives tormenting others."[49] The article shows that at least the alternative press was acutely aware of the linguistic strategies utilized in the mainstream press to gender drugs and that they took some offense at the attempt to portray addicts as somehow unmasculine.

Klaus Nuß, in a 1969 article in *Scheisse,* took this kind of critique even further, arguing that the attempt to label drug users as effeminate was evidence that the authoritarian nature of the German bourgeoisie had not been overcome.

> The Masses know that this minority clique is called hippies and can't be normal because they wear their hair long. For this reason they must be filthy, louse-ridden, and unhygienic. And you can become accepted that way. And if you don't spit, fight, provoke, insult, etc. But woe to he who defends himself or provokes back, and the masses see themselves driven into the corner, then come the old maxims. . . . "He belongs in a workhouse."—or: "We need another Hitler; he would send them all to the front—and right away!"[50]

While Nuß turns the tables on the middle classes by turning their negative attitudes toward drug users into a condemnation of a sort of authoritarian weakness, he goes further toward championing an

48. SSC, M613/1, "Stoff," *Germania,* No. 2, 8–9.
49. SSC, M613/1, "Staatsanwaltschaft & Hasch . . . ," *Päng,* No. 8–9, 6.
50. SSC, M613/1, "Philosophen—Götter: Menschen III. Klasse," *Scheisse,* February 1969.

overtly masculine response. "Against these crimes of individual authorities against the masses, the underground calls every citizen to defend yourself and therefore to take part in the rebellion. Because the state is still the masses, and they have both the right to self-determina-tion [*Selbstbestimmung*] and also to free choice. It rests entirely and solely in the hands of the masses, with the help of their own power, to enforce this right—your right."[51] The call to revolution could be made for the underground against the bourgeoisie.

Yet most of the alternative press that was associated with a clear political agenda (usually associated with various K-Gruppen or anar-chist collectives) saw drug use as counterrevolutionary. Drug use did not and could not fit in with their own views on a rugged, revolution-ary masculinity. The editorial collective of *Agit 883* took up the ques-tion of drug use in their twentieth number. Although they admitted that politically committed revolutionaries had experimented with drugs, they concluded that comrades could not take part in "politically effective work" while high and that, in the final analysis, "Hash can serve the liberation of individual needs, but, on the other hand, puts political work to sleep."[52] Indeed, the notions of the masculinity of the politically committed often more closely resembled a bourgeois moral-ity than the drug underground. A hedonistic masculinity found in the drug scene veered too far from the central notion of the political left—that the revolution was work—to be recognized as legitimate.

In perhaps the most interesting comment on masculinity and drug consumption in the alternative press, Raymond Martin, the editor of *Päng,* attempted to turn the biological argument about drugs and mas-culinity on its head. Martin had read about research that claimed mar-ijuana use reduced testosterone production in men, making them more feminine. Rather than countering this as an affront to his and other drug users' masculinity, Martin proclaimed the findings to be entirely positive because they forced men to step back from their "patriarchal standpoint." "Such low-testosterone men will hardly want to possess more power, or want to oppress or all the stupid things men do," Mar-tin argues. "For years it's been clear to me that the feminine world and

51. Ibid.

52. SSC, M613/11, Redaktionskollektiv "883," "Ebrach: eine Sauerei," *Agit 883,* No. 20, 4.

women have offered themselves alternatives from which we men could learn a lot. Yes, I have come so far that a matriarchal social order can serve as the solution to many problems."[53] Rather than defending masculinity from the power of science, he argues that any feminization caused by marijuana consumption can only be positive, that a new masculinity that recognized the positive aspects of femininity would be an improvement to current ideas of masculine normalcy.

As the preceding examples show, gendering drugs did not proceed in a linear manner that conclusively set out what was masculine and feminine. Indeed, inscribing masculinity on the category of drugs proved to be quite complicated and, in the end, ambivalent. Although the mainstream press tended to paint young addicts as victims, dealers became caught up in a much larger narrative about crime and crime fighters. And, at the same time, this hegemonic message did not go unchallenged. The alternative press and presumably members of the drug scene did not accept the notions put forward in the press and even challenged them openly.

Conclusion

Let us now return to the cartoon with which this chapter began. The striking aspect of this particular cartoon is not so much the story as the source. While this kind of morality tale would be completely expected in the tabloid press, this cartoon was actually placed within a story about the radical alternative group Release and published in the Berlin underground newspaper *Hundert Blumen*. This raises some fundamental questions. Why is the alternative press and a group that was more familiar than most with the experience of drug consumption repeating a narrative that would not be out of place in *Bild*? Why does a young woman artist, who presumably understands drug consumption intimately, during the initial expansion of the feminist movement, choose to tell this fundamentally conservative vision of gender and addiction?

The answer seems to lie in the power of narratives to define gender. Although little direct evidence on the reception of the narratives created and disseminated by either social scientists or the press exists, this

53. SSC, M613/1, Raymond Martin, "Marihuana verändert den Hormonhaushalt," *Päng*, No. 10, 11.

cartoon seems to suggest that even members of the drug scene were adapting their own experiences to broad narratives that helped explain not only drug addiction but the ways in which gender determined the experience of drug use as well. According to this cartoon, women drug users fell prey to their biology and their sex, falling almost inevitably into prostitution. Irina's cartoon recreated and reinforced a specific gendering of drugs. Yet, more important, this example shows the power of certain narratives to define the gender of drugs.

Social scientists asked certain questions because they were part of the common cultural lexicon that pointed to the breakdown of gender relationships and the family. Similarly, the press told certain stories that carried the weight of "truth" and explained to readers unfamiliar with the drug scene how drugs altered gender and how gender determined drug use. In both of these cases, drug use became a bulwark against changing gender roles. While the more extreme examples, such as prostitution, provided moral tales about the dangers of drug use, the more mundane questions, such as the question of the broken home, provided a simple explanation for a complex social phenomenon.

8. "Wowman! The World's Most Famous Drug-Dog"

Early in the summer of 1972, "Wowman, the world's most famous drug-dog" made his grand entrance tucked away in the pages of the children's comic book *Primo*. Though Wowman may have appeared to youngsters as simply a new comic strip featuring a police dog with a strange group of friends and an unusually strong penchant for bones, his significance was in fact far greater. Wowman was a central part of a federal initiative to harness the power of the advertising industry to turn kids off of drugs.

The success of consumerism in the postwar period drastically increased standards of living and created an unprecedented level of comfort for all Germans. Advertising acted as the engine for the production of consumer desire, convincing consumers of the value of their aspirations and guiding their consumer choices. Yet consumerism was also a Pandora's box. Advertising, the blunt tool of consumerism, had pried open the doors of consumer desire. But when it became evident at the end of the sixties and in the early seventies that untamed consumer desire could create very real social problems, the tools of advertising proved woefully inadequate to keep certain desires trapped within the box. The government had championed consumption as the key to a rising gross national product, and the advertising industry had promoted a belief that consumption was constitutive of individual identity, yet neither could control the desires unleashed. By examining the 1972 antidrug campaign, this paradox of consumerism comes to the surface. The West German government, locked in an ideological war with its East German foe, promoted a capitalist vision of modernity, but this vision and the instrumental, economic rationality upon which it was based contained contradictions that could not be resolved.

When faced with a rising incidence of drug consumption, the government turned to advertising to try and stem the tide, believing that rational actors, educated about the dangers of drug use, would turn their backs on irrational behavior. Yet the failures of the drug campaign illustrate the limits of economic rationality in the marketplace, the tension between public health and consumer desire in the postindustrial world, and the erratic power of advertising over consumer behavior. The antidrug campaign was a product of the modernization of West Germany, and its failures highlight complications involved in creating a Western consumer economy and the limits of state control within a postindustrial capitalist economy.

Advertising and Public Health Campaigns

The notion of a public health campaign against problem consumption certainly was not a new one in the 1970s. As early as the turn of the twentieth century, the German Association against the Misuse of Spirits (Deutscher Verein gegen den Mißbrauch geistiger Getränke) published temperance tracts, while its successor, the German Association against Alcohol Misuse (Deutscher Verein gegen den Alkoholmißbrauch), created a comprehensive educational alcohol abuse campaign for industrial workers and their families during the Weimar Republic.[1] The organized temperance movement continued into the National Socialist period, though increasingly alcoholics and drug abusers were seen as asocial enemies of the *Volksgemeinschaft* rather than as spiritually bankrupt people or victims of an illness. The public campaigns against alcohol abuse and smoking intensified during the Nazi period, increasingly focused on new problems such as the dangers of drinking and driving.[2]

After the war, public health campaigns against drinking and smoking showed remarkable continuity, both in substance and personnel. The continuity of institutions and personnel ensured a certain continuity of ideas, arguments, and images between the Weimar, Nazi, and postwar periods. Certain aspects of the National Socialist campaigns

---

1. Elisabeth Wienemann, *Vom Alkoholverbot zum Gesundheitsmanagement: Entwicklung der betrieblichen Suchtprävention 1800–2000* (Stuttgart: Ibidem, 2000), 340.

2. In 1937, for instance, Heinrich Himmler sent every licensed driver in Germany a letter deploring the habit of drunk driving. Proctor, *Nazi War on Cancer,* 145.

were patently offensive enough to be unrepeatable in the postwar period, particularly those that focused on the link between alcohol, tobacco, and racial degeneracy. For instance, in a 1941 illustration from the Nazi antismoking periodical *Reine Luft,* alcohol and tobacco are portrayed as the habits of profligate capitalists, Jews, American Indians, Africans, and prostitutes, leaving behind them a trail of burned cities, blood, and skulls. This kind of overtly racist imagery proved unacceptable in the 1950s, but the more common argument from the Nazi period that money spent on ephemeral pleasures like alcohol and cigarettes prevented useful social consumption remained remarkably similar. For example, another 1941 image from *Reine Luft* depicts a smoker letting the trappings of a better life—travel and consumer goods—go up in smoke. Twelve years later, a pamphlet published jointly by the Baden State Association against the Threat of Addiction (Baden Landesverband gegen die Suchtgefahren) and the Württemberg Office for Public Health for Protection against the Threat of Addiction (Württemberg Landesstelle für Volksgesundung zur Abwehr der Suchtgefahren) entitled "Can You Pass On It?" included the same sentiment and sensibility. The text tells the reader that the 9.5 billion marks spent yearly on tobacco and alcohol would be better spent on four hundred thousand new homes—a message that would have at least seemed persuasive during the housing crisis of the early 1950s. The same kind of consumer goods that were presented in 1941 reappear, including a train (the symbol of travel and tourism), a bicycle, and clothing. The message in these images point to the economic rationality that lay at the heart of public health campaigns: the purchase of tobacco and alcohol hampers the fulfillment of "proper" consumer desire. Consumption of certain consumer items should be promoted, but the consumption of wasteful, addictive substances serves as a drain on the nation's resources.

These campaigns of the forties and fifties took place before the introduction of modern social science techniques to measure the outcomes of public health campaigns. Current researchers have none of the statistical baggage of these later campaigns. The only measure of success or failure still available is the raw statistics on the sale of tobacco and alcohol over the period. From this perspective, the campaigns seem to have been a failure.

The public health campaigns of the forties and fifties give us some

Fig. 11. "Can You Pass On It?" A pamphlet from a 1953 Baden-Württemberg campaign against alcohol and tobacco consumption emphasizing the costs of unproductive consumption. (BAK, B142/404.)

TABLE 1. Alcohol and Tobacco Consumption in the Federal Republic, 1950–75

Year	Number of cigarettes per potential customer (age > 15)	Liters of beer per potential customer	Liters of hard liquor per potential customer
1950	622	48	1.4
1960	1,619	120	2.4
1970	2,529	184	3.9
1975	2,556	188	3.9

Source: Glatzer et al., eds., *Recent Social Trends in West Germany 1960–1990,* 441.

perspective on the antidrug campaigns of the seventies, but in many ways they were quite different, both in terms of the problem addressed and the means of tackling the problem. First and foremost, the illicit drug wave of the sixties and seventies was quite unlike the consumption of cigarettes and alcohol. Not only were the speed, hashish, and LSD of the latter period illegal, but they occupied a space in the economy that was fundamentally different from the corporate world of the tobacco and alcohol industries.

The growth in the illict drug market was in itself fairly astonishing. Yet perhaps more astounding was that this growth took place in the absence of the offensive arsenal of modern capitalism: the advertising industry. Although the point is obvious, it merits repetition: the drug trade grew without a single TV ad, without radio spots, without print ads, without product tie-ins, without direct mail, coupons, or giveaways.

It is particularly interesting then that the government turned to the advertising industry to convince consumers not to consume products that showed phenomenal market growth despite the lack of advertising. Why turn to the professional advertising world instead of having the members of the Federal Center for Health Education (Bundeszentrale für gesundheitliche Aufklärung, or BZgA) design and implement the program? Though the answer to this question is probably quite complicated, much of the explanation seems to rest with the growth, both in size and sophistication, of the advertising industry between the 1950s and the 1970s. This period saw significant changes in the scope and practice of advertising. Three of the industrywide transformations deserve special mention because they proved important to the design and implementation of public health campaigns and the antidrug campaign in particular: the triumph of the social sciences, the emergence of market segmentation, and the expansion of international advertising.

Transforming the Advertising World

Advertising and by extension public health campaigns underwent a radical transformation over the course of the 1950s and 1960s. This was true throughout the industrialized world, and although much of the impetus for this change came from the "consumers' paradise" of the United States, the new inflection of science-driven marketing and advertising spread rapidly on both sides of the Atlantic. Vance Packard's seminal 1957 book *The Hidden Persuaders* pointed to a not-so-secret secret that advertisers had increasingly turned to social psychologists and sociologists to help them "understand" consumers and consequently sell more goods. Perhaps the most important trend in advertising in the postwar period was this shift to approaching consumption as a science, the spread of the belief that desire could be measured and consequently tamed.[3] Though the German advertising agencies were often wary of the danger of "Americanization," the trend toward scientific market analysis emerged during the Weimar period and triumphed during the 1960s.[4] By the sixties, advertising provided a major source of revenue for the German mass media, and while the vast majority of advertising budgets were spent on newspaper and magazine ads, television advertising became an increasingly valuable sector over the course of the sixties.[5] By 1960, total advertising expenditure reached DM 2.2 billion;[6] this growth continued almost unabated through the 1960s. The expansion of market research was fed by the growth of advertising revenue, as advertisers demanded proof of the efficacy of advertising on consumer behavior. According to Karin Knop, this increase in accountability led to a strategic move from

3. Lizbeth Cohen, *A Consumers' Republic: The Politics of Mass Consumption in Postwar America* (New York: Alfred A. Knopf, 2003), 298.

4. Dirk Reinhardt sees the economic expansion of 1925–28 as the crucial period for the discovery of the consumer and the emergence of *Marketanalyse,* and he notes the establishment of a branch of the J. Walter Thompson agency in Berlin as the turning point of the move toward market research. See Dirk Reinhardt, *Von der Reklame zum Marketing: Geschichte der Wirtschaftswerbung in Deutschland* (Berlin: Akad. Verlag, 1993), 44–48.

5. Carter, *How German Is She?* 158–59. See also Christian Steininger, "Eleganz der Oberfläche: Werbung und die ökonomische Restauration deutscher Normalität," in *Die Kultur der fünfziger Jahre,* ed. Werner Faulstich (Munich: Wilhelm Fink, 2002), 181–98. For the breakdown of spending on various media, see Karin Knop, "Zwischen Afri-Cola-Rausch und dem Duft der großen weiten Welt: Werbung in den sechziger Jahren," in *Die Kultur der sechziger Jahre,* ed. Werner Faulstich (Munich: Wilhelm Fink, 2003), 246. The rapid growth of advertising after the 1948 currency reform led to the formation of the Zentralausschuss der Werbewirtschaft in 1949, and six years later the expansion of market research led to the creation of the Arbeitskreis für betriebswirtschaftliche Markt- und Absatzforschung, which acted as an industry group for market research firms such as the widely known Institut für Demoskopie Allensbach as well as the Intermarkt Gesellschaft für Markt- und Meinungsforschung, the latter of which later worked on the antidrug campaign. See International Chamber of Commerce, *Advertising: Conditions and Regulations in Various Countries,* 2d ed. (Basel: Verlag für Recht und Gesellschaft, 1964), D2.

6. International Chamber of Commerce, *Advertising,* D2.

advertising to marketing, as German advertising moved toward an Americanized "full-service agency" model.[7] And by the 1970s, the advertising industry had become a major economic player in Germany. Social science–driven advertising had become an omnipresent part of everyday life and, despite the agency of consumers, had become a significant force in shaping consumer desire.

Although the general rise in the "science" of marketing and the growth of the advertising industry played a large role in the consumer revolution of the 1960s, other more specific changes in the industry played a substantial role in redefining the relationship between consumption and identity. Specifically, in the 1960s advertising theory and practice shifted from appealing to the mass market toward focusing on market segmentation. Lizabeth Cohen has convincingly shown that after the recession of 1957–58 a "market segmentation revolution" took place in the U.S. advertising industry.[8] According to Cohen, the economic expansion of the 1950s increasingly brought industries into competition for a limited amount of consumer purchasing power. This crisis forced the advertising and marketing industries to rethink their strategy, which previously had focused on the average consumer or the average consumer unit, the household. As Cohen puts it, "executives had come to recognize that future profits—for their advertisers and hence themselves—depended on identifying market uniformity."[9] Over the course of the 1960s, advertisers aided by social scientists and social psychologists increasingly divided consumers into quantifiable "lifestyles" and sold images wrapped in goods.[10] Although much research in market segmentation in Germany still remains to be done, there is ample evidence that the same process was taking place on the Continent at roughly the same time; perusing any mass publication across the 1960s will illustrate this process.[11] Part of this shift toward

7. Knop, "Zwischen Afri-Cola-Rausch," 244.

8. Cohen, *Consumers' Republic*, 309–14.

9. Ibid., 307.

10. On this process in Germany, see Knop, "Zwischen Afri-Cola-Rausch," 246–68.

11. For an example of a German company's adoption of the lessons of market segmentation, see Harm G. Schröter, "Marketing als angewandte Sozialtechnik und Veränderungen im Konsumverhalten: Nivea als internationale Dachmarke 1960–1994," in *Europäische Konsumgeschichte: Zur Gesellschafts- und Kulturgeschichte des Konsums (18. bis 20. Jahrhundert)*, ed. Hannes Siegrist, Hartmut Kaelbe, and Jürgen Kocka (Frankfurt and New York: Campus, 1997), 615–48.

lifestyle advertising during the sixties was the result of the growth of youth culture, the student movement, and the various countercultures. Indeed, as Detlef Sigfried has pointed out, by the late fifties social scientists saw teenagers as "pioneers in the jungle of the consumer society."[12] Advertisers were forced to adopt new strategies to reach young consumers who had been heavily influenced by critiques of advertising as propaganda.[13] The industry adapted, and by the 1970s, much of the imagery of the counterculture had been appropriated by advertisers, and often young members of the counterculture helped advertisers reach this seemingly skeptical audience.[14]

In the realm of public health advertising, market segmentation failed to make significant inroads until the 1970s, when public health campaigners began to look toward the advertising world for new models of persuasive communication. Public health campaigns then began to target certain lifestyle groups in their research and especially in media campaigns.[15] When the BZgA began their national antidrug campaign in the early seventies, market segmentation was a guiding principle.

The third major shift in the advertising and marketing industry that greatly affected the early antidrug campaigns was the growth of multinational advertising agencies. Advertising, of course, was well established in the nineteenth century, but it was not until the postwar period that advertising became dominated by enormous global advertising agencies. When the BZgA began to plan its antidrug campaign, rather than employ a German-owned firm it turned to the American-owned J. Walter Thompson firm in Frankfurt to design the campaign. And even if it had given the contract to a German firm, the results would probably have differed only slightly. By the 1970s, national advertising styles had largely ceased to matter as advertising forms emerging from the United States increasingly became the international norm.[16]

12. Detlef Siegfried, "'Trau keinem über 30'? Konsens und Konflikt der Generationen in der Bundesrepublik der langen sechziger Jahre," *Aus Politik und Zeitgeschichte* B45 (2003): 28.

13. Knop, "Zwischen Afri-Cola-Rausch," 242–44.

14. See Marwick, *The Sixties,* 17.

15. See Ellen A. Wartelle and Patricia A. Stout, "The Evolution of Mass Media and Health Persuasion Models," in *Mass Media and Drug Prevention,* ed. William D. Crano and Michael Burgoon (Mahwah, NJ, and London: Lawrence Erlbaum, 2002), 19–34.

16. Victoria de Grazia, *Irresistible Empire: America's Advance through 20th-Century Europe* (Cambridge, MA: Belknap, 2005), 11.

These three innovations of the 1950s and 1960s—psychometrics, market segmentation, and internationalization—coalesced by the early 1970s. The government bureaucracy, though slow to adopt innovations, by the seventies realized the need for modern advertising techniques to fulfill its mission of "unselling" drugs. Rather than running the campaign themselves or through private welfare groups, as they had done in the past, the federal government turned to the vanguard of consumer capitalism to convince its young citizens not to consume. The remainder of the chapter will examine how they went about this, the effects of the campaign, and what this example can tell us about larger changes in advertising and the instrumental logic of public bureaucrats in their attempt to sway youth consumer behavior.

The Campaign

After considerable debate and under pressure for specific financial relief from the states, on 12 November 1970, the federal government finally published its first "Action Plan for the Struggle against Narcotics Misuse," a properly weighty title for a comprehensive plan. The Action Plan stressed a two-pronged approach to the drug problem. On the one hand, those who "conduct business in illegal drugs and narcotics and make a profit off the endangerment of others, particularly the young, while burdening society with the costs of remedying the damage caused by them," must be punished to the fullest extent of the law.[17] On the other hand, those "who became mixed up in the spell of drugs and narcotics frivolously and imprudently and cannot free themselves from them through their own power" ought to be offered social and medical assistance.[18]

Along with outlining the basic thrust of public policy for those already involved in the drug scene, the Action Plan called for a concerted antidrug campaign in an effort to prevent young people from taking up drug use, to "educate" the young about the "health danger and social harmfulness" of drugs.[19] In order to promote the public health, to rehabilitate the afflicted, to punish the guilty, and, not least, to alleviate the fiscal burden on the states, the federal government

17. Bundesministerium für Jugend, Familie und Gesundheit, *Dokumente zum Drogenproblem*, 99.
    18. Ibid., 100.
    19. Ibid.

pledged DM 1.5 million in immediate funding and promised to continue to help shoulder the costs of the drug war in the future. The campaign, as presented in the Action Plan, stressed creating informational materials, purchasing advertising, producing films, supporting various private welfare initiatives, and constructing an educational series for teachers and others with close contact to young people.[20]

When they began constructing the actual campaign, the BZgA began with a number of presuppositions. "The misuse of drugs is only a symptom of a complex problem, which can have both social and individual-constitutional psychological causes," they argued. "The drug problem must not be allowed to grow in isolation—it must be uncovered at the roots and combated."[21] Equally important, they realized that the problem needed to be approached with a deft hand, that even young teens often saw messages from the state as inherently repressive and dismissed them out of hand. Likewise, the BZgA concluded that widespread drug use would not disappear just because media messages told young people that drugs were bad for them.[22]

Acting on a tight budget, the BZgA adopted three foundational principals: minimize losses due to nonselective advertising, maximize consumer acceptance, and maximize cost-effectiveness.[23] Acting from these principles, the organizers divided the campaign into three primary target groups: parents and educators; teens over the age of fifteen; and the principal group, teens between the ages of twelve and fourteen. Having learned the lessons of the sixties about market segmentation, the campaign planners targeted specific messages and media at each group. For parents, educators, and social workers, a committee headed by Minister for Youth, Family, and Health Käte Strobel published a brochure entitled "Information on the Drug Problem" (*Informationen zum Drogen-Problem*). For older teens, the BZgA sought to exploit the explosive popularity of pop music celebrity and of music magazines by publishing "interviews" with musicians about the

20. Ibid., 103, 106–7. The specific eight-part plan laid out in the federal Action Plan closely resembles the recommendations of Heinz Westphal of the Ministry for Youth, Family, and Health outlined in a letter to the head of the chancellor's office on 16 July 1970, BAK B/141/37547.

21. BAK B310, B310/255, "Vorbemerkung," 1.

22. BAK B310, B310/255, "Vorbemerkung," 2.

23. Ibid., 3.

dangers of drugs. Finally, most of the campaign, most of the expense, and most of the media buys were directed at the younger teens. The BZgA saw this group of youngsters as the key to the success of the campaign. Viewing the older teens as already jaded by advertising, the media, and personal experience with drug users as well as being overly suspicious of the government and propaganda, the planners believed that they must reach this group of "potential drug users." Reaching this market, however, seemed more difficult than reaching the older group. One way was through schools, and there were curricula set up for teaching drug education.[24] But if the messages disseminated by schools were dismissed by these teens, what other media might prove efficacious? The BZgA settled on the idea of marketing antidrug messages through comic strips and through the radio, both of which offered the promise of reaching this very specific market segment. The messages aimed at each of these three groups were crafted to appeal to their preconceptions and prejudices and were pitched at a level appropriate to each group.

In today's world, more than thirty years into the war on drugs, most adults have some familiarity with the basics of drugs. This was not the case for most adults in the early seventies. Indeed, even the ignorance of young people in the early seventies is startling. For example, at the end of 1970, the Institute for Applied Social Science in Bonn-Bad Godesburg completed a representative survey of 1,009 Hamburg citizens on the drug problem. When asked if they personally knew someone who had ever consumed drugs, a shocking 81 percent of all respondents claimed they did not know a single user, and the percentage was even higher for those over age thirty-five.[25]

The authors of the brochure "Information on the Drug Problem" targeted just this kind of mass ignorance, perceiving it as a hindrance to rational, informed decision making. If parents knew more about drugs, the authors believed, they could help steer their charges down the right path. Children, on the other hand, would be less likely to try drugs in the first place if they were given the "scientific" facts. This kind of instrumental logic, focused on both adults and teens as "rational

24. BAK B310/508, Renate Fuchs et al., *Teilcurriculum für die Klassenstufen fünf bis acht: Zum Drogenproblem* (Köln: BZgA, 1973).

25. StAH, 135-1 VI, Staatliche Pressestelle VI, Institut für angewandte Sozialwissenschaften, "Meinungen in Hamburg zum Rauschgiftproblem," 1971.

consumers," permeated the discussions on the drug problem, not only at the BZgA but in the legislature, in the social science literature, and in the more intellectual public press as well. If only people understood the dangers of drugs, they would choose not to use them. Yet, in retrospect, this kind of enlightenment faith that an invisible hand of an informed, rational market could curb demand appears to be as fanciful as the horror stories in the boulevard papers.

Based on a brochure produced by the senator for work, health, and social welfare in Berlin, the "Information on the Drug Problem" pamphlet was for many their most reliable information on the physiological and psychological action of specific drugs, particularly when compared with the vitriolic hysteria spewed by the Springer press. The surprisingly measured tone of the brochure conformed to the consensus between the medical profession, the civil service, and the police: that factual information should be emphasized and that scaremongering often proved counterproductive. The BZgA believed that "The assumptions about drugs must be managed by imparting knowledge (professionally correct information about drugs) and by showing the alternatives to drug consumption."[26]

Despite a commitment to "science," however, many of the temperance tropes of inevitable organic decay, common since the nineteenth century, emerged as leitmotifs throughout the brochure. Though readers were asked to come to their own conclusions after reading the "facts" contained in the brochure, they were repeatedly faced with clichés. In her opening letter, for instance, Minister Käte Strobel opens with a recognition that "It is the nature of mankind to seek out new things beyond that which has been reached and is known and therefore to take on a certain risk. Enthusiasm, intoxication and personal ecstasy are not foreign to human nature."[27] This acknowledgment by a major figure in the federal government at the opening salvos of the drug war appears to be quite progressive. Yet after stressing that drug use can be a part of life, she slips into the familiar mantra of the temperance narrative, the drunkard's progress updated for the hashish generation: "Frequently, all too frequently, these drugs lead directly to illness, to social infirmity, and to death."[28]

26. BAK B310, B310/255, "Vorbemerkung," 3.
27. BAK, B310/236, "Information Drogen-Problem," 3.
28. Ibid., 3.

Deckname

„acid".

Herkunft, Verwendungsformen

Als Halluzinogene bezeichnet man Substanzen, die Sinneseindrücke verändern und Sinnestäuschungen hervorrufen.

Typische Vertreter:

LSD (Lysergsäurediäthylamid). Bestandteil des Mutterkorns, wird jetzt künstlich hergestellt.

Meskalin, Wirkstoff des Peyotl-Kaktus, seit Urzeiten in Mexiko und Südamerika, unter anderem bei religiösen Zeremonien, verwendet.

DOM (oder „STP"), synthetische Abkömmlinge des Amphetamins mit starker halluzinogener Wirkung.

Auf dem schwarzen Markt wird LSD in unterschiedlicher Konzentration und mit anderen Stoffen vermischt (Lösung auf Zuckerstückchen oder auf Löschpapier geträufelt und mit Stanniolpapier umwickelt) angeboten. Vermischt mit anderen Drogen, kommt LSD auch in Form von Tabletten und Kapseln vor. Meskalin wird illegal in Kapseln als weißliches Pulver oder in wäßriger, farbloser Lösung gehandelt.

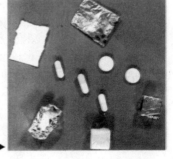

LSD auf Zucker und Löschpapier, in Tabletten und Kapseln

▶

Erlebnisse und Sinnestäuschungen können so bedrängend werden, daß es zu unverwarteten Fehlhandlungen (Selbstmordversuch, Fenstersturze) kommt.

Sowohl in chemischer als auch in physiologischer Hinsicht ist bei LSD noch vieles unerforscht, so daß äußerste Vorsicht geboten erscheint.

Schon relativ kurze Anwendung kann unter Umständen weitreichende Folgen haben. Noch ist ungeklärt, ob LSD Mißbildungen und Erbschäden auslöst. Hinweise darauf liegen jedoch vor.

Wirkung, Gefahren

LSD-Anhänger sprechen von der bewußtseinserweiternden, „offenbarenden", psychodelischen Wirkung der Droge. Schon mit kleinsten Dosen (¹/₁₀₀₀₀ Gramm) ist ein „Trip", eine „Reise", zu erzielen.

Der Verbraucher gerät dabei in einen Zustand gesteigerter nervlicher Erregbarkeit; seine Stimmung ist euphorisch gehoben oder auch depressiv

Angstrausch und Echorausch sind zusätzliche Gefahren bei den Halluzinogenen. Schon leichte Überdosierung oder eine vorübergehende besondere Empfindlichkeit können zu einem über zwölf und mehr Stunden andauernden Rauschzustand mit qualvollsten Angsterlebnissen führen (horror trip). Solche Entgleisungen können zu wirklichen Geistesstörungen führen. Bedrückend wird auch der unberechenbar eintretende „Echorausch" erlebt. Ohne neue Zuführung der Droge kommt es plötzlich zu Rauschzuständen von erheblicher Tiefe und langer Dauer.

Die Halluzinogene vor allem LSD und DOM, sind nicht, wie ihre Befürworter meinen, Wunderdrogen, sie sind wegen der Gewalt ihrer Einwirkung, ihrer Unberechenbarkeit und der Begleitgefahren in Wirklichkeit Wahnsinnsdrogen.

Fig. 12. A discussion of hallucinogens in the Federal Center for Health Education's pamphlet "Information on the Drug Problem." (BAK, B310/236.)

A similar tone emerges repeatedly throughout the brochure. In the general introduction, after confessing that "we live not only in a mechanized but at the same time a chemical world," the authors conclude with a paragraph so fantastic and spectacular that it deserves quoting at length:

> In this "chemical everyday life" it seems only to be a small step to try drugs that promise a trip with the clouds. This demonstrates the variable risk of these drugs. One risk is the same for all of them: in every case it is a matter of very serious intrusion. With such substances, the brain is forced into such abnormal functions that one can find a comparable state only in the mentally ill. Whomever would like to imagine what this means will reduce the risk of the use of such drugs.[29]

After this introduction, most of the rest of the brochure contains group-by-group explanations of different drugs, most of which oscillate between demonstrable "facts" (e.g., joints are hash cigarettes), politically motivated warnings (e.g., the claim that German statistics "confirm" that hashish consumption leads to "hard drug" use), and tepid moralizing (e.g., hallucinogens are not *Wunderdrogen* but rather *Wahnsinnsdrogen;* that is, they are not miracle drugs but rather insanity-inducing drugs).

After the journey through the drug classes, the final two sections give specific examples of the dangers of drugs.[30] The first of the two sections, entitled "Bitter Drug Experience," relates the stories of three young men who learned the lessons of drug use the hard way: a sixteen-year-old apprentice who graduated from hashish to LSD, lost his apprenticeship, and ended up in drug rehabilitation; a twenty-year-old technical draftsman who began using hash with friends but eventually realized the error of his ways and gave it up; and a twenty-year-old loner who left school and his parents' house, joined a commune, and was eventually arrested for robbing a store.[31] The final section contains an interview with a drug addict entitled "Shooting Up Makes You Happy and Dead," first published in *Underground* magazine in 1970.

29. Ibid., 4–5.
30. Ibid., 7–21.
31. BAK, B310/236, "Information Drogen-Problem," 25–26.

This interview is perhaps the most useful aspect of the brochure, as well as the only part not authored by the committee. The young addict's answer to the question "How would you characterize shooting up? An addiction?" rings much more true and less dogmatic than the rest of the pamphlet.

> For me it is a free choice (!?) Naturally there are people who have been persuaded to do it. I think that's shit. That people don't have any idea where they're leading themselves. I knew where I was leading myself. (?) Of course I'm addicted to drugs, but everyone's addicted to something. I've freed myself from thousands of addictions, and I've traded them for being addicted to drugs.[32]

The added emphasis by the authors here is interesting. It is the only place where punctuation is added in the entire brochure, though the punctuation serves not a grammatical function but rather as a form of commentary. It is as if the authors simply cannot let the addict tell his own story, as if this young man's story is literally incredible. The notion that addiction could be freely chosen is both extraordinarily provocative (!) and incomprehensible (?), while the idea that this young addict could have known where he was leading himself leaves the editors incredulous (?); he must be either disingenuous or self-deluded. In any case, he must not be allowed to speak without some challenge to his authority, without some indication that he is wrong, without some affirmation that addiction is a disease that leads to misery or death. The brochure lives and dies by this contradiction. The creators realize the limits of propaganda; they want to stress the "scientific" facts. Yet the brochure remains an attempt to persuade people not to use drugs. As such, counterarguments or even fragments that do not fit into this archetype must be questioned, confronted, and rejected. In the end, the brochure *is* propaganda, and try as the authors might to bend it into a simple statement of fact, the propaganda function trumps the truth value.

Judged on its own terms, however, the brochure was a success. It did what it set out to do: it provided "scientific" information to the woefully uninformed; it delivered the political message set out in the federal government's Action Plan; and, perhaps most important, it

32. Ibid., 27.

reached its audience and reinforced preexisting notions (that drugs were an imminent threat to the body and the mind). If the brochure satisfied its authors, its effect on the public was less than satisfactory. According to the market researchers hired by the BZgA, there were a number of significant problems with both the design of the brochure and the execution of the campaign.

After the publication of the brochure, the BZgA engaged the Institute for Market and Advertising Research in Cologne to research the effectiveness of the brochure on both adults and teens. Not surprisingly, the market research agency had a different view of the drug problem than the Ministry for Youth, Family, and Health. Rather than treating drugs as a social or cultural peculiarity, the agency began with the initial assumption that drug consumption "at the basic level cannot be differentiated from other behavior patterns and consumer habits."[33] This presupposition marked a significant departure from the government's approach. The government preferred to place drugs within the area of expertise of the physicians and criminologists rather than as part of the consumer sciences. After all, consumerism, at least since Ludwig Erhard's turn as finance minister, had been heralded as fundamentally good; drug consumption could not be seen as a good and, therefore, fell outside of the aegis of consumerism. If the state wanted to force an end to the drug trade, however, advertising and public relations experts were guided by market logic—that drugs were like other consumer goods. If they were products, they had a market, and, presumably, this market was organized by collective ideas that market researchers could uncover and manipulate.

The market analysis stressed the differences between the reception of young people and their parents' generation. Parents, the authors reported, tended to receive their information from the media, which had "demonized" drug consumption and consumers. As a result, their conclusions were skewed. Parents, for instance, believed that hashish and amphetamines caused hallucinations, even more so than LSD. Because of their "uninformed way of seeing drugs as equivalent," parents divided themselves from their children.[34] Young people, on the

33. BAK, B310/774, Institut für Markt- und Werbeforschung, "Der Aufklärungs-broschüren 'Information zum Drogenproblem' 'Perspektiven, Aussagen zum Drogenproblem' bei Jugendlichen und Erwachsenen," 5.

34. Ibid., 45.

other hand, proved to be much more informed and received their information from a number of sources (associations, brochures, books, etc.). Indeed, throughout the report young people are praised for being more "enlightened" about drug use than their parents.

The market researchers came to uncomfortable conclusions. They judged the brochure to be a failure, concluding that it "had a significantly weaker reception than comparable advertisements." And they cautioned that "this kind of information is in competition with all the other information flooding consumers everyday."[35] In addition to this reminder that antidrug messages had to compete with other media, the most important insight offered to the public health experts by the market researchers was the notion that information is not simply injected into consumers. According to the marketers, the disconnect between what the brochure had to say and what young people were hearing elsewhere led to "cognitive dissonance."[36] For instance, telling teens that hashish was as unsafe as heroin and LSD belied what they already knew. And ultimately, this dissonance led young people to reject everything they were told by the government because the brochure could not come to terms with their own experiences.

The market researchers collected and analyzed data collected from focus groups made up of both teenagers and adults. One thirty-six-year-old father from the middle class bemoaned the histrionic tone of the brochure, adding the sardonic postscript, "Do the authors actually have children in at-risk ages?" A working mother in her early forties proved to be less skeptical: "They write so well that even the unacquainted are well informed about the issue, we are introduced to the dangers as they actually are." The younger voices, on the other hand, highlighted the "cognitive dissonance" the researcher emphasized. A middle-class student, age fourteen, pointed out that young people often take drugs to shock their parents. "The experiences in it [the brochure] aren't very frightening. Rather an incitement," she stressed. "Then, there's mother and father falling from their stools when they hear that their kids smoke hash. Some really want that!!"[37]

The final conclusions from the market researchers were damning.

35. Ibid., 79.
36. Ibid., 31.
37. Ibid., 80–81.

Statistically, there was almost no change in opinions after reading the brochure, even immediately after reading it. The researchers questioned whether the brochure in its present form was an efficient medium and suggested that the BZgA consider lowering their expectations. In summary the institute concluded:

> Without wanting to repeat the individual conclusions in the overall results, here in conclusion we recommend that the theme, composition and realization of the "Anti-Drug Campaign" be fundamentally rethought and a coordinated total-strategy developed, which is not only fixated on narcotics but first and foremost also influences the remaining strong public opinion builders in the sense of the planned strategy. Nothing hinders the success of communication more than information that can be contradicted.[38]

In spite of these fundamental reservations, the brochure was published, and by 1973 approximately 2.5 million copies had been distributed. The report by the institute pointed out many of the problems with the text and layout, but it did not answer other fundamental questions about what happened to the brochure once it found its way out into the world. Two years after the initial design, the BZgA undertook a study of the brochure's distribution. They found enormous inefficiencies: groups had received double deliveries or none at all; some had been given far more copies than they could ever use; others could not keep enough in stock. For example, according to their records the BZgA had delivered 35,000 brochures to the Hamburg Work and Social Welfare Authority. But when they followed up during their distribution research they were told a fantastic story. The social worker charged with the distribution recalled how a large truck had arrived and how the office manager, the truck driver, and he had spent hours unloading boxes, so many that they feared the floor of their office would collapse. The office manager and the social worker then had to decide how they would ever get rid of the enormous number of brochures. They delivered boxes to every office they could think of. In a fit of desperation, the social worker even began taking his two daughters to the main train station in the evenings and handing the brochures out to anyone who would take them. Despite this mammoth effort, he

38. Ibid., 106.

still had many boxes left over. When asked by the interviewer if he thought that there had been 150,000 delivered, he answered, "Yes, at least!"[39]

Yet that only explains part of the distribution problem. Another problem was what the consumers would do with the brochures. The authors of the review gave examples of rampant skepticism. "For example, in the Jakob-Fugger-School they told us that after the brochures were distributed, the majority of them were found in the wastebaskets." The authors warned that students might use the information in unintended ways. "Because of this, the Tempelhof Health Office ended the trial of leaving brochures lying out by the porter's office for those interested. One had to come to the conclusion that after a time they were being picked up almost exclusively by youth who one would suspect were drug addicts or even dealers."[40]

So not only did distribution fail, but when it worked, the response was often dismissive or ironic. Even when people did read the material and absorb the message, there was no guarantee they would remember it. The instrumental logic of the rational consumer of information proved to be an organizing principle and a fundamental mistake. Given the "truth" about drugs, different groups could and did come to different conclusions. The brochures could be both informative to parents and a fetish object for young drug consumers; they could be deadly serious or ironically amusing, depending on the readers.

While the brochures fit into a fairly traditional public health model, the BZgA placed the direct advertising campaigns aimed at teens in the hands of the advertising world. Rather than designing and implementing these promotions, as they had done with the brochure, the BZgA turned the youth campaigns over to the J. Walter Thompson agency in Frankfurt. The relationship proved to be a complicated one, and the correspondence between the two organizations shows that working together was trying for both sides. The ad agency took over the primary role. They would design mock-ups, send them to the BZgA, and then wait for a critique. When the rules of design and advertising

---

39. BAK, B310/448, Walter Dörken, Lothar Gothe, and Marianne Schmid, *Bericht Zum Streuweg Der Broschüre "Information Zum Drogen-Problem"* (Cologne: Bundeszentrale für gesundheitliche Aufklärung, [1972]), 24.

40. Ibid., 15–16.

efficiency butted up against the demands of public health or the public health bureaucracy, the latter inevitably won.

A decision was made early on that the key group would be adolescents between the ages of twelve and fourteen. The rationale was that these children were still too young to begin experimenting with drugs and that if antidrug promoters waited until these youth were in their later teens, it would be too late and the cognitive dissonance would overwhelm the message of the advertising campaign. Even though they decided to focus on the younger group, they did want to attempt to reach older teens and particularly those who had already begun experimenting with drugs. They believed this market segment, at-risk teens, could best be reached by advertising in music magazines. They surmised, quite correctly, that rock music and drugs went hand in hand.[41] In order to reduce the cognitive dissonance, the advertisers at J. Walter Thompson decided to attempt to use the powerful link of drugs and music against itself. Rather than produce the "facts" about drugs and let them speak for themselves, like the model used in the brochure, they decided to run interviews with rock stars already associated with drugs, who would explain why they had quit and why drugs were a dead end. They assembled quite a lineup of artists to take part in the campaign: John Lennon; James Taylor; Grace Slick; Roger Waters from Pink Floyd; Pete Townshend and Roger Daltrey from the Who; Jon Hiseman, the drummer for Colosseum; as well as Rosemary Butler from the all-girl quartet Birtha.

The interviews, mostly excerpted from previous interviews, were run from June until December 1972 in a number of popular music magazines (*Musikexpress, Popfoto, Crash, ran, Musikboutique,* and *Pop*) and reprinted in school newspapers throughout Germany. These interviews—though the term *interview* normally implies honest, unscripted answers—presented an interesting moral dilemma for the BZgA, if not for the advertising agency. The dilemma, though it proved not to be much of an obstacle, was whether to run the interviews as journalism or as advertising. The crux of the problem rested in the acknowledgment that this information was, in fact, coming from the government. And if the young readers of these magazines knew that this was gov-

41. On the link between music and drugs, see Nicholas Knowles Bromell, *Tomorrow Never Knows: Rock and Psychedelics in the 1960s* (Chicago: University of Chicago Press, 2002).

ernment-sponsored information, would they simply reject it as propaganda? The preface to the documents in the Federal Archive notes specifically that the interviews were run as "editorially created advertisements" (*redaktionell gestaltete Anzeigen*) in order to "secure their acceptance by the target group."[42] The ad agency and the BZgA concluded that playing the interviews as straight "news" without any acknowledgment that the government was involved, and indeed paying for the media buy, was not a problem that would keep them up at night.

The ethical problems with this are evident. Does the government have a responsibility to citizens to differentiate information from official organs from news and entertainment from the private sphere? If not, how are citizens to differentiate between entertainment, which may lack the weight of government pronouncements, and propaganda? Or, on an even more cynical note, how are citizens to differentiate between "truth" and propaganda? In a democratic society that deemed a free press to be the cornerstone of protecting the population from a repetition of tyranny, the notion that the government would purposefully disguise government-sponsored information as journalism ought to have raised alarms within the bureaucracy; but this seems not to have been the case.

The interviews themselves are fairly predictable, generally a mixture of basic questions and a recitation of how drugs had negatively affected the interviewees' lives. Dolf Hartmann's interview with Pete Townshend and Roger Daltrey in December 1972 demonstrated the format at its least subtle. Hartmann notes how much success the Who had had in the sixties and asks Townshend what the worst times had been in the last decade. Townshend answers predictably:

Oh, we were totally freaked out then. Then the moment came when I couldn't believe in success any longer—and I reached for drugs at the same time. I just sat there forever and asked myself: "what is it actually all about?" . . . Drugs always lead people to the same thing: bad luck and problems. But drugs can't solve your problems—even when they promise you an answer.[43]

42. BAK B310, B310/255, "Vorbemerkung," 4.
43. BAK, B310/255.

Later, Hartmann notes that many musicians have posited a link between drug use and creativity and asks Roger Daltrey about his experience. Daltrey responds: "No! We took speed, smoked hash and 'grass'—but our music never needed it. It's similar to alcohol. You try it, it's good—and then . . ." Hartmannn interrupts: "Then perhaps the point comes when there's no longer a way back." Then Daltrey responds with a final flourish so cliché that even stoned teens would be hard-pressed to take it seriously: "Sure, I've lost a lot of friends that way."[44]

The interview with John Lennon, a peculiarly excerpted and translated version of his 1970 interview with *Rolling Stone* magazine, seems less scripted and proves to be more interesting, though the message seems out of place for government-sponsored propaganda.[45] After discussing John's early drug use, the unnamed interviewer—Jann Wenner—asks Lennon what he thinks about his early behavior. Rather than giving the kind of scripted answer evident in the Who interview, Lennon suggests that drug use is irresponsible when it distracts from revolutionary goals.

> Simple. We must recognize realities. There are still class differences, there are still weapons being sold to Africa and blacks murdered on the streets. The people still live in fucking poverty, nothing's changed. Only I've gotten older and a bunch of people are wandering around with long hair. Simple imitation isn't enough. One must think and then act. One must do something. I pulled "Lucy in the sky" out of the air. "Power to the people" should replace it.[46]

Though the interview is certainly an antidrug message, it seems peculiar that the German government in the summer of 1972, after the Red Army Faction bombings in May and the arrest of Andreas Baader and Holger Meins in June, would publicly acknowledge its preference for revolution over drug consumption. Certainly the government wanted to reduce, if not end, youth drug consumption, but even Willy Brandt would have taken issue with "Power to the people."

44. Ibid.

45. See Jann Wenner, ed., *Lennon Remembers: The Full Rolling Stone Interviews from 1970* (New York: Da Capo Press, 2000).

46. BAK, B310/255. This is a literal translation from the German. The original appears to be an excerpt from several different paragraphs of the original interview. The staff at J. Walter Thompson apparently borrowed from Lennon for effect rather than precision.

Zum Thema Drogen:

JOHN LENNON

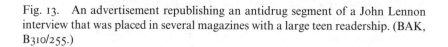

«Lucy in the sky» habe ich vom Himmel geholt.

FRAGE: Wann gingen die Beatles tatsächlich kaputt?
John: Nachdem Brian Epstein gestorben war, gab es einen Koller. Paul McCartney wollte an seine Stelle treten und uns führen. Aber was heisst schon führen? Zumal auch noch die Sache mit den Drogen dazukam.
FRAGE: Wie war das mit Deinem ersten Trip?
John: Unser Zahnarzt in London schmuggelte uns bei einem Abendessen in seinem Haus LSD unter. Er tat es uns heimlich in den Kaffee.
FRAGE: Wie lange hast Du dann Trips eingenommen?
John: Jahrelang.
FRAGE: Waren schlechte dabei?
John: Eine Menge, deswegen habe ich ja damit aufgehört. Ich konnte es einfach nicht mehr ertragen.
FRAGE: Hast Du auch andere Drogen genommen?
John: Ja. In der Kunstschule habe ich gesoffen. Dann in Hamburg nahm ich Pillen, die mir halfen, acht Stunden durchzuspielen, und bei «help» stieg ich auf Hasch um. Ich habe immer Aufputschmittel genommen. Die anderen auch, aber ich nahm immer mehr Pillen, mehr von allem, weil ich wahrscheinlich noch verrückter war. Ich war kaputt. Es war ein Ausverkauf.
FRAGE: Wie denkst Du heute darüber?
John: Ganz einfach. Wir müssen die Realitäten erkennen. Es gibt immer noch Klassenunterschiede, es werden immer noch Waffen nach Afrika verkauft und Schwarze auf der Strasse umgebracht. Die Leute leben immer noch in fucking Armut, nichts hat sich geändert. Nur ich bin älter geworden und ein Haufen Leute läuft mit langen Haaren herum. Einfach nachmachen reicht aber nicht. Man muss denken und dann handeln. Man muss was tun.
«Lucy in the sky» habe ich vom Himmel geholt. «Power to the people» soll sie ersetzen.

Fig. 13. An advertisement republishing an antidrug segment of a John Lennon interview that was placed in several magazines with a large teen readership. (BAK, B310/255.)

Yet these interviews posed little danger to the pillars of the state, as later market research showed. The follow-up survey of the target segment, fourteen- to seventeen-year-olds, showed that, other than John Lennon and James Taylor, most of these teens didn't know the artists. When asked if they had read that any of these artists had quit using drugs, the responses were abysmal. Only 12 percent of the sample had heard that John Lennon had turned his back on drugs, only 2 percent had heard the same for James Taylor, and the numbers went down from there. Almost 80 percent of the respondents had not read that any of the named musicians had quit using drugs. The market researchers concluded from this that, "Since the resonance of the ads is low and an amplification in the range is only possible to a limited extent, other alternatives to the ads employed should be discussed as well."[47] The authorities were no doubt disappointed with the success of the surreptitious propaganda, but they could be thankful that the lack of effectiveness ensured that there would be no demands for "Power to the people."

Wowman: The World's Most Famous Drug-Dog

These interviews were a sideshow to the main thrust of the campaign; the BZgA allocated the majority of the campaign's resources to reaching younger Germans, those who were deemed too young to have had much contact with drugs and who could be influenced by antidrug messages. The difficulty with reaching this quite specific market segment was finding a medium that would reach this group and doing so as economically as possible. Since 80 percent of youths between the ages of nine and fourteen read comics, the BZgA decided to create a recurring comic strip, to place the comic within an established comic book, and to produce radio tie-ins to reinforce brand recognition.[48]

The concept that the BZgA and the Thompson agency agreed upon seems in retrospect laughable, though perhaps this is not a dreadful characteristic for a comic series. The BZgA pitched the series this way:

> The lead character is "Wowman," the drug sniffing dog. His characteristic is that as soon as he "sniffs" drugs, he then becomes powerless; he is then no longer able to help his at-risk friends. This figure should be understood as a parable: Whoever misuses drugs is no longer able to solve the problems that can lead to drug consumption, among other things.[49]

After agreeing on the concept, the Thompson agency created mockups, which were then critiqued by the BZgA and sent back for revisions. This process went on until the BZgA was satisfied. The final product was a series entitled—without any sense of irony—"The Secret of the Underground Drug Plantation" (*Das Geheimnis der unterirdis-*

47. BAK, B310/247, Benad, IB3, "Ergebnisse einer Wiederholungsbefragung über Rauschmittelgebrauch bei Jugendlichen—Kurzbericht."
48. BAK B310, B310/255, "Vorbemerkung," 6.
49. Ibid.

Fig. 14. The title page for the first edition of Wowman comics. (BAK, B310/255.)

chen Drogenplantage). It ran sequentially over several months in *Primo Comics.* Like the interviews, the comics were inserted with other comic strips without any recognition that they had been created by the government and paid for from the public purse.[50]

The story is surprisingly humorous, though not always in the ways intended. The outlines of the story are classic comic book but with a psychedelic, early seventies twist. Wowman, the world's most famous drug-dog (all written in English, presumably for street credibility with ten-year-olds), and his human partner, Inspector (*Hauptwachmeister*) Knacke, try to foil a plan by the evil head of the drug underworld, Zaster, who looks remarkably like the caricatures of greedy capitalists from the Weimar period, and his hip but evil son, Zaster Junior. This caricature of Zaster as a gangster taps into a much older discourse prevalent in Germany since the First World War, in which middlemen—that is, capitalist distributors—act as stand-ins for the problems

50. Ibid., 7.

associated with capitalism. If only the distributors were not so greedy, dangerous, and so forth, then the system would work. Capitalism's failings were not endogenous but rather the result of Jews, foreigners, drug dealers, and so forth. This kind of logic remained a focal point not only for this campaign but also as a node of agreement in the larger debate over drugs in Germany during the seventies; the political parties, press, and population could not agree on all aspects of a plan to deal with drugs, but most could agree that, if only the traffickers (which often served as a shorthand for foreigners) were captured, drugs would go away.

Our hero, Wowman, has a certain addiction to bones and, when not foiling the plans of Zaster, prefers to sit and chew on them. The details of the seven-part series are too complicated to go into great detail here, but the choice of characters is interesting. In the second episode, after Knacke has been tricked into falling into the drug underworld, we are introduced to Wowman's eclectic band of friends—the presumably "at-risk" youths—as they sit around a low table with a large hookah resting on top. The gang of unlikely friends is making tea in the water pipe, the world's first "tea pipe," we're told. Wowman, however, would rather have a "bone pipe" (*Knochenpfeife*). Ali, "the little Muslim," leaves to make a bone pipe but falls into the trap laid by Zaster. The others soon follow and fall into the same trap: Rosa the young socialist, Uwe the sports expert, Blume and Taube the hippy pair, Yogi the Hari Krishna, and Johanna and Johannes the Jesus Freaks. The rest of the series follows Wowman as he journeys to the underworld to save his partner Knacke and his strange group of friends from Zaster's evil plans.[51]

The goal of the series was to convince young people not to use drugs. It certainly portrays the drug kingpins Zaster and his son as evil and shows how the "at-risk" friends ultimately reject drugs. But it remains unclear why the BZgA and the Thompson agency believed these comics would be successful at reducing drug consumption. The motley band of characters would have been quite recognizable at the time as stock characters from the counterculture, a panorama of teen culture, from the "normal" Uwe; through the socialists, hippies, and religious cult members; and even, surprisingly, Ali as a representation

51. BAK, B310/255.

Fig. 15.   Wowman's friends gather around the hookah. (BAK, B310/255.)

of Turkish immigration, which was connected in the public consciousness with the expansion of drug distribution. All these characters come off as sympathetic, and there is every reason to believe that this might induce drug experimentation rather than hinder it. After all, if Wowman's friends are socialists, hippies, Hari Krishnas, and Jesus Freaks, why would young people not also choose those types as models to emulate. Both the BZgA and the Thompson agency were aware of the tendency of media portrayals to backfire and provoke curiosity rather than abstinence, but they ultimately could not get around this contradiction. They had to try to "unsell" drug use, and the line between glamorization and demonization proved to be a very thin one.

The Thompson agency designed the campaign to be multifaceted, and the radio spots were meant to work with the comic books. The agency chose Radio Luxemburg to air the spots because of the popularity of this commercial sender with young people. The BZgA claimed that their Wowman spots could reach a potential audience of 1.5 million, 780,000 of whom were between the ages of fourteen and twenty-nine. And though statistics for listeners younger than fourteen years old were not kept, they estimated that 100,000 to 200,000 members of their target group would hear each spot. The Thompson agency understood the power of the radio medium well and was able to exploit it. The format of the spots followed a set pattern. Each five-minute spot focused on a single problem faced by young people. The audience would be asked to write to Wowman to help him solve the dilemma, and in order to increase listener loyalty, those who wrote in were entered into an album giveaway. At the end of the episode, the interviewer reminded listeners that they could follow Wowman's adventures in *Primo Comics,* "available at all newsstands."[52]

The first episode tackled the question, "Am I a coward if I don't smoke hash?" The tableau opens with Wowman exclaiming, "Listen up! There are 10 brand new Black Sabbath LPs to win!" Although this might have been a lightly veiled attempt to gain credibility with skeptical listeners, the rationale of telling children not to use drugs and then giving them albums from Black Sabbath—the authors of the song "Sweet Leaf"—seems dubious; it would appear that the Thompson agency was creating the kind of cognitive dissonance it was trying to avoid. After the speaker introduces the drug-sniffing dog and Inspector Knacke, the authors take care of one of the sticky problems with their main character by explaining that Wowman had learned to talk at a "special speech laboratory." Knacke then explains what a drug dealer is: "Incidentally, dealers are people who sell secret and illegal drugs. They buy hashish, for example, for relatively little money and then sell it for a lot." The narrator then asks who dealers sell to. "Mainly young people," of course, answers Knacke. The two then go on to discuss the central question, whether those who fail to smoke with friends are cowards. Wowman, unimpressed with the discussion, interjects:

> *Wowman:* You shouldn't talk about things you don't understand. There's nothing better than belonging to a clique of friends that have the same interests, who simply understand each other. And

52. BAK B310, B310/255, "Vorbemerkung," 7.

when one then says, come have a toke of my joint you can certainly come into conflict with your conscience.

Knacke: Incidentally, a joint is a hash-cigarette.

Wowman: Okay, okay! Something similar happened to me for the first time a few days ago. But before I tell you about it, I suggest that we play some music. And indeed from the LP that you can win today.

Wowman: Black Sabbath, Wow![53]

Up to this point, Wowman has told the children about dealers, reinforced the need for peers, explained what a joint is, and then cut to a Black Sabbath track—and this was considered a prophylaxis against drug consumption.

After the song, Wowman returns to his story about his friend Peter. The scene fades to a flashback. "The music is cool," Peter says. "Now a joint is the only thing missing." Wowman, in a voice-over, explains his weakness for drugs: "And before I could say that I always fall into such a state of powerlessness when I inhale drug smoke, Peter pulled out a joint, lit it and I flipped out." Peter then tries to pass the joint to a young girl. She declines, as does Klaus. Peter tries peer pressure: "Don't talk crap. Take a hit." But Klaus resists the pressure, giving the moral of the tale: "No. I don't have anything against you smoking hash. And you have to accept that I don't smoke it." Peter calls him a coward and shifts his attention to Dieter. The pressure is too much for Dieter, and he gives in. Wowman reappears in a voice-over.

Wowman: That's how my friends reacted. I'm interested in how our listeners would have reacted.

Announcer: Yes, dear listeners, simply write on a postcard what you would have done if someone had offered you a joint. Would you have accepted or turned it down? Explain why too. And don't forget to include the return address and your age!

Knacke: Each entry takes part in the raffle for the 10 Black Sabbath LPs.

Wowman: Please write to Wowman, W-O-W-M-A-N, Radio Luxemburg, the final day for entries is . . . Until next week at the same time![54]

53. BAK, B310/255.
54. Ibid.

A clear focus, material inducements, product tie-ins, listener participation—all these appear to be textbook modern advertising strategies. Yet most of the spots ring hollow. They pile stereotypes on top of clichés, and it is difficult to imagine that the listeners were moved either to take up drugs or to turn them down. Indeed the whole strategy, to have a talking drug dog convince children to "just say no," seems misguided.[55]

Even so, children did write in to attempt to help Wowman solve his friends' problems. Whether it was out of genuine interest or for the free records, one can only speculate. Rita Gross from Niederweiler, for example, wrote to Wowman about the conflict between Rolf and Willy. After explaining why Rolf and Willy failed to understand one another, Rita tells Wowman that he is too simplistic in his thinking.

> Rolf sees drugs as a balsam for his mental and emotional pain; in contradistinction to Willy, who believes that drugs are a harmful poison. He certainly is right about that, (because of burning out and so on!!) if he should succeed in helping his friend. *BUT IT REALLY DOESN'T HAPPEN THAT WAY!* Willy can't get away with such simple words. He must bring in substantial evidence in order to refute what Rolf thinks about smoking hash. Willy certainly has good intentions with Rolf and definitely also wants to help him, but how???
>
> There would be an opportunity to help Rolf, if he did things with many other young people and talked about his problem sometime. Then it could be that he allowed himself to be convinced and found an expert in the area of drugs and went into treatment with him. I think Willy is a good example for those who know drug addicts. He tackled the issue wrongly, but it can definitely be changed![56]

It is interesting and significant that Rita reproduces the same kind of instrumental logic that motivated the policymakers in the first place. Like the members of the federal government, Rita believes that, if only given the truth about drugs from "experts," individuals would make rational decisions. Michael Fuhr from Gniesenbach also showed sympathy for Willy. Michael opined that Willy should try again to talk to

55. Ibid.
56. Ibid.

Rolf about his problems, "but without screaming at him at the same time."[57] Most of the few remaining letters, which the BZgA selected as "representative," repeat these themes. They did not keep any letters from dissenting voices, though one could imagine that condemnatory or ironic letters were probably sent. Based on a review of the subsequent market research, however, there may not have been many more letters.

The market research proved unmistakably that any fears that the campaign might backfire and increase the number of young experimenters were unfounded. Almost no one read the comic strips; of those who did, almost no one remembered Wowman; and of those who did remember Wowman, almost no one remembered he was a dog, much less the world's most famous drug dog. Though one ought to be skeptical of statistics, the market research speaks volumes. Of the four main comic books that could have run the series—*Primo, Asterix, Micky Maus,* and *Fix und Foxi—Primo* was by far the least read by the target group (*Primo,* 30 percent; *Asterix,* 64 percent; *Micky Maus,* 70 percent; and *Fix und Foxi,* 64 percent). The BZgA and the Thompson agency picked the wrong comic, mainly because it was cheaper. Of the 30 percent who had read *Primo* in the previous half year, during which the series ran, only 3 percent had read it "regularly." When *Primo* readers were asked whether they could remember a comic strip named "Wowman," only 3 percent answered in the affirmative, and only 1 percent could identify Wowman as "the dog that sniffs drugs." The market researchers concluded that the campaign had been a failure. "In summary, it can be said that the specific education campaign against youth drug misuse in 1972 only found a very low resonance," they conceded. "A continuation of the campaign in the current form would certainly increase the resonance; however, it is questionable just how much of a decisive increase can succeed."[58] Yet the marketing experts recommended that the BZgA increase the intensity of the campaign and begin discussing alternative advertisements. Whether the marketers realized that the political imperatives would keep the campaign going despite the failures or they simply showed astounding hubris in the face of abject defeat is unclear.

57. Ibid.
58. BAK, B310/247, Benad, IB3, "Ergebnisse einer Wiederholungsbefragung," 24–26.

Conclusion

The 1972 youth drug campaign was a failure by any standard. Despite the best intentions of the government and the Thompson advertising firm, the campaign failed to reach the hearts and minds of the youth population, much less change them. Indeed, as the emphasis on cognitive dissonance shows, the campaigners were caught in an uphill battle. "Lifestyle," that peculiar object and product of marketing, had emerged over the sixties and seventies to offer a hermeneutic for understanding one's place in the world. For many young people, smoking a joint became a part of how they identified themselves—antiestablishment, part of a new generation, hip, cool, "flipped out." This message came from the media and from interaction with other people their own age. Wowman could do little to alter this fact. The advertisers, despite their wealth of knowledge of how to sell both products and lifestyles, could not "unsell" drugs.

Not only does this episode provide insight into the failures of advertising and the failures of government intervention, but it also forces us to ask questions about the instrumental logic that governed governmental policy in this case. Do individuals act rationally in their own economic or health interests? Does more factual information make for better consumers of products and more complicated notions such as health? The logic of advertising that emerged in the postwar period focused on creating micromarkets to which identity could be sold. Health officials borrowed from this model, trusting that the tools of the market could be used to "unsell" harmful goods or, conversely, to sell a new model of abstinence. The choices that guided the 1972 antidrug campaign continue to play a prominent role, not only in the war on drugs but in other public health issues as well. Governments still believe that, given the truth, consumers will make rational decisions. As we can see from this example, the notion of rational consumers may be more illusion than reality.

Epilogue

As we know, the story of drug consumption did not end in the middle of the 1970s. Yet the economic crisis that marked the end of the golden age had a profound effect on drug consumption: the heyday of consciousness expansion did not survive past mid-decade. While soft drug consumption continued to be widespread, a hard kernel of heroin users came to dominate the drug scene. Perhaps more important, the novelty of drug consumption wore off, and drug use took its place as a chronic social problem and a vivid symbol of the ambiguity of modernization. In fact, this symbolic capital that drug use and abuse accrued during the long sixties became a cultural icon that artists and filmmakers exploited. By the 1980s, it had become a powerful way for filmmakers to challenge the history of the Federal Republic and the process of modernization.

During the 1981–82 film season, two features were released that dealt specifically with drug addiction: Ulrich Edel's *Christiane F.—Wir Kinder vom Bahnhof Zoo* (We, the Children of Train Station Zoo) and Rainer Werner Fassbinder's *Die Sehnsucht der Veronika Voss* (Veronika Voss's Desire). *Christiane F.* proved extremely popular, breaking box office records for German language films. *Die Sehnsucht der Veronika Voss* marked the triumph of one of Germany's most influential directors, earning Fassbinder the Golden Bear award at the 1982 Berlin Film Festival.

The appearance of these two films in the first years of the eighties was no accident. At the end of the seventies, West Germany was wracked by a new wave of economic and political crises. Another economic downturn in 1979–80 pushed the unemployment level to heights unprecedented in the history of the Federal Republic, and stagflation led to further economic hardships among the working class. Young people faced dwindling possibilities; anarchist groups squatted in houses throughout the Federal Republic and frequently clashed with the police. This widespread disaffection over the fate of the economy led to the so-called *Wende* (turning point) in 1982, when over a decade of Social Democratic rule came to an end. Germany also experienced a second drug wave in the late 1970s and early 1980s. Hamburg witnessed rising rates of detoxification admissions in the hospitals, referrals to therapeutic communities, reported cases of hepatitis, and drug-related deaths.

It was in this atmosphere that Ulrich Edel and Rainer Werner Fassbinder turned to the theme of drug use. Edel sought to bring to the screen the story of a young woman's life as an allegory of the devastation caused by drug consumption. The result was a modern morality tale, a story of the degradation of a group of young West Berliners and the loss of innocence. Fassbinder, on the other hand, used the contemporary fears surrounding drug addiction to indict the Adenauer years. He used drug addiction to expose what he saw as the corruption of the *Wirtschaftswunderzeit* and to condemn West Germany's failure to overcome or at least to come to terms with the National Socialist past. Both of these films were a product of their times. Drug use had become an entrenched part of the urban landscape by the early eighties. Whereas Fassbinder sought to understand the failures of postwar reconstruction, Edel chose to show the destructive effects of the libertinism wrought by the cultural changes of the sixties and seventies. Yet both were ultimately disenchanted with the state of the Federal Republic. Far from seeing the process of modernization as a success story (*Erfolgsgeschichte*) or the metamorphosis into a "normal" Western country (*Wandlung nach Westen*), both saw this process as an allegory of corruption and disappointment.

Die Sehnsucht der Veronika Voss

Rainer Werner Fassbinder was no stranger to drug consumption. Fassbinder's notorious life often overshadowed his incredibly productive, if short, career as a filmmaker. His open homosexuality, his heavy drinking and drug use, as well as his often violent temper were legendary, leading his biographers to attempt to find some psychological, Freudian explanation for his provocative films.[1] These searches for

1. See, in particular, the less than flattering portrait of Fassbinder in Robert Katz, *Love Is Colder than Death: The Life and Times of Rainer Werner Fassbinder* (New York: Random House, 1987).

some Oedipal complex to elucidate Fassbinder's genius, as Thomas Elsaesser has argued, leave much to be desired.[2] Yet Fassbinder's life and his work are tied together, both embedded in the turbulent history of the sixties and seventies in West Germany. Fassbinder's remarkable FRG trilogy—*The Marriage of Maria Braun, Lola,* and *Veronika Voss*—marks one of the most imaginative critiques of the Federal Republic in any medium. These three films offer a uniquely accessible guide to the argument widely championed by the political Left throughout the sixties and seventies that German history was marked more by continuity than by rupture: that the Federal Republic had failed to overcome its Nazi origins and, at its most damning, that the Federal Republic remained even into the 1980s enmeshed in an authoritarianism that closely resembled the Nazi past. "I want with this film to give contemporary society something like a restoration of history," Fassbinder said of *Veronika Voss.* "Our democracy is one ordained at a certain time for the Western Zone; we didn't have to fight for it. Old patterns have a good chance of finding a way in—without the swastika, of course, but through being educated in the old ways. . . . I want to show how the 1950s shaped the people of the sixties—this collision of the establishment with the activists that resulted in the abnormality of terrorism."[3]

Though filmed last, *Veronika Voss* marks the chronological middle point of the trilogy. Set in the early fifties, it retells the story of Sybille Schmitz, an actress who had come to fame during the highpoint of the Ufa studio system. Schmitz had been a favorite of Goebbels during the thirties but had later been blacklisted. After the war, she could find little work and sought solace in alcohol and morphine. In 1955, Schmitz committed suicide by taking an overdose of sleeping pills. The subsequent investigation of the Munich physician Dr. Ursula Moritz, who had prescribed narcotics 723 times in less than three years, caused a considerable scandal.[4] Fassbinder was aware of Schmitz's early Ufa films and reportedly wanted to cast her as the mother in *The Bitter*

---

2. Thomas Elsaesser, *Fassbinder's Germany: History, Identity, Subject* (Amsterdam: Amsterdam University Press, 1996), 7–10.

3. Quoted in Laurence Kardish, ed., *Rainer Werner Fassbinder* (New York: Museum of Modern Art, 1997), 71.

4. Michael Töteberg, "Das süße Sterben," in *Die Sehnsucht der Veronika Voss: Ein Drehbuch für Rainer Werner Fassbinder,* ed. Peter Märthesheimer and Pea Fröhlich (Munich: Belleville, 1998), 129–30.

Tears of Petra von Kant in 1972, when he learned of her untimely death nearly twenty years after the fact.[5]

Veronika Voss is not, however, a direct retelling of the life of Sybille Schmitz. Even more than most of Fassbinder's films, this one sought to create a German version of a Hollywood melodrama, while injecting a political indictment of the Adenauer era and Fassbinder's own peculiar vision of German history. In addition to the influence of Douglas Sirk, Fassbinder appears to have looked to Billy Wilder and especially *Sunset Boulevard*. Indeed, *Veronika Voss* opens with Rosel Zech, whose haunting portrayal of Voss won her considerable acclaim, sitting in a darkened theater, watching herself and consequently her own past projected onto the screen—the aging star entranced by her own aura and that of the Nazi past, which she has never managed to escape.

Voss soon meets Krohn (Hilmar Thate), the journalist-detective who is infatuated with the faded beauty of the former Ufa star and serves the traditional role of male savior, though ultimately an ineffectual one. Krohn meets the former star on a rainy night and accompanies her to the office of Dr. Marianne Katz, a neurologist. Later that night, at home in bed with his girlfriend, Henriette (Cornelia Froboess), Krohn receives an invitation to tea with Voss the next afternoon. At their meeting, Voss tells Krohn of her impending return to the screen and fame, which are mostly a figment of her imagination. She also tricks him out of three hundred marks, ostensibly for a broach but actually to pay for her drug habit.

Krohn soon discovers Veronika's secret. Addicted to morphine, she has fallen under the spell of Dr. Katz (Annemarie Düringer), who, along with her manipulative assistant, makes her money by prescribing morphine to addicts, draining her victims of their life savings before engineering their ultimate demise. Katz's cruel scheme only works through a collusion with a member of the Ministry of Health and two African American soldiers.

Krohn and Henriette hatch a plot to expose the doctor. Henriette visits the doctor and receives a prescription for morphine, but the doctor's assistant discovers the plot to expose the doctor and runs Henriette over with her car. Krohn soon arrives with the police but is unable to convince them of foul play. Veronika Voss refuses to confirm

5. Elsaesser, *Fassbinder's Germany*, 112. See also Hellmuth Karasek, "Film: Ein deutscher Nostalgie-Frühling," *Spiegel* 36, no. 8 (1982): 199, 201.

Krohn's accusations to the police, but Katz, wary of Voss's relation-ship with Krohn, decides to end her "treatment," leaving Voss to over-dose on sleeping pills. Krohn, unable to prove any of his allegations, abandons the investigation and returns to sports reporting.

There is another subplot involving an elderly couple named Treibel, who are, like Voss, under Dr. Katz's care. They decide to take their own lives rather than live under the doctor's exploitative care. Unlike Voss's history, the Treibels' past is marked not by a longing for the Third Reich but rather by their experience in Treblinka. The Treibels mark Fassbinder's memorial to the victims of the Third Reich. Yet Fassbinder also sees Voss as a victim of the Nazi past. Wilhelm Roth argues that it is exactly this tension that motivates the film: Ufa and Treblinka are the keys to understanding Fassbinder's indictment of the Adenauer years. Both Voss and the Treibels are unable to adapt to life after the Third Reich. According to Ronald Hayman, Fassbinder "wants to set up a memorial to both victims of the camps and to those who prospered, like Veronika, under the Nazis, but find it hard to sur-vive in the Federal Republic."[6] Both the Treibels and Voss become vic-tims of the corrupt capitalism of the fifties.[7]

The critics were divided about *Veronika Voss.* Despite the film's suc-cess at the Berlin Film Festival, which culminated in Fassbinder's win-ning the Golden Bear (an award he had long coveted), *Veronika Voss* received mixed reviews. By the time the film was released, Fassbinder was at the height of his critical popularity and seen by many as the cen-tral figure in New German Cinema. Yet many critics saw the melo-drama as too melodramatic and believed it failed to reach the stan-dards of *The Marriage of Maria Braun.* Hellmuth Karasek, for example, in his review for *Der Spiegel,* bemoaned the lack of original-ity in the film and claimed that Fassbinder had fallen into a pattern of merely quoting his own work.[8] James Roy Macbean, writing in *Cineaste,* wrote that "this bleak, kitsch-laden film has little beyond its uncannily morbid self-referentiality to recommend it."[9] Though others

6. Ronald Hayman, *Fassbinder: Film Maker* (New York: Simon and Schuster, 1984), 113.
7. See Wilhelm Roth, "Die Sehnsucht der Veronika Voss," in *Rainer Werner Fassbinder,* ed. Peter Iden et al., 4th ed. (Munich: Carl Hanser, 1983).
8. Karasek, "Film," 199–200.
9. James Roy Macbean, "The Cinema as Self Portrait: The Final Films of R. W. Fass-binder," *Cineaste* 12, no. 4 (1983): 10. Macbean, in the kind of psychological argument that ties Rainer Werner Fassbinder to his films, argues that Veronika Voss "represents Fass-binder's attempt to come to grips with drug dependency" (12).

were less hostile, the film did not break any box office records and tends not to be considered one of Fassbinder's greatest achievements.[10]

Why did Fassbinder choose to use a story about drug abuse to close his indictment of the Adenauer era? Thomas Elsaesser argues that "*Veronika Voss* can be regarded either as a film about drugs (and in this respect offers some autobiographical speculations, if only insofar as Veronika is unable to maintain the creative force that the drugs so magically seemed to bestow on Fassbinder the director), or it can be seen as a film about cinema, in particular, the difficult transfer from the old Ufa cinema to the post-war West German movie business, and from Papa's Kino to the New German Cinema."[11] Elsaesser chose to pursue the latter line of inquiry. Yet *Veronika Voss* is undoubtedly also a film about drugs. Though Elsaesser is correct to note the autobiographical relationship between Fassbinder's filmic fascination with drugs and his own tortured relationship to illicit drug consumption, the production of *Veronika Voss* also represents the changing perception of drugs in German society.

Ronald Hayman argues that "Fassbinder tried to make drug-trafficking serve as an analogue for capitalistic commerce. The refrain of the song he uses on the soundtrack is: 'I owe my soul to the company store.'"[12] Voss certainly owes her soul to "the company store," personified by Dr. Katz, while economic corruption and the collusion of the government in the economy are represented by the relationship between Katz and the Health Authority representative. What Hayman fails to mention, though, is that this use of drug trafficking to indict the Wirtschaftswunder only works because the film was produced in the early eighties. By then, drugs had become a potent symbol of the "dark side" of capitalism and had taken a central place in the public conception of the problems of urban life on the other side of the "golden years." Faced with massive unemployment and the second recession in a decade as well as rising heroin consumption and increasing numbers of overdose fatalities, drugs by the early eighties had become a tangible sign of what had gone wrong. The psychedelic fashions of the sixties

10. For positive reviews, see Harlan Kennedy, "Fassbinder's Four Daughters," *Film Comment* 18, no. 5 (1982): 20–23, and Louis Skorecki, "L'amour tardif de l'actrice Veronika Voss," *Cahiers du Cinéma*, no. 339 (1982): 52–54.

11. Elsaesser, *Fassbinder's Germany*, 115.

12. Hayman, *Fassbinder*, 113.

had given way to an image of drug consumption that focused on death, decay, and waste.

Veronika Voss as both a film about drugs and a melodrama displays this changing attitude toward drugs. The public understanding of drug consumption as well as media representations had become by the late seventies melodramatic in their own right. Indeed, the conventions of representation of drug consumption had become their own form of melodrama, one that borrowed heavily from the temperance melodramas of the nineteenth century. The "truth" about drug addiction, which had been seriously challenged in the 1960s and early 1970s, had reemerged in a familiar form: drug addiction led inevitably to ruin. Fassbinder used the public understanding of drug addiction in the eighties and telescoped it back to the fifties. The financial and human corruption of the drug trade in the early eighties became a symbolic representation of the failures of reconstruction. From Ufa to Treblinka, drug addiction symbolized the failure to escape the long shadow of National Socialism.

On 10 June 1982, a mere 112 days after winning the Golden Bear for *Veronika Voss,* Fassbinder died of an apparent stroke after two days of binging on cocaine and sleeping pills. His relationship to drugs was a tangled one, full of contradictions. "Everyone must decide for himself," Fassbinder once wrote, "whether it is better to have a brief but more intensely felt existence or to live a long and ordinary life."[13] Fassbinder's life was certainly not ordinary, nor was it long.

Christiane F.—Wir Kinder vom Bahnhof Zoo

A year before *Veronika Voss* won the Golden Bear, another very different film about drugs was released in Germany. Directed by first-time director Ulrich Edel, *Christiane F.* failed to earn the critical accolades of Fassbinder's films, though it did win a viewers' award at the 1981 Montreal World Film Festival, beating out Fassbinder's *Lilli Marlene.* Yet the movie struck a chord with the German film audience and proved to be one of the most popular German films in history.

13. Quoted in Katz, *Love Is Colder than Death,* 114. See also Michael Tötenberg, ed., *Rainer Werner Fassbinder: Filme befreien den Kopf* (Frankfurt am Main: Fischer Taschenbuch, 1984), 91–93.

Released at the beginning of April 1981 in one hundred German cities, it quickly rose to the top of the ratings, displacing the American hit *Superman*. At the end of the month, over 1.8 million Germans had viewed the film.[14] By the end of the year, more than 3 million Germans had seen it, a number surpassed only by *Star Wars: The Empire Strikes Back* and Disney's *The Aristocats*.[15]

Edel's film was an adaptation of a story of a young drug user in Berlin, which had been published serially in *Stern* magazine beginning in September 1978. When the two reporters of the story, Kai Hermann and Horst Rieck, published their book in 1979 in the *Stern* book series, it became a best-seller, remaining at or near the top of the best-seller list for nearly half a decade. Within three years, the book had sold 1.3 million copies and been translated into ten languages.[16]

The film tells the story of Christiane (Natja Brunckhorst), who moves to the monstrous housing projects in Berlin-Gropiusstadt at the age of thirteen in 1975. The product of a broken home, Christiane, trapped in a modernist architectural nightmare, is forced to grow up in a world she fails to comprehend. As she meets new friends in her school, she becomes enmeshed in the nightlife that centers around the Sound disco. She begins experimenting with LSD but soon discovers that all of her friends have begun using heroin. Feeling abandoned and misunderstood at home, Christiane relies more and more on her friends and the scene at the Sound, where she meets and falls in love with Detlev (Thomas Haustein), a young male prostitute who plies his trade in train station Zoo.

Eventually, after a (fairly gratuitous) David Bowie concert, Christiane first tries heroin. Soon she begins shooting it. Despite her protestations that they are completely in control, Christiane and Detlev spend all their time getting and consuming heroin. Detlev lives in a horrendous junkie apartment and is forced to sell himself at the train station daily in order to pay for their habits.

Eventually the two decide that they must kick their habits. Their lengthy detoxification is the most disturbing scene in a film that pur-

14. Erika Fehse, "Die Kinder vom Bahnhof Zoo," in *Bilderreise Deutschland: Fotografien aus 50 Jahren*, ed. Johannes Willms (Hamburg: Campe Paperback, 1999), 102.

15. *Christiane F.* received the Goldene Leinwand award, which is only given to films with more than 3 million visitors.

16. Fehse, "Die Kinder vom Bahnhof Zoo," 102.

posefully attempts to be disconcerting. After detoxification, the two soon return to the scene and begin shooting up once more, despite the death of a friend and fellow junkie. Due to their growing tolerance and increasing need for drugs, Christiane is forced to begin turning tricks on the so-called *Babystrich* on Kurfürstendamm. Their lives become a vicious cycle of prostitution and shooting up, as the guilt drives Christiane and Detlev further apart. Eventually, Christiane's friend Babsi (Christiane Reichelt) dies from an overdose, becoming the youngest drug casualty in Berlin's history. After this event, Christiane's mother decides to send her to the Schleswig-Holstein countryside to live with relatives. The film ends with Christiane leaving for her exile, hopeful of recovery.

The film caused a considerable amount of controversy. Critics debated whether the movie, and the book, provided a cautionary tale that would keep young people from experimenting with drugs or whether the film fanned the flames of youthful curiosity. Herbert Riehl-Heyse, in his review for the *Süddeutsche Zeitung* claimed that the film, though meant to be a warning against the dangers of drug use, could work in the exact opposite manner, convincing children fed up with the boredom of their everyday life to try heroin. "In addition, if one can believe the film, the misfortune is not so bad," Riehl-Heyse wrote. "Prostitution is nasty, but one certainly earns money very easily. Addiction is dangerous, but hadn't Christiane been able to come 'clean' in the end, apparently without any help, through her own strength?"[17] Riehl-Heyse ended his polemic by accusing the distributor of using the controversy to promote his film, regardless of the social costs. Michael Schwarze, reviewing the film for the *Frankfurter Allgemeine,* largely concurred with this view of the film. "Certainly, he [Edel] displays what is otherwise concealed, the shadowy existence of fixers in subway stations, grubby toilets, but the film doesn't grab you, doesn't touch you, and doesn't especially shock you. 'Wir Kinder vom Bahnhof Zoo' is a film missing fury and weight."[18]

Gunar Hochheiden's review for the *Frankfurter Rundschau* was kinder to Edel's picture. Hochheiden believed that Edel's treatment of

17. Herbert Riehl-Heyse, "Wie vorbildlich ist Christiane F.?" *Süddeutsche Zeitung,* 3 April 1981.

18. Michael Schwarze, "Ohne Wut und Ohne Wucht," *Frankfurter Allgemeine,* 4 April 1981.

the book was authentic, arguing that the documentary distance employed by Edel made the film a valuable tool for teaching the dangers of drug consumption.[19] The reviewer for *Die Zeit,* Hans Blumenberg, agreed with Hochheiden's judgment that the film was a cautionary moral tale. Although he did not believe that Edel's film would lead young people to use drugs, he bemoaned the clinical nature of the film. "If the camera placement is a question of morality," Blumenberg wrote, "then Edel's moral appears to be the same as a ministerial bureaucrat: righteous, unimaginative, uninvolved." Blumenberg bemoaned the fact that Edel chose to create a morality play that would please "Frau Minister Huber, the Catholic Film Commission and the Women's Councils of all the parties in the Bundestag" rather than investigate the social causes of drug consumption—why drugs seemed to many young people as a way out of an otherwise banal, modern existence. Instead of creating a challenging film, like *Taxi Driver* or *Raging Bull,* Edel had created an educational film one might expect from a drug squad.[20]

The unprecedented popularity of the film and the criticism that surrounded its release culminated in a cover story by Wilhelm Bittorf in *Der Spiegel.* Bittorf saw *Wir Kinder vom Bahnhof Zoo* as the defining book of an entire generation. The book, he claimed, was the most read novel since Karl May's *Winnetou* and earned a place in the public imagination as influential as Goethe's *Werther.*[21] Though Bittorf believed that the debate over the effects of Christiane's story was overblown, he worried about the widespread, adolescent fascination with her life. The places shown in the movie—Christiane's childhood home in Gropiusstadt, the Sound discotheque, and especially the train station Zoo—had become modern stations of the cross, where young tourists would follow the path of Christiane's passion. Bittorf claimed that school classes on trips to Berlin would visit not only the Wall and the Reichstag but also the scenes of Christiane's downfall.[22]

Though Bittorf's claim that *Christiane F.* was the defining work of a new generation may be overstated, the book and film represented a

19. Gunar Hochheiden, "Stumpfe Nadel," *Frankfurter Rundschau,* 6 April 1981.

20. Hans Blumenberg, "Besonders wertvoll," *Die Zeit,* 3 April 1981.

21. Wilhelm Bittorf, "Irgendwas Irres muß laufen," *Der Spiegel* 35, no. 15 (1981): 230, 236–37.

22. Ibid., 242.

powerful individual story that clearly dominated the public consciousness of drug use, a consciousness that came of age in the second half of
the 1970s and continues to structure thinking about drugs up to the
present. *Christiane F.* still holds a central place in the understanding of
drug consumption in Germany and is still referred to when the issue of
drug consumption arises. The reasons for this do not necessarily rest in
the work itself, though the book in particular contains an interesting
mix of caution and fascination. Rather, the book and film express in a
tangible manner an understanding of drug consumption that had been
emerging since the introduction of heroin to the German drug scene in
1973. Christiane's story is the narrative version of the hard kernel argument championed by professionals dealing with drug addiction, with a
healthy dose of the slippery slope theory added. *Christiane F.* stands as
a reification of the modern drug problem. Its dominance attests to the
failures of the psychedelic imagination of the late sixties and the
growth of disillusion and drug use among children, who, dissatisfied
with their seemingly meaningless lives and the challenges of life after
the golden age, turned to drug use as a way out of the bourgeois society that seemed to offer them little.

Conclusion

In a sense, *Veronika Voss* and *Christiane F.* are both cautionary tales.
Fassbinder's film warns of the authoritarianism inherent in German
society, while Edel's movie advises young people of the danger of drug
addiction. In both movies drug addiction represented the breakdown
of German society. Voss's addiction was an addiction not only to
drugs but also to the image of the Nazi past. She failed to make the
transition out of fascism, much like German society. Trapped in a
world to which she could not adapt, she chose drug addiction as a way
to ease her own psychic pain. Manipulated by Katz and the complicit
state, she was a victim of both National Socialism and the Adenauer
era. Similarly, Christiane was a victim of the breakdown of German
society. Raised in a broken home and faced with the inhumane, imper-
sonal, and monotonous living conditions that were a legacy of reconstruction, she gravitated toward drug consumption as a way to miti-
gate the pressures of modern life. Drugs brought her a sense of
belonging she had not found in either the home or the rigid German

educational system. As the authors repeatedly point out, Christiane was a victim of a society that had lost its moorings.

Neither of these films would have made sense had they been produced even a decade earlier. The changes of the sixties and early seventies, both in terms of politics and culture, cast a long shadow over the following decades. Though Fassbinder believed that German society had not fundamentally reformed itself and that the nation remained a prisoner of its fascist past, Germany had changed drastically as a result of the cultural revolution of the sixties. In many cases this transformation was for the better. Yet alongside the positive changes wrought by the turmoil of the sixties grew new problems, which were only exacerbated by the economic decline after 1973.

Drug abuse represented only one of these unexpected consequences of the sixties. The initial euphoria surrounding the psychedelic revolution gave way to a drug scene that spawned Christiane's story. Although her life story became the public icon for drug abuse in Germany, hers was a tale that encapsulated the experiences of thousands of young Germans. The experience of drug addiction also shaped Fassbinder's view of the world as well as his films. Veronika Voss's drug addiction may have mirrored Fassbinder's own, but her addiction represented an indictment of German history specifically because drug addiction had, by the early eighties, become a remarkable symbol of the failings of modern society.

Select Bibliography

Archival Sources

Staatsarchiv Hamburg (StAH)
    JB Jugendbehörde
    BfI Behörde für Inneres
    GhB Gesundheitsbehörde
    BAS Behörde für Arbeit und Soziales
    BSB Behörde für Schule und Berufsbildung
    StPS Staatliche Pressestelle

Bundesarchiv Koblenz (BAK)
    BJ Bundesministerium der Justiz
    BfG Bundesminsterium für das Gesundheitswesen
    BZgA Bundeszentrale für gesundheitliche Aufklärung

Landesstelle gegen die Suchtgefahren Hamburg (LgS)
    LgSPS Pressestelle

Hamburg Behörde für Inneres (HBfI)
    K245 Landeskriminalamt, Rauschgiftdezernat

United Nations
    E/CN.7 Commission on Narcotics and Dangerous Drugs
    E/IT Illicit Traffic
    E/NR Summary of Annual Reports of Governments Relating to Narcotic Drugs and Psychotropic Substances
    E/NS Summary of Illicit Transactions and Seizures of Narcotic Drugs and Psychotropic Substances

League of Nations
    AC Committee on Narcotics and Dangerous Drugs

Stanford Library Special Collections (SSC)
    German Extraparliamentary Movement, 1967–84

Journals

Deutsche Medizinische Wochenschrift
Deutsche Polizei
Deutsches Ärzteblatt
Frankfurter Hefte
Hamburger Ärzteblatt
Hamburger Lehrerzeitung
Jugendschutz
Kriminalistik
Kursbuch

Nervenarzt
Neue Praxis: Kritische Zeitschrift für
    Sozialarbeit und Sozialpädagogik
Öffentliches Gesundheitswesen
Suchtgefahren
Theorie und Praxis der Sozialen Arbeit
Unsere Jugend
Zentralblatt für Jugendrecht und
    Jugendwohlfahrt

Magazines

Bravo
Konkret
Pardon
Praline

Der Spiegel
Spontan
Stern
Vörwarts

Newspapers

Bild
Bild am Sonntag
Hamburger Abendblatt
Hamburger Morgenpost
Frankfurter Allgemeine Zeitung

Frankfurter Rundschau
Süddeutsche Zeitung
Die Welt
Die Zeit

Underground Newspapers

Agit 883
Bambule
Floh
Germania
Hotcha
Humus
Hundert Blumen
International Times
Linkeck
Love

OZ
Päng
Peng: Provozeitschrift
Pot
Radikalinski
Roter Punkt
Scheisse
Song
Underground
Zero

Select Books and Articles

Albrecht, Willy. *Der sozialistische deutsche Studentenbund: Vom parteikonformen Studentenverband zum Repräsentanten der Neuen Linken.* Bonn: Verlag J. H. W. Dietz Nachfolger, 1994.

Ali, Tariq, and Susan Watkins. *1968: Marching in the Streets.* New York: Free Press, 1998.
Amendt, Günter. *Sucht Profit Sucht.* Frankfurt am Main: Zweitausendeins, 1984.
Amendt, Günter, and Ulli Stiehler. *Sucht Profit Sucht: Politische Ökonomie des Drogenhandels.* Frankfurt am Main: März, 1972.
Articus, Rüdiger, et al. *Die Beatles in Harburg.* Hamburg: Hamburger Museum für Archäologie und die Geschichte Harburgs, 1996.
Aust, Stefan. *Der Baader-Meinhof Komplex.* 10th ed. Hamburg: Hoffmann und Campe, 1988.
Avery, Peter, et al., eds. *The Cambridge History of Iran.* Volume 7, *From Nadir Shah to the Islamic Republic.* Cambridge: Cambridge University Press, 1991.
Bade, Klaus J. *Auswanderer—Wanderarbeiter—Gastarbeiter: Bevölkerung, Arbeitsmarkt und Wanderung in Deutschland seit der Mitte des 19. Jahrhunderts.* Vol. 2. Ostfildern: Scripta Mercaturae, 1984.
Baumann, Michael. *Wie alles Anfing = How It All Began.* Vancouver: Pulp Press, 1981.
Becker, Howard. *The Outsiders: Studies in the Sociology of Deviance.* New York: Free Press, 1963.
Becker, Walter. "Jugend und Rauschgift." *Therapie der Gegenwart* 107 (1968): 1395–403.
———. "Jugend und Sucht—aus dem Blickfeld der Jugendhilfe." *Zentralblatt für Jugendrecht und Jugendwohlfahrt* 54 (1967): 93–107.
———. "Die Neue Rauschgiftwelle." *Zentralblatt für Jugendrecht und Jugendwohlfahrt* 54 (1967): 360–64.
———. "Suchtgefahren in der Öffentlichkeit." *Therapeutische Gegenwartsfragen* 5 (1967): 656–62.
———, ed. *Jugend in der Rauschgiftwelle?* 4th ed. Hamm: Hoheneck, 1970.
Beeching, Jack. *The Chinese Opium Wars.* London: Hutchinson, 1975.
Berghahn, Volker. *The Americanization of West German Industry.* New York: Cambridge University Press, 1986.
Berghoff, Harmut. *Konsumpolitik: die Regulierung des privaten Verbrauchs im 20. Jahrhundert.* Göttingen: Vandenhoeck & Ruprecht, 1999.
———. "Population Change and Its Repercussions on the Social History of the Federal Republic." In *The Federal Republic of Germany since 1949: Politics, Society, and Economy before and after Unification,* ed. Klaus Larres and Panikos Panayi. London: Longman, 1996.
Bergmann, Peter. "The Specter of *Amerikanisierung,* 1840–1990." In *American Culture in Europe: Interdisciplinary Perspectives,* ed. Mike-Frank G. Epitropoulos and Victor Roudometof. London: Praeger, 1998.
Berridge, Virginia. "East End Opium Dens and Narcotic Use in Britain." *London Journal* 4 (1978): 4–28.
———. "Morality and Medical Science: Concepts of Narcotic Addiction in Britain, 1820–1926." *Annals of Science* 36 (1979): 67–85.
Bharier, Julian. *Economic Development in Iran, 1900–1970.* London: Oxford University Press, 1971.

Block, Alan. "European Drug Traffic and Traffickers between the Wars: The Policy of Suppression and Its Consequences." *Journal of Social History* 23 (1989): 315–38.

———. *Space, Time & Organized Crime.* 2d ed. London: Transaction, 1994.

Boelcke, Willi A. *Der Schwarzmarkt 1945–1948: vom Überleben nach dem Kriege.* Braunschweig: Westermann, 1986.

Bromell, Nicholas Knowles. *Tomorrow Never Knows: Rock and Psychedelics in the 1960s.* Chicago: University of Chicago Press, 2002.

Bruun, Kettil, et al. *The Gentlemen's Club: International Control of Drugs and Alcohol.* Chicago: University of Chicago Press, 1975.

Bundesarbeitstelle Aktion Jugendschutz. *Jugendschutz heute und morgen.* Hamm: Hoheneck-Verlag, 1961.

Bundeskriminalamt Wiesbaden, ed. *Organisiertes Verbrechen: Arbeitstagung des Bundeskriminalamtes Wiesbaden vom 21. Oktober bis 25. Oktober 1974.* Wiesbaden: Bundeskriminalamt, 1975.

———. *Rauschgift: Arbeitstagung im Bundeskriminalamt Wiesbaden vom 21. November bis 26. November 1955 über Bekämpfung von Rauschgiftdelikten.* Wiesbaden: Bundesdruckerei, 1956.

Carter, Erica. *How German Is She? Postwar West German Reconstruction and the Consuming Woman.* Ann Arbor: University of Michigan Press, 1997.

Casriel, Daniel. *Daytop: Three Addicts and Their Cure.* New York: Hill and Wang, 1971.

Castells, Manuel. *End of Millennium.* Vol. 3 of *The Information Age: Economy, Society, and Culture.* Oxford: Blackwell, 1998.

Caute, David. *The Year of the Barricades: A Journey through 1968.* New York: Harper & Row, 1988.

Charpentier, C-J. "The Use of Hashish and Opium in Afghanistan." *Anthropos* 68 (1973): 482–84.

Cohen, Lizabeth. *A Consumers' Republic: The Politics of Mass Consumption in Postwar America.* New York: Alfred A. Knopf, 2003.

Cohen, Stanley. *Folk Devils and Moral Panics: The Creation of the Mods and Rockers.* London: MacGibbon and Kee, 1972.

Confino, Alon, and Rudy Koshar. "Regimes of Consumer Culture: New Narratives in Twentieth-Century Germany History." *German History* 19 (2001): 135–61.

Courtwright, David. *Forces of Habit: Drugs and the Making of the Modern World.* Cambridge, MA: Harvard University Press, 2002.

Courtwright, David, et al. *Addicts Who Survived: An Oral History of Narcotic Use in America, 1923–1965.* Knoxville: University of Tennessee Press, 1989.

Crew, David. *Germans on Welfare.* Oxford: Oxford University Press, 1998.

———. "The Pathologies of Modernity: Detlev Peukert on Germany's Twentieth Century." *Social History* 17 (1992): 319–28.

Currie, Elliott. *Reckoning: Drugs, the Cities, and the American Future.* New York: Hill and Wang, 1993.

Daunton, Martin, and Matthew Hilton, eds. *The Politics of Consumption: Material Culture and Citizenship in Europe and America.* Oxford: Berg, 2001.

De Grazia, Victoria. "Changing Consumption Regimes in Europe, 1930–1970: Comparative Perspectives on the Distribution Problem." In *Getting and Spending: European and American Consumer Societies in the Twentieth Century,* ed. Susan Strasser, Charles McGovern, and Matthias Judt, 59–84. Cambridge: Cambridge University Press, 1998.

———. *Irresistible Empire: America's Advance through 20th-Century Europe.* Cambridge, MA: Belknap Press, 2005.

De Grazia, Victoria, and Ellen Furlough, eds. *The Sex of Things: Gender and Consumption in Historical Perspective.* Berkeley: University of California Press, 1996.

Dickinson, Edward Ross. "Biopolitics, Fascism, Democracy: Some Reflections on our Discourse about 'Modernity.'" *Central European History* 37 (2004): 1–48.

———. *The Politics of German Child Welfare from the Empire to the Federal Republic.* Cambridge, MA: Harvard University Press, 1996.

Dickinson, Robert. *Imprinting the Sticks: The Alternative Press beyond London.* Aldershot: Arena, 1997.

Doering-Manteuffel, Anselm. "Dimensionen von Amerikanisierung in der deutschen Gesellschaft." *Archiv für Sozialgeschichte* 35 (1995): 1–34.

———. "Transatlantic Exchange and Interaction—The Concept of Westernization." Paper presented at the conference American Impact on Western Europe: Americanization and Westernization in Transatlantic Perspective, German Historical Institute, 25–27 March 1999.

———. *Wie westlich sind die Deutschen? Amerikanisierung und Westernisierung im 20. Jahrhundert.* Göttingen: Vandenhoeck & Ruprecht, 1999.

Emig, Günther, et al., eds. *Die Alternativpresse: Kontroversen, Polemiken, Dokumente.* Augsburg: Maro, 1980.

Endore, Guy. *Synanon.* Garden City, NY: Doubleday, 1968.

Faulenbach, Bernd. "'Modernisierung' in der Bundesrepublik und in der DDR wahrend der 60er Jahre." *Zeitgeschichte* 25 (1998): 282–94.

Fay, Peter Ward. *The Opium War, 1840–1842.* Chapel Hill: University of North Carolina Press, 1975.

Fehrenbach, Heide. *Cinema in Democratizing Germany: Reconstructing National Identity after Hitler.* Chapel Hill: University of North Carolina Press, 1995.

Foucault, Michel. *Discipline and Punish: The Birth of the Prison.* Trans. Alan Sheridan. New York: Vintage Books, 1979.

Fountain, Nigel. *Underground: The London Alternative Press, 1966–74.* London: Routledge, 1988.

Frevert, Uta. *Women in German History: From Bourgeois Emancipation to Sexual Liberation.* Trans. Stuart McKinnon-Evans. New York: Berg, 1989.

Friman, H. Richard. *Narco-diplomacy: Exporting the U.S. War On Drugs.* Ithaca: Cornell University Press, 1996.

Fullbrook, Mary, *The Divided Nation: A History of Germany, 1918–1990.* New York: Oxford University Press, 1991.

———. *Interpretations of the Two Germanies, 1945–1990.* New York: St. Martin's, 2000.

Germany (West). *Bundesgesetze zum Schutz der Jugend in der Öffentlichkeit und über die Verbreitung jugendgefährdender Schriften.* Munich: Beck, 1954.

Glaser, Hermann. *Deutsche Kultur, 1945–2000.* Munich: Carl Hanser, 1997.

Green, Jonathon. *All Dressed Up: The Sixties and the Counter-culture.* London: Jonathan Cape, 1998.

Grotum, Thomas. *Die Halbstarken: zur Geschichte einer Jugendkultur der 50er Jahre.* New York: Campus, 1994.

Gusfield, Joseph R. *Contested Meanings: The Construction of Alcohol Problems.* Madison: University of Wisconsin Press, 1996.

Hall, Stuart, et al. *Policing the Crisis: Mugging, the State, and Law and Order.* London: Macmillan, 1978.

Hall, Stuart, and Tony Jefferson, eds. *Resistance through Rituals: Youth Subcultures in Post-war Britain.* London: Routledge, 1993.

Harding, Geoffrey. *Opiate Addiction, Morality and Medicine: From Moral Illness to Pathological Disease.* New York: St. Martin's, 1988.

Harris, George S. *Turkey: Coping with Crisis.* Boulder, CO: Westview, 1985.

Hauschildt, Elke. *Auf den richtigen Weg zwingen—: Trinkerfürsorge 1922 bis 1945.* Freiburg im Breisgau: Lambertus, 1995.

Hebdige, Dick. *Hiding in the Light: On Images and Things.* London: Routledge, 1988.

Hengartner, Thomas, and Christoph Maria Merki, eds. *Genußmittel: Ein kulturgeschichtliches Handbuch.* Frankfurt: Campus, 1999.

Herbert, Ulrich. *A History of Foreign Labor in Germany, 1880–1980: Seasonal Workers/Forced Laborers/Guest Workers.* Trans. William Templer. Ann Arbor: University of Michigan Press, 1990.

———, ed. *Wandlungsprozesse in Westdeutschland: Belastung, Intergration, Liberalisierung 1945–1980.* Göttingen: Wallstein, 2002.

Hermand, Jost. *Die Kultur der Bundesrepublik Deutschland 1965–85.* Munich: Nymphenburger, 1988.

———. *Pop International: Eine kritische Analyse.* Frankfurt am Main: Athenäum, 1971.

Heuer, Rolv, et al. *Helft Euch selbst! Der Release-Report gegen die Sucht.* Reinbek bei Hamburg: Rowohlt, 1971.

Homann, Ulf. *Das Haschischverbot: Gesellschaftliche Funktion und Wirkung.* Frankfurt am Main: Fischer-Taschenbuch-Verlag, 1972.

Hong, Young-Sun. *Welfare, Modernity, and the Weimar State: 1919–1933.* Princeton: Princeton University Press, 1998.

Hukeler, Karl. *Jugendschutz in öffentlich-rechtlicher Sicht.* Lucern: Fachgruppe Jugendschutz, Caritaszentrale, 1961.

Jantzen, Wolfgang. *Rocker und andere Probleme der Jugendkriminalität.* Wuppertal-Barmen: Jugenddienst, 1969.

Jarausch, Konrad, and Michael Geyer, eds. *Shattered Past: Reconstructing German Histories.* Princeton: Princeton University Press, 2003.

Jonnes, Jill. *Hep-Cats, Narcs, and Pipe Dreams: A History of America's Romance with Illegal Drugs.* New York: Scribner, 1996.

Käsmayr, Benno. *Die sogenannte "Alternativpresse": Ein Beispiel für Gegenöffentlichkeit in der BRD und im deutschsprachigen Ausland seit 1968.* Gersthofen: Maro, 1974.

Kazemi, Farhad. *Poverty and Revolution in Iran: The Migrant Poor, Urban Marginality, and Politics.* New York: New York University Press, 1980.

Klessmann, Christoph. *Die doppelte Staatsgründung: deutsche Geschichte 1945–1955.* Göttingen: Vandenhoeck & Ruprecht, 1982.

———. "Ein stolzes Schiff und krächzende Möwen: Die Geschichte der Bundesrepublik und ihre Kritiker." *Geschichte und Gesellschaft* 11 (1985): 476–94.

———. *Zwei Staaten, eine Nation: deutsche Geschichte 1955–1970.* Göttingen: Vandenhoeck & Ruprecht, 1988.

———, ed. *The Divided Past: Rewriting Post-war German History.* New York: Berg, 2001.

Klessmann, Christoph, and Georg Wagner, eds., *Das gespaltene Land: Leben in Deutschland 1945–1990: Texte und Dokumente zur Sozialgeschichte.* Munich: Beck, 1993.

Knop, Karin. "Zwischen Afri-Cola-Rausch und dem Duft der großen weiten Welt: Werbung in den sechziger Jahren." In *Die Kultur der sechziger Jahre,* ed. Werner Faulstich, 241–71. Munich: Wilhelm Fink, 2003.

Koenen, Gerd. *Das rote Jahrzehnt: Unsere kleine deutsche Kulturrevolution, 1967–1977.* Cologne: Kiepenheuer & Witsch, 2001.

———. *Vesper, Ensslin, Baader: Urszenen des deutschen Terrorismus.* Cologne: Kiepenheuer & Witsch, 2003.

Kohn, Marek. *Dope Girls: The Birth of the British Drug Underground.* London: Lawrence & Wishart, 1992.

Kosack, Godula. *Immigrant Workers and Class Structure in Western Europe.* 2d ed. Oxford: Oxford University Press, 1985.

Kosel, Margret. *Gammler Beatniks Provos: Die schleichende Revolution.* Frankfurt am Main: Verlag Bärmeier & Nikel, 1967.

Kreuzer, Arthur. *Drogen und Delinquenz: eine jugendkriminologisch-empirische Untersuchung der Erscheinungsformen und Zusammenhänge.* Wiesbaden: Akademische, 1975.

Kuhn, Helmet. *Jugend im Aufbruch: Zur revolutionären Bewegung unserer Zeit.* Munich: Kösel-Verlag, 1970.

Labin, Suzanne. *Hippies, Drogues et Sexe.* Paris: La Table Ronde, 1970.

Lamour, Catherine, and Michel R. Lamberti. *The International Connection: Opium from Growers to Pushers.* Trans. Peter and Betty Ross. New York: Pantheon Books, 1974.

Leonhardt, Rudolf Walter. *Haschisch-Report: Dokumente und Fakten zur Beurteilung eines sogenannten Rauschgifts.* Munich: R. Piper, 1970.

———. *Wer wirft den ersten Stein?—Minoritäten in einer züchtigen Gesellschaft.* Munich: R. Piper, 1969.

Linton, Derek S. *"Who Has the Youth Has the Future": The Campaign to Save Young Workers in Imperial Germany.* Cambridge: Cambridge University Press, 1991.

Lüdtke, Alf, ed. *The History of Everyday Life: Reconstructing Historical Experiences and Ways of Life.* Trans. William Templer. Princeton: Princeton University Press, 1995.

Lüdtke, Alf, Inge Marssolek, and Adelheid von Saldern, eds. *Amerikanisierung: Traum und Alptraum im Deutschland des 20. Jahrhunderts.* Stuttgart: Steiner, 1996.

Luger, Kurt. *Die konsumierte Rebellion: Geschichte der Jugendkultur 1945–1990.* Vienna: Österreicher Kunst- und Kulturverlag, 1991.

Maase, Kaspar. *Bravo Amerika: Erkundigungen zur Jugendkultur der Bundesrepublik in den fünfziger Jahren.* Hamburg: Junius, 1992.

Maase, Kaspar. "Roll over, Beethoven! The 'Americanization' of West German Youths and the Emergence of a New Cultural Balance." Discussion paper at the Hamburger Institut für Sozialforschung, 1992.

Mäckelburg, Gerhard, and Hans-Jürgen Wolter. *Jugendkriminalität in Hamburg: Ein Bericht des Landeskriminalamtes über Umfang, Erscheinungsformen und Ursachen der Jugendkriminalität mit einer Übersicht über die statistische Entwicklung der Jahre 1963 bis 1974.* Hamburg: Landeskriminalamt, 1975.

Marwick, Arthur. *The Sixties.* Oxford: Oxford University Press, 1998.

Massing, Michael. *The Fix.* New York: Simon & Schuster, 1998.

McCormick, Richard. *Politics of the Self: Feminism and the Postmodern in West German Literature and Film.* Princeton: Princeton University Press, 1991.

McCoy, Alfred W. "Coercion and Its Unintended Consequences: A Study of Heroin Trafficking in Southeast and South West Asia." *Crime, Law & Social Change* 33 (2000): 191–224.

———. *The Politics of Heroin: CIA Complicity in the Global Drug Trade.* Brooklyn, NY: Lawrence Hill Books, 1991.

McDonald, Maryon. ed. *Gender, Drink, and Drugs.* Oxford: Berg, 1994.

Mehnert, Klaus. *Twilight of the Young: The Radical Movements of the 1960s and Their Legacy.* New York: Holt, Rinehart, and Winston, 1976.

Mintz, Sidney. *Sweetness and Power: The Place of Sugar in Modern History.* New York: Viking, 1985.

Moeller, Robert G., ed. *West Germany under Construction: Politics, Society, and Culture in the Adenauer Era.* Ann Arbor: University of Michigan Press, 1997.

Morgan, H. Wayne. *Drugs in America: A Social History, 1800–1980.* Syracuse: Syracuse University Press, 1981.

Moscow, Alvin. *Merchants of Heroin: An In-Depth Portrayal of Business in the Underworld.* New York: Dial Press, 1968.

Musto, David. *The American Disease: Origins of Narcotic Control.* Exp. ed. New York: Oxford University Press, 1987.

Nadelman, Ethan. *Cops across Borders: The Internationalization of U.S. Criminal Law Enforcement.* University Park: Pennsylvania State University Press, 1993.

Nelson, Elizabeth. *The British Counter-Culture, 1966–73: A Study of the Underground Press.* New York: St. Martin's, 1989.

Neumann, Nicolaus, ed. *Hasch und andere Trips: Fakten, Infomationen, Analysen.* Hamburg: Konkret, 1970.

Neville, Richard. *Play Power: Exploring the International Underground.* New York: Random House, 1970.

Parssinen, Terry, and K. Kerner. "Development of the Disease Model of Drug Addiction in Britain, 1870–1926." *Medical History* 24 (1980): 275–96.

Petersen, Klaus. "The Harmful Publications (Young Persons) Act of 1926. Literary Censorship and the Politics of Morality in the Weimar Republic." *German Studies Review* 15 (1992): 505–23.

Peukert, Detlev J. K. *Grenzen der Sozialdisziplinierung: Aufstieg und Krise der deutschen Jugendfürsorge 1878 bis 1932.* Cologne: Bund, 1986.

———. "Die 'Letzten Menschen': Beobachtungen zur Kulturkritik im Geschichtsbild Max Webers." *Geschichte und Gesellschaft* 12 (1986): 425–42.

———. *Max Webers Diagnose der Moderne.* Göttingen: Vandenhoeck & Ruprecht, 1989.

Pieper, Werner. *Nazis on Speed—Drogen im 3. Reich.* Vol. 1. Löhrbach: Grüne Kraft, 2002.

Plant, Martin A. *Drug Users in an English Town.* London: Tavistock, 1975.

Poiger, Uta. "Beyond 'Modernization' and 'Colonization.'" *Diplomatic History* 23 (1999): 45–56.

———. *Jazz, Rock, and Rebels: Cold War Politics and American Culture in a Divided Germany.* Berkeley: University of California Press, 2000.

———. "Rock 'n' Roll, Female Sexuality, and the Cold War Battle over German Identities." *Journal of Modern History* 68 (1996): 577–606.

Pommerin, Reiner, ed. *The American Impact on Postwar Germany.* Providence and Oxford: Berghahn Books, 1995.

Poroy, Ibrahim I. "An Economic Model of Opium Consumption in Iran and Turkey during the Nineteenth Century." Paper presented at the annual meeting of the Middle East Studies Association, Seattle, 4–7 November 1981.

Proctor, Robert. *The Nazi War on Cancer.* Princeton: Princeton University Press, 1999.

Reinhardt, Dirk. *Von der Reklame zum Marketing: Geschichte der Wirtschaftswerbung in Deutschland.* Berlin: Akademische, 1993.

Rist, Ray C. *Guestworkers in Germany: The Prospects for Pluralism.* New York: Praeger, 1978.

Röhl, Klaus Rainer. *Fünf Finger sind keine Faust.* Cologne: Verlag Kiepenheuer & Witsch, 1974.

Rush, James. *Opium to Java: Revenue Farming and Chinese Enterprise in Colonial Indonesia, 1860–1910.* Ithaca: Cornell University Press, 1990.

Sayres, Sohnya, et al. *The 60s without Apology.* Minneapolis: University of Minnesota Press, 1984.

Schildt, Axel. *Ankunft im Westen: Ein Essay zur Erfolgsgeschichte der Bundesrepublik.* Frankfurt am Main: S. Fischer, 1999.

———. "Beyond the 60's—Finally Arrived in the West? Notes on the Americanization of Culture in West Germany." Paper presented at the conference American Impact on Western Europe: Americanization and Westernization in Transatlantic Perspective, German Historical Institute, 25–27 March 1999.

———. *Moderne Zeiten: Freizeit, Massenmedien und "Zeitgeist" in der Bundesrepublik der 50er Jahre.* Hamburg: Christians, 1995.

Schildt, Axel, Detlev Siegfried, and Karl Christian Lammers, eds. *Dynamische Zeiten: Die 60er Jahre in den beiden deutschen Gesellschaften.* Hamburg: Hans Christians, 2000.

Schildt, Axel, and Arnold Sywottek, eds. *Modernizierung im Wiederaufbau: Die westdeutsche Gesellschaft der 50er Jahre.* Bonn: J. H. W. Dietz, 1993.

Schivelbusch, Wolfgang. *Tastes of Paradise: A Social History of Spices, Stimulants, and Intoxicants.* New York: Pantheon, 1992.

Schmid, Martin. *Drogenhilfe in Deutschland: Entstehung und Entwicklung 1970–2000.* Frankfurt am Main: Campus, 2003.

Schmidbauer, Wolfgang, and Jürgen vom Scheidt. *Handbuch der Rauschdrogen.* Munich: Nyphenburger, 1971.

Schmidt, Jan. *From Anatolia to Indonesia: Opium Trade and the Dutch Community of Izmir, 1820–1940.* Istanbul: Nederlands Historisch-Archaeologisch Instituut, 1998.

Schulenburg, Lutz, ed. *Das Leben andern, die Welt verändern! 1968 Dokumente und Berichte.* Hamburg: Edition Nautilus, 1998.

Siegfried, Detlef. "'Trau keinem über 30'? Konsens und Konflikt der Generationen in der Bundesrepublik der langen sechziger Jahre." *Aus Politik und Zeitgeschichte* B45 (2003): 25–32.

Siegrist, Hannes, Harmut Kaelbe, and Jürgen Kocka, eds. *Europäische Konsumgeschichte: Zur Gesellschafts- und Kulturgeschichte des Konsums 18. bis 20. Jahrhundert.* Frankfurt and New York: Campus, 1997.

Simon, Titus. *Rocker in der Bundesrepublik: eine Subkultur zwischen Jugendprotest und Traditionsbildung.* Weinheim: Deutscher Studien, 1989.

Spence, Jonathan. "Opium." In *Chinese Roundabout: Essays in History and Culture.* New York: W. W. Norton, 1992.

Spode, Hasso, ed. *Goldstrand und Teutonengrill: Kultur- und Sozialgeschichte des Tourismus in Deutschland 1945 bis 1989.* Berlin: W. Moser, Verlag für universitäre Kommunikation, 1996.

Stares, Paul B. *Global Habit: The Drug Problem in a Borderless World.* Washington, DC: Brookings Institution, 1996.

Stearns, Peter. "Stages of Consumerism: Recent Work on the Issue of Periodization." *Journal of Modern History* 69 (1997): 102–17.

Steininger, Christian. "Eleganz der Oberfläche: Werbung und die ökonomische

Restauration deutscher Normalität." In *Die Kultur der fünfziger Jahre,* ed. Werner Faulstich, 181–98. Munich: Wilhelm Fink, 2002.

Stieg, Margaret F. "The 1926 German Law to Protect Youth against Trash and Dirt: Moral Protectionism in a Democracy." *Central European History* 23 (1990): 22–56.

Sugarman, Barry. *Daytop Village: A Therapeutic Community.* New York: Holt, Rinehart, and Winston, 1974.

Sywottek, Arnold. "The Americanization of Everyday Life? Trends in Consumer and Leisure-Time Behaviors." In *America and the Shaping of German Society, 1945–1955,* ed. Michael Ermarth. Oxford: Providence, 1993.

Taylor, Arnold. *American Diplomacy and the Narcotics Traffic, 1900–1939.* Durham, NC: Duke University Press, 1969.

Tomory, David. *A Season in Heaven: True Tales from the Road to Kathmandu.* London: Lonely Planet Publications, 1998.

Trocki, Carl. *Opium, Empire, and the Global Political Economy: A Study of the Asian Opium Trade, 1750–1950.* London: Routledge, 1999.

Uesseler, Rolf. *Die 68er: "Macht kaputt, was Euch kaputt macht!"* Munich: Wilhelm Heyne, 1998.

Varon, Jeremy. "'Shadowboxing the Apocalypse': New Left Violence in the United States and West Germany." PhD diss., Cornell University, 1998.

von Dirke, Sabina. *All Power to the Imagination! The West German Counterculture from the Student Movement to the Greens.* Lincoln: University of Nebraska Press, 1997.

von Hirschheydt, Ute. "Erfahrungen mit jungen Rauschmittelkonsumenten: Deskriptiv phänomenologisch Darstellung der Drogenszene eines Hamburger Kollektivs." PhD diss., Fachbereich Medizin der Universität Hamburg, 1972.

Vuckovacki, Vera. *Endstation Kathmandu.* N.p.: blick + bild Verlag, 1972.

Wartelle, Ellen A., and Patricia A. Stout. "The Evolution of Mass Media and Health Persuasion Models." In *Mass Media and Drug Prevention,* ed. William D. Crano and Michael Burgoon, 19–34. Mahwah, NJ, and London: Lawrence Erlbaum, 2002.

Wegner, Werner. *"Balkan-Route" contra "Seidenstrasse": Die tödlichen Rauschgiftstraßen von Asien nach Westeuropa.* Berlin: Schmidt-Römhild: 1996.

Weinhauer, Klaus. *Schutzpolizei in der Bundesrepublik: zwischen Bürgerkrieg und innerer Sicherheit: die turbulenten sechiziger Jahre.* Paderborn: Schöningh, 2003.

Wendiggensen, Paul. "Hamburger Drogenkonsumenten in Kliniken, Haftanstalten und der Drogenszene: Ergebnisse einer deskriptiv-statistischen Untersuchung." PhD diss., Fachbereich Medizin der Universität Hamburg, 1972.

Wienemann, Elisabeth. *Vom Alkoholverbot zum Gesundheitsmanagement: Entwicklung der betrieblichen Suchtprävention 1800–2000.* Stuttgart: Ibidem, 2000.

Wildt, Michael. *Der Traum vom Sattwerden: Hunger und Protest, Schwarzmarkt und Selbsthilfe.* Hamburg: VSA-Verlag, 1986.

————. "Plurality of Taste: Food and Consumption in West Germany during the 1950s." *History Workshop Journal* 39 (1995): 22–41.

————. *Vom kleinen Wohlstand: Eine Konsumgeschichte der fünfziger Jahre.* Frankfurt am Main: Fischer Taschenbuch, 1996.

Willet, Ralph. *The Americanization of Germany, 1945–1949.* New York: Routledge, 1989.

Willis, Paul E. *Profane Culture.* London: Routledge, 1978.

Winslow, Charles. *Lebanon: War and Politics in a Fragmented Society.* London: Routledge, 1996.

Yablonsky, Lewis. *The Tunnel Back.* New York: Macmillan, 1965.

Index